Greek Marseille and Mediterranean Celtic Region

LANG
Classical
Studies

Daniel H. Garrison
General Editor

Vol. 20

This book is a volume in a Peter Lang monograph series.
Every volume is peer reviewed and meets
the highest quality standards for content and production.

PETER LANG
New York • Bern • Frankfurt • Berlin
Brussels • Vienna • Oxford • Warsaw

Greek Marseille and Mediterranean Celtic Region

Edited by
SOPHIE BOUFFIER and
DOMINIQUE GARCIA

PETER LANG
New York • Bern • Frankfurt • Berlin
Brussels • Vienna • Oxford • Warsaw

Library of Congress Cataloging-in-Publication Data

Names: Collin Bouffier, Sophie, editor. | Garcia, Dominique, editor.
Title: Greek Marseille and Mediterranean Celtic region /
edited by Sophie Bouffier, Dominique Garcia.
Description: New York: Peter Lang.
Series: Lang classical studies; vol. 20 | ISSN 0891-4087
Includes bibliographical references.
Identifiers: LCCN 2015041782 | ISBN 978-1-4331-3204-9 (hardcover: alk. paper)
ISBN 978-1-4539-1689-6 (ebook pdf) | ISBN 978-1-4331-3962-8 (epub)
ISBN 978-1-4331-3963-5 (mobi) | DOI 10.3726/978-1-4539-1689-6
Subjects: LCSH: Marseille (France)—History. | Greeks—France—Marseille.
Gauls—France—Marseille. | Ligurians—France—Marseille.
Romans—France—Marseille.
Marseille (France)—Relations—Mediterranean Region.
Mediterranean Region—Relations—France—Marseille.
Classification: LCC DC801.M37 G74 | DDC 936.4/91202—dc23
LC record available at http://lccn.loc.gov/2015041782

Bibliographic information published by **Die Deutsche Nationalbibliothek**.
Die Deutsche Nationalbibliothek lists this publication in the "Deutsche
Nationalbibliografie"; detailed bibliographic data are available
on the Internet at http://dnb.d-nb.de/.

Table of Contents

Introduction   1
    SOPHIE BOUFFIER AND DOMINIQUE GARCIA

1. The Littorals in Southern Gaul: State of the Issue   7
    PHILIPPE LEVEAU

2. Greeks, Celts and Ligurians in South-East Gaul:
Ethnicity and Archaeology   39
    SOPHIE BOUFFIER AND DOMINIQUE GARCIA

3. Territorial Variations: Natives and Greeks in the
Mediterranean Celtic Region   55
    DOMINIQUE GARCIA AND SOPHIE BOUFFIER

4. The Exchanges on the Coastline of Southern Gaul in the First Iron Age:
From the Hellenisation Concept to That of Mediterraneisation   77
    DOMINIQUE GARCIA AND JEAN-CHRISTOPHE SOURISSEAU

5. The Sources of Greek Marseille and of Its Territory: The Ethnica *of*
Stephanus of Byzantium and the Lexicographical References   91
    MARC BOUIRON

6. Territories of the Massaliot Identity: Conservatism or
Political and Moral Loosening?   117
    SOPHIE BOUFFIER AND EMMANUÈLE CAIRE

7. Marseille: An Ionian City in the Greek West   139
    HENRI TRÉZINY

8. *At the Frontiers of Massalian Territory: Greek and Indigenous Rhythms from the Seventh to Second Century BC* 151
  LOUP BERNARD, SOPHIE BOUFFIER AND DELPHINE ISOARDI

9. *The Cults of Greek Marseille* 183
  ANTOINE HERMARY

10. *The Territories In-between: Marseille, Rome and the Gauls* 193
  RACHEL FEIG VISHNIA

11. *Marseille Territories of Exchanges* 205
  MARIE-BRIGITTE CARRE

12. *Greek Marseille and the Gauls of the South: Quite Different Funeral Practices (Fifth–Second Centuries BC)* 223
  BERNARD DEDET

13. *Land Allotment and Ancient Vineyards around Marseille* 249
  PHILIPPE BOISSINOT

14. *The Greco-Massaliot Shipwrecks in the Place Jules-Verne in Marseille and the Evolution of Greek Ship Construction from the Sixth to the Fourth Century BC* 263
  PATRICE POMEY

15. *Protohistoric Mediterranean Gaul as a Middle Ground* 281
  MICHEL BATS

Contributors 301

Introduction

SOPHIE BOUFFIER AND DOMINIQUE GARCIA

This book is the synthesis of recent works conducted by archaeologists and historians over the past 25 years in Southern Gaul and on the territory of the Greek city of Marseille. It shows an overview of the different issues behind the circulations between Greeks from Phocaea and Celtic populations, from the occupation of the territory of Massalia before the foundation of the Greek city to the Roman period. This reflection on a key region of the Euro-Mediterranean space rests on the analysis of archaeological findings (urban excavations, spatial studies, analysis of necropolis, of submarine remains and of paleo-environmental data…) and reviewing the ancient literary documentation.

Whereas studies generally pertain to the evolution of the region from the Greek viewpoint, by looking for the possible signs of Hellenisation and the mutations officially provoked by the arrival of an Aegean population, the authors have purposely moved the focus on the indigenous (Celtic and Ligurian) populations and offer an innovative insight in the textual as well as archaeological documentation by scrutinising the political, economic and cultural fields of the relationships between the Greek migrants and the populations they started to meet at the end of the seventh century BC. Various fields of the exchanges between these populations are examined and give rise to chapters associated with a synthetic bibliography and a choice of unpublished illustrations. The book is thus broken down into fourteen chapters, written by specialists in Greek, Gallic and Roman societies, who may be archaeologists as well as philologists, who have produced the research on Massalia and its region over the last twenty-five years.

Philippe Leveau first of all takes stock of the results of the paleo-environmental studies dedicated to the Provence milieu before Sophie Bouffier and Dominique Garcia go back over the ethnogenesis and structuring processes of the Celtic societies in contact with the Greeks by using the anthropological models. The traditional approach to the History of Southern Gaul sets the date of foundation of Massalia, that is 600 BC, as a pivotal position for the whole reflection by considering an anterior and a posterior period, which had to be bound together. This position finds its main origin in the conception of the colonial phenomena, particularly those relating to the Greek world, imposed by the Moderns since at least the nineteenth century. This marked approach has grooved concepts such as the Hellenisation of the South of Gaul (by Fernand Benoît) with consequently the idea of a binary confrontation between Greeks from Massalia and natives. Dominique Garcia and Jean-Christophe Sourisseau endeavour to go beyond the concept of Hellenisation so as to tackle that of Mediterraneisation building the analysis of exchanges on the Gallic coastline.

The analysis of the text sources of Greek Massalia and of its territory covers two chapters; the one on the political and social history of Massalia, often neglected by politologists, revisited by Sophie Bouffier and Emmanuèle Caire by reshaping the view suggested by ancient testimonies, emphasising the specificity of the Massaliot regime and society. They recontextualise the founding texts of Aristoteles throughout the work of that philosopher before reintegrating the customs and usages of the Massaliots in a general environment, characteristic of the culture of the Greek world. Marc Bouiron, now in charge of the study of the *Ethnica* of Stephanus Byzantinus, proposes a new, rich and systematically structured method for reading the text.

The last three decades have seen considerable increase in the volume of research on the city and the territory of Massalia. From a city without monuments and without a territory, Massalia has become a Greek city like the others, even if certain aspects of its organisation are still eluding us. A chapter, written by Henri Tréziny, a major specialist of Greek urbanism, thus presents an overview of the urban topography of Greek Massalia and offers comparisons with other so-called colonial cities of the Western Mediterranean region. The renewed field researches on the Marseille territory also enables us to address, according to several approaches, the modes and the rates of settlement by exploring the frontiers of the Marseille territories in the seventh–fifth centuries BC (works of Loup Bernard, Sophie Bouffier, Delphine Isoardi). The archaeological exploration of the Marseille terroirs by Philippe Boissinot has enabled us to unearth the traces of the ancient vineyards and thus to evaluate the spatial extension of a wine economy which the ancient texts and the commercial amphorae had already permitted scholars to apprehend correctly. The indigenous counterparts (in particular cereals) are also put forward by the study of the storage structures such as granaries and silos (Dominique Garcia).

The book includes a chapter on the cults of that ancient city, impregnated with its Phocaean and Ionian, and on those of its neighbours. Antoine Hermany, the author of numerous articles on the Marseille cults, offers to update the information at our disposal. Bernard Dedet proposes a comparison between the indigenous funeral practices and those recognised in the necropoles of Greek Marseille.

But, as stressed by ancient sources, Massalia is first and foremost a maritime power, which came more than once to the rescue of its Roman ally before it fell under its domination. To form a tie between Greek and Roman Marseille, Michel Bats' paper is based on Onomastic, Ancient Literature and Hellenistic Sculpture to propose an analysis of Massaliot society at the dawn of the Roman Conquest.

In this view, Massalia maintains with the other cities relationships which may be sometimes peaceful, sometimes conflictual, studied by the late Rachel Feig-Vishnia in the context of the relations between Massalia and Rome: she suggests in particular that the control of the Gallic tribes, on both sides of the Alps, may have provided a link between both cities before Rome pacified the route between Spain and Italy in the aftermath of the second Punic War. She emphasises, irony of history, that Massalia would probably have largely benefited from the pacification of Gaul by Caesar...but its poor political choice resulted in the loss of its independence.

From then on, Massalia has been a Roman city: the study and the putting in perspective of the material documentation proposed by Marie-Brigitte Carre give an overview of the "Marseille territories of exchanges" which substantially mitigates our view of text data on their own. To form a tie between Greek and Roman Marseille, Michel Bats' paper is based on Onomastic, Ancient Literature and Hellenistic Sculpture to propose an analysis of Massaliot society at the dawn of the Roman Conquest.

Finally, to complete this update of the Massaliot issues and results, the book proposes a commented bibliography and a webography which will enable English-speaking students and researchers to gain knowledge of the works and research tools developed by the French teams and their partners.

This work has been produced within the framework of the Unit of Excellence LabexMed—Social Sciences and Humanities at the heart of multidisciplinary research for the Mediterranean—which holds the following reference 10-LABX-0090.

This work has benefited from a state grant administered by the Agence Nationale de la Recherche for the project Investissements d'Avenir A*MIDEX which holds the reference n°ANR-11-IDEX-0001-02.

Web Resources and Supplementary Bibliography

http://syslat.on-rev.com/
http://ccj.cnrs.fr/
http://www.asm.cnrs.fr/spip.php?article61
http://www.inrap.fr/
http://www.culturecommunication.gouv.fr/Politiques-ministerielles/Archeologie
http://archeologie.culture.fr/
http://epmp.huma-num.fr/bibliographie/
http://www.bibracte.fr/fr/approfondir/ressources-documentaires/le-centre-de-docu
   mentation
http://www.archeo.ens.fr/spip.php?article680

Arcelin, P., 1986, Le territoire de Marseille dans son contexte indigène. *In*: *Le territoire de Marseille grecque*, Actes de la table ronde d'Aix-en-Provence, 1985, Collection Etudes massaliètes 1, 43–104.

Barruol, G., 1969, *Les peuples préromains du sud-est de la Gaule. Etude de géographie historique*, Paris, De Boccard, 408p.

Bats, M., éd., 1990, *Les amphores de Marseille grecque (Actes table ronde de Lattes, 1989)*, Collection Etudes massaliètes 2, 294p.

Bresson, A., Rouillard, P., éd., 1993,—*L'Emporion*, Paris, de Boccard, 247p.

Brun, P., Chaume, B., 1997, *Vix et les éphémères principautés celtiques. Les Vie–Ve siècles avant J.-C. en Europe centre-occidentale*, Paris, Errance, 408p.

Buxo, R., Py, M., 2001, La viticulture en Gaule à l'âge du Fer, *Gallia*, 2001, 58, 29–43.

Chausserie-Laprée, J., dir., 2000, Le temps des Gaulois en Provence, Martigues, Musée Ziem, 279 p.

Clavel-Lévêque, M., 1977, *Marseille grecque, Le dynamisme d'un impérialisme marchand*, Jeanne-Laffite, Marseille, 215 p.

Delamarre, X., 2001, *Dictionnaire de la langue gauloise*, Paris, Errance, 352 p.

Gailledrat, E., 1997, *Les Ibères de l'Ebre à l'Hérault*, Lattes, Aralo, 336 p.

Gailledrat, E., Taffanel, O., 2002, *Le Cayla de Mailhac (Aude)*, Lattes, Aralo, 272 p.

Gailledrat, E., *et al*, 2000, Nouvelles données sur l'habitat protohistorique de Mailhac (Aude) au premier âge du Fer (VIIe-Ve s. av. J.-C.), *In*: *L'hàbitat protohistoric a Catalunya, Rossello i Llenguadoc Occidental*. Gérone, 173–184.

Goudineau, Chr., 1998, *Regard sur la Gaule*, Paris, Errance, 379 p.

Gras, M., 1995, *La Méditerranée archaïque*, Paris, A. Colin, 192 p.

Janin, Th., 2006, Systèmes chronologiques et groupes culturels dans le midi de la France de la fin de l'âge du Bronze à la fondation de Marseille : communautés indigènes et premières importations, *In : Gli Etruschi da Genova ad Ampurias*. Pise-Rome, 93–102.

Louis, M., Taffanel, O., 1955, *Le premier âge du Fer languedocien, I, Les habitats*, Institut d'Etudes Ligures, Bordighera-Montpellier, 207 p.

Louis, M., Taffanel, O., 1958, *Le premier âge du Fer languedocien, II, Les nécropoles à incinération*, Institut d'Etudes Ligures, Bordighera-Montpellier, 262 p.

Louis, M., Taffanel, O., 1960, *Le premier âge du Fer languedocien, III, Les tumulus, conclusions.* Institut d'Etudes Ligures, Bordighera-Montpellier, 423 p.

Marichal, R., Rébé, I., 2003, *Les origines de Ruscino (Château-Roussillon, Perpignan, Pyrénées-orientales) du Néolithique au premier âge du Fer*, Lattes, 300 p.

Monteil, M., 1999, *Nîmes antique et sa proche campagne*, Lattes, 528 p.

Py, M., 1990, *Culture, économie et sociétés protohistoriques dans la région nimoise*, Rome, Ec.Franç., 2 vol., 957 p.

Py, M., dir., 1999, Recherches sur le quatrième siècle avant notre ère à Lattes, *Lattara*, 12, 680 p.

Roman, Y., 1997, *Histoire de la Gaule. VIe siècle av. J.-C.–Ier siècle ap. J.-C*, Paris, Fayard, 791 p.

Rouillard, P., 1991, *Les Grecs et la Péninsule ibérique du VIIIe au IVe siècle avant Jésus-Christ*, Paris, de Boccard, 467 p.

1. The Littorals in Southern Gaul: State of the Issue

Philippe Leveau

Research on the natural history of the littorals of Southern Gaul considered in their relation with the archaeological data and more especially for the ancient period benefits from a proven tradition which dates back to the conference organised by Roland Paskoff and Pol Trousset in *Les déplacements des lignes de rivages en Méditerranée d'après les données de l'archéologie* (1987). Incidentally, it only replaced partially the synthesis of the British geographer Catherine Delano-Smith (1979). In the following years, littoral geomorphology studies saw a remarkable development thanks to the impetus given in Languedoc by the works of Paul Ambert (1987, 1995, 2000, 2001) and, in Provence, by those of Mireille Provansal (1988, 1993, 1999) and of Christophe Morhange (1995, 1998, 2000, 2015), relayed by a new generation of researchers who, in their wake, have worked closely with archaeologists, not only on sites of interest on French littorals, but also on those of the rest of the Mediterranean region. One of them could undoubtedly have produced a statement of the works in progress giving a better overview of the new perspectives opened by these collaborations. But archaeologists are not only passive users of researchers on littoral morphology. They contribute to the development of them by prospections and excavations on a terrestrial environment on aggraded sectors and in a marine environment on sites which were drowned by the rebound of the sea level. For Provence and Languedoc, numerous articles and several books have provided the demonstration of the usefulness of these collaborations. This article intends to review their breakthroughs.

The Natural Processes: Accumulation and Erosion Dynamics

For a generation, the systematic use of isotopic dating methods permitted by the decrease in costs and the allocation of financing has completely renewed the history of littorals. Room should be left to the works of Ch. Morhange who opened research on the littorals of the Mediterranean region by a systematic use of the bioindicators which happen to be those we can actually date. But the latter are not the only ones and, generally speaking, the knowledge of the evolution of the littorals benefits from all the research procedures developed by environmental geosciences to study anthropisation phenomena. They have ensured the independence of the history of environment with respect to those of societies and removed the exclusivity of written sources. They have upset the theories which had been proposed before from the single archaeological and historical data.

Those which had been elaborated in the nineteenth century are outdated and should only be of interest for the history of science. They are still sparking the regional imagination and have triggered reconstructions, some of which are still in use. Echoing Albert Grenier who, already in 1931, wrote in his *Manuel* that, if the facts noted by Ernest Desjardin (1876) were interesting, "neither of them should have his theories reported any longer." Paul-Marie Duval reminded forty years later about the exaggerated character of their restitutions (Duval 1971, 149). However, a usual book, *L'Atlas historique*, published in 1969 (Baratier et al. 1969), again reproduced the map of the Rhône delta proposed in the nineteenth century by that historian. Closer to us still, they are invoked as an admissible hypothesis on the question of the Hérault delta (Ugolini in Fiches 2002, 531).

The current geomorphology of the littorals throws a light on the accumulation and erosion processes conditioning the existence and the visibility of littoral sites. These are connected to the opposite processes of the erosion caused by the tide attacking the shore and of the accumulation of sediments carried by watercourses at the mouths and distributed over the coasts by marine currents. Between the tenth and the fourth millennium BC, the postglacial rebound of the sea level associated with global warming had caused the valleys dug by rivers to be flooded and the shoreline to be moved back. But, in the Holocene Age, from the Neolithic Age, its slowing down enabled the alluvial contributions to compensate for it and the shoreline to move forward. Thus, during the 2500 years elapsed since the end of the first Iron Age, the rise of the water body reached 1.30 m on our coasts, which corresponds to an average of 0.33 cm/year, but it stabilised in fact some 500 years ago (Morhange et al. 1998), so that on most coasts, the sedimentary contributions of the watercourses associated with the erosion of their watersheds have largely balanced out the attack of littorals by the sea. Consequently, the shorelines have moved forward and littoral sites are now inland. This process reflects two salient features of current littoral archaeology. Hitherto mainly submarine, this archaeology has spread to a terrestrial environment. Such evolution is accompanied by a close dependence to geomorphological studies which account for the taphonomy of littoral sites. Geoarchaeology is now an inescapable part of the archaeological approach to littoral sites (Morhange et al. 2015).

Two natural factors reflect the diverse situations observed on the shores of Southern Gaul. The first factor refers to geology and opposes the littorals of the Maritime Alps and Provence to those of Languedoc. In the East of the Rhône River, the little extension of the littoral plateau does not enable the development of alluvial plains. Indeed, once the rias invaded by the postglacial rebound of the sea level have been filled, the sediments which reached the deltas and have been mobilised by marine currents are evacuated into the deep marine basins and cease to feed the littorals. In the West of the Rhône River, the extension of the littoral plateau reflects a different evolution and considerable progradation of the shoreline. The second factor is of climatic order and explains the importance of chronological breaks. The increase in temperatures and conversely their decrease have had an influence on the melting ice and on the pace of the sea level rebound. The degradation or the improvement of the regional climatic conditions act upon the erosion of the sides and condition the quantity of the sediments reaching the littorals and the littoral currents take over and deposit along the coasts. But to both these factors should be added a third, that is, the anthropisation of the watersheds which may either increase the sediment load due to an aggressive agricultural enhancement or decrease said load by developing sides or watercourses retaining the sediments. Consequently, between the end of the first Iron Age and the current time, littorals have seen phases of moving forward and backward causing discontinuities in the preservation of archaeological sites.

The Coasts of Provence from the Maritime
Alps to the Rhône River

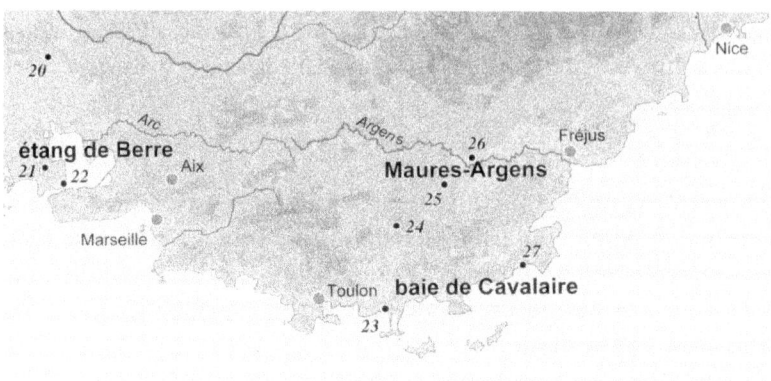

Figure 1. The Southern Gaul Coastline from the *Alpae Maritimae* Province to the Rhône (from Fiches & Raynaud 2010; fig. 1 p. 125). 21: Saint-Blaise; 22: *Maritima Avaticorum* (Tholon Martigues?); 23 Olbia; 27: Pardigon (Cavalaire).

From the Baie des Anges to the Argens Delta

In the East, in the Maritime Alps, the process described was most efficient in the rias deeply incised by the watercourses running down from the Alps or the mountain ranges of the Provence foreland. The shoreline essentially reached its current position as early as the end of the second millennium BC and later on the extension of the littoral alluvial strip connecting the mouth plains was reduced. The littoral is formed from a succession of low alluvial plains at the gulf bottom, separated by mulls. These are, from East to West, between the *Tropaeum Augusti* at the Western boundary of the Ligurian country and the mountain range of the Esterel, *Baie des Anges*, separated by the *Cap d'Antibes* from the *Golfe Juan* and the *Golfe de Napoule* beyond the *Cap Croisette* and the Lerins islands. Neither the position nor the nature of the port facilities associated with the colony of *Nikaia* are known. Only two texts are available which qualify the Roman *Nicia*, for one as a *portus* (the Acts of the council of Arles in 314), for the other as a *plagia* (*Antoninus' maritime Itinerary* around 500).

It is in this context that at a discussed date, the Marseille colony of Antipolis was implanted in the East of the rock mountain range of *Cap d'Antibes* on the bank of a cove dominated in the North by the mull of Fort Carré, Saint-Roch cove. This cove is sheltered from the Mistral which here has a South-west orientation and from the sea currents by two rocky islets. It was a lagoon separated from the sea by a sandy belt. But in the Neolithic Age, the belt was broken and the lagoon became a bay, gradually clogged with sand (Sivan 2013). Ancient discoveries in currently aggraded areas, observations in submarine prospection or on aerial photos have provided partial reconstruction of the history of the harbour area. The only ancient developments built which have been identified are salting tubs. No pontoon or quay has been discovered. But the slope of the embankment enabled the docking of small tonnage boats and the excavation of a shipwreck enables us to specify the dimensions thereof: that of an average size sailing boat (20–22 m in length) (Daveau 2013). On the other side of *Cap d'Antibes*, on the littoral of *Golfe Juan*, the contributions of a watercourse have sealed off a lagoon which had formed behind a sandy littoral belt. It was at the origin a shower water lagoon. But at the end of the Bronze Age, the partial dismantling of the belt had enabled the penetration of salty marine waters. A preventive archaeology intervention has enabled us to identify one of the few known developments on these littorals during Roman times: a seawall had been raised at the bottom of the lagoon to protect a stony space which had supposedly been used for salt production (Daveau and Sivan, 2010).

The Argens Delta

In the West, in the department of the Var, the Esterel and Maures mountain ranges are separated by the Argens valley. The delta of this watercourse, whose valley give access to the inside of Provence, had drawn the attention of historians and archaeologists in the last century because of the Fréjus site *(Forum Julii)*, a location of one of the Augustan colonies of Southern Gaul and a harbour of the Roman military fleet, clogged with sand. The progress of the shoreline is associated with the combined contributions of this river which collects the water from the depression delineating the Maures mountain range and that of the Reyran running down from the Esterel. As such, it contributes to the natural factors of erosion (lithology, climate), anthropic factors of weakening of the slopes like agropastoral activities, forest exploitation and human interventions on runoff. In the nineteenth century, Ch. Lenthéric had dedicated a landmark study to the position of Fréjus and to the Argens mouth (Lenthéric 1876). It was then considered that the harbour had been dug in a lagoon or a littoral swamp and that it was connected to the sea by a canal. This image of the Argens mouth was still admitted in the 1990s when the researches on landscape archaeology on the lower plain of Argens were initiated (Fiches et al. 1995).

Michel Dubar had proposed a hypothesis for locating the shoreline at three moments of the history of the filling of the ria, in the Bronze Age, at the beginning of the fifth century BC and in the middle of the first century BC, based on a mathematical model for filling the ria which assumed that the littoral progressed regularly along an arc of a circle (Dubar 2004). This model was established from an assessment of the width of the valley and of five radiocarbon datings performed on two sediment core samples. This modelling was the starting point of programmes that the archaeologists have carried out in collaboration with him and with the geomorphologists of Aix. The results of the last of them, coordinated by Frédérique Bertoncello, reflect the deep modification of our previous vision of the places with which the valley was filled. The latter has been neither regular nor uniform. The progradation of the shoreline has been dissymmetrical. It was faster on the North flank of the plain because of the contributions of the Reyran. A wet area persisted in the centre of the valley, in the sector of the Esclapes, so that during Roman times, a bridge had been built to join the Maures mountain range from a diverticulum of the Aurelian route. In the alluvial plain, the levels of the Iron Age are situated between 4 and 10 m in depth, which accounts for the absence of site dating from that time. In the Southern part of the valley, between the fourth and the second century, a littoral belt delineated a lagoon opened to the sea. During Roman times, the lagoon of Villepey, on the bank of which a military camp had been built, construed as that of the fleet, remained in communication with the sea and there was still a lagoon in the High Middle Ages, whereas the ria is sealed off in the North (Excoffon et al. 2010; Bertoncello et al. 2014).

The difference in the paces with which the terminal part of the ria was filled reflects the harbour position occupied at one moment in time of their history by both agglomerations of the delta, the Escaravatiers for the protohistorical period and Fréjus for the Roman period. The main protohistorical agglomeration of the Argens is situated at the Escaravatiers on a sandstone mound 1 km away from the lagoon of the Esclapes then opened to the sea. Implanted at the junction of the sixth and fifth centuries, this site constitutes "the best-known Ligurian centre by archaeology in the coastal area of Eastern Provence". The nature of its occupation leads us to interpret it as one of the locations controlled by the Ligurian populations who threatened the commerce in Marseille rather than a relay of that commerce (Fiches et al. 1995, 230). When it was built, the port of *Forum Julii* was situated at the bottom of a marine bay protected by the rocky mound of Saint-Antoine. It communicated directly with the sea. What was considered as the Southern quay of the access channel to the port is now construed as a jetty developed in the first third of the first century AD to protect the port from being clogged with sand. The archaeological and sedimentological data have thus led scholars to abandon the assumption of a development of the Roman port of Fréjus in a lagoon connected to the sea by a canal which may be preceded by an outer port.

From the Delta of the Argens to the Natural Harbour of Marseille

At the West of the mouth of the Argens, the rocky littoral of the Maures mountain range includes a number of bays delineated by its rocky outcrops, at the bottom of which small alluvial plains have formed. They have housed ancient port facilities named by Antoninus' maritime itinerary and which remain to be discovered: these are *Golfe de Saint-Tropez* where he sited the *sinus sambracitanus,* Pampelonne cove between *Cap Camara* and *Cap Piner,* Cavalaire bay, the cape of which would have sheltered the *portus of Heraclea Caccabria* and, in the West of the Maures cornice, Lavandou bay. All of them have sheltered port facilities. Moreover, at the Western outlet of the "Permian depression", the main axis of circulation between the primary mountain range of the Maures and the mountain ranges of calcareous Provence, separated by the outlet, the sediments torn off from these mountain ranges and carried by the Gapeau its affluent, the Real Martin, have formed a littoral plain at the South of which Giens double tombolo separates two natural harbours: in the East, the natural harbour of Hyères, delimited in the South by its islands, in the West the natural harbour of Giens and of Toulon, protected by the peninsula of Saint-Mandrier. The research conducted by the geomorphologists charts the environmental reasons which explain the different destinies of both ports of this portion of the Var littoral, that is, the Marseille trading post of *Olbia* and the Roman port of *Telo Martius* (Pasqualini 2000).

The Marseille people had implanted their colony of Olbia in Provence on the littoral plateau at the foot of a sandstone hill, at the base of Giens double sandy tombolo (Brun 1999, 437–461; Bats 2006). As explained by Michel Pasqualini: "It is difficult to imagine today that there had been a port in *Olbia*. Its beach exposed to the mistral, the necessity to cross the Western tip of Giens and to come back and reach *Olbia* from the East, which is almost impossible according to the wind orientation, the absence of any protected berthing, are as many arguments which render this possibility hardly credible." Between 1996 and 1998, the joint researches of Luc Long and of Claude Vella have reflected this paradoxon. They have shown that in the West of the Western tombolo, there had been a paleotombolo connected towards the North with the continent by a belt of dune sandstone which has disappeared under the effect of active tides in the natural harbour under a prevailing wind. *Olbia* was founded at the bottom of a lagoon situated between this paleotombolo and the current tombolo. It opened to the sea through graus. The Greek port was probably situated against the Eastern rampart of the city at the outlet of a brook. Between the fourth century BC and the first century AD, the filling of this sector by the brook emerging therein accounts for the Roman port facilities built downstream whereas the tombolo which protected the lagoon and the sandstone belt were already partially eroded. Two thousand years later, the pier erected to protect the inlet to the port is totally drowned off the Almanarre shore (Long & Vella 2003). An analogous evolution of the littoral leading to the disappearance of lagoons sheltering port facilities is at the West in the Laurons on the littoral of the Nerthe and in Fos at the outlet of the Marius canal (Vella et al. 2000).

In Toulon, excavations caused by major urban works have enabled the discovery of Roman port facilities realised under very different natural conditions. The *Telo Martius portus* was situated in a natural harbour delineated by the Saint-Mandrier Cape in the West and the Couronne Cape in the East, by the bank of little coastal plain at the back of a bay, formed by the alluvions carried by the Las and Eygoutier Rivers. Both these rivers, whose waters fed swamps, flowed into the natural harbour at that place before Vauban diverted them to prevent the harbour from being filled. No hard ancient development has been unearthed. The embarkations berthed at wooden wharves arranged perpendicular to the bank and unloaded their cargos there. The strand properly speaking was stabilised by tree trunks retaining embankments. As on other ancient ports, excavations and geoarchaeology enable us to monitor the progress of the strand and the fossilisation of the Roman developments as they were being filled by the alluvion contributions of both rivers and urban waste (Brun 1999, 799–806, 816–818; Pasqualini 2000, 37).

Tauroeis colony *(Tauroention, Tauroentum)* that Marseille would have established against the Ligurians is located on an eminence, the Citadel of the Brusc, in the West of the peninsula of Cap Sicié. The site, lying at the North of the small Embiez archipelago provides a good shelter for shallow-draft ships (Brun 1999, 726–738). Its position reminds of Olbia, with the fundamental difference of exposure to marine erosion. The three other ancient harbour sites known on the littoral between Cap Sicié and Bec de l'Aigle occupy a position at the back of creeks: the *villa maritima* of Baumelles built above the cove and the Madrague small harbour at Saint-Cyr sur Mer, on a tidal flat (Brun 1999, 639–652), the *Citharista portus,* quite probably situated by the old La Ciotat harbour and the Prè cove occupied by the shipbuilding yards and the *Carsicis portus,* situated in Cassis at the back of a bay surrounded by the mountain ranges of the Calanques in the West and of Cap Canaille in the East. The cliffs towering over that bay are highly attacked by the sea. The remains of a *villa maritima* partially sunken in the Arène cove by a collapse are perfect examples of this situation (Rothé & Tréziny 2005, 794–796).

Marseille

In the West of the mountain range of the Calanques, the Phocaeans founders of *Massalia* had installed their harbour at the foot of the colonial rampart on the North bank of an East/West orientation calanque dug perpendicular to the strand of the natural harbour in the clay and sandstone facies of the Stampian marls of the basin of Marseille. In the 1990s, further to excavations initiated as of 1945 by the developments of the Vieux-Port, Marseille played a laboratory role in the elaboration of the collaboration protocols between archaeology and geosciences. Building upon the structures which enabled assessment of the vertical mobility of the marine level, Ch. Morhange elaborated a methodology which was applied to the studies of rocky littorals and which enabled understanding of the evolution of the ancient harbour basins and to write the natural history thereof (Mariner 2009, 15–16; Morhange et al. 2015). The modelling-based reconstruction of coastal circulation threw light on the location of ancient harbour facilities. Both ends of the Northern bank, in the West the sector between the Fort Saint-Jean and the City hall which saw the first harbour facilities and in the East the horn of the harbour in the area of La Bourse are the most protected sectors from a mistral wind NW 340° and of its effects on the currents (Millet et al. 2000). It started to be filled by the sediments torn off from its sides around 1500 BC, that is, long before the arrival of the Phocaeans. But the progradation of the strand on the different banks of the calanque was faster on the North bank due to the presence of the city, while slower on the East bank and around the city. A swamp still exists on this side which, as seems to be the case in Antibes, was even affected by a transgression at the end of Antiquity (Morhange & Weydert 1995).

From Marseille to the Rhône Delta: The Littoral of the Nerthe and the Access to the Pond of Berre

Between Marseille and the Pond of Berre, along the littoral of the chain link of the Nerthe, rocky mulls and creeks alternate which constitute as many natural harbours. In its East-West orientation Southern part, these creeks are sheltered from the Western winds, but exposed to offshore tides in case of an Eastern wind. They saw various developments in connection with occupations and a littoral life which can be monitored since the beginning of the Iron Age on both mulls of Tamaris and of L'Arquet where the equipment discovered testifies to the contacts with the first navigators who frequented these coasts (Gateau 1996, 261–262). These creeks were used for shipping stones extracted from littoral quarries mentioned by Strabon (*Geography*, IV, 6) which employed for building works in Marseille (Pedini 2013). In Roman times, these mulls and the associated creeks hosted the *villae maritimae* erected by Italians or rich Marseille people. The harbour facilities associated with that of Seynèmes-les-Laurons have been recognised in the cove of the Laurons on the Western part of this littoral, where it inflects towards the North. Three seawalls protected the harbour facilities from the Western tides (Vella et al. 2000, 43–44). But it is not the only one: another one was recognised in Carry-le-Rouet (Gateau 1996, 157–158). They are part of a series completed by that of La Baumasse in the West of the Caronte canal.

This watercourse, 6.5 kilometres in length and 250 metres in width, communicates the water body of the Pond of Berre with the sea. In the Middle Ages and in the modern era, this space was occupied by a 1.5 km-wide lagoon, perhaps the *Kainos* mentioned by Ptolemy, which was particularly interesting for its salt works and its fisheries. In the nineteenth century, the dredging works which have permitted the access of marine ships increased its depth to 10 m. They have turned the area upside down and in particular destroyed the lake villages of the Salins de Ferrières and of the Abion, dating from the Late Bronze Age (Gateau 1996, 224–226). These sites are only known by the collection of material found at the surface and the possibility of discovering ancient developments seemed to be ruled out. Nevertheless, the recent researches of Frédéric Leroy (2010) have shown that there were still stakes corresponding to developments. As early as in the Iron Age, islets associated with the aggradations had slowed down the hydrological exchanges and progressively closed the pass until the operation of the Pond was relatively independent from the general maritime level. Since the 1980s, excavations conducted by Jean Chausserie-Laprée have enabled scholars to monitor the history of the successive villages of the Iron Age on the island of Martigues and controlled the inlet thereof. The oldest dates back to the beginning of the fifth century BC. M. Provansal has shown that if maintaining the site above water was vastly due to the successive contributions of materials by the inhabitants, the origin of the island where these villages were installed was linked with the particular significance of the sludgy sedimentation in contact with the pond and the sea (Provansal 1988, 12–13). Based on current knowledge, it must be admitted that as of the Iron Age, the water body of the Pond of Berre operated independently of that of the sea (Provansal 1993) and that the penetration of marine ships was impossible.

The Pond of Berre, whose inlet was controlled by these protohistoric sites, is a lagoon of brackish water which covers 15,000 has (Leveau 1996), halfway between the delta of the Rhône and Marseille. A consensus was found around an identification between this pond and the *stagnum mastromela* (Barruol 1969), rather than the *Stomalimné* (literally the Pond of the mout[1]), the lagoon rich with oysters and fish that Strabo (*Geography*, IV, 1, 8) situated in the East of the mouth of the Rhône. Since the rebound of sea water, 7000 years ago, sediments have accumulated there and the water body is being filled. Its maximal depth remains smaller than 10 m (Leveau & Provansal 1993). However, it can be observed that the filling speed has remained quite moderate, at least in the South basin, inasmuch as the quantity of alluvions brought by the Arc and the Touloubre Rivers, although reinforced by the Durancian contributions of the EDF canal, is still smaller than what can be discharged into the ponds of the Languedoc littoral by the rivers running down from the Cevennes mountains. In the nineteenth century, the connection of the lagoon to the sea caused the salinity of the Pond to increase. The data of fauna preserved in sediments show that its salinity rate has remained equivalent to that of the sea up to the end of the Roman era. A reduction might have taken place in the High Middle Ages, which would reflect that the Caronte Pass had been clogged up. This observation is important since it enables us to assume that the Pond was not accessible to marine ships.

The Delta of the Rhône

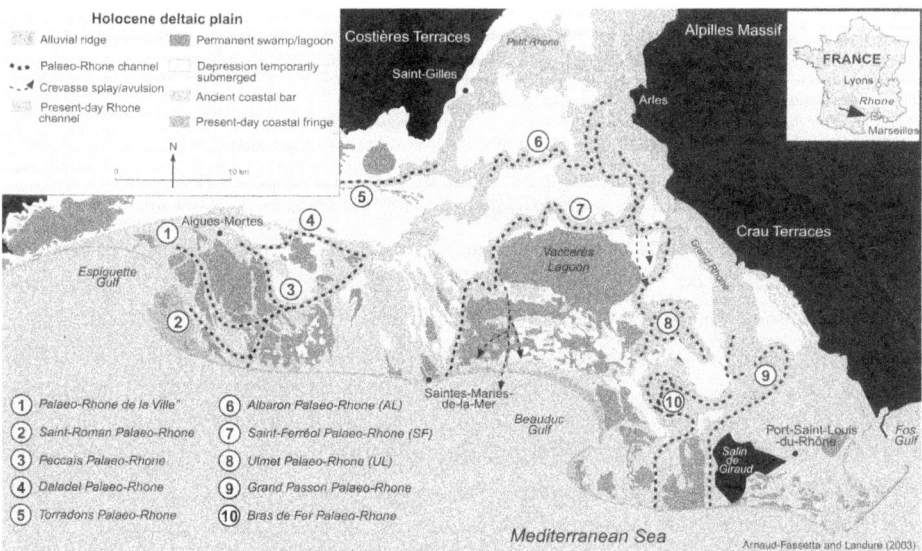

Figure 2. Hydrogeomorphological and palaeohydrographical changes in the Rhône Delta during the last millennia. Paleo and present-day channel (Arnaud-Fassetta 2004, fig. 2, p. 67).

Further West, the central issue is that of access to the Rhône, the main navigable pathway towards the inside of the continent, well-known to ancient navigators. The recent works of Patrice Arcelin (1995) on the site of Arles, at the head of the delta, have shown that although the first traces of occupation of the site date to the years 650–600, a major settlement appeared on the rock no sooner than one century later, around 540–530. For the second Iron Age, the account of the crossing of the Rhône by Hannibal drew attention to the significance of navigation on the river as early as the third century BC (Leveau 2003). The ease with which the Carthaginian chief acquired the ships he needed (barges, but also ships adapted to fluvio-maritime navigation) suggests that the Rhône was used for navigation. As regards the opportunities offered by the river during the Iron Age, the issue is explained by the recent works of Aix-based geomorphologists developed under the guidance of M. Provansal (2008). In the wake of the works of Alain L'Homer on the Western part of the delta, his works, those of Gilles Arnaud-Fassetta (2004) and of C. Vella (Vella et al. 2008) have renewed our knowledge on the Camargue and the Fos gulf. Although these works are still tributary of the historical cut between the Languedoc and Provence parts of the delta, they give a coherent vision of navigation in the delta of the Rhône and have fuelled the thinking of archae-ologists and historians (Landuré & Pasqualini 2004; Leveau 2004b).

Saint-Blaise and the Sea

Situated between the Pond of Berre and the Rhône, in the area of the ponds, the site of Saint-Blaise is the starting point of the terrestrial pathway which follows the basin of the South of the Crau River and leads to the North towards the Rhône valley. The prominence of an Etruscan and Greek material led archaeolo-gists to imagine the existence of a harbour at the foot of the *Oppidum*.

This hypothesis reflected the singularity of a site whose ancient name remains a subject of debate: only the medieval denomination, *Ugium*, is ensured; *Mastromela / Mastramellé / Mastrabala* is only the most plausible name. F. Benoit also suggested an identification of Saint-Blaise with the *Her-aclea* named by Stephanus of Byzantium, but Pliny placed this site in the delta of the Rhône *(Heracleam oppidum in ostio Rhodani fuisse, HN, 3, 34)* (Benoit 1965, 97–98). In fact, none of the ponds it dominated, neither the pond of Lavalduc nor that of the Engrenier, whose bottoms are situated respectively 8 m and 14.50 m below the 0 NGF, have communicated directly with one another and even less with the sea, at least since the end of the Bronze Age. Consequently, these cannot claim to be the elements of a proto-historical harbour complex (Trément 1999).

The East of the Delta from the Fos Gulf to the Camargue

In the East of Berre's pond, the topography of the littoral is governed by a complex series of causes whose works in question throw a light on their respective prominence and their interferences. Already evoked, the first of the factors is the rebound of the sea level which has occurred over time scales on the order of thousands of years. The second, more properly speaking geological factor is the subsiding tectonic which makes it worse. Long suspected, it was put in evidence by the works of C. Vella who, from an inventory of the archaeological structures dated on the littoral strip comprised between Marseille and the Camargue shows the local character of the submersion of the Northern part of the Fos gulf since the beginning of the era (Vella 2002, 106). These natural factors, which combine to explain the recession of the shoreline, are balanced out variably by the considerable sediment contributions of the Rhône triggered by the erosion of the watershed of the river (95,500 km²). In the Neolithic Age, 6,000 years ago, the distance between le Rocher de l'Hauture and the shoreline lay some twelve kilometres in the South of Arles; it had doubled in Roman times.

The history of the occupation of the soil in the delta is now better known by the works conducted in Camargue (Landuré and Pasqualini 2004) and, on the river, upstream in the plain of Arles. Before its mouth, the current Rhône divides into two arms which diverge upstream of Arles: the Grand-Rhône which built the arrow, which confers his current aspect to the delta of the Rhône and the Petit-Rhône (Leveau 2014).

The protohistorical period is poorly known. The ancient sources vary considerably as regards the number of the mouths prior to the beginning of our era. A rhyme of the Argonauts by Apollonios of Rhodes (IV, 634) (third century BC) alludes to seven mouths, whereas they would be six in number according to Posidonios and five in number according to Diodorus of Sicily (first century) (5, 25), Polybius quoting Timaeus (second century BC) and Festus Avienus (fourth century). The evolution would then be as follows: in the fourth century BC (Pytheas), five mouths would have been in operation; in the middle of the second century, they were only two in number (which is the current figure). Twenty years later, the occurrence of a mouth gave the delta the configuration which was its own in Roman times, the best known because we have the description of Strabo and iconographic testimonies. The river had then three mouth arms. The main arm lies in the East of the Rhône, called the Ulmet River. The Rhône of Saint-Ferréol ran in the North and the West of today's Vaccarès. In the West, a third arm corresponding to the Rhône of Peccaïs, in the extension of that of Albaron, emerged about 5 km behind the current shoreline. The progress of the coastline was due to the sediment contributions of these arms which built deltaic lobes and its recession was caused by the displacement of these arms or the decrease in their contributions. The arm of Saint-Ferréol remained functional during the ancient period, but the main flow ran along the arm of Ulmet, extended by the arm of Fer which grew from strength to strength from the fourth century. Later on, the appearance of the Grand-Rhône, further East still, was responsible for the recession of the shoreline in this central sector. Downstream, according to the ease of evacuation of the sediment load, the river changed styles and described meanders.

The approach to the coast and the entry of the ships into the river are governed by the position and the height of the bar of the mouth so that the ships are more or less likely to get stranded. This difficulty was taken into account by ancient mariners, as stated quite clearly by Strabo in the abstract where he evoked the conditions in which Marius was led to dig his famous canal between 104 and 102 BC. The aim was to remedy the difficulties associated with an episode that occurred precisely at that time and which probably modified the layout of the mouths. The opening of the canal of Marius resulted in the installation of the station of *Fossae Marianae* at its maritime outlet. At the end of the Antiquity, on the Table of Peutinger, that station is represented by a thumbnail whose size is equal to that of Ostia. But, for the time being, we know hardly anything about this agglomeration and its related developments. The traces of the outlet of the canal into the Fos Gulf have been effaced by the fluctuations of the shoreline (Vella et al. 1999) and the building works of the Fos harbour have erased what remained of it in the West. However, archaeological structures remain on the beach of Cavaou and at a small depth in the cove of Saint-Gervais, which had been first construed as ship hangers, but which are probably warehouses (Vella et al. 2000). On the current shoreline, at the Estagnon, Frédéric Marty excavated a development formed of wooden crates filled with amphorae and separated from canals (Marty 2007). In the East of the tip of Saint-Gervais opened the Pond of the Estomac now isolated from the sea by a 1.5 km dam protecting the road and the Fos canal at Port de Bouc. F. Benoit considered that he could have formed an outer port of Fos. According to C. Vella, for whom this pond would have housed the main harbour, this assumption can be taken into account (Vella et al. 2000, 45). First oriented Northwest/Southeast, the coast is inflected in the East and took a North-South direction up to Port-de-Bouc, at the inlet of the canal of Caronte. Halfway between them, the Pointe de la Baumasse houses a cove along which a maritime villa was erected. Unfortunately, it has been almost completely destroyed by marine erosion. But in the nineteenth century, its ruins were large enough so that many thought they corresponded to *Stomalimné* which would have been a city, that is, *Maritima Avaticorum* (Gateau et al. 1996, 268–269; Trément 1999, 280–281).

The *Fossae Marianae* were probably in use no longer than one and a half centuries, possibly two. Two hypotheses have been ventured to explain their demise. According to one, perhaps as soon as in the first century, a modification in the bar of the mouth would have rendered entry into the river again directly accessible to ships. But it may also have been a technical change: The ships entering the Rhône River would have been relieved from a portion of their cargo before the bar of the mouth. The cartography of the shipwrecks realised by L. Long effectively shows that ships "got stranded on the bars and the sandbanks usually clogging the mouths", preferably in a sector comprised between the West of the Petit-Rhône and the mouth of the Rhône of Saint-Ferréol around Saintes-Maries-de-la-Mer where most of the 29 listed shipwrecks and most of the limestone blocks have been discovered. Opposite that mouth, the presence of a large number of Roman anchors would point to a secluded anchorage (Long et al. 2002, 163; Long 2013). But for the time being, nothing enables us to conclude whether the ships ran up the river or were unloaded on flat-bottom light boats.

The Petite-Camargue and the Western Part of the Delta

At the end of the 1990s, the knowledge of the Western part of the delta of the Rhône was related to the works of A. L'Homer who had been entrusted with the realisation of the different geological maps of the area. The successive surveys on Saintes-Maries-de-la-Mer (L'Homer 1975), Arles (L'Homer 1987) and the Grau-du-Roi (L'Homer 1993) propose interpretations on the complex relations between the Petit-Rhône and the arms of Albaron, of Peccaïs and of Canavère, between the successive Western arms of the Rhône, between the latter and the two coastal rivers whose mouths concern the same area: Vidourle and Vistre. These works have been used in particular by Jean Cabot in the monograph he has dedicated to the Petite-Camargue. Building upon the data made available to him by A. L'Homer, he situated "at the beginning of our era, a first layout of the Petit-Rhône [which] ran through Saliers and then turned towards the immense lagoon comprised between the Costières in the North and the ancient littoral belt of Sylveréal. But farther West, it received the Vistre and the Vidourle Rivers,

which formed their own delta" (Cabot 1991, 12). A. L'Homer worked on
an era and under conditions which did not enable him to use chronological
data which were as accurate as those obtained on the littoral belts and in
the swamps of the Eastern part of the delta. He was thus prompted to use
archaeological sources and written sources. For the period of interest, the
former are related to the neighbouring sites of Espeyran and of Saint-Gilles
(in Provost et al. 1999).

The issue was repeated by Tony Rey. Indeed, he focuses on the study of the
area situated in the North of the paleo-belt of the Sables or of Sylveréal which
delineated lagoon spaces at a time when the paleo-gulf of Aigues-Mortes was
still open water. From 6500 years BC to Roman times, the progradation of
the deltaic plain of the Petite-Camargue took place between this belt and the
embankment of the Costières. The sediments come from a rift feeding the
fossil arm of the Rhône of the Tourradons (Rey et al. 2005). These works
throw a light on the conditions under which both sites of Espeyran (Saint-
Gilles) in the East and of the Caylar at the confluent of the Rhône and of
the Vistre in the West have developed at the end of the Costière, in contact
with the littoral plain and alongside the lagoon. The first one would be the
trading post of *Rhodanousia* whose name appears in the Pseudo-Scymnus
(*Periegesis*, 2006, 216) and by Stephanus of Byzantium in his *Ethnic studies* as
"the city of Massalia". The second, recently discovered, would be *Virinnae*,
one of the agglomerations quoted on the geographical inscription of Nîmes
(*CIL* XII, 3362). Its role as a trading post at the Eastern end of a long lagoon
area was poorly known before geo-archaeological studies reported the fast
environmental mutations (Roure 2010). It is on this side of the delta that
the first canal is situated, mentioned in written sources, including the *fossa
gothica* which reputedly had been dug by the Visigoth Kings, but which may
also have been the extension of previous works. Its layout did not seem to be
extremely rational. The purpose might have been to secure direct access to
the sea from Saint-Gilles through the arm of the Peccaïs (Cabot 1991).

The Coasts of West of the Rhône: Languedoc and Roussillon

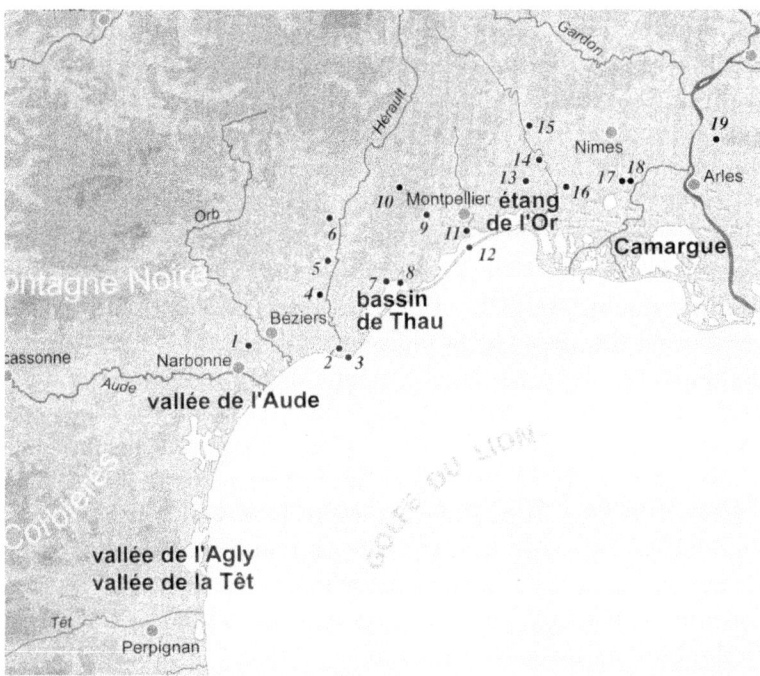

Figure 3. The Coasts of Southern Gaul West of the Rhône (from Fiches & Raynaud 2010, fig. 1, 25). 1—Ensérune. 2—Agde. 3—Embonne. 7—Loupian. 8—Balaruc-les-Bains. 11—Lattes. 12—Maguelonne. 16—Psalmodi. 17—Espeyran. 18—Saint-Gilles.

Between the Rhône and the Hérault Rivers: The "endolagunar" Navigation

In the West of the Rhône, on the archaeological plan, the problematic of the littoral is governed by the old assumption of an "endolagunar" navigation between the deltas of the Rhône and Aude. E. Desjardins indeed admitted the existence of a long water body formed of an uninterrupted series of ponds communicating with the Rhône and the Durance and traversed by the boats of the utriculariae, the *Rubresus* (Desjardins 1876). Formulated at the time when, in the absence of isotopic date, the historians of the littoral only had written sources, this proposition has been repeated and discussed regularly. In fact, the toponym, *Rubresus* (Pomponius Mela, *De Chorografia*, II, 5, 6) or *Rubresus Helice palus* (Festus Avienus, *Ora Maritima*, v. 490) or still *Rubrensis* (Pliny the Elder, *Nat. Hist.*) rather applies to the ponds of the region of Narbonne also named *Narbonitis* (Strabo, *Geography*, IV, 1,

6; Stephanus of Byzantium, *Ethnic studies*). Let us evoke the area of interest here, Claude Raynaud (in Provost et al. 1999, 81–82) identifies it with the *"stagnum Lattara,* the pond of Lattes" described by Pliny and depicts it as "a beautiful navigable pathway connected to the sea through graus". For the ancient period, Espeyran and Lattes, where the corporation of the *fabri et utricularii Lattarenses* (AE 1966, 247) is attested, would thus have been situated on an internal littoral…studded with more modest facilities and traversed by flat-bottom ferry boats up to the delta of the Aude. The interest for this littoral is currently reinforced by the recent borings carried out by Michel Py and Réjane Roure on the site of the Cailar which henceforth seems to have been a (new) lagunar trading post (Py and Roure 2002, 208–209; Roure 2010).

The works of the geomorphologists throw a light on the issue of the maritime circulation along the laguna littoral of the Languedoc and concern the area of the Hérault. Chronologically, the first contributions were made by Paul Ambert (1987). But, to stick to a descriptive rationale from East to West, we shall start with the works of Christophe Jorda on the delta of the Lez and the harbours of Lattes. The littoral of Lattes where the research was coordinated by Philippe Blanchemanche is that on which the most numerous and most accurate data are available (Blanchemanche et al. 2003). Ch. Jorda has demonstrated that the agglomeration had settled on "a residual mound flush with the Pre-Chassean detritic cone, alongside the laguna" (Jorda 2002, 173). This mound which seems to correspond to a pebbly lobe of the Lez set up in the Neolithic Age has been extended in different places at the expense of the lagoon: in front of the Southern gate of the city where the excavations of the harbour have unearthed a harbour facility "in the wake of a low-sloping seabed" (Garcia & Vallet 2002, 71). A first facility would hence have been implanted close to a beach surrounded by a dune formation. Later on, on the urban nucleus properly speaking, the accumulation of structures over a long period, at the rate of one metre per century in average, caused the formation of a tell. The Bronze Age had been characterised by the relative stability of the plain. In the Iron Age, the filling of the lagoon remained minimal, probably because the Lez succeeded in evacuating its sediments. Such conditions are obviously favourable to the development of the harbour activities. D. Garcia stresses the possible interest, in that laguna context, of the installation of a harbour at the mouth of a coastal river: "the current generated by the river permanently or during seasonal floods has probably enabled to create a natural channel in the axis of its confluent, thereby making access to the shoreline easier" (Garcia 2002, 216).

In the West, the history of the littoral between the pond of Mauguio and the Hérault River has been subject to several studies due to P. Ambert.

He insists on the essential distinction to be established between the ponds of L'Or in the East and of Thau in the West: the first belongs to the series of ponds filling up the considerable sediment contributions carried from littoral watercourses running down from the Cevenol foothills, here the Vidourle River; the second receives limited contributions due to its narrow watershed. This major particularity sets it apart from the just mentioned Languedoc ponds as well as from the Roussillon ponds of Sigean and of Salses. It explains that the sedimentation rates at the bottom of the pond have not wiped off the pre-existing morphological irregularities (Ambert 2001, 48) and it reflects the discovery of immersed protohistorical facilities by F. Leroy further to his subaquatic prospections (2010). In this area, the formation of the littoral belt which closes the pond started in the Neolithic Age (7000 BP) with the Holo-cene slow-down of the rising sea level. At the end of the second millennium BC, it would have been close to -2 m NGF.

Farther West still, we find the Hérault River, a major fluvial axis in Languedoc, whose mouth is occupied by Agde, a fluvial and marine harbour which, as soon as at the beginning of the Iron Age attracted the navigators (Ropiot 2003a; Ugolini 2010). The attractive assumption of a long water body connecting the mouths of the Rhône and of the Hérault Rivers accounts for the importance of the debate centred on what P. Ambert (1995) called the "pseudo-insularity of the Agde volcano in Greek and Roman times". The insu-larity of this volcano had indeed been assumed by historians who, building on the indisputable innundability of the corridor of the Sept-Fonds between the Agde volcano and the Pond of Thau in the Northeast, thought that they were dealing with a river: it would be the heir of the Eastern branch of a paleo-delta of the Hérault (Ugolini in Fiches 2002, 349–351). This old assumption was based upon the reading of Ptolemy: Monique Clavel-Lévêque (1970, 105) already observed that "the centre of the delta was occupied by the acropolis, to the extent that Ptolemy (II, 10, 21) could consider Agde as an island". Indeed he mentions twice *Agatha* in his *Geographical guide,* first as a city between the Hérault and the Sète Mountain, then as an island. This dupli-cation evokes a passage of Artemidorus about *Alônis* on the Eastern coast of Spain. Pierre Moret whose interest was raised by it has shown the wording *nésos kai polis* is a formulary expression, specific to the style of the stretches which, according to him, admits only one interpretation, that is, that of a city established on an island (Moret in Badie et al. 2000, 245). Actually, *nésos* does not necessarily designate a space completely surrounded with water. Polybius uses it about the confluent of the Isère and of the Rhône; so does Strabo about Egyptian sites (Leveau 2003, 28 n. 14). For the time being, it is not possible either to invoke the archaeological argument that the discovery of an ancient canal would provide. Although it did not have the aspect of a delta enclosing the Agde volcano, the mouth of the Hérault did not have the same shape as today. At the height of the marine post-glacial rebound, the lower valley of the Hérault was occupied by a gradually aggraded vast gulf and transformed in the Holocene Age into a lagoon by a littoral belt. In the absence of systematic research, its precise depth and extension in the first Iron Age remain rather hypothetical. But pierced with graus, it secured more favourable conditions to navigation than the main mouth which is more or less regularly clogged by the formation of unstable bars. The works of C. Raynaud and those of Languedoc Medievalists have shown that, during the ancient and medieval times, as regards human occupation, this portion of the Languedoc littoral was perfectly integrated to the life of the hinterland (Bourin-Derruau et al. 2001, 418). This character differentiates it clearly from Camargue, even after the rectification relative to its occupation brought by the recent research (Landuré & Pasqualini 2004).

We may have a tendency to project into the past the deltaic progradation which succeeded to a phase of relative stability of the shoreline: it seems to have been considerable as of the end of the Middle Ages in combination of the pejoration of the Little Glacial Age. Nevertheless the continuity and the accessibility of the water body behind the Languedoc littoral belts required continuous developments. In the East, the passage towards the Rhône was made more or less precarious by the quantity of sediments discharged by the Vidourle and the Vistre. As written by J. Cabot (1991, 12), the circulation between the ponds of Mauguio and of Scamander depended on the regular maintenance of discharge canals. In fact, the aim is to clearly differentiate on the one hand the intensity of the social life organised around these water bodies and on the other hand the use of these water bodies for a direct connection between the deltas of the Rhône and the Aude. The latter raises a debate: two solutions of continuity seem to have subsisted, in the East, towards Arles, on the side of the delta and, in the West, at the level of the Agde volcano, towards Béziers and Narbonne beyond. This debate between local and regional is not specific to this maritime façade; it can be found on other laguna littorals, as well as on the Atlantic on the estuary of the Gironde (Bouet 2003).

The Mouth of the Aude and the Gulf of Narbonne

In the West, the littoral of Béziers has been nourished by the contributions of the Hérault and those of the Orb. In protohistorical and historical times, the Orb built a three-arm swampy mouth at the location of the littoral lagoons behind a dune belt (Ugolini & Olive, 2012, 80; Ropiot 2003b).

This delta would have lasted up to the eleventh century. Unlike its neighbour Narbonne, Béziers, which towers over it, seemed to owe its prominence to the installation of the Roman military colony, without connection with any maritime access of significance. But archaeological data have led Daniela Ugolini and Christian Olive to "place Béziers among the three main cities of the French Mediterranean arc, on a par with Arles and Marseille" in the Iron Age (Mazière et al. 2001, 88). The site would have been frequented at an early stage by Greek navigators (Ugolini & Olive 2012). If proven right, this assumption would completely renew our approach to a site whose prominence was acknowledged in protohistorical times, but which was considered essentially for its position of the littoral terrestrial pathway.

As a starting point of the Aquitaine isthmus towards the Garonne valley which provides its Western outlet, the mouth of the Aude, the *Atax* of the ancients, occupies in the geography of the Southern Gaul a position comparable to that of the Rhône. The physiognomy of the littoral has been thoroughly modified by a recent backfill whose prominence undermines most of the reconstructions suggested. Nowadays, the river flows into the sea halfway between Béziers and Narbonne in the North of the Clape whereas, in Antiquity, two branches seem to have coexisted on both sides of the mountain range. In the Iron Age, in the sector of the "Narbonne gulf" whose backfilling by the river and by the Berre had barely started, the existence of a vast water body would have favoured the inland penetration of the ships. Two major sites could supposedly access it. The first one is Montlaurès, a possible capital city of the Elisycs, now situated 15 km inland on an isolated limestone hill culminating 52 m above the lower plain of the Aude whose altitude ranges between 7 and 9 m (Chazelle *in* Dellong 2002, 466–485). Today, the river flows 2 km away. In Roman Antiquity, a swamp fed by major karstic sources lay at the foot of the hill. But this swamp was not necessarily in direct connection with the Aude. Although the geoarchaeological research has shown that an ancient paleocanal may have existed 1 km away from the site (Rescanières 2002, 46), the hypothesis of a fluvial harbour remains to be demonstrated. Pech Maho in Sigean, the second site occupies the extremity of a small plateau towering over the Berre and a lagoon, now clogged up, which in Antiquity communicated with the sea. Between the middle of the sixth century and the end of the second century BC, it was used as a "pier and a relay for cabotage ship along the coasts" (Gailledrat 2010, 350; 2012). But Ensérune, today inland, may have been close to the maritime littoral, although not a harbour site (Fiches 2002). Its position with respect to the sea is governed by the considerable aggradations in the delta of the Aude.

Nowadays, Narbonne lies some twelve kilometres from the sea in a fluviomaritime plain clogged by the contributions of the Aude, in the West of the hill of La Clape. In the early 1990s, an important campaign of borings directed by Jean Guilaine (1995) have produced a quantity of data to assert that in a period related to the recent Prehistory and the Bronze Age, "it was an island and the mull of Narbonne formed a peninsula twice and a half larger than the current Pond of Thau…However, the age when the laguna-marine water body was closed totally is still unknown (between the Chalcolithic and the Antiquity?)" (Rescanières 2002, 45). Its position at the extremity of the lower valley of the Aude supported the idea that, in Antiquity, from Sallèles, the river would have joined the sea through two branches forming a kind of delta on both sides of the La Clape: an arm would have followed in the North the current course of the Aude and a second arm, in the South, would have joined the sea in the area currently occupied by the ponds. The numerous text testimonies, the contributions of the geotechnical borings realised on the current urban site and those of a campaign of borings in the delta of the Aude, show that in Roman times, it was a mull between two water bodies (Ambert 2000). There was still a swamp at the foot of the urban enclosure in the third century.

In 2002, Sébastien Rescanières published an update on the question in the introduction to the volume *Narbonne* of the Archaeological Map of Gaul (Rescanières 2002). Since 2008, new research has thoroughly renewed the case. P. Ambert thought that the Robine running through the city took its rise in the digging of a canal when the Roman city was created. But recent excavations have put in evidence the presence of the river in the third century BC, which suggests that the Robine originated from an arm of the river (Jorda 2013, 135–145). The research underway has thoroughly renewed the knowledge on what was the major harbour of Narbonne Gaul. Excavations conducted in the South of La Clape, in the West of the Pond of Gruissan, in the context of a Collective Research project on the ancient harbours of Narbonne coordinated by Corinne Sanchez and Marie-Pierre Jézégou, have unearthed two jetties enclosing a river, some fifty metres wide. Fifteen to 25 m wide, they were arranged as carriageways. A 4m deep bed enabled deep draught navigation. Thus, "the excavations of Castelou and of Mandira today enable to know the outlet of the Aude in the lagoon" (Sanchez et al. 2014). Outposts probably existed at these places. But, if the channel part could be maintained by a dredging system, it was far more difficult to preserve the circulation of marine ships in the vast lagoon water body being backfilled into which the arm of the Aude and the Berre flowed (Sanchez & Jézégou 2014). This backfilling is quick. Indeed, between Leucate and

Port-la-Nouvelle, the convergence of the littoral drifts explains the progra-dation of the shoreline unlike that of the Pond of Thau (Larue et al. 2009). In the South of the Ponds of Narbonne and of the delta of the Aude, the lido of the plain of the Roussillon is fed by the littoral drift which redistri-butes to the North the sand sediments rejected by the Pyrenean watercourses, the Tech, the Têt and the Agly. Max Guy identified in the Coussoules, in the North of Leucate-la-Franqui, an ancient littoral belt (Guy 1987). Since this pioneering work, the outlines of the natural history of this lido have been enlightened by the geomorphological research in progress since the 1990s. The lagoon of Salses-Leucate was closed in Roman times. Behind the lido, the wet areas in the lagoon and the banks of the internal ponds of the Roussillon were highly attractive for agricultural and pastoral communi-ties having adapted techniques (Ropiot 2012). Between that period and now, the backfilling of the lagoons and the progress of the littoral are associated with erosive crises, the most recent and the important of which corresponds to the Little Glacial Age as in Languedoc (Carozza et al. 2010). The impact of sedimentation in that period is probably responsible for the absence of archaeological data on the littoral life which accounts for the portion of the maritime activities of *Ruscino* and of *Illiberis*. For the time being, the only data available come from submarine archaeology, mainly from the rocky part of the coast (Kotarba et al. 2007, 622–641).

Conclusion: Littoral Archaeology and Wetland Archaeology

The purpose of this overview is to present the evolution of research on Mediterranean shorelines since the 1950s. Between that time and the 1990s, its main actor has been submarine archaeology whose foundations were laid by Fernand Benoit for France and Nino Lamboglia for Italy. As of the 1990s, the carrying out of major urban excavation sites in preventive archaeology has given rise to harbour archaeology in a terrestrial environ-ment. It has benefited from the intervention of geomorphologists to whom harbour excavations offered the opportunity of adjusting their works on the variations of the sea level and on those of the shoreline with greater accu-racy than that given by isotopic chronologies. Completed by core sampling, these littoral geomorphology works enable us to reconstruct the position of the harbours in a shoreline configuration which has now disappeared. These enlighten the choices made in their implantation to suit the needs of commerce or fishing, the navigation conditions governed by the wind and the marine currents, and to suit the capacities of the ships. At the same time, they give hindsight into the complexity of the environmental mutations which have neglected harbour sites: progradation of the littoral in the case of Escaravatiers and of Fréjus at the outlet of Argens, Espeyran and Saint-Gilles on the Western margin of the delta of the Rhône, Lattes abandoned to the benefit of Maguelone and of Narbonne in the delta of the Aude; erosion of a littoral belt in the case of *Olbia;* displacement of a mouth arm into that of *Fossae Marianae.*

These breakthroughs open a new perspective in archaeological research which thus widens from the shoreline and the harbour site to the littoral, that is, from the shoreline to the geographical space of the littoral. Well contextualised on the geographical plane as well as on the historical plane, an archaeology of the Mediterranean littorals opens an original chapter of landscape archaeology in wet areas, *Wetland Archaeology*, which started in Northern Europe as soon as in the 1950s and fine-tuned methodologies based on textual history, on population, plot and landscape archaeology, as well as on paleoenvironmental, in particular paleobotanical and hydrosedimentary studies. These works benefit from the three main advantages of the wet zones: the preservation of organic matter, the coexistence of archaeological data and of environmental data which provides an integrated approach to the nature/culture relationship and the dating opportunities offered by organic remains, in particular thanks to dendrochronology. But it will be reminded that the testimony of environmental data should not be opposed to that of written sources. The reconstructions of Desjardins are obsolete. But, in the case of the delta of the Rhône, he was correct in suggesting that their contradictions noted successive states of an evolving delta.

Listing the written sources bearing upon the area between Marseille and Aigues-Mortes without interpreting them "in the light of the actual or assumed knowledge, on the ancient topography of the delta", H. Tréziny observed that these sources "refer to remote perspectives and do not describe the same reality". He showed that if some of their contradictions were due to mistakes, the context shows that they often express "different concerns" (Tréziny 2004). Thus Strabo and Pomponius Mela evoke the Plaine-de-Pierres (which is the Crau) in a description of the littoral. Further on, Strabo signals salt works which would be "in the middle". In this description, this environment is not that of the plain, as put forward in the translations. There may never have been salt works in Crau and the allusion obviously refers to those of Saint-Blaise (Leveau 2004a). The same observation can be made about the written sources pertaining to the *Rubresus,* the port of Narbonne and the delta of the Aude (Ropiot 2011). To different extents, Strabo, Ptolemy, *the Maritime Itinerary* from Rome to Arles, locating certain stations or the *Ora maritima,* the poem of Avienus inspired by ancient stretches illustrate these difficulties. The pluridisciplinary approach enables, if not always to answer the questions, at least to review the writings, to correct their interpretation and, building upon them, to improve their translation and their comments.

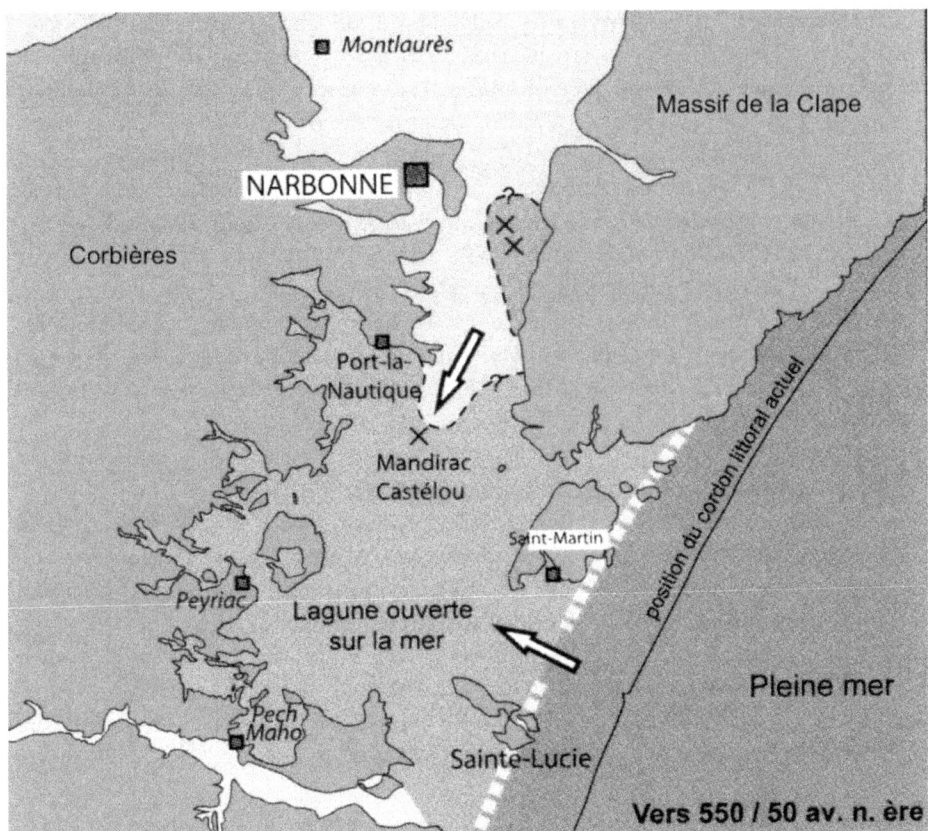

Figure 4. The ponds of Narbonne and the major archaeological sites (from Sanchez and Jezegou 2014, 126, fig. 1). In antiquity the passage of the sea to the lagoon was between New Port and Narbonne (shipwrecks).

Note

1. In Greek, *stoma* designates the mouth. The two oldest occurrences of this name date from 1467 (folio XXVI mentioning for Johan Gay "una pineda confrontant avec lestang de lestomas) and 1501 (folio LXX for Georges Niyel and André Challie "un pra après del pont de Nostro Damo confrontant ambe lo prat de Monsegnour de Fos et ambe lestang de lestomac") in two registers of the community of Fos (ADBR B 1142). According to Jean Rostaing, the origin of this toponym is pre-Latin (information courteously communicated by J. Ph. Lagrue).

Bibliography

Ambert, P., 1987, Modification des paysages en Languedoc central, état actuel des connaissances. In: *Déplacements des lignes de rivage en Méditerranée d'après les données de l'archéologie*, Aix-en-Provence 5–7 septembre 1985, Paris, CNRS.

Ambert, P., 1995, La branche orientale du delta de l'Hérault ou de l'insularité du volcan d'Agde à l'époque gréco-romaine. Hypothèses archéologiques et données géologiques. In: *Sur les pas des Grecs en Occident, Études Massaliètes*, Arles, Errance, 4, 105–112.

Ambert, P., 2000, Narbonne Antique et ses ports, géomorphologie et archéologie, certitudes et hypothèses, *Revue Archéologique de Narbonnaise*, 33, 295–307.

Ambert, P., 2001, Géologie et géomorphologie des pays de l'étang de Thau et de la basse vallée de l'Hérault. In: Lugand & Bermond, 48–57.

Arcelin, P., 1995, Arles protohistorique, centre d'échanges économiques et culturels. In: P. Arcelin, M. Bats, D. Garcia, G. Marchand & M. Schwaller (eds.), *Sur les pas des Grecs en Occident (Hommages à André Nickels)*, Paris-Lattes, Errance-ADAM, Études massaliètes 4, 325–338.

Arnaud-Fassetta, G., 2004, Le rôle du fleuve: les formations alluviales et la variation du risque fluvial depuis 5000 ans. In: Landuré & Pasqualini, 65–77.

Badie, A., Gailledrat, E., Moret, P. et al., 2000, *Le site antique de la Picola à Santa Pola, Alicante*, Paris, éd. Recherches sur les civilisations, Madrid, Casa de Velázquez, 379p.

Baratier, E., Duby, G. & Hildesheim, E., 1969, *Atlas historique Provence, Comtat Venaissin, principauté de Monaco, comté de Nice*, Paris, Armand Colin, 220p.

Barruol, G., 1969, *Les peuples préromains du sud-est de la Gaule. Essai de géographie historique*, Paris, E. De Boccard, 408p.

Bats, M. (ed.), 2006, Olbia *de Provence à l'époque romaine*, Aix-en-Provence, Edisud, 476p.

Benoit, F., 1965, *Recherches sur l'hellénisation du Midi de la Gaule*, Aix-en-Provence, Ophrys, 220p.

Bertoncello, F., Devillers, B., Bonnet, S., Guillon, B., Bouby, L. & Delhon, C., 2014, Mobilité des paysages littoraux et peuplement dans la basse vallée de l'Argens (Var, France) au cours de l'Holocène, *Quaternaire*, 25, (1), 23–44.

Blanchemanche, P., Berger, J.-F., Chabal, L., Jorda, C., Jung, C. & Raynaud, C., 2003, Le littoral languedocien durant l'Holocène: milieu et peuplement entre Lez et Vidourle (Hérault, Gard). In: F-D. Vivien, J. Burnouf, B. Villalba & T. Muxart (eds.), *Des milieux et des hommes: fragments d'histoires croisées. Bilan du Programme PEVS/SEDD*, Elsevier, Collection Environnement, 79–92.

Blondel, J., Barruol, G. & Vianet, R., 2013, *L'Encyclopédie de la Camargue*, Paris, Buchet Chastel, 351p.

Bouet, A., 2003, La mort de Barzan et la naissance du *Litus Saxonicum*. In: J.P. Bost, J.M. Roddaz & F. Tassaux, *Itinéraire de Saintes à Dougga. Mélanges offerts à Louis Maurin*. Bordeaux, Ausonius, E. De Boccard, 95–114.

Bourrin-Derruau, M., Le Blévec, D., Raynaud, C. & Schneider, L., 2001, Le littoral languedocien au Moyen Âge. In: *Castrum 7, Zones côtières et plaines littorales dans le monde méditerranéen au Moyen Âge: défense, peuplement, mise en valeur*, Rome, 23–26 octobre, Rome-Madrid, Ecole Française de Rome, Casa de Velázquez, 345–423.

Brun, J.-P. & Borréani, M. (dir.), 1999, *Le Var 83/1 et 2*, Carte Archéologique de la Gaule, Paris, Académie des Inscriptions et des Belles Lettres, 984p.

Burnouf, J. & Leveau, P. (eds.), 2004, *Fleuves et marais, une histoire au croisement de la nature et de la culture. Sociétés préindustrielles et milieux fluviaux, lacustres et palustres: pratiques sociales et hydrosystèmes*, Aix-en-Provence, Éditions du CTHS, 493p.

Cabot, J., 1991, *Anciens ports et moulins de Petite-Camargue*, Montpellier, Presses du Languedoc, 123p.

Carozza, J.-M., Puig, C., Valette, Ph. & Odiot, T., 2010, La plaine du Roussillon au cours de l'Holocène: apports d'une démarche géoarchéologique et géomorphologique à la connaissance des interactions homme-milieu. In: Delestre & Marchesi 2010, 37–46.

Chausserie-Laprée, J. (ed.), 1988, Le village gaulois de Martigues, *Dossiers Histoire et archéologie*, n°128, 98p.

Clavel-Lévêque, M., 1970, *Béziers et son territoire dans l'Antiquité*, Paris, Les Belles Lettres, 664p.

Daveau, I., 2013, Le port antique d'Antibes: les premiers résultats de la fouille du Préaux Pêcheurs. In: *Aux origines d'Antibes. Antiquité et Haut Moyen Âge*, Antibes, 89–92.

Daveau & Sivan, O., 2010, Les aménagements lagunaires du Bas-Lauvert à Antibes. In: Delestre & Marchesi, 55–60.

Delano Smith, C., 1979, *Western Mediterranean Europe. A historical Geography of Italy, Spain and Southern France since the Neolithic*, London and New York, Academic Press, 453p.

Delestre, X. & Marchesi, H., 2010, *Archéologie des rivages méditerranéens*, Paris, Errance, 532p.

Dellong, E., 2002, *Narbonne et le Narbonnais, 11/1*, Carte Archéologique de la Gaule, Paris, Académie des Inscriptions et des Belles Lettres, 704p.

Desjardins, E., 1876, *Géographie historique et administrative de la Gaule romaine*, t.1, *Introduction et géographie physique comparée. Époque romaine-époque actuelle*, Paris, Hachette, 475p.

Dubar, M., 2004, L'édification de la plaine deltaïque du Bas Argens (Var, France) durant la Protohistoire et l'Antiquité. Application d'un modèle numérique 2D à l'archéologie, *Méditerranée*, 1 (2), 47–54.

Duval, P. M., 1971, *La Gaule jusqu'au milieu du Ve siècle*, Paris, Picard, 865p.

Excoffon, P., Bonnet, S., Devillers, B. & Berger, J.-F., 2010, L'évolution du trait de côte aux abords de Fréjus, de sa fondation jusqu'à la fin du Ier s. après J.-C. In: Delestre & Marchesi, 47–53.

Fiches, J.-L. (ed.), 2002, *Les agglomérations gallo-romaines en Languedoc-Roussillon*, MAM 13-14, Lattara, 2 vol.

Fiches, J.-L., 2002, Ensérune. In: Fiches (ed.) 2002, 218–234.

Fiches, J.-L., Bérato, J., Brentachalof, D., Chouquer, G., Dubar, M., Gazenbeek, M., Latour, J. & Rogers, G.B., 1995, Habitats de l'Âge du Fer et structures agraires d'époque romaine aux Escaravatiers (Puget-sur-Argens, Var), *Gallia*, 205–261.

Fiches J.-L., Raynaud C., Le peuplement littoral de la fin de l'âge du Fer. In : X. Delestre et H. Marchesi (dir.) 2010 – Archéologie des rivages méditerranéens : 50 ans de recherche. Actes du colloque, Paris, Errance, 123–130.

Gailledrat, E., 2010, Pech Maho (Sigean, Aude): de l'emporion au sanctuaire. In: Delestre & Marchesi, 349–355.

Gailledrat, E., 2012, Pech Maho, comptoir lagunaire de l'Âge du fer (VIᵉ–IIIᵉ siècle avant notre ère), Maugio (Les Carnets du Parc n°12).

Garcia, D., 2001, Le port de *Lattara*, de l'emporion protohistorique au *vicus* portuaire de la *Civitas* des *Volcae Arecomici*. In: Garcia & Vallet, 215–223.

Garcia, D. & Vallet, L. (eds.), 2002, *L'espace portuaire de Lattes antique*, Lattara 15, 223p.

Gateau, F., 1996, *L'Étang-de-Berre. 13/1*, Carte Archéologique de la Gaule, Paris, Académie des Inscriptions et des Belles Lettres, 380p.

Grenier, A., 1931, *Manuel d'archéologie gallo-romaine: 1. Généralités*, Paris, Picard 619p.

Guilaine, J. (ed.), 1995, *Temps et espace dans le bassin de l'Aude du néolithique à l'âge du Fer*, Centre d'Anthropologie, Toulouse 442p.

Guy, M., 1987, Chronologie relative et explications des formes d'anciens rivages d'après leurs images aériennes. In: *Déplacements des lignes de rivage en Méditerranée (Colloque international CNRS, Aix-en-Provence, 1985)*, Éd. CNRS, Paris, 45–58.

Jorda, Ch., 2002, La zone portuaire de *Lattara*, entre Lez et étang. Indice d'un rivage lagunaire autour du changement d'ère. In: Garcia & Vallet, 171–179.

Jorda, Ch., 2013, Études paléoenvironnementales. In: O. Ginouvez (coord.), *14 Quai d'Alsace*, Rapport d'opération archéologique de fin de fouilles, Inrap, 135–145.

Kotarba, J., Castellvi, G., Mazière, F., 2007, *Carte archéologique de la Gaule 66, : Les Pyrénées Orientales*, Paris, Académie des Inscriptions et Belles-Lettres 712p.

Larue, J.-P., Bouabdallah, M. & Étienne, R., 2009, Un littoral sableux en progradation: le lido entre Leucate et Port-la-Nouvelle (Aude, Golfe du Lion, France*), Physio-Géo Géographie, physique, et environnement*, 3, 151–173.

L'Homer, A., 1975, *Notice explicative de la feuille Saintes-Maries-de-la-Mer à 1/50 000*, Orléans, Éditions du Service géologique national, 34p.

L'Homer, A., 1987, *Notice explicative de la feuille Arles à 1/50 000*, Orléans, Éditions du Service géologique national, 72p.

L'Homer, A., 1993, *Notice explicative de la feuille Le Grau du Roi à 1/50 000*, Orléans, Éditions du Service géologique national, 93p.

Landuré, C. & Pasqualini, M., 2004, *Delta du Rhône. Camargue antique et médiévale, Bulletin Archéologique de Provence, supplément 2*, Aix-en-Provence, 334p.

Lenthéric, C., 1876, *Villes mortes du golfe du Lion*, Paris, Plon, 524p.

Leroy, F., 2010, Les habitats littoraux protohistoriques des côtes de Méditerranée nord-occidentale. In: Delestre & Marchesi, 137–148.

Leveau, Ph., 1996, Introduction. In: Gateau, 67–97.

Leveau, Ph., 2003, Le franchissement du Rhône par Hannibal: le chenal et la navigation fluviale à la fin de l'âge du Fer, *Revue Archéologique*, 25–50.

Leveau, P., 2004a, L'herbe et la pierre dans les textes anciens sur la Crau: Relire les sources écrites, *Ecologia Mediterranea*. 30,1, 25–33.

Leveau, P., 2004b, La cité romaine d'Arles et le Rhône. La romanisation d'un espace deltaïque, *American Journal of Archaeology*, 108, 349–375.

Leveau, P., 2014, Le Rhône romain dans sa basse plaine et dans le delta. Variations territoriales, sociétales et environnementales, *Revue Archéologique de Narbonnaise*, 45, 9–34.

Leveau, P. & Provansal, M., 1993, *Archéologie et Environnement de la Montagne-Sainte Victoire aux Alpilles*, Aix-en-Provence, Publications de l'Université de Provence, 551p.

Long, L. & Vella, C. 2003, Du nouveau sur le paysage de Giens au Néolithique et sur le port d'*Olbia*. Recherches sous-marines récentes devant l'Almanarre (Hyères, Var). In: M. Pasqualini, P. Arnauld & C. Varaldo (eds.), *Des îles à la côte. Histoire du peuplement des îles de l'Antiquité au Moyen-Age (Provence, Alpes Maritimes, Ligurie, Toscane)*. Aix-en-Provence, 165–173.

Long, L., 2013, Un port antique aux Saintes-Marie de la Mer?. In: Blondel, Barruol & Vianet, 203.

Long, L., Rico, Ch. & Domergue, C., 2002, Les épaves de Camargue et le commerce maritime du fer en Méditerranée occidentale (Ier s. av. J.-C.—Ier s. ap. J.-C.). *L'Africa romana*, 14, Sassari Rome, 161–188.

Lugand, M. & Bermond, I., 2001, *Agde et le bassin de Thau. 34/2*, Carte Archéologique de la Gaule, Paris, Académie des Inscriptions et des Belles Lettres, 448p.

Mariner, N., 2009, *Géoarchéologie des ports antiques du Liban*, Paris, L'Harmattan, 259p.

Marty, F., 2007, Fos-sur-Mer. L'Estagnon, *Bilan scientifique 2007*, Aix-en-Provence, Service régional de l'Archéologie, 136–139.

Mazière, F., Olive, Ch. & Ugolini, D., 2001, Esquisse du territoire de Béziers (VIe–Ve s. av. J.-C.). In: A.M. Ortega & R. Plana-Mallart (dir.), *Territori politic i territori rural durant l'edat del Ferro a la Mediterrània Occidental. Acters de la Taula Rodona celebrada a Ullastret*, Girona, 87–114.

Millet, B., Blanc, F., Morhange, C., 2000, Modélisation numérique de la circulation des eaux dans le Vieux-Port de Marseille vers 600 avant J.-C., *Méditerranée*, 61–64.

Morhange, C. (ed.), 1995, Les origines de Marseille. Environnement et archéologie, *Méditerranée*, 82, 3.4.

Morhange, C. (ed.), 2000, Ports antiques et paléoenvironnements littoraux, *Méditerranée*, t. 94, 1.2.

Morhange, C., Marriner, N. & Carayon, N., 2015, The geoarchaeology of ancient Mediterranean harbours, G. Arnaud-Fassetta & N. Carcaud (eds), *French geoarchaeology in the 21ˢᵗ century*, Paris, CNRS Editions, 311p.

Morhange, C., Provansal, M., Vella, C., Arnaud, P., Bourcier, M. & Laborel, J., 1998, Montée relative du niveau de la mer et mouvements du sol à l'Holocène en Basse Provence (France, Méditerranée), *Annales de géographie*, n° 600, 139–159.

Morhange, Ch. & Weydert, N., 1995, 5000 ans de dégradation de l'environnement au Lacydon de Marseille. In: Morhange 1995, 53–62.

Paskoff, R. & Trousset, P., 1987, *Les déplacements des lignes de rivages en Méditerranée d'après les données de l'archéologie*, Aix-en-Provence 5–7 septembre 1985, Paris, CNRS, 225p.

Pasqualini, M., 2000, Les ports antiques d'*Olbia* (Hyères) et Toulon. Environnement historique et géographique. In: Morhange 2000, 33–38.

Pedini, C., 2013, *Les carrières de la Couronne de l'Antiquité à l'époque contemporaine*, Arles-Aix-en Provence, Errance, Bibliothèque d'Archéologie méditerranéenne et Africaine du Centre Camille Jullian 14, 316p.

Provansal, M., 1988, Géomorphologie du site de Martigues. In: J. Chausserie-Laprée (ed.) Le quartier de l'Ile à Martigues, *Dossiers Histoire et Archéologie*, 128, 12–13.

Provansal, M., 1993, Les littoraux holocènes de l'Étang de Berre. In: Leveau & Provansal, 279–284.

Provansal, M., 2008, Le contexte physique: du Rhône aux plaines, de la ville à la Camargue. In: J.M. Rouquette, *Arles, histoire, territoires et cultures*, 33–50.

Provansal, M., Berger, J.-F., Bravard, J.-P., Salvador, P.-G., Arnaud-Fasseta G., Bruneton, N H. & Verot-Bourrely, A., 1999, Le régime du Rhône dans l'Antiquité et au Haut-Moyen Âge, *Gallia*, 56, 13–32.

Provost, M. et al., 1999, *Le Gard, 30/2–3*, Carte Archéologique de la Gaule, Maison des Sciences de l'Homme, Paris, 400p.

Py, M. & Roure, R., 2002, Le Cailar (Gard). Un nouveau comptoir lagunaire protohistorique au confluent du Rhône et du Vistre, *Documents d'Archéologie Méridionale*, 25, 171–214.

Rescanières, S., 2002, Essai sur le cadre géographique antique du Narbonnais. In: E. Dellong, *Narbonne et le Narbonnais, 11/1*, Maison des Sciences de l'Homme, Paris, 44–51.

Rey, T., Lefevre, D. & Vella, C., 2005, Données nouvelles sur les lobes deltaïques du paléogolfe d'Aigues-Mortes à l'Holocène (Petite-Camargue, France), *Quaternaire*, 16 (4), 329–338.

Ropiot, V., 2003a, La question du port fluvial d'Agde et le trafic de l'Hérault durant l'âge du Fer (VIe–IIe s. av. n.è.). In: *Puertos fluviales antiguos: Ciudad, Desarrollo e infraestructuras, IV jornadas de arqueologia subaquatique*, Valence, 213–225.

Ropiot, V., 2003b, Trois exemples d'axes fluviaux en Languedoc occidental et en Roussillon du VIe au Ve s. av. n.è., *Dialogues d'Histoire Ancienne*, 29/1, 77–107.

Ropiot, V., 2011, Narbonne et ses ports dans les sources antiques. In: C. Sanchez & M.P. Jézégou (eds.). *Espaces littoraux et zones portuaires de Narbonne et sa région dans l'Antiquité*, Lattes, 17–20 (Monographies d'Archéologie Méditerranéenne 20).

Ropiot, V., 2012, Habitats et zones humides entre l'Hérault et le Ter du IXe s. au début du IIe s. av. n. è. Bilan des connaissances et essai de synthèse. In: V. Ropiot, C. Puig & F. Mazière (eds.), *Les plaines littorales en Méditerranée nord-occidentale. Regards croisés d'histoire, d'archéologie et de géographie de la Protohistoire au Moyen Âge*. Actes de la table ronde de Capestang (Hérault), 16–17 novembre 2007. Editions Monique Mergoil, 111–128.

Rothé, M.-P. & Tréziny, H. (eds.), 2005, *Marseille et ses alentours, 13/3*, Carte Archéologique de la Gaule, Académie des Inscriptions et des Belles Lettres, Paris, 925p.

Roure, R., 2010, Grecs et non-Grecs en Languedoc oriental: Espeyran, Le Cailar et la question de *Rhodanousia*. In: H. Tréziny (ed.), *Grecs et non Grecs de la Catalogne à la mer Noire*, Aix-en-Provence, 2010, Bibliothèque d'Archéologie méditerranéenne et Africaine du Centre Camille Jullian 3, 681–688.

Sanchez, C., Faïsse, C., Jezegou, M.-P., & Mathe V., 2014, Le système portuaire de Narbonne antique: approche géoarchéologique. In: L. Mercuri, R. Gonzalez Villaescusa & F. Bertoncello, *Implantations humaines et milieu littoral méditerranéen*, APDCA, Antibes 2014, 125–136.

Sanchez, C. & Jezegou, M.-P., 2014, *Les ports antiques de Narbonne*, Maugio (Les carnets du Parc n°15).

Sivan, O., 2013, Évolution paysagère de l'anse Saint-Roch depuis la fin de la dernière glaciation. In: *Aux origines d'Antibes. Antiquité et Haut Moyen Âge*, Antibes-Cinisello Balsamo, Musée d'archéologie-Silvana Editoriale, 20–23.

Trément, F., 1999, *Archéologie d'un paysage. Les Étangs de Saint-Blaise (Bouches-du-Rhône)*, DAF 74, Paris, Éditions de la Maison des Sciences de l'Homme.

Tréziny, H., 2004, Sources écrites grecques et latines. In: Landuré & Pasqualini 2004, 93–104.

Tréziny, H., ed, *Grecs et indigènes de la Catalogne à la mer Noire*. Paris/Aix, Errance/CCJ, BiAMA 3, 2010, 326 p.

Ugolini, D., 2002, *Agatha*-Agde. In: Fiches (ed.) 2002, 346–370.

Ugolini, D., 2010, Présences étrangères méditerranéennes sur la côte du Languedoc-Roussillon durant l'âge du Fer : de la fréquentation commerciale aux implantations durables, Pallas 84, 83–110.

Ugolini, D. & Olive C. 2012, *Béziers. 34/4*, Carte Archéologique de la Gaule, Maison des Sciences de l'Homme, Paris.

Vella, C., 2002, Évolution paléogéographique du littoral de Fos et du delta du Rhône: implications archéologiques. In: L. Rivet & M. Sciallano (eds.), *Vivre, produire et échanger: reflets méditerranéens*, Monique Mergoil, Montagnac, 103–114.

Vella, C., Leveau Ph. & Provansal M., 1999, Les dynamiques littorales du Golfe de Fos et le canal de Marius, *Gallia*, 56, 131–139.

Vella, C., Provansal M., Long L. & Bourcier M., 2000, Contexte géomorphologique de trois ports antiques provençaux: Fos, Les Laurons, Olbia, *Méditerranée*, 1.2, 39–46.

Vella, C., Fleury, T., Gensous, B., Labaune, C. & Tesson, M., 2008, Grandes séquences Holocènes et discontinuités sédimentaires dans le delta du Rhône. In: M. Desmet, M. Magny & F. Mocci, *Du climat à l'homme. Dynamique Holocène de l'environnement,* 155–166.

2. Greeks, Celts and Ligurians in South-East Gaul: Ethnicity and Archaeology

Sophie Bouffier and Dominique Garcia

Recent syntheses concerning the Celtic Mediterranean (Py 1993; Garcia 2014), or south-east Gaul (Chausserie-Laprée 2000), present lucid analyses of material culture, the dynamic nature of Mediterranean exchange networks, the rise of the urban phenomenon, and the impact of humans on the natural environment. On the other hand, since the pioneering work of Guy Barruol (1969), the study of pre-Roman Provençal peoples has not been subject to re-examination. Modern anthropological perspectives allow us to clarify the development of these pre-literate populations. It is this approach that we wish to develop in this paper; associating a critical historical approach with the philological and archaeological data (Poutignat & Streiff-Fenart 1995; Amselle & M'Bokolo 1999). The Celts and Ligurians of southeast Gaul are analyzed, not as immutable entities, nor as stable divisions of humanity, but as the product of contingent historical, social, political, and economic processes, in which the Greek merchants and migrants played a determining role.

People, Cultures and Nationalism

In nineteenth-century Europe, the development of ethnic nationalism involved a degenerate use of a large number of ethnonyms based on ancient or medieval written sources (Geary 2002). A large proportion of twentieth century European historical discourse was guided by this limited approach to the history of its peoples. Indeed, one concept of civilization, which was common at the end of nineteenth century, was directly applied by researchers like Heinrich Schliemann, or Arthur J. Evans within Minoan or Mycenaean archaeology. However, following the publication of Edward B. Tylor's work (1871), the concept of people was defined as a culture and a territory and the concept of culture as the diffusion of objects associated with this culture ("guiding fossils" constituting whole or part of the "material culture"). Some kind of "guiding fossils" only corresponded to one "people", that were representative of invasion, migration or conquest...This analysis could lead to the development of nationalist discourses, or even racist ones, such as those of Gustaf Kossinna (1911, 137): "Cultural regions as defined by archaeological material always coincide with tribes or a particular people".

For Protohistory, it was the Frenchman Gabriel de Mortillet, who during an excursion as part of the 5th congress of anthropology and of prehistoric archaeology of Bologna in 1871, identified some "Gauls" in Marzabotto (Emilie-Romagna), through a comparison of the weapons and ornaments from the necropolis (swords, iron lances and bronze fibulae) with the material found in the Champagne region. He thus "invented" Celtic archaeology. At the same conference, the Swede, Hans Hildebrand, proposed a terminology for the European Iron Age in 1874. Two distinct chronological phases were identified; the early and the late Iron Ages, with which two geographically distinct archaeological cultures were associated: Hallstatt in Austria, and La Tène in Switzerland. It is amusing to note that the development of La Tène culture in the north of the alpine arc was attributed to the influence of Greek Marseille. In France, Joseph Déchelette in his *Manuel d'Archéologie Préhistorique, Celtique et Gallo-Romaine* (1927), supported this definition of this culture which he saw as having its origins in Hallstatt. He went on to evaluate its expansion through the distribution of archaeological material, and associated this with the notion of a civilization; in this instance, that of the Celts and the Gauls as developed by Henri d'Arbois de Jubainville in his book *Les premiers habitants de l'Europe* (1894). Joseph Déchelette considered that the Celtic homeland was in the Upper Danube basin, whereas Camille Jullian considered their origin to be in Northern Germany and the Danish peninsula islands, across to the coasts of the North Sea. Little by little, the Celts were defined as a pan-European people whose origins were situated in the northern alpine arc. As a result of invasions and migrations, they moved out over a great part of central and Western Europe, whilst the ancient texts only mention the expansion of certain groups towards the Italian peninsula, the central Danube area, or the Balkans (for example Livius, *History*, V). Movements of Celtic populations towards the Atlantic, the British Isles, southern Gaul, or the Iberian Peninsula, which are still evoked today, were only assumptions that were not supported by the texts, and largely contradicted by archaeology, which emphasized the power of Celtic peoples, who came to destroy primitive tribes, in particular, the Ligurians. Within this extremely ideological discourse, southeastern Gaul appeared as a liminal zone, both geographically and culturally, whose barbarian tribes were colonized by the Greeks from 600 BC, and then by the Celts from the fourth century BC.

Celts and Galates

The current etymological assessments of the term Keltiké do not suggest a Celtic origin for the word. It is most likely that during the Early Iron Age, and even later, most of the Celtic populations of central-Western Europe did not consider themselves as "Celtic" and certainly did not feel that they belonged to such a broad group. In 1987, Colin Renfrew drew attention to the importance of a passage by Strabo: "This, then, is what I have to say about the people who inhabit the dominion of Narbonitis, whom the men of former times named 'Celtae'; and it was from the Celtae, I think, that the Galatae as a whole were by the Greeks called 'Celti' on account of the fame of the Celtae, or it may also be that the Massiliotes, as well as other Greek neighbours, contributed to this result, on account of their proximity" (IV, 1, 14; transl. Jones, Loeb, 1949). He then stressed that it is completely plausible that the first Barbarians to have had contacts with the Greek population in the colony of Massalia (Marseille) belonged to a tribe whose ethnonym was *Keltoi* or its equivalent. The Greeks would have then extended the use of this term to all the Barbarians in this area (Renfrew 1987, 264). This implies indeed that it was not the inhabitants who defined themselves as *Celts*, but this ethnonym was imposed from outside of the group.

Indeed, as a part of the interest in the semantic analysis and the origins of the word, Greek geographers and historians sought to explain the names of the people in Gaul, Iberia and in Germany. The explanations were generally founded on an original myth; based on legendary characters, or on a linguistic interpretation of a particular term. In all of these cases, it was a question of incorporating the realities of other people's characteristics into the Greek perception of the world, to recover that which appeared to be beyond their view of the world. Both the Celt and Galate ethnic groups were assimilated with one other from the first century BC onwards; a notable instance of this was Caesar's *Bellum Gallicum*: "…a people called in their own tongue *Celtae*, in the latin *Galli* […]"(I, 1). According to this documentation, from the fifth century BC onwards, the Greek tradition proposed an explanation of these terms, and this interpretation continued to diversify until the Byzantine period.

There was an early etymological definition of the word Celt, and according to Dionysius of Halicarnassus, who produced an inventory of all of the known etymologies of *Celtus* (*Roman Antiquities*, 14.1.3: transl. Cary E.

Loeb, 1950). "There are also some who say that when the first Greeks came to this region that their ships, driven by a violent wind, came to land in the Gallic Gulf, and that the men upon reaching shore called the country *Celsika* (*Kelsikê*) because of their experience. Later generations, through changing one letter, called it *Celtica*". The noun had its origins in a Greek pun based on the Greek verb "*kellein*", which means to reach the shore: the aorist, which evoked the moment when Greeks arrived at the shore as "*ekelsan*", from which the qualifying adjective was derived. This employed the radical ending of the aorist, kels- and the suffix -ikos, which was used for the formation of ethnic names (Chantraine 1956, 102–105). This explanation is related to maritime vocabulary and has parallels in the etymology of the word *Massalia*, as proposed by Timaeus during the fourth century BC: Here a local fisherman, *halieus*, was asked by the Phocaean pilot to moor the boat, *Massai* (F. Jacoby, *FGrH*, 3B, N°566, F72, p. 622, *ap.* St. De Byz., *s.v.* Massalia).

In this version, which we have recently discussed elsewhere (Garcia 2014, 20–24), Celtic is thus perceived as a space that extended from the northwestern Mediterranean littoral towards the interior of the European continent. Thus, we can see how this view is diametrically opposed to that privileged by recent historiography, where the Celtic civilization is presented as endemic to central Europe; an origin from which successive migrations occurred, this view thus contradicts many archaeological hypotheses.

Other traditional Greek versions have much more ideological foundations. The most apparently neutral of these is that considered by Dionysius of Halicarnassus (*Roman Antiquities*, 14.1.3): "The whole country is called by the Greeks by the common name *Celtika* (*Celsikê*) according to some, from a giant Celtus who ruled there". This is comparable with the myths known for the barbarian regions, where strange sovereigns, with non-Greek physical and behavioural characteristics, were often fought by Greek heroes. Thus in Heracles' journey through Libya, Iberia, Sicily, and Greece, he confronted giants or monsters, such as Antaeus, Eryx, Lacinios or Croton. Diodorus of Sicily, in his *Historical Library*, (4, 17–25), stresses in particular: "But the giants were present in Iberia and notably in Italy at the same time, where the historian situates the combat with the giants". Confronted with a reality that eluded them, the Greeks developed an alternative image that was more or less belligerent and at the same time accessible in their conceptual discourse. This myth has allowed some to develop anthropological interpretations. Colette Jourdain-Annequin observed from her readings of the works of Jean-Pierre Vernant, Pierre Vidal-Naquet and Marcel Detienne (1989, 313 and n. 482) that the limits of *oikoumene* (inhabited land) are comparable with *eschatiai* (borders) of the civic territories, uncultivated fallow grounds and *agriai*, both wild and rural; this is where young Greeks had to pass initiation tests, which allowed them to reach adulthood and become a citizen.

In addition, it appears logical to associate Heracles, patron of Greek civilization, with the Celtic, Galatian and Ligurian populations. Having left for the West in search of Geryon's oxen, he met a number of natives, thus this journey was a precursor to the relationship that developed between the Greeks and the barbarian populations in what was an unknown part of the Mediterranean. The account of his exploits is quite detailed: Hesiod, in his *Theogony*, blissfully refers to the monsters that the hero faced (V. 287–291; 979–983). Apollodor us, whose account was studied by C. Jourdain-Annequin, describes Heracles' journey in two lines: "[…] he came to Liguria, where Ialetion and Dercynus, sons of Poseidon, attempt to rob him of the kine, but he killed them and went on his way through Tyrrhenia" (*Hist. Lib*, II.110–111; transl. J. G. Frazer, Loeb, 1961). For the first time we find the matrimonial legend in the texts of Dionysius of Halicarnassus and Diodorus of Sicily.

The first laconically indicates: "others, however, have a legend that to Hercules and Asteropê, the daughter of Atlas, were born two sons, Iberus and Celtus, who gave their own names to the lands which they ruled."

The second offers a more detailed account: "Now Celtica was ruled in ancient times, so we are told, by a renowned man who had a daughter who was of unusual stature and far excelled in beauty all the other maidens. But she, because of her strength of body and marvellous comeliness, was so haughty that she kept refusing every man who wooed her in marriage, since she believed that no one of her wooers was worthy of her. Now in the course of his campaign against Geryones, Heracles visited Celtica and founded there the city of Alesia, and the maiden, on seeing Heracles, wondered at his prowess and his bodily superiority and accepted his embraces with all eagerness, her parents having given their consent. From this union she bore to Heracles a son named Galas, who far surpassed all the youths of the tribe in quality of spirit and strength of body. And when he had attained to man's estate and had succeeded to the throne of his fathers, he subdued a large part of the neighbouring territory and accomplished great feats in war. Becoming renowned for his bravery, he called his subjects Galatae or Gauls after himself, and these in turn gave their name to all of Galatia and Gauls" (V. 24; transl. Oldfather C. H., Loeb, 1952).

Finally, there is a third variation from Parthenius of Nicaea contemporary with Augustus: "It is said that Heracles, when he brought from Erytheia the Geryone heifers, passed through the land of the Celts, and arrived at Bretannos's. This prince had a daughter called Celtine. Falling in love with Heracles, she hid his heifers, and she would not return them to him unless they slept together. The hero, keen to save his heifers, and also struck by the beauty of the girl, married her, and some time later their son, Celtus was born from whom the Celts took their name" (*Of the Sorrows of Love*, 30, Celtine).

Heracles' journey to the West is particularly evident in the *Historical Library* and has been the subject of many studies (Jourdain-Annequin 1989). The anthropological interpretation underlines the civilizing role of the hero who brings Greek culture to everywhere he visits: It opposes "a savage nature that is closed to man with an open nature for his greatest good, an untamed infested nature with a purified nature characterised by agriculture; this untamed nature is disorganized whilst tamed nature is organized according to the needs of life in the society and in the City" (Jourdain-Annequin 1989, 313). Nevertheless, in Gaul, the hero does nothing but pass and engender; it is his son who civilizes while pacifying, contrary to what happened in Sicily or Greece where he himself instituted Hellenic cultic traditions. This son was called Celtus, descended from Atlas, or Galas/Galatus, who was born from an unknown native. This was hardly important, as the Greeks organized their mythical geography around their discovery of the world. In the first instance, the Greeks established peaceful relationships with some peoples, these probably corresponded with phases of pre-colonial contact, and this served to legitimise the authorities already in place. They sometimes placed certain families at the head of the local society; these groups maintained political and religious power, and they held the monopoly over trade with the Greeks. We can thus bring the diodorean version of the myth regarding the foundation of Massalia into focus, where the Phocaean, Protis, marries the king's daughter, on her own initiative. In both cases, the indigenous peoples who favourably accommodate the Greek representatives seem like special barbarians: they stand out due to their size and their beauty, as well as by their behaviour, which is identical to that of the Homeric heroes (the practice banqueting, marriage dowries…). Approval from reigning families is apparent only in Gaul and Italy, where the Heracles-Hercules relationship was very close. As the historiographers of the Dorian hero have already indicated, this is not just a fortuitous characteristic. The myth was only known from the time of Caesar's conquest of the Gauls and Diodorus emphasises the analogy that existed between the two heroes (*Hist. Lib* IV.19), and made Caesar a second Heracles; both were descendants of the gods, benefiting from an apotheosis.

One can also link these two last versions with a third, suggested by Dionysius of Halicarnassus. This is based upon another chronicle common in the Greek tradition: "Others state that there is a river Celtus rising in the Pyrenees, after which the neighbouring region at first, and in time the rest of the land as well, was called Celtica" (D.H., *AR* 14.1). This was attested to in Homer's river genealogies, which made reigning families the legitimate authorities in the region. Thus, one of Achilles' adversaries, Asteropeus, is Pelegon's son, "They say that the country received its name from Illyrius, the son of Polyphemus; for the Cyclops Polyphemus and his wife, Galatea, had three sons, Celtus, Illyrius, and Galas, all of whom migrated from Sicily and ruled over the peoples called after them Celts, Illyrians and Galatians" (D.H., *loc. cit.;*). Samias is Meander's daughter (Paus. 7.4.1); Olynthos, Strymons' son (Conon, apud Phot. *Bibl.* 186), Euthymos, Caecinos' son (Paus. 2.6.4); even in Greece, Argos, founder of the homonymous city, is the son of the River Inachos (Asclépiades, apud Apollod. Bibl. II.6.). These genealogies demonstrate the local aristocracies' desire to defend their native origins, which is the foundation for their power, within these sedentary societies. The affirmation that the Celts originated from their own soil, in their own territory, via a river that gushed from the depths of Gaia, legitimised their presence in the region, before uniting them through marriage with Greeks who journeyed through this area.

The fourth version offered by the Greek texts is the most original, and was probably intended to be read in one specific context, that of the relationship between Gaul and Sicily. Starting from the fifth century BC, here, a genealogical myth connects both of these areas.

According to the Byzantine *Etymologicon Magnum* collection, during the fourth to third centuries Timaeus recounted how the Cyclops Polyphemus and the Galatean nymph had a son named Galatus, who gave his name to the country: "Galatia, territory; it received its name, as Timaeus said, from Galatus, Cyclop's and Galatea's son" (in Jacoby, *FGrH*, 3B, n°566, F69, p. 621). Logically, one can suspect Timaeus's patriotism; this historian came from the land where the Cyclops and the nymph legend was located, below Etna, next to the approaches to the Tauroménion and Naxos rocks. But Appian, in his *Roman History* (X, 1–2), reconsiders this version regarding the Illyrians: "They say that the country received its name from Illyrius, the son of Polyphemus; for the Cyclops Polyphemus and his wife, Galatea, had three sons, Celtus, Illyrius, and Galas, all of whom migrated from Sicily and ruled over the peoples called after them Celts, Illyrians and Galatians" (D.H., *loc. cit.*). The relationship between Sicilian Greeks and the Celts during the period of Dionysius the Elder was studied for a long time: at the end of the fifth century, the tyrant of Syracuse had to resort to using Celtic mercenaries, and Timaeus' version would consider the military bonds that were established at this time (Tagliamonte 1994, 136). Some saw this as an anti-Etruscan alliance, but at that time, the Etruscans no longer represented a danger to Dionysius the Elder, who faced the Italic and Carthaginian populations.

In the case of Dionysius, he tends to find experienced warriors when the Greeks needed them (Collin Bouffier 1999). Actually this group of soldiers who proved their skill in the Italian peninsula do not seem to defend the same stakes and interests as the Syracusan tyrant. Even if it does not appear until the fourth century BC onwards in our literary sources, it is probably necessary to see this myth as having a more ancient source, one relating to connections between Celts and Sicilians, and showing an interest in other types of activity, in particular trade.

The relative importance of trade between the South and Sicily during the archaic period was undoubtedly underestimated at the expense of trade with Etruria, or eastern Greece. Recent data tends to support strong Sicilian links, both economic and cultural. "Greek" vases (cups and skyphoi) from seventh century BC from the Celtic Mediterranean (Garcia 2014, 24) Mailhac and Montlaurès in Aude, Agde in Hérault, Sanilhac in Gard, Saint-Blaise in Bouches-du-Rhône have been associated with Italian workshops from southern or central Italy by A. Nickels (1989, 455), or more recently with Etruscan workshops by M. Gras (2000, 233). However a Sicilian origin is not ruled out: Results of physicochemical analyses recently obtained from an geometric cup from Saint Blaise implies a northwestern Sicilian origin—sector of the Messinian Strait. These documents sometimes associated with objects that were inspired by the Phoenicians could support the idea of Phoenician commercial activity from the eighth century BC. Furthermore a recent exhibition highlighted the cultural relations between Gaul and Sicily since the Archaic period (Verger & Pernet 2013).

Wine amphora, known as ionio-massiliotes, which are common on the southernmost Early Iron Age sites are now considered to be Greek, based on the results of petromineralogic analyses (Abbas 1999). According to J.-C. Sourisseau other amphora recognized in the northwestern Mediterranean, in particular the Corinthians B, would usually have been produced in Sybaris. In archaeological contexts, these wine containers are often accompanied by fine vases, in particular cups referred to as "Ionian B2" including a large proportion that were probably manufactured in southern Italy and Sicily (also in the sector of the Strait) according to Thierry Van Compernolle.

Conversely, Mediterranean objects from the seventh to sixth century BC, normally made from bronze, have recently been identified in Sicily: in Megara Hyblaea (Tomb 660: conical button of type Grand-Basin I: Verger 2000, 402) or in the sacred deposit of Sciacca (an assemblage of launacians objects: bracelets, heels...: Guilaine 2000, 428 and Verger & Pernet 2013). They testify to an early phase (Bronze Age) of continuous commercial activity of relations direct between two lands.

Ligurians

Among the fragments of Hecateus of Miletus (documents from the end of the sixth century BC) preserved in the *Ethnika* by Stephanus Byzantius, the word "Ligurian" appears for the first time about our region; in particular in fragments 61 ("Elisyques: ethnos of the Ligurians. Hecataeus in *Europe*") and 62 ("Massalia: *polis* of the Ligystic, downwards Celtike, colony of the Phocaeans. Hecataeus in *Europe*"). An early date (end of sixth century BC), is attested to by quite precise evidence that reflects ethnic (Elisyques forming a part of the Ligurian group) and territorial hierarchy (Marseille is included as a part of the Ligurian region, which is itself Celtic). This evidence has not always been taken into account. Current geopolitical notions too often influence modern authors. For example, some have sought to juxtapose ethnic or territorial information drawn from ancient texts. However, the work of geographers and anthropologists proposes the concept of "piled territories", and they reject a reading which privileges inter-, or supra-ethnic rivalries and the notion of a limited territory defined by a closed linear border.

In order to discover the origin of the word "Ligyen/Ligure" we need to look to the Greeks: Even if ancient writers had already posed themselves the question, and proposed solutions that were more or less whimsical. One of the most interesting was that made by Stephanus Byzantius, who argued that the term was derived from the name of a river, the Liguros. We have seen how river-based genealogy is an important element in the Greek tradition when talking about the Celts. Twentieth-century historians have also considered the transposition of the name from the Ligurians, who were known as "Eastern" (in Asia). Nino Lamboglia considered that the term had an indigenous basis. The formation of the word "Liguria" would be based on the pre-Roman meaning of *liga*, which signified "the marsh". This area would have extended from the marshy zones stretching from the Gulf of Lion. He also noted the toponym, "Livière" (named *Liguria* by Grégoire de Tour, sixth century), located close to Narbonne, and thus proposed an extension of the term to this area as well. Ligurians would thus be the people of the marsh, as Lattes (Latera) in the Languedoc, or Arles (Arelate) in Provence are both cities "in front of" (*are*) "the marsh" (*late*). However, if the Gallic term *late* (or *lati*) is recognized in the area that was defined as Ligurian—and was widely known in the Celtic world to indicate the word "marsh", the pre-Roman origin for the word *liga*, proposed by Nino Lamboglia, remains poorly understood, even if we can recognise it in *Liger* (the Loire); this river's etymology remains enigmatic. Finally, historiography has often emphasised the fact that the Ligurians who fought on the side of Marius' troops at the time of the battle of Aix-en-Provence in 102 BC against the Teutons and Ambrons were known as *Ambrones* (Plutarchus, *Marius*, 19).

Recently, Pascal Arnaud (2001) reconsidered a hypothesis initially proposed by Camille Jullian (1909, 112): The Greek name for the Ligurians could not be an approximation of the Greek transliteration or homophonic name that was actually used by an indigenous people, but the appliance of a Greek term. According to P. Arnaud, the Ligurians (Ligyens in the Greek transcription) meant "the squealers" or "the loudmouths", and they would have been saddled with a nickname whose undertone was not so different from the term "barbarian". More precisely, we feel that the term *lygies* means "high-pitched", which is likely to be the sound of the harp, or the voice of the sirens who are associated with this word in the archaic Greek texts (Hesiod, *Theog.*, 275; 518). It is thus this characteristic that would have been retained by the Greeks and that would be the origin of the ethnonym Ligyens (Ligures, according to the Latin authors). One can thus deduce that Liguria would have been the Celtic area visited by the Greeks: a littoral zone, where direct contact between the Greeks and these "Men with the high-pitched voices", would have occurred. Thus, we are far from Amédée Thierry's proposition (*Histoire des Gaulois*, 1926): he saw the Ligurians as Iberian invaders who supplanted the Celts. On the other hand, Camille Jullian, in his *Histoire de la Gaule*, followed Roget de Belloguet (*Ethnogénie gauloise*, 1861) and affirmed the indigenous character of the Ligurian populations. Scholars who compared the material evidence with the literary sources were more embarrassed. In his *Manuel d'archéologie préhistorique, celtique et gallo-romaine* (1927, 150), Joseph Déchelette clearly noted: "The results from all of these observations of Hallstatt tumuli in the Rhône area show that Ligurian funerary sites in this territory hardly differed from those belonging to the Celts". A similar example, chosen from other post-war research, that is to say Jean Jannoray's analysis (1955, 380), today appears particularly pertinent: "(…) si les archéologues n'ont guère de peine, parmi les vestiges architecturaux et le matériel céramique ou métallique dont ils disposent pour faire l'étude des civilisations préromaines entre Rhône et Pyrénées depuis le premier âge du Fer, à marquer certaines similitudes avec la culture de la péninsule Ibérique ou à discerner les rapports hallstattiens, ceux de La Tène et ceux du monde grec, ils se sont montrés impuissants jusqu'ici à dire en quoi consiste la part ligure, sauf à appeler de ce nom tout ce qui se révèle indigène (…)". Albert Grenier (1931, 163) had already noted the difficulty in distinguishing the two groups; the Ligurians having been compared to the Gallic groups, "presque de même langue qu'eux et de même origine…"

Segobriges and Salyens

The Segobriges form another group that is characteristic of the Early Iron Age. We know them because, according to the legend, the Phocaeans "founded Marseille amongst Ligurians and the wild people of Gaul" in their territory (even if the occurrence is late: Justin, *Epitome of the Philippic History of Pompeius Trogus*, 43. 3). The Celtic origin for the name "Segobriges" is not in doubt; it refers not only to "victory" (*sego-*), but also to "force" (*brigo*). A hierarchy is also present here: The Greek city was created (from the littoral towards the hinterland) in the Segobriges' territory, amongst the Ligurians, in the Gaul's homeland. We should note that the only site in Marseille that testifies to a pre-600 BC occupation is Baou de Saint-Marcel, an oppidum located approximately 7 km from Vieux Port, at the outlet of the Huveaune valley.

The Pseudo-Scylax, which dates from at least the fourth century BC (with a possible late sixth-century date) reports that: "3. Ligurians and Iberian. After the Iberians, the Ligurians and Iberians were mixed up to the Rhône. Navigation along the Ligurians zone, from Emporion to the east of the Rhône, took two days and a night. 4. Ligurians. Beyond the Rhône followed the Ligurians until Antion. In this area, we find the Greek city of Massalia with its harbour (…)" (*Periplous*, 3, 4). The coastal area, from the northeast of the Iberian Peninsula to the north of the Tyrrhenian Sea, is divided here into three spaces: Settlement of this area between the Pyrenees and the Rhône has been the subject of much writing. This reflects the results of archaeological research that has been undertaken over a twenty-year period in these areas. From the seventh century BC there was a progressive iberianisation of Roussillon and Languedoc, which stopped at about 400 BC with the foundation of the Greek colony of Agathè/Agde. This town, established at the mouth of the river Hérault became an area of contact between "the Iberian lands and the harsh Ligurians" (Avienus, *Ora maritima*, 612). Here, we employ the term "iberianisation" as a synonym for a progressive development within the local populations, where cultural elements (including language) and economic characteristics (including crafts and agriculture) were shared following a period of exchange. In this instance, exchange was primarily commercial with the Phenico-Punic sphere, in particular, the Iberian Levant. The fact that the colony of *Agathè* was situated on the border between these two spaces, as a pawn on the Massalian chessboard, justifies the Greeks' situating this place in Liguria, as did Stephanus Byzantius, Euxodus Rhodiensis, or Philo Byblius.

Celto-Ligurians

The *Periegese* from Pseudo-Scymnus (around 199–219), the origins of which date back to the fourth century BC, gives us a good description of Liguria (5.167). It is defined as a coastal area, stretching from Emporion to Tyrrhenian people. Previously, the same author stated the Celtic people after the Iberian one and made the Celts the most important people in the West. One also sees here the concept of a layered territory: Ligurie is a littoral area within the Celtic sphere. Later, Polybius placed the Ligurians in a zone from Massalia to Pisa, in what he calls the Apennine (*History*, 2.16.1). This includes the pre-Alps and the first highland areas located to the north of Massalia. He also reported that the Massalians asked Rome for assistance against the Ligurians (*History*, 33.7.8); thus the two tribes were given names of a Celtic origin (Oxybians and Deciates). One finds similar precision in Pliny when he gives us the list of Ligurian groups from the extreme West: "Of the Ligurian beyond The Alps the most famous are the Sallui, Deciates and Oxubi" (*n.h.*, 3, 47; Pralon 1998). They already appeared in Strabo's *Geography* (IV, 6, 3) where we are told: "But through the early writers of the Greeks call the Sallyes 'Leagues', and the country which the Massiliotes hold 'Ligustica', later writers name them 'Celtoligurians', and attach to their territory all the level country as Luerio and the Rhodanus". Logically, Strabo "brings up to date" older data. He tells us that the Salyens are now recognized as a specific people known as the "Ligurians", and that the term "Celto-Ligurian" was used by the Greeks during his lifetime (Arnaud 2001; Bats 2003). The designation "Celto-Ligurian" was often interpreted as a diverse concept. Some modern authors have used this designation to support the assumption that during the Late Iron Age populations from "Ligurian stock" were enriched by important human and cultural contributions from the said "historical Celts". However, as Michel Py has recently suggested (2003), the archaeological documentation and the texts concerning southern Gaul do not allow us to support such an assumption. However, it seems possible (without defining it as an absolute rule) that the first element of the name was an adjective, and the second, a substantive, which could only indicate the ethnic origin. The Celto-Ligurians would be thus the Ligurians of the Celts. One finds here an alternative for "above" or "among" within the description employed by the more ancient writers. Ligurians are the indigenous people with whom the Greeks had direct contact. They occupy an interface, a pacified zone that facilitates communications and thus trade towards the outlying areas.

For the Celtic Mediterranean, the later written sources, in particular Pliny (*Natural History*, 3, 31–37) and Strabo (*Geography*, 4), present us with a list of important "peoples" who tend to occupy limited territories around one oppidum. This really presents us with information regarding the management of space related to conquest, rather than a real division of these existing communities. Broader ethnic groups are also mentioned (for example, Volques Tectosages in the western Languedoc, the Volques Arecomiques in the eastern Languedoc, the Salyens in western Provence, the Cavares in the area around Avignon, and the Voconces around Vaison). These represent ethnic confederations that emerged from existing economic networks, and co-federal religious centres, or military alliances.

Conclusions

Beyond this inevitably synthetic panorama regarding the ethnogenesis of pre-Roman populations in the Celtic Mediterranean, it is useful to insist on the problems or even the dangers for archaeologists or historians when combining certain ideas too hastily. Indeed, by adopting an anthropological reading of the ancient sources, we have evoked concepts of civilization and archaeological culture; these concepts have deeply marked, or even stunted, the history of the study of the protohistoric societies during the twentieth century.

According to us it is probably from the second half of the seventh century BC, when the Greek explorer-merchants approached the coasts of the Gulf of Lyon that the populations of the northwestern Mediterranean were called Ligurians, and that this space was named as a Celtic area. Slowly but surely, this term took on a broader relevance and was applied to a large proportion of Central and Western Europe. Even at the end of the eighth century BC, with the appearance of the first iron objects and then the development of the iron and steel industry, one notes important socio-economic developments that did not have decisive consequences for ethnicity. Communities, which one can describe as tribes, exerted control over quite limited territories (a few thousand km^2) over one or more valleys (like the Elisyques in Languedoc), a plateau or a small catchment (e.g., the Segobriges). The increase in trade and the development of complex settlement patterns led to the evolution of cultural-economic spheres, which stimulated ethnic developments, particularly among the Iberians and Ligurians. Here, ethnicity seems to be a social and psychological phenomenon associated with a cultural construction. Newly controlled space was thus named "Celtic"; a territory that had been *approached*—this was akin to a geographical concept, and Liguria—was a *frequented space*—a place of exchange and of confrontation. During the Late Iron Age, the internal evolution of indigenous groups, and the geopolitical stakes for classical societies, manifested themselves among the Mediterranean Celts with the development of confederations such as that of Salyens.

Bibliography

Abbas, G., 1999, *Identifications pétrominéralogiques des productions céramiques anciennes. Application aux amphores de Grande Grèce*, PhD Montpellier.

Amselle, J.-L. & M'Bokolo, E. (dir.) 1999, *Au cœur de l'ethnie: ethnies, tribalisme et Etat en Afrique*, Paris, La Découverte, 2nd edition (1985), 225p.

Arnaud, P., 2001, "Les Ligures: la construction d'un concept géographique et ses étapes de l'époque archaïque *à l'empire romain". In: Origines gentium. Actes de 3 séminaires tenus à Bordeaux en 1997 et 1998*, Bordeaux, Ausonius, 227–263.

Barruol, G., 1969, *Les peuples préromains du sud-est de la Gaule. Etude de géographie historique*, Paris, E. De Boccard, 408p.

Bats, M., 2003, "Ligyens et salyens d'Hécatée à Strabon". In: *Peuples et territoires en Gaule méditerranéenne. Hommages à Guy Barruol* (Montpellier), *RAN Sup. 35*, 147–166.

Chantraine, P., 1956, *Etudes sur le vocabulaire grec (Etudes et commentaires, XXIV)*. Paris.

Chausserie-Laprée, J., (ed.) 2000, *Le temps des Gaulois en Provence*, Martigues: Ville de Martigues; Images en Manœuvres Editions, 279p.

Collin Bouffier, S., 1999, Denys l'Ancien et la guerre. In: P. Brun (dir.), *Guerres et Sociétés dans les mondes grecs (490–322)*, Paris, Ed. du Temps, 1999, 55–72.

Garcia, D., 2014, *La Celtique méditerranéenne. Habitats et sociétés en Languedoc et en Provence du VIIIe au IIe siècle av. J.-C.*, Arles, Errance [2nd edition edited and improved, 2004], 250p.

Geary, P.J., 2002, *The Myth of Nations, the Medieval Origins of Europe*, Princeton, Princeton University Press, 199p.

Gras, M., 2000, Les Etrusques et la Gaule méditerranéenne. In: *Mailhac et le premier âge du Fer en Europe occidentale. Actes du colloque international de Carcassonne*, Lattes, Association pour la recherche archéologique en Languedoc oriental, 229–242.

Grenier, A., 1931, *Manuel d'archéologie préhistorique, celtique et gallo-romaine*, vol. 1, *Généralités et travaux militaires*, Paris, Picard, 619p.

Guilaine, J., 2000, Le Sud de la Gaule et les relations méditerranéennes et atlantiques. In: *Mailhac et le premier âge du Fer en Europe occidentale. Actes du colloque international de Carcassonne*, Lattes, Association pour la recherche archéologique en Languedoc oriental, 229–242.

Hildebrand, H., 1874, *Sur les commencements de l'âge du fer en Europe. In: Congrès International d'Anthropologie et d'Archéologie Préhistorique*. Stockholm, 592–601.

Jannoray, J., 1955, *Ensérune, contribution à l'étude des civilisations préromaines de la Gaule méridionale*, Paris, E. De Boccard, 490p.

Jourdain-Annequin, C., 1989, *Héraclès aux portes du soir: Mythe et Histoire*, Paris, Les Belles Lettres, 729p.

Jullian, C., 1909, *Histoire de la Gaule*, III. *La conquête romaine et les premières invasions germaniques*, Paris, Hachette, 607p.

Kossinna, G., 1911, *Der Herkunft der Germanen zur Methode der Siedlungsarchäologie* Würzburg, *Kabitzsch*, 30p.

Nickels, A. (ed.), 1989, *Agde. La nécropole du premier âge du Fer*, *RAN Sup. 19*, Paris, Ed. CNRS, 498p.

Poutignat, P. & Streiff-Fenart, J., 1995, *Théories de l'ethnicité*, Paris, PUF, 270p (3d ed, 2008).

Pralon, D., 1998, "Les Salyens dans les textes grecs anciens" (Congrès d'Entremont, Aix-en-Provence, octobre 1996), Documents d'Archéologie Méridionale 21, 1998, 21–26.

Py, M., 1993, *Les Gaulois du Midi*, Paris, Hachette, 288p.

Py, M., 2003, "Les Celtes du Midi". In: *Peuples et territoires en Gaule méditerranéenne. Hommages à Guy Barruol* (Montpellier), *RAN Sup. 35*, 303–322.

Renfrew, C., 1987, *Archaelogy and Language: The Puzzle of Indo-European Origins*, London, J. Cape, 346p.

Tagliamonte, G., 1994, *I figli di Marte. Mobilità mercenari e mercenariato italici in Magna Grecia e in Sicilia*, Tyrrhenica, III, Archeologica, Rome, G. Bretschneider, 294p.

Tylor, E.B., 1871, *Primitive Culture: Researches into the Development of Mythology, Philosophy, religion, Language, art and Custom* (1924 7th ed.), New York, Brentano's, 2 vol.

Verger, S., 2000, "Des objets languedociens et hallstattiens dans le sanctuaire d'Héra à Pérachora (Corinthe)". In: *Mailhac et le premier âge du Fer en Europe occidentale. Actes du colloque international de Carcassonne* (Lattes), Association pour la recherche archéologique en Languedoc oriental, 287–514.

Verger, S. & Pernet, L. (dir.), 2013, *Une Odyssée gauloise. Parures de femmes à l'origine des premiers échanges entre la Grèce et la Gaule*, Exposition Lattes, Arles, Errance, 2013, 399p.

3. Territorial Variations: Natives and Greeks in the Mediterranean Celtic Region

DOMINIQUE GARCIA AND SOPHIE BOUFFIER

From the space perceived and travelled by the native communities towards lands developed and dominated politically by the Greeks from Marseille, the South-East of France saw between the end of the eighth century BC and the beginning of the fifth century BC, a notable evolution in the determination of the territories at the pace of the decisive social transformations from Protohistory to modern history.

Let us be frank: even if they are frequently called upon, the ancient texts, admittedly rare and lacunar, only provide partial information on the nature of the first interethnic contacts or on the mutations experienced by the local communities. However, through the evocation of proper nouns, these accounts designate, distinguish and situate the main actors in presence, the actual or imagined power struggles and, consequently, for this part of the West, vaguely depict the frameworks of these new geopolitical stakes. In this contribution, we shall first of all focus on the native "strata" to query the texts pertaining to the foundation of Marseille: may we assume that they also transmit facts or local customs liable to enrich our perception of how the Celtic society was structured and how it controlled its territories? But before, as regards the phase prior to the urbanisation process, we shall sum up the main field data we managed to acquire, as we have already analysed and interpreted them (Garcia 2014).

Native Territorial Spaces before the Urbanisation Phase

From the End of the Bronze Age...

In the South of France, from the lagunar region to the first craggy foothills, the localisation of the metal fields in the end of the Bronze Age and in the beginning of the Iron Age reflects a wide variety of travelled and exploited territories. The diversity of the types of recognised sites is quite significant: agglomerations on heights or on plains, dwellings grouped in small numbers, grottoes, isolated settlements...The occupancy areas of agglomerations are variable, but generally extremely small: from 0.1 to 30 hectares, with 1 hectare on average. Certain sites reveal proto-urban fixtures: enclosures in the form of rampart(?) in Mailhac (Aude) or of pitch in Carsac (Aude), retaining walls as in the Baou-Roux (Bouches-du-Rhône), for example. Others, the largest in number, indicate blatant, but still incomplete sedentarity. The food economy seems to be founded on agro-pastoral practices where the share of cattle raising apparently dominates.

We are here quite certainly dealing with societies based on a "domestic way of production". This system aspires to exclude any relation of (economic hence political) dependence with respect to the neighbouring groups but, according to the ethnological observations (Sahlins 1976), it is fundamentally hostile to the formation of surplus. However, though the word market may be excessive, (neighbouring or remote) groups are involved in more or less intense relations of exchange of goods. We have suggested (Garcia 2000) to reconcile both archaeological as well as environmental data for describing the agrarian slash and burn systems (also designated as "long fallow"). In this system, the cultures are practised in various wooded media and installed on fields previously cleared by burning. The plots thus provided are grown only for one, two or three years, rarely more; after which, they are left as a wooded fallow field for one or several decades before they are cleared and cultivated again. This agrarian practice has always been accompanied by a strong demographic growth and continued as long as there remained accessible wooded terrains, never cleared hitherto. Eventually, this system led to a double crisis, ecological (deforestation, erosion) and subsistence, only overshadowed by the introduction of the fallow and light ploughing system, whose generalisation in the South of France did not seem older than the middle of the sixth century BC.

The main tooling of this type of rudimentary and little differentiated agriculture is composed of axes accompanied by burrowing rods and little hoes as regional archaeological examples show us. In her study on the forest in Languedoc from the end of the Neolithic Age to Late Antiquity,

Lucie Chabal (1997, 77) notes that before the arrival of iron soil-working tools, which alone enable stubble-burning of fallow fields and of grassland, the forest cover was quite ill-suited for agriculture. In the system of slash and burn cultures, the populations are generally sedentary but are led to move after a few years. The cleared spaces lend themselves to breeding activities which constitute an appreciable complement of activity. Villages of foresters and growers are composed of "families", related or not, forming as many units of production and consumption. The low productivity of agricultural work reduces the possibilities of social differentiation: artisans, shopkeepers, and warriors still take part in the agricultural tasks, whereas the political and religious functions are filled by a small number of people whose level of consumption is hardly higher than that of the other villagers. Whereas the demographic growth ratio is high, the villages rarely include more than one thousand inhabitants since, beyond that, the returns would not be sufficient to meet the needs of the population. De facto, the times of demographic boom saw the "spawning" of new villages (by subdivision and migration).

Among the socio-archaeological models proposed by anthropologists, the "acephalous tribal" mode of organisation (Sahlins 1976; Jonhson & Earle 2000) or a "semi-State controlled lineage-type" organisation (Testart 2005) may correspond to the archaeological documentation. In this system dominated by the domestic mode of production and where each household has a behaviour aiming solely at the satisfaction of its own requirements, the only work division was governed, in each unit, by sex. These are hence fundamentally egalitarian societies, without a sovereign, incapable of collective works organised in common although one of the rare centrifugal elements may be religion or at least ritual activity. These groups are fractionated as soon as they reach a few hundred individuals.

Obviously, the model of "system of slash and burn cultures" has been suggested as a hypothesis and will correspond to all the instances but seem to operate from the lagunar sectors to the Alpine foothills of the Central Massif and the Pyrenees. The phenomenon of semi-sedentarity associated with the practice of inverted transhumance, a model proposed by Michel Py (1993, 78) would only be a component of the global model adapted to certain lagoon sectors. In the semi-mountain or "causse" sectors, other agrarian modes can be evoked: traditional transhumance before the Aude hinterland (Gasco 1987), permanent installations in middle-altitude areas linked with pastoral, agricultural or mining practices, for example. For most dwellings in these regions, the practice of active hunting completing the intake of meat food is illustrated by frequent bone remains of wild faunas.

In the state of research (from formal documentation analysis to the model suggested), everything seems to justify for a majority of these populations of the end of the Bronze Age, the absence of booming urbanisation (subsistence economy, relative sedentarity, little stratified society, for example). However, certain rites like the Baou-Roux in Provence, Roque-de-Viou or *Sextentio(?)* in Eastern Languedoc, Mailhac or Carsac in Western Languedoc have a substantially different documentation. They are at the centre of a more diversified land, their extent is greater, and they have arrangements reflecting some mid- to long-term investment (Baou-Roux terrace, Mailhac rampart(?), Carsac ditch, for example). Their situation seems to control a soil but also a pass route. Other sites may also be associated with this series, like Saint-Blaise (Bouches-du-Rhône) and Le Cluzel (Haute-Garonne), for example. It seems fair to say that certain populations of the end of the Bronze Age evolved (without external influxes) towards some degree of urbanisation. Why not "proto-urban" centres already using a more performing agriculture (with fallow fields or light animal-drawn cultivation), practising mid- or long-distance exchanges (of metal, for example), with an increasing structure from a political viewpoint and even providing a kind of pre-writing (pictograms of the Mailhacian I)? Their geographical situation suggests that they played a regional part by controlling the circulation of people and of goods.

According to Marcel Mazoyer and Laurence Roudart (1997, 116), in the sub-current societies, practising this type of economy, apart from lodgings, the adjoining gardens and the possible perennial plantations, subject of a regular right of usage akin to a kind of private property, the village territory is open to the right of usage of all families. Every family is assigned every year, by the competent village authority, cultivable wooded plots meeting its needs. This right of usage extinguishes with the last harvest and the plots abandoned to long-term wooded fallow land return to public domain. As long as the village territory is little populated and the lands to be cleared are overabundant, this right of usage is even easily granted to possible newcomers. This right of temporary usage tends to become a right of permanent usage when perennial plantations are set up, or also when, due to the increase in population or to the degradation of a portion of the lands, the time during which the land lies fallow reduces so that the exploitation of a plot by the same family tends to become continuous.

The settling mode does not suggest therefore any set territorial grip. Communities are groups limited to a few families who exploit a limited land for no more than a single generation. This relative sedentarity and this community fragmentation would be responsible for the apparent homogeneity, on vast geographical spaces, of the Southern cultures of the Late Bronze Age

IIIb (Janin 2000). In addition to the space which was temporarily exploited for agricultural purposes, the authority of the populations, communities of people or cultural groups was probably exercised over a vast collection of communication paths marked with precise indicators (watering holes, tombs, for example), zones of extraction of raw materials (ores, salt, for example) only on a delineated space, encompassing lodgings, lands and curtilages. Similarly, it can be deduced that the feeling of property related to the livestock rather than to the soil: in this type of society (cf. lastly Kaplan 2012) the herds constitute a capital, generally managed collectively, and which grows naturally with reproduction whereas the few cultivated fields form family properties whose harvests provide the income. De facto, in these societies of pastoral tradition, property is distinct from territory: the largest surface area of the plots can be occupied by different groups according to the seasons. As shown for the central Languedoc (Garcia 1995), we can venture the hypothesis that the territories of the little hierarchised village communities of the Late Bronze Age IIIb were discontinuous and temporary, included in a landscape marked by the presence of isolated sepultures and of necropoles, which are as many benchmarks in a territory that was felt and experienced rather than dominated; a kind of "archipelago territory" to repeat the expression of the ethnogeographer Edmond Bernus (1999).

For this period, nothing prevents from proposing a matrilineal at/or matriarchal system. Indeed, no masculine and/or warlike supremacy is visible in sculpture (Py 2010, Garcia 2013) and armament (Beylier 2012, 2013), whereas archaeology suggests the presence of women enjoying a privileged status, on the basis of deposits of bronze objects and of tombs (Verger & Pernet dir. 2013).

...to the Beginning of the Iron Age

For the 725–700/600–550 BC period, there is a high contrast between the apparent continuity of the material culture (in particular the ceramic furniture) and the substantial modifications of forms of habitat. Indeed, several facts may be put forward as regards soil occupancy, which denote a breakup, let alone a crisis. We shall observe first of all the abandonment of numerous sites, regardless whether they are agglomerations of relatively great height like Cayla of Mailhac or Carsac in Aude, Saint-Blaise in the Bouches-du-Rhône or Le Pègue in the Drôme, or of smaller fields in Languedoc or in Provence. The list would be too long to mention all of them, but we cannot fail to notice that not a single Southern protohistoric site is known whose stratigraphy does not include any hiatus between 750 and 550 BC.

However, if the seventh century BC is a breakup century, it is also that of remarkable technical innovation or borrowings—in particular the use of iron (Janin & Chardenon 1998)—on the one hand and that of the first contacts with the Mediterranean "shopkeepers" on the other hand (Garcia & Sourisseau *infra*). These are significant events, almost concomitant but of different origins: their impact was to be decisive on the development of societies of recent Protohistory. Unlike bronze, the use of iron renders the production of tools and weapons less dependent on remote extraction centres and permits extended usage of metal, especially in agriculture. For the historians and agronomists, the introduction of iron in agriculture constitutes a true technical revolution (Sigaut 1998); its use is indispensable to the practice of stubble-burning and more generally to the development of a performing, possibly surplus agriculture.

The organisation of Mediterranean commerce has been largely analysed over the last years, but it ought to be emphasised that it started at a time when the local populations seem to lack dynamism and when their ways of life and of production were most permeable to evolution. Certain sites created or reoccupied ("redynamised") at the end of the seventh century or at the beginning of the sixth century BC (Carsac, La Liquière, Saint-Blaise, Le Mont-Garou, for example) exhibit, by their topographic situation and their economy, one or several original characters about, later on, to become the norm: implantation on heights, presence of an enclosure, and opening-up to the Mediterranean commerce, for example.

In order to venture an embryo of explanation for this kind of breakup between 725 and 625 BC, We first ruled out (Garcia 2014) the hypotheses based on natural causes whose action would have weakened these populations directly. Indeed, no notable marker has been observed in the paleo-environmental analyses available to us, unless in the lagoon sector, where a few sites have been abandoned, probably further to critical aggradations caused by the alluvions of rivers (Chabal 1997, 103). We have also rejected warlike explanations: we do not have testimonies about invasion, major conflicts or great battles which would have swept these societies. The study of the material culture, the pursuit of the previous funeral practices, often on the same premises, do not support this assumption. The most probable reasons may result from a series of unfavourable conjunctions precisely around the lifestyles of these Early Iron Age populations: Indeed, eventually, the system of slash and burn cultures leads to a double ecological crisis (deforestation, erosion possibly degradation of the climate as well as subsistence). This crisis which could have affected the Southern populations as of the last third of the eighth century BC, in one or two generations, had only been outperformed by the generalisation of the fallow and light animal-drawn cultivation system during the second half of the seventh century BC, as permitted by the control of the iron industry and boosted by the Mediterranean merchant economy (Garcia & Sourisseau *infra*).

The Mediterranean Celtic region saw the emergence, after the apparent homogeneity of the Mailhacian culture of the Late Bronze Age IIIb, of several cultural and certain ethnic assemblies which were seemingly to last throughout the Iron age (Garcia & Vital 2006): the Grand-Bassin I facies in the West of the Hérault (Nickels, Marchand, & Schwaller 1989), the Suspendien facies in the Eastern Languedoc and beyond that, up to the Alpilles (Py et al. 1984), a facies of Western Provence and a Low Alpine facies. This crisis, if not breakup, phase may well have triggered the development process of the ethnic collections, as a result of the new lifestyles after abandoning the practice of slash and burn agriculture and of the social reorganisation (emerging proto-chieftainships) among populations, always with contacts with the Mediterranean merchants in the background. Paradoxically, there would be geographical spreading of the populations and strengthened identity feelings.

The space would then be more largely invested and the perennity of the territory marked by funerary and/or cultural spaces (Garcia 2013). This dynamic is not specific to this region: anthropologists and historians agree in thinking that ethnicity is a "supra-historical and quasi natural element in a group, as a quality inherent to the belonging acquired once for all at birth; but rather like a social identity built on specific politico-historical circumstances in a continuous dialectic process which emphasises that 'us' is constructed in opposition to 'them'". The ethnic territories which seem to form during the first Iron Age are composed of three piled up spaces corresponding to lands which are occupied and exploited in quite a discontinuous way, limited by boundary spaces and in the centre of which are implanted funerary structures, isolated tombs or necropoles. These sepultures are the markers of these ethnic territories: for these populations of relative sedentarity, they come across as an identity space, asserting the spatial grip of these human groups, a process prior to a strengthening political territory resulting from these emerging ethnic groups (Garcia & Vital 2006).

These populations would then have left the "tribal acephalous" (egalitarian and probably matriarchal) mode of organisation to come closer to a system of "proto-chieftainship" with a "*Big Man*" (Sahlins 1976; Johnson & Earle 2000) or/then of "simple chieftainship (Johnson & Earle 2000) characterised by the union of local groups of a given region into a political institution dominated by an aristocrat (Brun & Ruby 2008). In these societies, tribal chiefs are capable of acquiring powers within parenthood networks at the cost of major overwork efforts to meet the reciprocity and prodigality obligations. The *Big Men* can be surrounded by a clientele available for cooperative works (the implementation of fortifications, for example). These societies are however little hierarchised and the force of inertia inherent in the domestic mode of production leads to a revival of social segmentation during periodic crises. According to Marshall Sahlins, the *Big Man* provides the illustration of a kind of minimum degree in the continuous curve of the political power, which gradually would lead to the primitive royalties. The *Great Man*-type societies are directly derived from "acephalous" societies, but here the power acquired by an individual is transmissible, the result is then an aristocratic tribal system.

This period would see the introduction of a patriarchal and, according to the texts we shall evoke below, matrilineal system. This masculine supremacy is visible through the heroic statuary (Py 2011; Garcia 2013) but also in the funerary documentation illustrated by tombs of "chiefs" (sepultures associating a warlike panoply and rich accompaniment furniture) (Girard dir. 2013) but also by that of young adolescents, possibly children (Dedet 2008) as for example in Castelnau-de-Guers (Hérault) (Janin 2013) or Pertuis (Vaucluse) (Garcia 2013b). The latter graves, of armed defunct youth whose sepulture benefits from the deposit of exotic objects may be the expression of the hereditary transmission of power. Contrapuntally, the disappearance of privileged feminine tombs and of rich women adornments, hitherto used in the South-East, can be noted.

Thus, the archaeological data, enlightened by the anthropological models, may enable us to address the ethnogenesis of the Segobriges and the assumed location of the village of Gyptis/Petta. The latter can only be a low density settlement, with a flexible territorial grip and capable of granting an external group a right of usage on its land. The attribution of this right rests with the king which, hence, really exerts a political role: it controls this ethnic territory and manages the development of its settlement. Through certain young ladies of its lineage, it would organise periodically a kind of spawning. A modelling of this (more social than economic) territorial dynamic, can be suggested. The village is placed at the centre of its territory: this is a deforested space, developed for exclusively local needs, probably over less than 5 km in radius, that is, less than one hour's walk from the houses. This farming space forms a landscape which can be perceived directly from the habitat; on a flat field, the horizon can be seen up to approximately 3 miles.

It is beyond this first territorial crown, that is, at the curtilages of the ethnic territory that a new settlement can be created, by spawning. The links of different (physical, symbolical, for example) natures between the different settlements are then ensured by the paths and routes traced for a long time for pastoral purposes, but also by lineage links between the different communities and, finally, by federating funerary or cultural assemblies. Progressively, this dynamic was going to structure the territory and construct the cultural identity of the group.

"...on whose territory they meditated to found a city and ask him for his friendship" Justin (Abstract of Philippic histories)

After these few reflections on the territorial dynamic of the Southern communities of the Late Bronze Age and the Early Iron Age as can be assumed from the archaeological data, how can we read the arrival of the Phocaeans in the Marseille territory? How can the preserved Greek and Latin texts on the accession of these regions to "great History" be read? Can they enlighten possible mutations? What model of society and what type of political, social and territorial organisation did the Greeks bring as luggage?

When the Phocaeans, aristocrat adventurers, merchants seeking raw materials, rare in Ionia, or others, arrive in the Gulf of Lion, during the seventh century BC, the Greek cities of the Aegean world are still in the making: that it is so little known about their political evolution or their social structures, their event-driven history, except that some of the Greek communities from Minor Asia felt sufficiently threatened by the Lydian invaders, according to the later texts, to launch into migrations leading to the foundation of *apoikiai*, 'communities remote from the house', that we like to call colonies for simplification purposes. As regards the West, such is the case of Siris a little before Marseille (Strabo, 6.14), whereas Miletus sends contingents to the Black Sea, probably further to prospective and limited explorations. The rare testimonies written about these foundations are late and reconstructed *a posteriori* in ideological perspectives, possibly associated with myths including semi-Gods, like Heracles or Jason, or Homeric heroes returning to Troy, in *Nostoi* well-known in Italy and in Adriatic Sea.

Most of the time, these foundation accounts evoke violent installations where Greeks and local populations fight each other (for example in Sicily: Thucydides. VI.3–5; in Magna Graecia, Diodorus of Sicily, *Bibl. Hist.*, 8, frgts), where the Greeks prove cunning or betray their interlocutors to arrogate the property of the place (for example in Locrii Epizephyrii, in Magna Graecia: Polybius, *Hist.*, 12.V.6). Conversely, according to the text tradition, the Phocaean expansion, regardless whether Eastern or Western, in Lampsacus (Plutarch, *Virtues of women*, 255; Polianus, *War tricks*, 8.37) or in Marseille *(infra)*, rests on the peaceful encounter between the Greeks and the natives; in Lampsacus, founded one generation before Marseille, "There was in Phocaea two twin brothers of the race of Codrides, called Phobos and Blepsos. Phobos was the first to throw himself from the rocks of Leucadia into the sea, according to the accounts of Charon of Lampsacus. His power and his rank placed him apart with a king. For his own business, he sailed to Parium when he struck a friendship with Mandron, king of the Bebrykes, nicknamed Pithyossenians and rescued him in the war against harassing neighbouring people. Mandron, when Phobos was about to leave, offered him with profuse show of friendship a portion of the city and of its territory should he want to move to Pithyossa with Phocaean settlers. Phobos persuaded his fellow citizens to do so and sent his brother to Pithyossa at the head of the settlers and Mandron placed at their disposal what he had promised, as they expected", as Plutarch recounts. In Marseille, Justin like Aristotle reveals a similar process. And Herodotus evoked the same type of relation, in the famous passage on the stay of Phocaeans with Arganthonios, the king of Tartessos, who proposed them to settle in his kingdom to deliver them from the Barbarian threat (*Investigations*, I.163). We may see there a repetitive scheme, resulting from an intention of the Phocaeans to homogenise the facts or to come across in a favourable light, and not to give any credit thereto. But we may question the rest of the story proposed by Plutarch and Alienus, evoking the degraded relations between the Greeks and the Bebrykes. The insistence of authors as varied as Herodotus, Aristotle or even if they came later, Plutarch and Trogus Pompeius who relied on diversified sources, now gone, as well as the forms of trade presented as the first Greek settlements in the remotest Western regions (see in particular Moret & Rouillard 2012; Plana Mallart 2012) emphasise relations such as *philia* (friendship) and *xenia* (hospitality), which structured the movements of these Greeks at archaic times. The presence of Phocaeans in Naucratis reflects the same opinion. And precisely the repetitive process seems to highlight the operating mode of these Phocaean elites and the objectives pursued in the first colonial settlements.

To consider the example of interest here, that of Marseille, we think that the documents refer to certain historical realities and consequently that they integrate knowledge of indigenous communities. To do so, it is easier to start from elements of the text of Justin by "completing" it, sometimes by the version of Aristotle.

The name of the Segobriges, rare in literature (two occurrences) is etymologically clear: it designates the population of the hill/the mount or the victorious (*sego*) fortress (*briga*) (Delamarre 2003). In this respect, the ethnonym refers to a specific and limited community which extended its supremacy over a wider area. The name of the group carries within it the act of passage from a polynuclear community with egalitarian structuration towards a hierarchy-based proto-urban society. It refers therefore to a virtual domination, possibly a de facto domination of these Segobriges over other ethnic groups that the Greek or Latin texts do not even mention. We always have a tendency to read the relations between Greeks and natives in terms of ethnos versus ethnos; by encompassing all the local populations under the same vocable of native; however, if we read in parallel the text on the Lampsacus foundation or if we take into account the complexity of the Celtic worlds in which the Greeks settle, we must consider the possibility that there is no ethnic unit and that the relations can be so conflictual between the Segobriges and the others as between the Greeks and the Celts, the wedding of a high-lineage daughter then appearing as a means to seal a political, perhaps military alliance in a vaster system. This community is supposedly run by king Nannus: the anthroponym Nannus (Nanos—in Greek, the dwarf) has rapidly been interpreted as a nickname associated with a possible physical characteristic, but it can also be construed as a way to qualify (in the context of the hierarchy of Greek social structures) the status of the chief of the native community: a little king, a petty king.

The territory of the Segobriges, bordered by the Mediterranean Sea and connected to the communication pathways towards the Alps and the Rhône Valley, economically under-harvested, constitutes an ideal space for the settlement of the little group of Phocaeans: Its inhabitants were specific, possibly privileged hosts, for the first two generations. Neither a competitor, nor a rival, it may be ventured that the Phocaean colonial dynamic (whose network forms in itself another form of "archipelago territory") seems to accompany the social and territorial evolution of the local communities. This equilibrium will probably be broken (if not counteracted) only by the arrival of new migrants (Gras 1995) in the second half of the sixth century BC.

The wedding is presented as fitting with a custom in which the daughter of the king must choose her husband among the guests of a banquet. The pretenders may be, in all or in part, villagers or men of a rank close to that of the king's daughter, but belonging to neighbouring and allied groups. The first instance may illustrate a kind of "spawning" as we propose it in view of the archaeological data: a young couple of superior rank (at least by the spouse), accompanied by individuals of the same generation, would go and found a new village on the community territory. Practice would provide a demographic regulation and an appropriation of space (a "colonisation") associated with an extension of the political grip of the lineage. The second, more dynamic case, is not very far: The king's daughter chooses her spouse among the high-ranking men of the neighbouring village units. This is what is suggested by the fact that the head of the Greek expedition is naturally invited to the banquet: He is not coming to "distort competition" with the locals but, due to his status, he is admitted to take part in the ceremony. It is the local king who organises and invites; he thus marks the power of the paternal group. The king's daughter chooses among the aspirants, but de facto she is offered to another community and with a portion of the paternal territory in her dowry: this wedding therefore testifies to a form of dependence of the husband's group as regards Nannus and acts an intercommunity union. It has been noted (Pralon 1992, 53) that we generally translate the verb *synoikein* (he cohabited) also quite vaguely: "He lived with his wife". For Didier Pralon, the term cannot fail to evoke synoecism, the reunion by Thesaeus of the attic demes formerly dispersed or still the joint foundation of colonies. For Henri Tréziny, the expression seems pleonastic, but the verb used, *synoikein*, is interesting: it may serve to designate the cohabitation not only between two people, but also between two groups, and some thought it was the symbolic expression of a cohabitation, at least in the first generation, between Greeks and Gauls. Didier Pralon has also insisted on the epic character of this outstanding wedding, by integrating it in a tradition of Indo-European myths, recognisable in the Homeric saga, from the free choices of Helena or of Penelope; we shall not come back to that. But contrary to what takes place in Marseille, the heroines of the saga leave the father's home for the husband's, as young spouses would do in most Aegean Greek weddings. They join the *oikos*, their father-in-law's household, and contribute to enlarging the patrilineal clan, put in evidence by the works of the anthropologists (Todd 2011, 313–335; Homer *Odyssey* III.31–41; 395–404; IV, 3–12). In the Aegean Greek world, there is no spawning, as we suggest here, but a strengthened paternal *oikos*, by the aggregation of the new couples after the wedding, a structure which perpetuates in the classical era, and which is sanctuarised by usages, possibly laws imposing upon the young generations to look after their parents and to pay for the funerary rites for the previous generations. As already emphasised (Leduc 1991), the Greek wedding, as of the archaic time, rests on an organising principle which consists of a gracious donation from a woman and of a number of immovable and movable goods. The dowry that comes with the spouse and which will be returned in case of couple separation is intended for strengthening the social and hence political power of the *génos*.

The colonisation phenomenon toppled this pattern by breaking the parenthood links and by causing, out of necessity, the sons to scatter away, like the two founders of Marseille, Prôtis and Simos. The need to secure the durability of the lineage as well as of the community obliges the newcomers to accept the host's operating mode, which in this instance also corresponds to their wishes. It is only in a second stage, in all cases with the arrival of Phocaean families fleeing the Persian invasion in 546, that the immigrants probably defended the social structures of the metropole with greater fierceness.

With Aristotle (*apud* Athenaeus), the maiden logically bears a name of Celtic origin, which has never been stressed. This name, Petta, is quite close (Delamarre 2003, 249–250) to insular Celtic *peth* and to Breton *pezh* 'thing' < *petâ (piece, portion, part, fraction, ramification) attested in Medieval Latin (eighth century) in the form *petia* 'piece of land'. De facto, the name Petta expresses a certain polysemy: Petta is both a "*good catch*" (since endowed with a *piece of land*) and hence a *part* of paternal territory, but she is also a *piece* from the bloodline of the native group which illustrates a *ramification* of the lineage. This proposition may be reinforced by the change in name narrated by legend: according to Aristotle "[…] Euxenos took her as his wife and lived with her, changing her name into Aristoxena. There is in Massalia a family (*génos*) descended from that woman, still now, called Protiads. Since Prôtis was the son of Euxenos and of Aristoxena". Thus, in a second stage, the patrilineal Greek practice breaks the link from the matrilineal group of Nannus and installs a new lineage, that of the Protiads, the son of the 'good host' and of the 'best of hostesses'. The apparition of a *génos*, in the original meaning of the word, the descendance, the lineage by birth and its continuity underline the integration in the Greek parenthood system, but at the same time, we observe that the text of Aristotle specifies that the *génos* of the Protiads comes from Petta/Aristoxena, and not from Euxenos, as would be conceived generally in a Greek, even colonial, city. Generally, as outlined (Duplouy 2006, 39–43), the ascendance runs through the father or the paternal ancestor, regardless whether in the Homeric saga or in the Athenian city, where genealogies are based first of all on the recuperation of the masculine family past. Thus, Aeneas traces her paternal ancestors back to Zeus, to the seventh generation (*Il.* 20. 200–241), and Diomedes evokes the race of his forefathers without mentioning the name of his mother (*Il.*14.113–127). The mother is mentioned only if she is a divinity, Thetis for Achilles, Aphrodite for Aeneas. The identity was long given by the father, as emphasised by the epigraphy of the Greek cities, for example for the West, Selinunte, Syracuse or Megara Hyblaea at the archaic and classical times (Collin Bouffier 2010). Even at the end of the archaic time, the city of Athens, through Clisthenes, seeks to erase from the identity card of the citizen his patronym to replace it with his demotic name, his geographical and administrative origin, such usage was to remain in force even in the democratic city.

Under the authority of the chosen one, the newly constituted community settles and develops in a space offered by the woman's lineage. As we have suggested, the matrimonial system thus reproduced reflects a trade law by crossing different native groups who privileged a lineage but also a form of land transmission and attribution through the dowry, and the conclusion of political alliance and/or the extension of a group's authority. Indeed, in its native practices, the village of Nannus might be the group who provided women: at the origin of the lineage, the strongest one from a demographic viewpoint, it would spawn over a territory that he would progressively control.

This instance is known through anthropology (Leach 1978 quoted by Bonte & Izard 2004, 40): for example with the Kachins in Burma, the women providing groups are superior to the takers (we are dealing here with feminine hypogamy) and the matrimonial system is then at the heart of the social and political dynamic of the hierarchised society.

Globally, this system seems to have persisted to the middle of the sixth century BC, as testified by the relation of the Comanus episode (4–5): "At the death of Nannus, the king of the Segobriges, who had given the Phocaeans a place to found their city, since his son Comanus had taken his place, a petty king declared unto him that one day Massalia would cause the ruin of the neighbouring peoples and that it had to be nipped in the bud, lest it would grow from strength to strength and ultimately defeat him (…). Similarly, these Massalians, who then seemed to be tenants, would one day rule the country (…). But a woman, a King's relative, betrayed the conspiracy. She was having an affair with a young Greek". Indeed, the lineage of Nannus still seems to occupy the apex of the hierarchy of the native community (the other representatives of the other settlements are designated as petty kings...), matrimonial exchanges continue and the Greeks are still considered as "tenants" of the native territory. Up to the extinction of the Segobrige authority, the local groups seem to have been governed by a matrilocal and probably matrilineal tradition ("from host he became a son-in-law and received from his father-in-law a location to found a city") even if the authority is held by men: the family settles on the spouse's territory and the descendance is directly linked with the mother's family. The situation probably changed after the taking of Phocaea by the Persians, when the mass arrival of entire families compelled the new community to re-examine its usages so as to integrate them and to reconcile them with the models in force in Phocaea, which also seems to attest to the political evolution of the Massaliot city. The opening of the regime to those who are worthy, then to the older sons, the younger sons of ruling families, at times unspecified by our sources, but prior to Aristotle, reflects a social and political mutation which integrates the Phocaean city in the Greek political *koinè* (cf. Bouffier & Caire *infra*).

From a politico-social viewpoint, if we take for example the typology of societies suggested by Jared Diamond (2000, 391–437), we may venture, for the territory of future Massalia, the assumption of the existence of a chieftainship (the Segobriges) governed in a centralised way (the village of Nannus) by a hereditary authority (the lineage of Nannus) spawning in a matrilineal and matrilocal way, during the creation of small village units formed of a few tens of people placed under the authority of *big men* (the petty kings of the text). The whole process is placed under a divine "control" appreciated by the king ("as the father accepted the presence of the maiden, thinking that the donation had been made with the consent of the divinity").

As we have emphasised, the fact that the name Segobrige vanishes from the sources (and consequently that the community does not constitute a geopolitical stake any longer) is linked, as of the second half of the 6th century BC with the demographic (and hence economic) development of Marseille. At that stage, the lineage of the Protiads has arguably "ingested" that king Nannus and the extension of the land around Marseille, dedicated to speculative cultures as of that period, had integrated the Segobrige land totally or partially. But if Segobrige "females" disappear and if their territory is mostly dominated by the Massaliots, this was due to cause, beyond to *chôra*, a political reorganisation of the Celtic communities.

Indeed, the sources tell us (Justin, 43.4–5)—probably in the fourth century BC, since the action takes place a little after the plundering of Delphes—that "Massalia again flourished with its famous exploits, its abundant resources and its glorious young forces, when the neighbouring peoples joined forces all of a sudden to destroy the name of the Massalians, as for putting out a fire threatening all of them. They unanimously chose the petty king Catumandus as their chief". As written clearly by Jared Diamond (2007, 431) "History and archaeology have highlighted numerous instances where small units were amalgamated into larger ones. This switch is never driven by small unthreatened societies freely deciding to merge so as to promote the happiness of their citizens. The heads of the small like the larger societies are jealous of their independence and of their prerogatives. Amalgamations take place in two ways rather: by merging, under the threat of an external force or by a conquest in due form". It is the first instance that the Catumandus episode seems to illustrate; it might prefigure the formation of the Salyan confederation: the stage of intermediary social organisation prior to the forms of Archaic state (Brun & Ruby 2008, 84–86). We know that an apparition led Catumandus to backpedal and that further to that surrender the Celtic chief deposited in a Massaliot sanctuary a golden torques: a highly symbolical tribute indeed.

This example would thus comply with what is observed in other regions invested by the Greeks: Magna Graecia or Illyria are familiar with this phenomenon of structuring local communities who eventually threatened the Greek cities and whom only the Roman intervention could jugulate.

"From them consequently, the Gauls learnt, by giving up and by softening the Barbary, the usage of a more cultured life, the cultivation of fields and to enclose the cities with ramparts" Justin (Abstract of the Philippic histories)

After the start of the Massaliot economy in the 550–530s BC and the Phocaean will to control the Gaul Mediterranean shoreline and the low valley of the Rhône, we can note a spectacular development of the sedentary habitat along the river up to Lyon and, somewhere else, on a littoral strip of approximately 50 km in width. This type of agglomeration reflects the will to control and to exploit complementary lands; it marks the abandonment of slash and burn agriculture to the benefit of the generalised fallow system and light animal-drawn cultivation. These sites, often of small and medium importance, were probably managed by chieftainship communities. The native elites knew how to surround themselves with a clientele who could be called upon for collective works, for example for building enclosures. In the necropoles, the emergence of a large number of weapons (offensive iron weapons and defensive bronze weapons) in most masculine sepultures (Beylier 2012) indicates that the defence was at this stage entrusted with all the men of the community, rather than the sole privilege of a cast of warriors (Sanmarti 1993, 20). This period is also marked by an increased social hierarchisation in the Southeast of France where only the exceptional individuals benefit from a *tumulus* (Dedet 2000, 145–146) as well as in West Languedoc where the study of the Elisyc necropoles shows "an acute pyramidal social structuration" (Janin 2000, 128).

This habitat network was set up in two stages. The first is marked by the grouping of populations in sedentary habitats which occupy spaces with varied potentialities predominantly, generally the edges of foothills or of valleys, possibly the mouth of the rivers. These sedentary settlements reflect the adoption of new agrarian practices and are accompanied by a sensitive demographic boom (Garcia & Isoardi 2010). The second stage is triggered by the Mediterranean (Phoenician, Etruscan, but especially Phocaean) commercial activity which reinforced the role of the lagoon sites and of the river mouths by conferring them an economic role, that of product trade and management centres (storage, transfilling, for example). This resulted in the first waves of diffusion of products, hence the flows of goods and of people between the coastline and the hinterland, along the natural circulation routes, in particular the valleys of the main coastal rivers. Both of these movements were expressed in the creation of numerous sites, especially in the last third of the sixth century BC and the first quarter of the fifth century BC.

Conclusion

This work has enabled us to throw a new light on the Marseille territories, but also along the same lines, on the Mediterranean Celts. For the first half of the sixth century BC, the archaeological and literary data suggest an integration of the Greek community within the Celtic society. After a contact phase, the small group of Phocaeans implants itself in the native territory according to a social and economic pattern which, all in all, does not seem to differ much from that of its origins. They constitute a demographic component likely to worry the local populations. Conversely, progressively, they were going to occupy a specific land (that of the "Calanques"—coves), little coveted by the local peasants and breeders, and by the import of exotic products (wine in particular), they reinforce the power of the natives whose space they share. In so doing, the foundation of Marseille merely connects two systems: on the one hand, a network of Phocaean foundations partially consecutive to the demographic boom of the cities of Eastern Greece and the search for metals and, on the other hand, the Celtic Southern "archipelago" whose political point of equilibrium rests on the capture and the redistribution of prestige goods.

It is only after the taking of Phocaea by the Persians and the probable arrival of Greek migrants that the territorial dynamic was going to evolve notably. Rapidly, Marseille would develop a speculative agriculture devoted to vineyards and olive trees, and strengthen its trade with a cereal-growing native world. This involved controlling the Massaliot land and its marshes, and grabbing the territory of the Segobriges. The latter would then be slaved to the setters and/or repelled by a newly defined *chôra:* a king of "heard-of" people, they would miss the Marche of History.

Beyond "Marseille and its surroundings", as a counterpoint to the territorial control and the organisation of the Massaliot commercial maritime network, the other native communities of the Southeast were going to experience a radical change in their lifestyle which, as often in the evolutions of the modes of settlement (Le Bras 2000), did not result from a strong cause or a strong combination of significant causes, but from a tenuous adjustment of two opposite forces: those of the development of the Celtic principalities (Brun & Chaume 2013), "emerging countries" of Central-Western Europe, and those of the structuring of the Emporia commerce. Thus, the Ligurian ethnic identity was going to assert itself in a reshaped geopolitical framework (Bouffier & Garcia supra).

Indeed, the Mediterranean Celtic region was first of all going to be the scene of the habitat "moving closer to the shoreline", due to the attractiveness of the Massaliots, judging by the creation of numerous maritime, lagunar and fluvial sites. Secondly, there was a kind of "Mediterraneisation", that is, whereby the Mediterranean Celts adopted new cultural (the consumption of wine in particular), social (proto-urban lifestyles) and economic (the development of cereal growing especially) frameworks. In fact, and it is no small paradox, both ethnic groups could (co)exist and thrive only by linking and integrating themselves in two networks going far beyond their territorial base: that of Emporia commerce for the Massaliots and that of the Mediterranean region towards the Celtic principalities for the Celto-Ligurians.

Translations According to the Texts Analysed and Commented in Pralon 1992

1) The Greek text of Aristotle (frag. 549 Rose) according to a quotation of Athenaeus of Naucratis.

"The Phocaean Euxenos was the guest of the king Nanos (such was the name of that king). Nanos celebrated the wedding of his daughter whereas Euxenos for some reason or the other happened to be present. He invited him to the banquet.

The wedding unfurled as follows: After the meal, the young girl had to enter and give a cup of temperate beverage to whom she chose among the pretenders attending. The one to whom she handed the cup had to become her husband.

The young girl therefore enters and, either by chance or for any other reason, gives [the cup] to Euxenos. The young girl's name was Petta. Further to that event, as the father accepted Euxenos as his daughter's husband, thinking that the donation had been made with the consent of the divinity, Euxenos took her as his wife and change her name into Aristoxena, There is in Massalia a family (*génos*) descended from that woman, still now, called Protiads. Since Prôtis was the son of Euxenos and of Aristoxena".

2) The Latin text of Trogus Pompeius (*Philippic histories of Trogus Pompeius* XLIII, 3), according to abridged version by Justin.

"Thus, they were to consult the king of the Segobriges, named Nannos, on whose territory they contemplated to found a city and asked for his friendship.

Still, on that precise day, the king was busy organising the wedding of his daughter Gyptis whom, according to his people's custom, he was going to grant in marriage once she had chosen a son-in-law during the festive board.

And since all the pretenders had been invited to the wedding, the Greek hosts were also welcome to join the banquet.

Then, the young girl was introduced and, as her father had ordered her to offer water to the one she would choose for her husband, then she ignored all the others, turned towards the Greeks and offered water to Prôtis, who from host became son-in-law and received from his father-in-law a location to found a city".

Bibliography

Bats, M., 1999, Identités ethno-culturelles et espaces en Gaule méditerranéenne (principalement aux VIe et Ve s. avant J.-C.). In: *Confini e frontiera nella grecità d'occidente*. Atti del trentasettesimo Convegno di studi sulla Magna Grecia, Taranto, 3–6 ottobre 1997, Tarente, Istituto per la storia e l'archeologia della Magna Grecia, 381–418.

Bernus, E., 1999, Nomades sans frontières ou territoires sans frontières? In: J. Bonnemaison, L. Cambrezy, L. Quinty-Bourgeois (dir.), *Les territoires de l'identité. Le territoire, lien ou frontière?* Paris, L'Harmattan, 33–42.

Beylier, A., 2012, *L'armement et le guerrier en Méditerranée nord-occidentale au premier âge du Fer*. Lattes, Adal, 500p. (*Monographie d'Archéologie Méditerranéenne*, 31).

Beylier, A., 2013, Armes et panoplies individuelles du premier âge du Fer. In: B. Girard (dir.), *Au fil de l'épée. Armes et guerriers en pays celte méditerranéen*. Nîmes, école antique éd., 37–44.

Boissinot, Ph., 2011, L'ethnicité en mode régressif, de l'âge du Fer à l'âge du Bronze. Quelques problèmes épistémologiques. In: D. Garcia (dir.), *L'âge du Bronze en Méditerranée. Recherches récentes*. Paris, Errance, 171–192.

Bonte, P. & Izard, M. (dir.), 2004, *Dictionnaire de l'ethnologie et de l'anthropologie*. Paris, PUF, 842p.

Brun, P. & Chaume, B., 2013, Une éphémère tentative d'urbanisation en Europe centre-occidentale durant les VIe et Ve siècles av. J.C.? *SPF*, 2013, 110, 2, 319–352.

Brun, P. & Ruby, P., 2008, *L'âge du Fer en France. Premières villes, premiers Etats*. Paris, La Découverte, 177p.

Chabal, L., 1997, *Forêts et sociétés en Languedoc*. Paris, DAF, 63, 189p.

Collin Bouffier, S., 2010, Parentés et spécificités culturelles en Sicile grecque à travers les tablettes de malédiction. In: N. Cusumano, D. Bonanno, C. Bonnet (eds.), *Alleanze e Parentele. Le affinità elettive nella storiografia sulla Sicilia greca*. Palerme, colloque international 14–15 avril 2010, 89–112.

Bouffier, S. & Garcia, D., *supra*, Greeks, Celts and Ligurians in South-East Gaul: Ethnicity and Archaeology. In: S. Bouffier & D. Garcia (dir.), *Greek Marseille and Mediterranean Celtic Region*.

Dedet, B., 2000, Images sociales de la mort dans le Sud-Est de la France au premier âge du Fer. In: T. Janin (ed.), *Mailhac et le premier âge du Fer en Europe occidentale*. Lattes, Adal, 133–155 (*Monographie d'Archéologie Méditerranéenne, 7*).

Dedet, B., 2008, *Les enfants dans la société protohistorique, l'exemple du sud de la France*. Rome, FR, 400p.

Delamarre, X., 2013, *Dictionnaire de la langue gauloise. Une approche linguistique du vieux-celtique continental*, Paris, Errance, 440p. (reed.).

Diamond, J., 2000, *De l'inégalité parmi les sociétés*. Paris, Gallimard, 492p.

Duplouy, A., 2006, *Le prestige des élites. Recherches sur les modes de reconnaissance sociale en Grèce entre les Xe et Ve siècles avant J.-C.* Paris, les Belles Lettres, 414p.

Garcia, D., 1995, Le territoire d'Agde grecque et l'occupation du sol en Languedoc central. In: *Sur les pas des Grecs en Occident*. Collection Études Massaliètes, 4, 137–167.

Garcia, D., 2000, Economie et réseau urbain protohistoriques dans le Nord-Est du monde ibérique (Roussillon et Languedoc occidental) (Vie–IIe s. av. J.-C.). In: *Ibers. Agricultors, artesans i comerciants. III Reunio sobre Economia en el Mon Ibèric, Valencia 24–27 novembre 1999*. Valencia, 69–79 (suppl. 3 à SAGVNTVM-PLAV).

Garcia, D., 2013, Monuments cultuels du premier âge du Fer méridional. Evolution, transformations, destructions. *DocArchéoMérid*, 34 (2011), 341–349.

Garcia, D., 2013b, L'enfant armé de l'Agnel (Pertuis, Vaucluse). In: B. Girard (dir.), *Au fil de l'épée. Armes et guerriers en pays celte méditerranéen*. Nîmes, école antique éd., 257–259.

Garcia, D., 2014, *La Celtique méditerranéenne. Habitats et sociétés en Languedoc et en Provence du VIIIe au IIe siècle av. J.-C.* Arles, Actes Sud /Errance, 250p. (2nd edition edited and improved, 2004).

Garcia, D. & Isoardi, D., 2010, Variations démographiques et capacités de production des céréales en Celtique méditerranéenne: le rôle de Marseille grecque. In: H. Tréziny (ed.), *Grecs et indigènes de la Catalogne à la mer Noire*. Paris/Aix, Errance/CCJ, BiAMA 3, 2010, 403–424.

Garcia, D. & Sourisseau, J.-C., *infra*, The exchanges on the coastline of the southern Gaul in the first Iron Age: From the hellenisation concept to that of Mediterraneisation. In: S. Bouffier & D. Garcia (dir.), *Greek Marseille and Mediterranean Celtic Region*.

Garcia, D. & Vital, J., 2006, Dynamiques culturelles de l'âge du Bronze et de l'âge du Fer dans le sud-est de la Gaule. Actes de la table ronde de Bologne, 28–29 mai 2005 organisée dans le cadre du thème *Celtes et Gaulois, l'archéologie face à l'histoire*. Glux-en-Glenne: Bibracte, Centre archéologique européen, 63–80 (Bibracte; 12/2).

Gasco, J., 1997, Etapes connues dans l'évolution agro-pastorale de la Montagne d'Alaric (Aude), de la Préhistoire récente à la période historique. In: *La dynamique des paysages protohistoriques, antiques, médiévaux et modernes*, Antibes, APDCA, 557–576.

Girard, B. (dir.), 2013, *Au fil de l'épée. Armes et guerriers en pays celte méditerranéen*. Nîmes, école antique éd., 416p.

Gras, M., 1995, L'arrivée d'immigrés à Marseille au milieu du VIe s. av. J.-C. In: *Sur les pas des Grecs en Occident*. Collection *études Massaliètes*, 4, 363–366.

Janin, T., 2000, Nécropoles et sociétés élisyques: les communautés du premier âge du Fer en Languedoc occidental. In: *Mailhac et le premier âge du Fer en Europe occidentale*. Lattes, 118–131 (MAM 7).

Janin, T., 2013, La sépulture à incinération de Saint-Antoine (Castelnau-de-Guers, Hérault). In: B. Girard (dir.), *Au fil de l'épée. Armes et guerriers en pays celte méditerranéen*. Nîmes, école antique éd., 273–274.

Janin, T. & Chardenon, N., 1998, Les premiers objets en fer en Languedoc occidental et en Roussillon. In: M. Feugère & V. Serneels (eds.), *Recherches sur l'économie de fer en Méditerranée nord-occidentale*, Montagnac, Monique Mergoil éd., 56–64.

Johnson, A.W. & Earle, T., 2000, *The Evolution of Human Societies*. Stanford, Stanford University Press, 1987, 456p. (2nd Ed.).

Kaplan, R.D., 2012, *The Revenge of Geography: What the Map Tells Us About Coming Conflicts and the Battle Against Fate*. New York, Random House, 403p.

Leduc, C., 1990, Comment la donner en mariage? La mariée en pays grec (IXe–IVe s. av. J.-C. In: P. Schmitt-Pantel (dir.), *Histoire des Femmes. L'Antiquité*, Paris, Plon, 1991 (Bari, Laterza, 1990), 259–318.

Le Bras, H., 2000, *Essai de géométrie sociale*. Paris, éditions Odile Jacob, 300p.

Mazoyer, M. & Roudart L., 1997, *Histoire des agricultures du monde. Du Néolithique à la crise contemporaine*. Paris, Le Seuil, 534p.

Moret, P. & Rouillard, P., 2012, Diasporas grecques: le cas de la péninsule Ibérique. In: S. Bouffier (ed.), *Diasporas grecques en Méditerranée. Du détroit de Gibraltar à l'Indus, VIIIe s. av. J.-C.—IIIe s. av. J.-C.*, Paris, Armand Colin, 149–159.

Nickels, A., en collaboration avec Marchand G. & Schwaller M., 1989, *Agde. La nécropole du premier âge du Fer*. Paris, CNRS, 498 p. (suppl. à la *RANarb*, 19).

Plana Mallart, R., 2012, La présence grecque et ses effets dans le nord-est de la Péninsule ibérique (VIIe-début du IVe siècle avant n. è.), *Pallas*, 157–178.

Pralon, D., 1992, La légende de la fondation de Marseille. In: M. Bats, G. Bertucchi, G. Congès & H. Tréziny (dir.), *Marseille grecque et la Gaule, Actes du Colloque international d'Histoire et d'Archéologie et du Ve Congrès archéologique de Gaule méridionale (Marseille, 18–23 novembre 1990)*. Lattes/Aix-en-Provence, ADAM-PUP, 51–56 (EtMassa, 3).

Py, M., 1993, *Les Gaulois du Midi. De la fin de l'âge du Bronze à la conquête romaine*. Paris, Hachette, 288p.

Py, M., 2010, *La sculpture gauloise méridionale*. Paris, Errance, 200p.

Py, M., Sauzet, P. & Tendille, C., 1984, *La Liquière, village du Ier âge du Fer*. Paris, CNRS, 364p. (suppl. 11 à la *RANarb*).

Sahlins, M., 1976, *Âge de pierre, âge d'abondance. L'économie des sociétés primitives*, Paris, Gallimard, 420p.

Sanmarti-Grego, J., 1993, Grecs et Ibères à Emporion. Notes sur la population indigène de l'Empordà et des territoires limitrophes. *Documents d'Archéologie Méridionale*, 16, 19–25.

Sigaut, F., 1988, L'évolution technique des agricultures européennes avant l'époque industrielle, *Revue Archéologique du Centre de la France*, 27–1, 61–94.

Testart, A., 2005, *Éléments de classification des sociétés*. Paris, Errance, 160p.

Todd, E., 2011, L'origine des systèmes *familiaux. Tome 1. L'Eurasie.* Paris, Gallimard, 355p.

Tréziny, H., 2008, La maison de Gyptis, In: J.E. Brochier, A. Guilcher & M. Pagni (eds.), *Archéologies de Provence et d'ailleurs. Mélanges offerts à G. Congès et G. Sauzade.* Aix-en-Provence, APA, 285–289.

Verger, S. & Pernet, L. (dir.), 2013, *Une Odyssée gauloise*. Arles, Errance, 400p.

4. The Exchanges on the Coastline of Southern Gaul in the First Iron Age: From the Hellenisation Concept to That of Mediterraneisation

DOMINIQUE GARCIA AND JEAN-CHRISTOPHE SOURISSEAU

Introduction

The traditional approach to the history of Southern Gaul sets the date of foundation of Marseille, that is, 600 BC, as a turning point in any pondering process wherein a before and an after are bound to be connected. This position is the heir of a history of research which goes vastly beyond the framework of the South of Gaul and the 50 years which are given to analyse here. It finds its main origin in the conception of the so-called colonial phenomena, particularly those relative to the Greek world that the Modern have imposed since at least the nineteenth century. The first occurrence of that conception can be found in the very vocabulary, since to speak of colonies to designate the settlements of Greeks in the West and in the Black Sea between the eighth and the sixth centuries BC is not only an anachronism in itself (it is the transposition of a Latin word, *colonia*, which translates a very different Roman reality), it is also an important element in the construction of the justification of the contemporary colonial phenomena, especially in North Africa, which mainly rests on the idea of the contribution of the civilisation and of the profusion to non-civilised populations: whereas the ancient colonial phenomenon not only appears as a model, but also as a golden age. In the Archaic Greek model, there is no clear political connection between the metropolitan city and the colonial city: it is a fundamental distinction since it enables us to reject the idea of a political and/or economic project in what is still called the Archaic Greek colonial phenomenon. And all the old debates on, for example, the distinction between agrarian colonies and settlement colonies are de facto today outdated since they rest on that at least partial confusion between Greek *apoikia* and Roman *colonia* (Etienne 2010, with earlier bibliography). From there, we may become aware of the difficulty of taking stock of the research relative to the economic exchanges in Southern Gaul, between Greeks and indigenes in the first Iron Age, when we measure the historiographical weight of that very widespread confusion in the historical and archaeological research of the twentieth century. Building upon that connoted approach, concepts such the Hellenisation of the South of Gaul have been grooved (Benoît 1965) with consequently the idea of a binary confrontation between Marseille Greeks and indigenes (the Southern Gauls being perceived as a relatively coherent whole) and whose cultural, economic or political evolution of the local groups was obligatorily associated with the confrontation of the Marseille Greek involved in that space (Garcia 2000).

Before the Foundation of Marseille, Exchanges and Contacts

On Symbolic Objects, but Especially Mediterranean Cultural Baggage

It is generally admitted that before 700 BC, the Southern societies of the beginning of the Iron Age had maintained very few relationships with the Mediterranean cultures. It is in itself, in the context of the Western Mediterranean region, an originality to single out since in Southern Italy or in Sicily as well as in Etruria, the proximity of the Greek colonial establishments has favoured since at least the middle of the eighth century, phenomena of economic and cultural contacts which generated deep transformation processes of the indigenous societies. The same observation could in fact be in Western Sicily, in Sardinia, in the area of the Straits of Gibraltar or along the coasts of the Iberian Levant where the Phoenician influence has deeply and durably marked the indigenous societies since at least the beginning of the eighth century. The explanation most often put forward by the researchers is the geographical isolation of the Gallic South, the remotest space from the major Western colonial focal points, whether Greek or Phoenician, while forgetting that as early as the ninth century BC the Nuragical communities of Sardinia maintained, at a date anterior to the first exogenous implantations in the Western Mediterranean region, exchange relationships with the

Villanovan community of the Tyrrhenian façade characterised by circulation of metallic objects and probably as well by individual mobilities (Gras 1985).

In the South, it is perhaps in this context of direct exchanges that the presence of fibulae supposedly discovered on various Languedoc (Janin 2006) or Provence sites and dated to the eighth century should be put in perspective. Their early discovery, which no recent finding could back up, nevertheless casts doubts on the credibility with which their place of discovery was stated but, taking into account the elements just mentioned, they should not be rejected *a priori* as was done for a long time, considering that the emergence of these contacts must have been associated with the Greek or Phoenician implantations in the South of the Western Mediterranean region. Recently, J. Guilaine and S. Verger (2008) have restated the terms of the debate while insisting on the variety of the available sources, in particular the 'orientalising' (rather than Iberian) iconography of the stelae of Sextantio (Hérault) and of Bioux (Vaucluse), or on the discovery of the deposit belt of the Motte in Agde. If these exogenous contributions and influences affecting the Southern communities before the seventh century BC come across as discontinuous and varied, the scrutiny of adornment elements of the feminine tomb 517 of the necropolis of San Montano of Pithecusses (dated from the last quarter of the eighth century) throws a new light: at the heart of one of the first Greek colonial experiments whose political, cultural and ethnical complexity is perceived today, the Gauls are not insignificant. Around the middle of the seventh century BC, the witnesses of these Mediterranean circulations are still quite limited in number but clearly attested as shown by the discovery of Mediterranean imports in very rare funerary contexts in Languedoc, as in Agde (Hérault) and in Mailhac (Aude) (Janin 2003). As for East of the river Rhône, these discoveries should be complemented by a proto-Corinthian cup in Antibes (Alpes-Maritimes) and a *skyphos* of ancient Corinthian time in Bollène (Vaucluse). These are lathed vases associated with the service of liquids and more precisely, in a Greek or Etruscan context, the service of wine. These objects have been interpreted as the tangible signs of prestige goods exchanged between indigenous elites and Mediterranean merchants, following the model of Homeric *praxis*, in which the personal relationship between partners recognising each other as of equivalent social (and therefore probably high) rank induces the exceptional character of the signs of the exchange, at least for the receiving part, and would hence account for their rarity. For some, their (secondary) funerary usage would constitute a new form of expression of the status of the associated defuncts, with the reinterpretation, in a Gallic native context, of the signs carrying a Greek or Etruscan aristocratic ideology linked with collective consumptions of wine, without the product in question being attested.

The possible identification of a fifth exogenous object in the Agde necropolis excavated by André Nickels (Nickels et al. 1989) enables us to enrich the reflection. S. Verger (2010) recently claimed that the large iron knife of tomb 202 was an exogenous object with indeed no equivalent in regional typologies and for which he offered a very convincing comparison in the sanctuary of Betalemi in Gela in Southeastern Sicily. These large knives are generally associated with sacrificial butchery and hence to gestures which, put back in the context of this type of exchange, refer to Mediterranean sacrificial practices associated with hospitality rites, a necessary corollary of the Homeric *praxis*. But who are these partners with whom the regional communities or at least their elites have maintained exchange relationships probably involving traffic? The first hypothesis, assuming that these objects were Greek, with several origins suggested, came from A. Nickels, venturing vague Greek connections. M. Gras (2000), hypothesising an Etruscan origin for some of these vases, envisaged for his own part not so much an Etruscan connection properly speaking, but an exchange network the origin of which would be situated in the Tyrrhenian Sea, travelled at that time by Greeks and Etruscans and perhaps even other partners.

The publications of B. Bouloumié on the Archaic material of Saint-Blaise (1992) and, especially taking stock of the collections of the site, even if they do not allow for the moment clear characterisation of the stratigraphical horizon of the seventh century still authorise to identify a few rare objects to be situated around the middle, for some, or during the second half of the seventh century, for others. These are again vases associated with the service of drinks (drinking and pouring vases), but the quite diverse origins of the identified objects might back up the hypothesis of M. Gras of Tyrrhenian networks, since Greek vases of various (Eastern and Western) origins and Etruscan vases are combined. However, other clues tend to cloud this pattern, like the presence of local modelled vases of Phoenician typology in the necropolis of Mailhac, down to the detail of bearing the red varnish characteristic of the traditional Phoenician prototypes, whereas no imported piece, which might have served as a model, was found on location, at least for the time being (Gailledrat 2000). The discovery on the same site of a stone lion, although quite damaged but well characterised, whose comparison models refer to the Iberian Levant deeply studded with Phoenician cultural elements, has enabled Eric Gailledrat (Gailledrat & Bessac 2000) to formulate the hypothesis of the expression of a local orientalising phenomenon, which would also put in perspective the vases previously evoked among which an *askos* in the form of a bird, a remote cousin of forms known in a Greek and Phoenician Mediterranean context since far more ancient times and which constitute one of the characteristic objects of the orientalising phenomenon. If the hypothesis seems to be founded, it makes the situation apparently more complex than we had envisaged at the start, since we would only have to admit contributions from the West and not anymore only from the Tyrrhenian space in the East, but it especially supplies the elements of a global coherence to break free from the initial issue. Indeed, if the idea of orientalising expression must be adopted, in spite of the limited character of the phenomenon, we must follow the analysis to the end and design a polymorphic phenomenon made of individual mobilities or of small groups carrying with them not only a few objects with a high symbolic value, but especially a Mediterranean cultural baggage of artistic, technical possibly even political type.

Gallic Products Which Are Not Only Compensations

In this area affected by the Mediterranean influences, the resources in copper, silver or gold are not negligible and the deposits of bronze objects (the majority of which date back to the second half of the seventh century and to the first half of the sixth century) have been designated several times as potential compensations, in particular by J. Guilaine and M. Gras. Bronze appears as a driving element between the Mediterranean world and Gaul, but not solely in the context of a strict economic analysis. The Gallic metallurgy of the first Iron Age finds an explicit illustration with the so-called Launacian deposits, by the name of the series of bronze objects discovered in the nineteenth century in Launac (Fabrègues, Hérault) containing generally several tens to several hundreds of objects and of ingots made of copper metal. In the Hérault hinterland (in Péret or Saint-Saturnin for example), the habitat— cupriferous field—object and ingot deposit relation is established with certainty. The deposits are substantially composed of ingots and of axe-ingots made from copper extracted on site and from bronze coins collected.

The deposit of Roquecourbe in Saint-Saturnin (the most important after that of the eponym Launacian site) was contained in a bronze situla, probably of Etruscan origin. These copper and bronze objects would then be transported towards the coast. Several deposits have been found along natural communication pathways and close to the coastline (Vias, Loupian, Launac). The submarine site of Rochelongue, situated 600m off the shore of Agde (probably a shipwreck), was discovered in 1964. It enabled collection of more than 800 kg of copper, lead and tin ingots and a batch of more than 177 bronze objects. The product of this metallurgical and, from a mass perspective, far more accessorily recovery activity, had then to be exported towards the active commercial centres of Etruria and of Greece, essentially to be remelted to the benefit of the local craftsmanship. In this sense, the word 'Launacian' should be used rather for characterising an original economic phenomenon—the development of the native metallurgical production intended for exchange—than for designating regional cultural assemblages. The recent revelation by Stéphane Verger of Mediterranean circulation of bronze objects of diverse nature and origin (but in many ways comparable to the composition of these famous deposits) opens new perspectives and falls quite easily in line with the pattern we have just evoked. Obviously, we shall not dwell here on all the items of this complex file but simply to sum up the main elements of interest for our reflection today. The low valleys of the Aude and the Hérault are known for concentrating numerous deposits of bronze objects: elements of adornment, tools, weapons and ingots. If numerous objects are of regional origin, certain reveal continental influences or origins (Massif Central, Jura). Certain of these types of objects, of Gallic origin, have been recognised in the deposits of sanctuaries of Sicily and of Greece by S. Verger (2000). The interface role of central Languedoc, as a mining production area, but also an area of exchanges and of contacts, is emphasised. We might suggest that the Gallic objects discovered in the sanctuaries in Greece, in Sicily but also at the mouth of the l'Elne are the visible, ritualised part, the one dedicated to gods, of a larger diffusion activity.

A First "Mediterraneisation"

In total, the way we may perceive this history of the Southern communities before the foundation of Marseille has evolved quite a lot in 50 years. The traditional observation was that of irregular, isolated and exceptional contacts (almost accidents in a way), according to an idea founded on a few objects, admittedly symbolic but so rare in view of the volumes of the following period that they therefore have been relegated to the rank of pre-colonial relations.

It can be analysed today in quite a different manner. Although the material culture is only hardly marked by external contributions, the fact of the matter is that the Southern native communities knew about the existence of a vaster Mediterranean space than the horizon of the coast strip they occupy. This new perception of the space goes hand in hand with an at least partially Mediterranean community in which the natives of Southern Gaul take part. We can see in fact, before the foundation of Marseille, a phenomenon of first "Mediterraneisation" of Southern Gaul, an admittedly vague concept

(Morris 2003) since the hierarchisation of the phenomena and their relative chronology are themselves still vague, but which at least partially overlaps the concept of "connectivity" dearest to Horden and Purcell (2000).

Beyond concepts, to situate the main occurrence of such a phenomenon around the middle and during the second half of the seventh century seems quite satisfactory when we know moreover the interest of certain Western Greek poets, such as Stesichoros of Himera, for conceptualising the Western Mediterranean space.

Exchanges and Contacts, from the Foundation of Marseille to 400 BC

The Foundation of Marseille in the Context of Confronting Mediterranean and Regional Contexts

Although we have limited the extent (or at least the idea we had of its importance), the foundation of Marseille around 600 BC remains a primordial event: for the first time, a Greek community settles durably in Gaul and is going, de facto, to establish regular relationships with the local communities for several centuries. Nevertheless, the point is to know to what extent this event is not only the visible part of the associated phenomena of diverse nature and which historically may be even more structuring.

In the first place, it is the massive arrival of imported wine, in that particular instance essentially Etruscan wine, which towards the end of the seventh or the very beginning of the sixth century is the major sign of the rapid mutation affecting the Southern communities; whereas the foundation of Marseille can only be perceived in this context as an indirect consequence of the deep and rapid changes who modify the organisation of the traffics in the Western Mediterranean region.

What is the situation? As we said, around the end of the seventh century or the beginning of the sixth century (and the chronological debate has not been settled yet, but it does not matter), a regular and relatively important distribution of wine to communities who had apparently ignored its use so far emerged and developed rapidly in Southern Gaul. This is the implementation of new contacts based on the exchange of manufactured products (wine in particular) against basic necessities (cereals, metal, slaves, for example).

Several reading levels of the phenomenon can be envisaged. From a strictly Mediterranean viewpoint, these circulations of products cannot be dissociated from an unheard-of situation characterised by new emerging forms of exchanges. Up to 525, *Massalia* is admittedly a Greek city but its operating mode is linked with the rhythms of the Archaic *emporia* in the northwestern Mediterranean region: that is, a physical but limited presence in space (of the Greek blocks) and a commerce largely constituted of Etruscan products. In this context, are the Massaliots essential partners in the *Emporia* alongside the other Greeks and the Etruscans, possibly the Western Phoenicians? Not obligatorily. They are first and foremost the prime movers of regional commerce, brokers rather than producers.

Around 540 BC, the beginning of the diffusion of the Massaliot wine growing productions, associated with the probable arrival of Phocaean immigrants in Marseille (Gras 1995), and the implementation of the Marseillais commercial network (Bats al. 1992; Morel 1983) triggered the boom of the business activity of the city. This is a major turning point with the economic and political control of the Massaliot territory.

Greek Demand, Indigenous Cereals and New Economic Frameworks

A probable modification of the economic activity of *Massalia* and its demographic boom have caused the development of the indigenous cereal growing whose production surplus was going to feed a structured exchange network: The Gallic corn was meant to remedy the lack and the shortage of cereals of the Massaliot *chôra* (Strabo, IV, 1, 5) but also take part in a wide Mediterranean traffic associating other cities. Redistribution centres situated close to the coastline, native places for commerce and transhipment counterbalance the production premises of the Provence and Languedoc hinterland. But beyond the establishment of these South-North economic exchanges, we realise that upheavals affect the very organisation of the native societies whose most relevant expression is this dense habitat network unfurling as of the end of the sixth century BC (Garcia 2004).

In so doing, far more than native town-planning criteria (difficult to establish and to recognise on the field, one ought to emphasise the revealing conditions of the changes in lifestyles and premises which have been necessary to that urbanisation and that increasing power of the urban functions. Four at least seem to have been united and supported the Gallic growth. In the first instance, the presence of federative elements (in particular religious) which have enabled us to draw and to crystallise the native populations on these sites. Then, the emergence of a political power, i.e., of a class of leaders capable of organising the use of the surplus by the non-productive population: this power also enables us to impose a certain stability favourable to the production and to the circulation of foodstuffs. Thirdly, the possibility of an agricultural surplus capable of feeding the non-producers. Hence the necessity of the valorisation of a land and the exploitation of an *umland*. But the larger the agglomeration the less it may be content with its immediate hinterland, hence the necessity of a wider-scope tribute and of a larger-scale interregional commerce. Finally, the establishment and the control of its commercial activities: commerce is integral part of the city and, for the largest, it implied the presence of a class of merchants specialised in the collection and the redistribution of foodstuffs, with its body of specialists dedicated to storage, transport, book-keeping, and possibly the organisation of a market.

The Gallic agglomerations come across for the vast majority as production structures implanted within complementary lands wherein the culture of cereals and of legumes seems to prevail: it is quite a novelty. The organisation of the agrarian space in the context of a fallow system and light animal-drawn cultivation goes hand in hand with the boom of cities in the Southern Gaul. As we have just outlined, the cereals (in particular bearded barley) are not solely a term of the exchange; they are already a decisive marker (before the development of vineyards and olive trees) of the social, economic and cultural transformations experienced by the populations of the South of France from the middle of the Iron Age: the Mediterraneisation of an agrarian system, the reflect of a rapid transformation of the premises and lifestyles. The emergence of specialised cultures (vineyard in the *chôra* of Marseille, cereals on the native lands) constitutes a decisive threshold in the anthropisation of the natural geosystems. The speculative character of these productions marks for its own part an essential step in the evolution of the economic practices of both communities.

Finally, such an ethnical partition on a restricted geographical space, where the agrarian production departs from the self-sufficiency principle, implies a certain geopolitical stability, hence the adoption of commonly admitted rules.

A Massaliot market system, which lasted at least, with twists and turns, up to the second Punic War, and whose native integration (in two stages) was summed up perfectly by Justin (XLIII, 4): "4,1. Consequently, the Gauls learned from them how to live in a more civilised way, after softening and forsaking their Barbarian ways; they learned to cultivate fields and to surround cities with ramparts; 2 they also became accustomed to live governed by laws, not compelled by arms, to cut vineyards, to plant olive trees, and men like things reflected that blinding change to the extent that one could have thought that Gaul had been transported to Greece instead of the Greeks having emigrated to Gaul."

On Cereals...

The archaeology of the storage means, with recent archaecarpological syntheses (Bouby 2010) remains the best means of apprehending the evolution of cereal production. Indeed, statistically absent from the furniture exposed during the excavation of the Languedoc and Provence habitats prior to 500 BC, the *pithoi*—vases essentially reserved for the storage of cereals—represented, in the middle of the fifth century BC, from 25 to 35% of the furniture on the indigenous Southern sites. This progression of the frequency rates was accompanied by an increase of the volumes. The first granaries appeared at the same time. If the supra-family management of the granaries with a loose or a *pithoi* storage is not ensured, it is undeniable for the long-term cereal reserves formed by the silo fields of the Western Languedoc (Aumes, Montfau, Ensérune) and of the Roussillon (Ruscino, Elne for example) where the volume of certain specimens may reach 350 hl. This increased phenomenon of the cereal storage capacities of the Southern sites (especially in the Languedoc, apparently) was connected with the Mediterranean commerce, especially around Marseille. This is confirmed by the almost parallel evolution of the consumption of Greek wine, as attested by the presence of Massaliot wine amphorae, in the native world. All things considered, this phenomenon suggests (directly or indirectly) the significant modifications of the structures of indigenous societies: total sedentarisation, new agrarian practices, stock management and control, and early signs of work specialisation.

...and of Lead

For that period, in addition to the terms of the exchange, quite different from those recognised before the foundation of Marseille, certain documents provide information on the very modalities of commerce.

Such is the case in particular of the commercial inscriptions engraved on lead blades (regardless whether they are in Etruscan, in Pech-Maho in the Aude, and quoting for the first time the name of Marseille *(Mataliai)* in that language, or in Ionian, on the other side of the same document, but mentioning indigenous intermediaries as early as the second quarter of the fifth century (Lejeune et al. 1988) or even much more recently and in Iberian, in the region of Narbonne-Béziers or in Ibero-Greek in Elne. The lead inscribed in Greek discovered on the trading post of Sigean is a contract underwritten between merchants, one of them an Ionian (Heronoios) who is probably the writer and signatory of the document. It mentions the purchase (or the rental) of a boat *(akation)* or the purchase of its cargo and stipulates the presence of witnesses whose names are of local origin—Iberians of Languedoc or of Catalonia: Basiguerros, Bleruas, Golo. biur, Segedon, Nauaruas and Nalbe(…)n. *The akation* (or its contents) was purchased in an *emporion*. But the hypothesis of Jean Pouilloux (Pouilloux 1988) should be reminded, for whom the redactor of the text is only a go-between (a *metabolos*), accountable for the money paid to its native principals, which led him to write out the minutes of the whole case.

In Lattes (Hérault) recent discoveries have enriched this case (Bats 2010). When replenishing the soil of an edifice built around 430 BC and when backfilling the same zone, two lead blades inscribed in Greek were discovered. On the first part, we are dealing with a claim for payment in staters with two Greek characters, perhaps brokers installed in Lattes, Kleosthenes and Kleanax. The second one seems to allude to another type of product to be purchased, such as cereals *(sitos)*. We should also evoke the discovery outside our study area, on the Greek site in *Emporion*, of a lead blade engraved in Archaic Ionian and dated from the second half of the sixth century BC. It relates the instructions of the merchant asking a "colleague" to move (again a *metabolos?*) on an indigenous commercial premise called Saiganthe (*Sagunto?*) where he will have to make contact with a third merchant bearing an indigenous name: Baspedas(?). To the latter, he will have to offer the towing of a boat and the transport of goods; he finishes by specifying the (negotiable) conditions of this traffic (Asencio & Sanmarti 1998). The bulk of these documents (to which we must today add the discoveries of Elne, Ruscino) was then about to prohibit considering the exchange activities in a too primitive light which, in the South of France, associated Etruscans, Greeks, Iberians of the Southeast and natives. They are the testimony that these exchanges (probably the largest) were governed by written contracts.

This implies (as written by Fr. Salviat as early as 1988) "a contract law, a jurisdictional system and a civic control" admitted by the different partners and not only by the Greeks. We should admit that natives had accepted, possibly adopted for their own transactions, a system of Mediterranean commercial law. When it comes to new economic practices, we shall easily recognise this loan but at the cost of a relatively structured vision of at least a portion of the exchange modes in a protohistoric environment.

Conclusions

We need to acknowledge the interest raised by the primordial syntheses of Jean Jannoray (1955) and Fernand Benoît (1965) throughout the second part of the twentieth century; they have supplied a structuring framework for research on Southern Gaul and the Greek presence in the region. The development of the works of protohistorians since the 1970s, in particular those of P. Arcelin, B. Dedet and M. Py, has constituted a benchmark in terms of documentation and of analyses whereas in parallel the Marseille archaeology guided methods and issues in different ways (overview in Bats et al. 1992; Hermary et al. 1999). André Nickels (1988) or Jean-Paul Morel (1983) were among the rare scholars to try and combine these geographical as well as cultural or methodological approaches and to lay the foundations of new issues by privileging cultural interactions, breaking de facto the traditional moulds. Southern Gaul provides today a privileged study field which deserves putting the documentation in perspective by adopting a systemic analysis and rejecting Hellenising or "indigenist" approaches. As such, the reintegration of pre-Roman archaeology of Southern Gaul in a wide Mediterranean context constitutes a drastic change of paradigm. In this context, the cases of Saint-Blaise ("city of Marseille"), Lattes (indigenous site) or of Béziers ("forgotten Greek city") can be seen in a far more enriching light, as reflected in their Mediterranean diversity, composed not only of mobilities of products but also of men and of concepts (Py 2009; Tréziny 2010).

Bibliography

Asencio i Villaro, D. & Sanmarti i Grego, J., 1998, Consideracions metodologiques en relacio a l'estudi de las activitats comercials en época protohistorica. In: *Comerç i vies de comunicacio (1000aC.–700dC.)*. Puigcerdà, Institut d'Estudis Ceretans, 17–32.

Bats, M. et al. (ed.), 1992, *Marseille grecque et la Gaule*. Etudes Massaliètes 3, Lattes-Aix-en-Provence, 497 p.

Bats, M., 2010, L'écriture à Lattes. In: L. Pernet & M. Py (eds.), *Les objets racontent Lattara*. Paris, Errance, 26–30.

Benoît, F., 1965, *Recherches sur l'hellénisation du Midi de la Gaule*, Aix-en-Provence, éd. Orphys 331 p.

Bouby, L., 2010, *Agriculture dans le bassin du Rhône du Bronze final à l'Antiquité*. Toulouse, thèse EHESS, 3 vol. 650 p.

Bouloumié, B., 1992, *Saint-Blaise (fouilles Henri Rolland). L'habitat protohistorique. Les céramiques grecques*. Aix-en-Provence 279 p.

Etienne, R. (ed.), 2010, *La Méditerranée au VIIe siècle av. J.-C. (essais d'analyses archéologiques)*, Paris 442 p.

Gailledrat, E., 2000, Courants commerciaux et partenaires méditerranéens entre le Languedoc occidental et la Péninsule Ibérique au Premier Age du Fer (VIIe–Ve s. av. J.-C.). In: T. Janin (ed.), *Mailhac et le Premier Age du Fer en Europe occidentale. Hommages à Odette et Jean Taffanel*. Lattes, 261–270.

Gailledrat, E. & Bessac, J.-Cl., 2000, Découverte d'un ensemble sculpté du Premier Age du Fer à Mailhac (Aude). In: T. Janin (ed.), *Mailhac et le Premier Age du Fer en Europe occidentale. Hommages à Odette et Jean Taffanel*. Lattes, 291–303.

Garcia, D., 2000, Le temps des chercheurs. In: J. Chausserie-Lapree, *Le temps des Gaulois en Provence*. Martigues, 12–17.

Garcia, D., 2004, *La Celtique méditerranéenne. Habitats et sociétés en Languedoc et en Provence du VIIIe au IIe siècle av. J.-C.*, Paris, Errance. (second edition, edited and improved, 2014) 248 p.

Garcia, D. & Isoardi, D., 2010, Variations démographiques et capacités de production des céréales en Celtique méditerranéenne: le rôle de Marseille grecque. In: H. Tréziny (ed.), *Grecs et indigènes de la Catalogne à la mer Noire*. Paris/Aix, Errance/CCJ, BiAMA 3, 2010, 403–424.

Guilaine, J. & Verger, S., 2008, La Gaule et la Méditerranée. In: S. Celestino et al., *Contacto cultural entre el Mediterràneo y al Atlàntico (siglos XII–VIII). La precolonizacion a debate*. Madrid, CSIC, 219–238.

Gras, M., 1985, *Trafics tyrrhéniens archaïques*, Paris-Rome (BEFAR, 258) 773 p.

Gras, M., 1995, L'arrivée d'immigrés à Marseille au milieu du VIe s. av. J.-C. In: *Sur les pas des Grecs en Occident*, Études Massaliètes 4, Arles, Errance, 363–366.

Gras, M., 2000, Les Etrusques et la Gaule méditerranéenne. In: T. Janin (ed.), *Mailhac et le Premier Age du Fer en Europe occidentale. Hommages à Odette et Jean Taffanel*. Lattes, 229–241.

Hermary, A., Hesnard, A. & Tréziny, H., 1999, *Marseille grecque. La cité phocéenne (600–49 avant J.-C.)*. Paris, Errance 181 p.

Horden, P. & Purcell, N., 2000, *The Corrupting sea: a study of Mediterranean history*. Malden, Wiley-Blackwell 761 p.

Janin, T., 2003, Importations, modèles méditerranéens et faciès orientalisant dans le sud de la France: l'exemple du Languedoc occidental au VIIe s. av. n. è. In: *Les Etrusques en France. Archéologie et collections*. Lattes, 19–22.

Janin, T., 2006, Systèmes chronologiques et groupes culturels dans le Midi de la France de la fin de l'Age du Bronze à la fondation de Marseille: communautés indigènes et premières importations. In: *Gli Etruschi da Genova ad Ampurias, Atti del XXIV Convegno di Studi Etruschi ed Italici (Marseille-Lattes, 2002)*. Pise-Rome, 93–102.

Jannoray, J., 1955, *Ensérune, contribution à l'étude des civilisations préromaines de la Gaule méridionale*. Paris, de Boccard (BEFAR 181) 490 p.

Lejeune, M., Pouilloux, J, & Solier, Y, 1988, Etrusque et ionien archaïques sur un plomb de Pech-Maho (Aude). *Revue archéologique de Narbonnaise*, 21, -19–60

Morel, J.-P., 1983, Les relations économiques dans l'Occident grec. In: *Modes de contacts et processus de transformation dans les sociétés anciennes*. Rome (Coll. EfR 67), 549–580.

Morris, I., 2003, Mediterraneanization. *Mediterranean Historical Review*, 18.2, 30–55.

Nickels, A., 1988, Contribution des fouilles de l'arrière-pays d'Agde à l'étude du problème des rapports entre Grecs et indigènes en Languedoc (VIe–Ve siècles). *Mefra*, 96, 141–157.

Nickels, A., Marchand, G. & Schwaller, M., 1989, *Agde, la nécropole du Premier Age du fer*. Paris, CNRS (RANarb, Suppl. 19) 522 p.

Pouilloux, J., 1988, Un agent commercial souvent ignoré: le *métabolos*. *Cahier d'Histoire*, XXXII, 413–417.

Py, M., 2009, *Lattara, Lattes, Hérault. Comptoir gaulois méditerranéen entre Étrusques, Grecs et Romains*. Paris, Errance 352 p.

Salviat, F., 1988, Tablettes de plomb inscrites à Emporion et à Sigean. *RANarb*, 21, 1–2.

Trézny, H. (ed.), 2010, *Grecs et indigènes de la Catalogne à la mer Noire*. Paris/Aix-en-Provence, Errance/CCJ, BiAMA 3, 326 p.

Verger, S., 2000, Des objets languedociens et hallstattiens dans le sanctuaire d'Héra à Pérachora (Corinthe). In: T. Janin, (ed.), *Mailhac et le Premier Age du Fer en Europe occidentale. Hommages à Odette et Jean Taffanel*. Lattes, 387–414.

Verger, S., 2010, Archéologie du couchant d'été. In: J.P. Le Bihan & J.P. Guillaumet (eds.), *Routes du monde et passage obligés de la protohistoire au Haut Moyen Age*. Quimper, 293–337.

Verger, S. & Pernet, L. (ed.), 2013, *Une odyssée gauloise. Parures de femmes à l'origine des premiers échanges entre la Grèce et la Gaule*, Paris, Errance 400 p.

Zurbach, J., 2012, Mobilités, réseaux, ethnicité. Bilan et perspectives. In: L. Capdetrey & J. Zurbach (eds.), *Mobilités grecques. Mouvements, réseaux, contacts en Méditerranée, de l'époque archaïque à l'époque hellénistique*, Bordeaux, 261–273.

5. The Sources of Greek Marseille and of Its Territory: The Ethnica of Stephanus of Byzantium and the Lexicographical References

Marc Bouiron

The *Ethnica* of Stephanus of Byzantium form an indispensable book when we study the references of the ancient authors relating to places known or inhabited in Antiquity. This lexicon with geographical character has indeed kept a single piece of information. In the context of the study of Marseille and its territory, it seems important to analyse the notice of Massalia as it has been preserved, and beyond, to examine a few references related to the Massaliot territory. However, taking into account the numerous references made to the lexicon of the *Ethnica* without the authors knowing its nature exactly, it has appeared necessary, first of all, to describe the nature of the book transmitted to us, to understand the way this text has been abbreviated and how Stephanus of Byzantium designed his *Ethnica*. This reflection takes place in the wider context of a PhD thesis on "Stephanus Byzantinus as a source for Western Europe", under the direction of Arnaud Zucker (CEPAM-UNS) and Dominique Garcia (CCJ-AMU), wherein we shall find a far more detailed argumentation.

The Ethnica *of Stephanus of Byzantium*

We know for a fact that Stephanus of Byzantium described its lexicon in the years 530–540 (Honingmann 1929, col. 2372–2374; Billerbeck et al. 2006, 3*; Bouiron 2012, § 8–12). The indices have long been known but have been blurred so far by the mention of an abridged edition, written out as early as in Justinian time by some Hermolaus, to whom was wrongly attributed the *Epitome* with which we are familiar (we shall designate thus the work in our possession in order to distinguish it from the book of origin).

The Transmission of the Text and Its Epitomisation

A notice of the *Souda* (Adler ε 3048) mentions a *grammatikos* by the name of Hermolaus, the author of a summary of the book by Stephanus of Byzantium, dedicated to Justin. It has long been considered to grant clear anteriority to the work of origin and that the text in our possession had probably been written at a very early date. Still, such is not the case; Hermolaus is most certainly a "successor" of Stephanus of Byzantium, who gave a partial edition of the *Ethnica* at the end of the reign of Justin. The text in our possession originates, if we are not mistaken, from the work of Byzantine copyists and epitomisers, which started during the eleventh century with the first transliteration of the work of origin (passage of a manuscript of late Antiquity, written in non-accentuated uncials into a manuscript in accentuated lower case letters) and continued until the late Middle Ages. Indeed, the oldest manuscripts in our possession date from the end of the fifteenth century; they attest to the presence at that time of an archetype manuscript (non-preserved) which served for reproducing all the copies that we know.

The detailed study of the subsisting text enables us to put in evidence differentiated abbreviation phases, taking into account the breakdown of the *Ethnica* into 60 books (Bouiron 2012, § 67–73). Without going into the details of the argument, it can be noted that after the transliteration of the work of origin, it was abridged for the first time at the beginning of the twelfth century. This epitome is used by Eustathius of Thessalonica in his Comments on the *Illiad* or Dionysius the Periegete. It was followed by a second abbreviation (in the first half of the thirteenth century?) then again, in a third step, by a new reduction of the text which comes across almost in the form of a summary. It should be noted that each of the abbreviations reduces to a third the previous text. In this process, the first abridged version started with wiping out the quotations, then the mentions of authors as well as the grammatical indications were completely isolated.

Finally, the archetype manuscript, probably lost since the sixteenth century and on the basis of which all the known manuscripts (and the princeps edition of *Aldus*) have been copied, must have been composed of the different parts still subsisting in the fifteenth century both from the first epitome (for books 1 to 3 and 58 to 60), of the third abstract for books 29–30 and

40–50 (and perhaps 14 and 35) and of the second abstract for the remainder. Let us also note the disappearance of books 24, 28 and 37.

This precise analysis of our *Epitome*, here summed up, is fundamental to understanding the degree of preservation of any notice *according to the book of origin*. For more details, we refer to the table we have listed, so as to define the abbreviation phase of each primitive book (Bouiron 2012, § 85, tab. V). But it is not sufficient to understand the preserved text of the notices; we also need to take into account the nature of the information generally contained in the lexicon.

The Work of a Grammarian

Stephanus of Byzantium worked as a grammarian and not as a geographer or a historian. His book follows the work of another grammarian of the fifth century of our era, Oros of Alexandria. For the *Ethnica*, he certainly used simultaneously his orthographic treatise, his *Attic lexicon* and his book *On the formation of ethnica*. The latter, probably the latest of the books of Oros, contained the whole doctrine derived from Herodianus and criticised by late grammarians like Eudaimon of Pelusa and Arcadius of Antioch. It is quite certainly through this work that Stephanus of Byzantium quoted and used Herodianus, by using the indications of construction of ethnonyms. This explains the grammatical indications on the formation of the ethnica, quite present in the first books of the *Epitome*.

Conversely, the very form of the notices does not seem to be specific to Oros nor even to Stephanus of Byzantium. Thus their organisation, in particular the presence of a piece of information of chrono-mythological type immediately after the initial geographical determination, can be found in other older lexica, although perhaps less systematically. If Oros probably provides very useful grammatical information for Stephanus of Byzantium, he does not form the substrate of the text of the notices. The *Etymologicum Genuinum*, composed in the ninth century, supplies blatant evidence: for the woman *Aiguptos*, it offers a text of Oros different from that of the *Epitome*. The notices of populations seem also to have been treated distinctly. It is too long here to give the detail of the argumentation but we have emphasised that all of the notices (like indeed a portion of the work of Oros) could rest on a lexicon-source from the middle of the second century of our era that we also found quasi-integrally in the *Ethnica*.

In the work of Stephanus of Byzantium, the contribution of his predecessor Eugenius of Augustopolis, a grammarian from the end of the fifth century, has never been analysed in detail. It might be slightly more important that the sole mention preserved from this grammarian in the *Epitome* could lead us to think. We suggest that Stephanus of Byzantium may have used, on top of his *Assorted lexicon*, his work entitled *On the names of temples* for the references related to sanctuaries of divinities, and perhaps his book *On the -ia names*.

We cannot detail here the arguments confirming these hypotheses, but it clearly appears that Stephanus of Byzantium is part of a long knowledge transmission chain going back to the Alexandrine time and relying first of all on the works of his immediate predecessors.

The Direct and Indirect Authors

Understanding the book of the Stephanus of Byzantium involves first of all the identification of the source-authors that he may have used to fill his lexicon. We shall define two major categories: those he has read directly to find the information of interest, in particular geographers, and from which he has "skinned" the texts (in the archival sense of the term); and those he quoted from second or third hand. Among all these authors, regardless whether direct or indirect, some have probably acted as go-betweens that granted access to older authors forming the basic material of his notices. These authors could be read directly by himself or used by intermediate authors (we think here for example to grammarians such as Epaphroditus or Didymus *Chalcenterus).*

Among the authors that Stephanus of Byzantium used directly, we find a few late grammarians such as Oros of Alexandria and Eugenius of Augustopolis, as we have said, less certainly Herodianus, rather used through the filter of Oros (but its work was still largely accessible in the sixth century). He also read a few geographers such as Strabo, Pausanias or Marcianus of Heraclea, who come across as often mentioned, regardless of whether their name has been kept or not in the *Epitome.*

Conversely, he never mentions authors whose work we have kept, such as Dion Cassius, Diodorus of Sicily, Lucian of Samosata or Gallienus of Pergamum; whereas the borrowings are quite anecdotic and indirect as for Ptolemy and Plutarch.

Due to a probable usage of a very detailed basic lexicographical text, which may date back to the second century of our year it is difficult to know whether Stephanus of Byzantium directly used authors such as Polybius, Thucydides and Herodotus whose texts were still accessible at the time. The references encountered in the *Epitome* seem however to originate from the source-lexicon. The question is raised crucially for Hecataeus, who is the most frequently quoted author (304 times in the text in our possession) but we do not think he could be read directly in the sixth century.

The Information Contained in the Lexicon

The reading key of the book of Stephanus of Byzantium can be found in the notion of "derived form" of a name, in the antique grammatical sense. It refers to the complete title of the original work (Billerbeck al. 2006, 5*; Bouiron 2012 § 6): "On the names of the cities and of the islands, of the populations and the demes, and of the places; and, as regards them, the cases of homonymy and the cases of name change, as well as the ethnical, topical and ktetical derived names" ("περὶ πόλεων, νήσων τε καὶ ἐθνῶν δήμων τε καὶ τόπων καὶ ὁμωνυμίας αὐτῶν καὶ μετονομασίας καὶ τῶν ἐντεῦθεν παρηγμένων ἐθνικῶν τε καὶ τοπικῶν <τε> καὶ κτητικῶν ὀνομάτων"). The way the title has been built should be noted for better understanding of each of the notices. We are dealing with a listing of successive elements coordinated by καὶ; inside each of the main listings, the secondary juxtaposition is indicated by τε καὶ.

We shall find in his book notices whose names (1) have homonyms or (2) have changed names, or, by far the most frequent case, (3) possess derived forms of the initial toponym. This is fundamental to understanding this work and explains why a very large number of toponyms presents in the old geographical works (for example the *Geography* of Strabo, although abundantly quoted) are not reproduced here: Stephanus of Byzantium did not find the names of the inhabitants or of people derived from the toponym and therefore has not kept them. The presence of notices only related to populations without any lexical form, designed as derivatives from geographical names as such, and which therefore fall into the grammatical category of the work, should also be noted.

The detailed analysis of the whole *Epitome* enables us to put in evidence four large categories of names (which we designate, generically, by the neologism "geonym") subject of a lemme in the lexicon of Stephanus of Byzantium. They form the heart of the information collected in the lexicon.

The first, largest category corresponds to the names of place: Regardless whether it is a city, a village, a river, etc. The list is very long and goes from the smallest element (χωρίον or κώμη) to the widest (the continent for Europe, Libya or Asia). Their high frequency confers to the book the tonality of a "conventional" geographical lexicon, a kind of dictionary of all the toponyms. These notices still contain a "derived" form, in the sense of antique grammarians, that is, an ethnical, a feminine or a (possessive) ktetical name. Their complex organisation will be studied more in detail below.

The second category of information concerns the names of populations, considered as we said as derived names.

The third understands the names of the demes and of the attic tribes. Although disseminated throughout the book, they are organised in a similar and specific manner. The names of these demes and tribes may be reconciled with other geonyms whose name is similar and that appear as such in plurial notices encompassing several homonymous toponyms.

The last category relates to general definitions, geographical in the broadest sense. When studying the lexicon in detail, we have discovered that it contains notices corresponding to the generic terms themselves designating the geographical connection. They are either purely geographical (γῆ, land; ἤπειρος, continent; θάλασσα, sea; νῆσος, island; πεδίον, plain) or associated with human occupation (κώμη, village; λιμήν, port; οἶκος, habitant; πόλις, city; φῦλον, gender; χώρα, region), or finally specific to the Athenian space (δῆμος, deme; φρατρία, brotherhood; φυλή, political tribe). They are themselves structured as the remainder of the notices and contain the names of the inhabitants and the other derived forms. Stephanus of Byzantium has probably compiled an older source (the source-lexicon?), perhaps through the lexicographical works of Oros of Alexandria.

Finally, we should mention the presence of specific information within these notices, such as places of worship (a category grouped in the antique authors under the name of *temenika*), proverbs and indications of cities of birth or of death of famous characters that may, for each of them, originate from previous compilations.

All these elements nest into each other according to the pattern defined by the author for the construction of his notices, which we are now going to analyse.

The Basic Structuration of the Notices

The general structuration of the notices can be put in evidence thanks to the analysis of the *Epitome*. We shall specify below using letters the internal breakdowns of the notices common to all the notices.

For the most complete notices (those with a toponym and derived forms), Stephanus of Byzantium gives first of all the general, compulsory and usually quite short, geographical definition (which we shall note [A]), which indicates the nature of the toponym and its localisation.

It is followed, each time it was possible to find adequate information, by a paragraph on the (often mythological) origin of the name and the history of the toponym [B]. It should be noted that this part does not appear explicitly in the title and could be understood as an extension of the geographical determination, in an "etymological" form which was fashionable during Antiquity; the systematic character of this data has however led us to distinguish it. The author then gives the variations of the name [C], divided in two sub-parts: the homonymies [C1] and the name changes ("metonomasies") [C2].

Then comes the derived form of the ethnica [D]. As for the toponyms, Stephanus of Byzantium outlines all the spelling variations. The general title then indicates solely the treatment of the possessive (ktetical) names [E] but these derived forms are not the only ones, since we often find here the feminine names, considered as variations of the ethnica [E1], alongside the ktetical names properly speaking [E2].

Finally, certain notices contain two series of complementary information [F]: the one, general [F1] consists of true digression on expression; the second [F2], derived from grammarians, "repentants" or information which should have be situated normally in a previous section.

As we have said, a second large category of notices can be found in the *Ethnica*: these are the ones starting directly with an ethnical name (generally a people) and wherein the lemme is a derived form. These notices are organised on the pattern of the previous notices with the ethnical name [Da], sometimes followed by a small chrono-mythological paragraph [Db] as for the toponyms. The spelling variations [Dc] are followed by the feminine [E1] and ktetical [E2] forms, which may be extended in turn by the complementary information [F1] and [F2].

Finally, notices whose lemme corresponds to several different places can also be found. These notices, which we shall designate as plurial notices, are quite numerous in the work of Stephanus of Byzantium and are organised in three different manners. The first one consists of juxtaposing the notices, whereas each of the units has its different columns (in particular its ethnical character). The second method includes processing the other homonymous toponyms in the column of name variations [C]; this implies that the form of the ethnical form is the same, since it is then common to all the geonyms. The third one consists in placing the piece of information into the residual column [F].

The Notice on Massalia in the Ethnica

After having established the exact nature of the text preserved and the type of information contained in the *Ethnica*, we can analyse the notice of the *Epitome* for Massalia. We shall supply the text first of all with its translation, then the analysis of its different constituents. Finally, a comparison with the mentions of Eustathius of Thessalonica, who used a still little abridged epitome of Stephanus of Byzantium, will enable us to see whether a more complete text can be reconstructed.

The Notice in the Epitome

The notice on Massalia belongs to book 30, available to us solely in its most reduced version. We have kept, theoretically, only 12% of the original text. Needless to say this notice is abridged and even therefore may have been rendered incomprehensible.

We shall supply first of all the text in which we have numbered the sentences and revealed the internal organisation, followed by the critical apparatus (according to Meineke's edition). In the translation, we have indicated in square brackets the probable authors from whom the references are derived. Finally, we have followed up on each of the sentences with a detailed comment.

Μασσαλία· [A] |1| πόλις τῆς Λιγυστικῆς[a] κατὰ τὴν Κελτικήν, [B] ἄποικος Φωκαέων. |2| **Ἑκαταῖος** *Εὐρώπῃ*. |3| **Τίμαιος** δέ φησιν ὅτι προσπλέων ὁ κυβερνήτης καὶ ἰδὼν ἁλιέα ἐκέλευσε[b] μάσσαι[c] τὸ ἀπόγειον[d] σχοινίον· μάσσαι[c] γὰρ τὸ δῆσαί[e] φασιν Αἰολεῖς· ἀπὸ γοῦν[f] τοῦ ἁλιέως καὶ τοῦ μάσσαι[c] ὠνόμασται. [D] |4| τὸ ἐθνικὸν *Μασσαλιώτης* καὶ *Μασσαλιεύς* [E] καὶ *Μασσαλία* καὶ *Μασσαλιῶτις* γυνή.

a) Λιγυστικῆς Holtmann: Λιβυστικῆς *mss.*—b) ἐκέλευσε Meineke (*ex* Eust. *Com. Dion* 75): κελεῦσαι *mss.*—c) μάσσαι Meineke (*ex* Eust.): μᾶσαι *mss.*—d) ἀπόγειον *mss*: ἀπόγαιον Eust.—e) δῆσαί Meineke (*ex* Eust.): ἐκδῆσαι *mss.*—f) γοῦν R: οὖν V.

> *Massalia:* [A] city of the Ligystica [*Hecataeus?*] at the level of the Celtic world [*Abstract of Artemidorus,* **Strabo?**], [B] foundations of the Phocaeans. **Hecataeus** in *Europa*. **Timaeus** says that the pilot as he approached and saw a fisherman, asked him to attach the mooring line to the land; indeed, the Eolians say '*massai*' for '*dêsai*' (to attach). It takes its name therefore from '*halieus*' and '*massai*'. [D] The ethnical form is rendered as *Massaliôtês* [**Strabo?**] and *Massalieus* and [E1] *Massalia* and *Massaliôtis* [**Strabo?**] In the feminine.

[A] |1|: the geographical determination is double, which probably results from the juxtaposition of two distinct pieces of information, joined through the abbreviation process. The first one is specific to archaic and classical authors; we shall here give the precedence to Hecataeus, whose major role as the source of the *Ethnica* is known, and who is mentioned further. The indication is interesting since it does not refer to a possession of the city by a given people but situates it within a territory, which Hecataeus calls Ligystica and where the Ligyans live.

The second determination, "at the level of the Celtic world" might derive either from the *Geography* of Strabo or from the *Abstract of Artemidorus* by Marcianus. Both these works are indeed direct sources of Stephanus of Byzantium: Strabo is quoted 218 times, the *Abstract of Artemidorus* between 20 and 40 times (we cannot differentiate the abstract from the original when there is only the name of Artemidorus). In the latter's work, the *Geographical descriptions*, the Celtic world corresponds to more continental Gaul, but we know that Marcianus has "updated" the geographical determination of a number of toponyms. Such indication should probably be traced back, in the context of the lexicon, beyond the middle of the second century BC.

The original notice therefore contained a first determination, then completed by several authors who placed Marseille in Ligystica (Polybe?) or in the Celtic world (Artemidorus? Strabo; for this author, the whole of Gaul is denominated thus). Most probably, quotations backed up these different references. However, there is no point here to multiply the number of authors used by Stephanus of Byzantium for this sole geographical determination.

[B] |1–2|: The mention of a foundation of Phocaea, most probably derived from Hecataeus, also refers to the pseudo-Scymnus (v. 210), but also to a whole series of authors of Thucydides (I, 13, 6) to Favorinus of Arles (fr. 96, 12). The position of the mention of Hecataeus, probably due to the reduction of the text of Stephanus of Byzantium, makes him the author both of the geographical determination (city of Ligystica) and of the foundation by the Phocaeans.

|3|: The false etymology of Massalia has been kept by the successive abbreviators of Stephanus of Byzantium. It rightfully belongs here and matches the chrono-mythographical references providing the origin of the city as well as of the name it bears. The last abbreviator could have decided to delete this information but the anecdotic aspect prevailed. The end of the notice suffered de facto far more from the successive abbreviations.

[D] |4|: The reduction of the summary has proved fatal to the correct understanding of this paragraph. It juxtaposes several distinct forms. The beginning is dedicated to the ethnical form (with forms such as Μασσαλιώτης and Μασσαλιεύς) then to a particular form (of the *chôra*? Μασσαλία) which is identical to the name of the city and to the feminine form (Μασσαλιῶτις).

The form Μασσαλιώτης is present in a very large number of authors, quite often to define the origin of Pytheas and Euthymenes. Among those mentioned, usually by Stephanus of Byzantium, the first is Strabo (II, 5, 8 and 30; III, 4, 6, 8 and 17; IV, 1, 3, 5–6 and 8–10, 14; 2, 1; VIIa, 1, 2; VII, 3, 1; XII, 8, 11; XIV, 2, 10), followed by Pausanias (X, 8, 6–7; 18, 7), the pseudo-Scymnus (v. 203, 250), Polybius (III, 41, 9; 95, 7; XXXIV, 10, 7), Aelianus (*De nat.* V, 38; XIII, 16; *Varia hist.* II, 38), Appianus (*Iber.* 55) and Marcianus (*Per. Men.*, § 2). This ethnical form appears in the very title of the work of Aristoteles (ἡ Μασσαλιωτῶν Πολιτεία) and in his *Poetica* (1457a).

The other form for the masculine, Μασσαλιεύς, is not mentioned by any authors we know. It ought perhaps to be attributed to one of the Hellenistic geographers or historians present in the *Ethnica*: Eudoxus of Cnidus, Timaeus, Theopompus, Ephorus or Eratosthenes. Ephorus is mentioned 60 times in total in the *Epitome*, almost always for its *Histories* but never about the Western Mediterranean region (with the exception of Sicily). Theopompus lists a number of cities and populations, probably situated in the Iberic peninsula or in Ligystica, in book 43 constituting an excursus of his *Philippicae*. Timaeus of Tauromenion is quoted only four times in the *Epitome*, and under conditions alluding to a very indirect use. In addition to Massalia, it is nominated twice for a geonym of Sicily (*Ataburion* and *Eukarpeia*) and once for a people of Epirus (*Argurînoi*), a mention which originates from the grammarian Theonius (second century). For *Eukarpeia*, F. Jacoby (*FrGrHist* 566 F 24b) suggests attributing this mention to Polemon and adding <πρός> (against) before the name of Timaeus. All these mentions are therefore indirect. Eratosthenes of Cyrene is hardly ever mentioned: a single time for this *Geographical descriptions* (and still solely in the notice *Durrachion* preserved from the original manuscript of the *Ethnica*), twice for poetical works (Erigone and Hermes) and six times for the *Galaticae*. It is probably Eudoxus of Cnidus who stood the most chances of being quoted here: we have kept one reference relating to the city of *Agathê* (Agde) and he has the particularity of often using ethnical forms ending with -εύς.

The Ionian form Μασσαλιήτης found in Polybius (XXXIII, 8, 2; 9, 1–2; 10, 12, fragments reported by Constantinus Porphyrogenitus), Athenaeus (I, 48; IV, 36; X, 33; XI, 103) and Appianus (*Ital.* VIII, 3) and, for the authors who are not quoted in the *Ethnica*, Plutarch (*Marius* XXI, 7) and Diodorus of Sicily (XIV, 93, 5). Stephanus of Byzantium, in the least abridged portion of the *Epitome*, refers to the ethnical form of *Aiginai*: "τὸ δὲ πολιήτης πλεονασμὸν ἔχει τοῦ η, ὡς τὸ μυθιήτης, ὅπερ οὐδ' ἐθνικόν, καὶ τὸ Ἰουλιήτης ἀπὸ τοῦ Ἰουλίτης. τὸ δὲ Βαργυλιήτης καὶ Μασσαλιήτης τέτραπται" (the *poliêtês* has an additional êta, just like *muthiêtês*, which is not an ethnical form, and *Iouliêtês* with respect to *Ioulitês*, but for *Barguliêtês* and *Massaliêtês* this is a letter modification). We also found this form in the notice of Massalia with the same grammatical indication, which seems to derive from the formal comparison work carried out by Oros of Alexandria.

[E]: There remains the issue of the vocable Μασσαλία in this column, which does not match the very name of Marseille. We may assume that it is either a feminine form (but which is not backed up anywhere else) or more probably the name "Massalia", in the sense of "land of Marseille", a word popularised by the exhibition catalogue *Voyage en Massalie* in 1990. It may be the meaning of the expression we find in Dionysius the Periegete (v. 75), when he speaks of the "γαῖα Μασσαλίη", explained in another form by the pseudo-Aristoteles (*Mirab.* p. 837b): "ἐν τῇ τῶν Μασσαλιωτῶν χώρᾳ" (in the *chôra* of the Marseillais). Stephanus of Byzantium probably signalled here the use made by Artemidorus of this word, as can be seen below (§ 4).

The form *Massaliôtis* is only indicated by Strabo (IV, 2, 3: "Μασσαλιώτιδος"), not in the sense of a feminine form, but with that of "Massalia/land of Massalia"; he also uses (IV, 1, 12) the word Μασσαλιωτική that P. Thollard (2009, 35) translates in the same manner as *Massaliotis*.

We could also find the ktetical form (μασσαλιωτική), present in Strabo (IV, 1, 6 and 12; 6, 3 and 11), the pseudo Scymnus (v. 146), Polybius (III, 41, 5 and exceptionally in its Ionian form μασσαλιητική in III, 95, 6), Aelianus (*De nat.* XIII, 16; *Varia hist.* II, 38) and, for the authors not read by Stephanus of Byzantium, Gallienus (*De sanitate tuenda*, vol. 6 p. 282 etc., for example) and Aelius Aristides (*Aigyp.* p. 353). Let us mention finally the topical form Μασσαλίηθεν in Lucianus (*Toxaris*, 24) which could be used as well by Stephanus of Byzantium in another author since Lucianus is never quoted in the *Epitome*.

Other mentions, in particular in Byzantine erudites, however enable us to reconstruct some portions which have disappeared from notice during the abbreviation process.

The Notice of Troizen

Several mentions of Marseille are present in the *Epitome*. One of them relates more particularly to our object, that of the city of *Troizen*. Well-known to those working on the Massaliot *chora*, this text has been written about extensively (Brunel 1945, Gras 2003). First of all, we shall give the text of the *Epitome* (this is a plural notice):

I-[A] |1| πόλις Πελοποννήσου, [B] ἀπὸ Τροιζῆνος τοῦ Πέλοπος. [C] ἐκαλεῖτο δὲ Ἀφροδισιάς καὶ Σαρωνία καὶ Ποσειδωνιάς καὶ Ἀπολλωνιάς καὶ Ἀνθανίς. [D] |2| τὸ ἐθνικὸν Τροιζήνιος καὶ Τροιζηνία, καὶ Τροιζηνίς, καὶ οὐδέτερον Τροιζήνιον.

II-[A] |3| ἔστι καὶ ἄλλη Τροιζήν ἐν Μασσαλίᾳ τῆς Ἰταλίας, [C] ἣν **Χάραξ** Τροιζηνίδα χώραν φησί.

Troizen: I-[A] |1|. City of the Peloponnese, denominated after Trezene, son of Pelops. [C] It is also called Aphrodisias, Sarônia, Posidonias, Apollonias and Anthanis. [D] |2|. The ethnical form is *Troizênios*, the feminine form *Troizênia* and *Troisênis*, and the neutral form *Troizênion*.

II-[A] |3|. There exists another *Troizen* in Massalia of Italy, which **Charax** designates as the territory *Troizênis*.

This notice originates from book 54, preserved in our *Epitome* in the version of the second abstract, corresponding to a more reduced text than that read by Eustathius of Thessalonica. It is a plurial notice which handles in the third part a *Troizên* situated in the Peloponnese (Trezene, Τροιζήνα now). For the second toponym of this name, the text seems to be clear: there exists a city called *Troizên* which is situated in the territory belonging to Marseille, situated in Italy. The author who is mentioned for the region (Troizênis, formed as Massaliôtis), Charax of Pergamo, is a historian of Roman time (around 130–140), quoted 47 times by Stephanus of Byzantium; we think that these references originate from the source-lexicon in the middle of the second century AD. It authored both *Hellenica* and *Chronicles*. In the *Epitome*, the *Chronicles* are used for the Allobroges (*s.v. Allubruges*) and the Salyans (*s.v. Salues*). It seems hence quite possible that this mention relates to a possession of Marseille situated beyond the Var, a river marking the limits of Italy in the second to first centuries BC, as stated by Strabo (IV, 1, 9).

The version of Eustathius (*Com. Iliad.* v. 561, vol. 1, p. 442) is similar; he says:

Τροιζὴν δὲ πόλις οὐκ ἄσημος, ὑπερκειμένη θαλάσσης πεντεκαίδεκα στάδια, ἧς πρόκειται νησίδιον· καλεῖται δὲ ἀπὸ Τροιζῆνος, υἱοῦ Πέλοπος. ἡ δ᾽ αὐτή ποτε καὶ Ἀφροδισιὰς καὶ Σαρωνία καὶ ἢ Ποσειδωνία ἢ Ποσειδωνιάς, ὡς ἱερά, φασί, Ποσειδῶνος· καὶ Ἀπολλωνιὰς δέ. ἔστι δέ, φασί, καὶ ἑτέρα ἐν Ἰταλίᾳ Μασσαλιωτική

> *Troizên* is a famous city, looking across the sea from which it is fifteen stadia away, in front of which an islet extends, it is named after Trezene, son of Pelops. It was also called *Aphrodisias*, *Sarônia*, or *Poseidônia* or *Poseidônia* as a sanctuary, probably of Poseidon; also *Apollonia*. There is supposedly another Marseille in Italy.

Both forms (in Massalia, of Marseille) are distinct, but Eustathius used to repeat the very words of Stephanus of Byzantium (here for example ἑτέρα replaces ἄλλη): The form used in Charax perhaps seemed less understandable to a twelfth-century Greek.

However, it seems difficult to imagine that the author of the quite general *Chronicles* indicates a place name that is absolutely not known elsewhere. The solution is probably given by another notice in the *Epitome*, the Chalkis'one (in the least abbreviated part of the work). There is indeed, in this plural notice, a specific place name "καὶ πόλις Χαλκῖτις ἐν Μεσσαπίᾳ τῆς Ἰταλίας": "and *Chalkîtis* city in Italy's Messapia" formulation necessary because there is another Messapia / Messapion in Viotia (sv *Messapion* and *Boiotia*). We knows also two other cities attached to the "Messapia" *Amazonia* (sv *Amazones*) and *Sallentia* (sv).

The very close formulation likely gives the key to the puzzle: the Μασσαλίᾳ form may correspond to a misreading of Μεσσαπίᾳ. The fact that Eustathius of Thessalonica repeats the same error means that it already exists in the first abstract and goes back certainly to a misreading of uncials in transliteration (ΜΕϹϹΑΠΙΑ read ΜΑϹϹΑΛΙΑ). The Π was here confused with a Λ and perhaps a little automatic reading of the entire word caused this error. In our hypothesis this Troizen is in fact in Italy, in the region near Taranto. So we can not keep this form for the *chôra* of Massalia.

The References from the Comment on the Iliad of Eustathius of Thessalonica

We know that Eustathius of Thessalonica, before he became archbishop of Thessaloniki in the last quarter of the twelfth century, wrote several commentaries on the *Illiad*, the *Odyssey* and Dionysius the Periegete, in which he uses a very large number of authors, such as Strabo (whom he calls ὁ Γεωγράφος, the geographer) or Stephanus of Byzantium (ὁ τὰ Ἐθνικὰ γράψας, the author of the *Ethnica*). For the latter, we also know through one of his references that he uses an epitome. We were able to put in evidence that it is quite probably the first abstract (Bouiron 2012, § 132), still rather complete, which is quite precious for us.

However, Eustathius has a particular use of the different authors in his comments. We have scrutinised the way he quotes Stephanus of Byzantium: he gives the text often in disorder, using certain words only, changing others. We may quote for example the use of "son of" whereas the original text employs the genitive: thus we may compare the *Epitome* (*s.v. Gelônos*): ἀπὸ Γελωνοῦ τοῦ Ἡρακλέους and in Eustathius of Thessalonica (*Com. Dion.* v. 310): ἀπὸ Γελωνοῦ (…) υἱὸς δὲ Ἡρακλέος. The transformations are numerous, except when he explicitly gives a quotation of the text he had before him (but the case is quite rare). It is hence not always obvious how to reconstruct faithfully the text of Stephanus of Byzantium on the basis of the indications provided by Eustathius.

The first mention relating to Massalia is derived from the *Comment on the Iliad* (v. 549, vol. 3, p. 251):

τὸ δὲ 'ἀγροιῶται' ἀπὸ τοῦ ἀγρόται γίνεται κατὰ διπλῆν ἐπένθεσιν τοῦ τε ι καὶ τοῦ ω μεγάλου, δοκεῖ δὲ ὑποκρίνασθαι τοῦτο ἀναλογίαν τῶν προπαραληγομένων μόνῳ τῷ ι οἷον Στρατιώτης, Ἀμβρακιώτης, Μασσαλιώτης

The name *agriôtai*—rural—is formed from *agrotai*, by double insertion of a vowel, iota and omega, and this phenomenon probably proceeds from an analogy with having only an iota at the antepenultimate syllable, for example *Stratiôtês, Ambrakiôtês, Massaliôtês.*

There is a mention of grammatical type resting on ethnical forms, but relating to a common name.

In Stephanus of Byzantium, we find comparisons between ethnical forms in -ωτης:

καὶ Οἰχαλιώτης ὡς Ἀμβρακιώτης <καὶ> Σικελιώτης

And *Oichaliôtês* formed as *Ambrakiôtês* <and> *Sikeliôtês*) (*s.v. Oichalia*)

τὰ γὰρ εἰς ια θηλυκὰ καὶ εἰς ιον οὐδέτερα διὰ τοῦ ωτης ποιεῖ τὰ ἐθνικά, Σικελιώτης Πηλιώτης Indeed, the feminine form in *-ia* and the neutral in *-ion* have ethnical forms in *-ôtês*, such as *Sikeliôtês* and *Pêliôtês* (*s.v. Ambrakia*).

Besides, this latter rule may apply for the name of the Marseillais. Another rule can be found in the Canons of the grammarian Theodosius (§ 245), but relates to the accentuation of words ending with *-ôtês.*

Around the beginning of the ninth century, Georgios Choeroboscos also points out two rules, the one (*De orth.* p. 262) for *stratiôtês:*

Στρατιώτης· ι, παρὰ τὸ στρατιὰ, καὶ τὸ ω μέγα· τὰ διὰ τοῦ ωτης ἀρσενικὰ διὰ τοῦ ω μεγάλου γράφεται· ἢ καθαρεύει ἡ παραλήγουσα· οἷον, στρατιώτης· κυβεριώτης· τοξιώτης

Stratiôtês: with an iota, derived from *stratia*, and an omega; the masculine forms ending with *-ôtês* are written with an omega, or the penultimate is preceded by a vowel; for example *stratiôtês, kuberiôtês* and *toxiôtês.*

The second (*id.* p. 169) for *Askalônitês:*

Ἀσκαλωνίτης· διὰ τοῦ ι τὸ νι· τὰ γὰρ εἰς της λήγοντα ὑπὲρ δύο συλλαβὰς βαρύτονα, εἴτε ἁπλᾶ, εἴτε σύνθετα, μὴ ἔχοντα ἀντιπαρακείμενον τὸ ο, μήτε ἀπὸ πρωτοτύπου τὸ ε, μήτε ἀπὸ πλεονασμοῦ τὸ ι, ἑνὶ φωνήεντι παραλήγεται· οἷον, Ἀσκαλωνίτης· μνηματίτης· σημαίνει δὲ τὸν ἐπιτάφιον λόγον· πολίτης· μυθίτης, σημαίνει δὲ τὸν στασιαστήν· τεμενίτης· Σικελιώτης· στρατιώτης

Askalônitês: -ni- with an iota; indeed, the words ending with *-tês*, with more than two non-accentuated syllables on the final one, regardless these words are simple or compound, when they do not have a root ending with omi-cron, nor an epsilon at the end of the radical, nor a double iota, have a vowel at the end of the penultimate; for example *Askalônitês, mnêmatitês* (which means eulogy), *politês, muthitês* (which means seditious), *temenitês, Sikeliôtês, stratiôtês.*

We do not find here the rules defining the ethnical forms pointed out by Stephanus of Byzantium. All these examples relate to formation modalities of names (and their accentuation) which typically pertain to the grammarian Herodianus, either read directly or via the filter of late Antiquity grammarians.

Two other mentions, in the *Comment on the Iliad*, relate to the form *Massaliêtês*. The first (*Com. Iliad.* v. 786–806, vol. 1, 544) gives little information: οὐ δήπου γὰρ φυσικῶς ἐνταῦθα ἔγκειται, ὡς ἐν τῷ Μασσαλία Μασσαλιήτης καὶ τοῖς τοιούτοις

Indeed, it is most certainly not situated there naturally, as in *Massalia Massaliêtês* etc.

This is a rapid comment (by Eustathius or interpolated?) appended as a note to the initial text, regarding the addition of an êta to a word which does contain any.

The second mention (*Com. Iliad.* v. 49, vol. 1, 742) is related directly to an Ionian form, according to the grammarian Herodianus. This indica-tion could also be found in Stephanus of Byzantium, possibly via Oros of Alexandria: "καὶ γὰρ καὶ Ὅμηρος τὸν πολίτην πολιήτην φησίν, ὅπερ Ἰωνικὸν εἶναι δοκεῖ κατὰ τὸ Μασσαλιήτης, Ἀπολλωνιήτης, οἰκιήτης, ἃ κεῖνται παρὰ τῷ Ἡρωδιανῷ. δύναται δὲ ἐκεῖνο καὶ ἀπὸ τοῦ πολιά γενέσθαι τροπῇ τοῦ α εἰς η"

And indeed, Homer says *poliêtês* for *politês*, a form which seems to be Ionian going by the forms *Massaliêtês, Apollôniêtês, oikiêtês*, that can be seen in Herodianus. But this may be derived from the ancient phenomenon where the vowel alpha was changed to êta.

References from the Comment of Dionysius the Periegete by Eustathius of Thessalonica

The last mention of Eustathius of Thessalonica is the most interesting. It is a comment on the poem of Dionysius the Periegete (v. 120–140), a versified description of the whole of the Oikoumene which was highly praised as a literary work in Antiquity and Byzantine times. The poetical form has always been quite successful, in particular since it enables better memorisation of a text.

Let us first of all present the initial text (v. 74–75, translation according to M. Bats, CAG, p. 148 n° 25):

τὸν δὲ μετ' ἐκδέχεται Γαλάτης ῥόος, ἔνθα τε γαῖα
Μασσαλίη τετάνυσται, ἐπίστροφον ὅρμον ἔχουσα.
Then comes the Gulf of Gaul, and there the land
of Massalia extends, which possesses a curved harbour

The comment of Eustathius of Thessalonica is a mix between diverse indications and those from Stephanus of Byzantium (even if he does not indicate it explicitly). Here is the text and its translation:

ὅτι καὶ ἡ *Μασσαλία* γαλατική ἐστι, Φωκεῖς δὲ ᾤκησαν αὐτὴν, οἱ ἐκ τῆς ἕω φυγόντες τὴν τοῦ Κύρου δουλείαν. καὶ ὅτι ὅρμον ἡ *Μασσαλία* ἔχει ἐπίστροφον, ὃ ἔστι περιφερῆ, περίδρομον καὶ καμπύλον, ἢ οὗ ἐπιστρέφονται οἱ ναυτιλλόμενοι. ἀγαθὸς γὰρ τοῖς *Μασσαλιώταις* λιμὴν ὁ Λακύδων. τὸ δὲ ἐπίστροφος καὶ παρ' Ὁμήρῳ κεῖται, ὅπου λέγει ὅτι καὶ Ὀδυσσεὺς ἐπίστροφος ἦν ἀνθρώπων. φασὶ δὲ τοὺς *Μασσαλιεῖς* εὐδοκιμῆσαί ποτε περί τε ὀργανοποιΐαν καὶ ναυτικὴν παρασκευήν. ἔστι δὲ οὐ μόνον χώρα *Μασσαλία*, ἀλλὰ καὶ πόλις Λιγύων περί που τὴν Κελτικήν, ἐτυμολογουμένη ἀπὸ τοῦ μάσσαι, ὃ ἔστιν ἐκδῆσαι, Αἰολικῶς, καὶ ἀπό τινος ἁλιέως. προσπλέων γάρ, φασιν, ὁ τῶν ἀποίκων Φωκαέων κυβερνήτης καὶ ἰδὼν ἐκεῖ ἁλιέα, ἐκέλευσε μάσσαι, ἤτοι δῆσαι, τὸ ἀπόγαιον πεῖσμα· ὅθεν καὶ ἡ πόλις *Μασσαλία*, παρὰ τὸ μάσσειν καὶ τὸν ἁλιέα.

> It should be noted that Massalia is Gallic, founded by the Phocaeans, from the East where they wanted to escape from the yoke of Cyrus. It should be noted that Massalia has an "epistrophos" mooring post, i.e. "rounded, circular and curved in" or "where the sailors make an about turn". The Massaliots have indeed a good harbour, the Lacydon. The word 'epistrophos' can also be found in Homer, when he says that Ulysses is an 'epistrophos' (visitor). The Marseillais are said to always having been renowned for the production of machines and the equipment of vessels. There exists not only the territory (*chôra*) Massalia, but also the city of the Ligyans, of the Celtic side, that etymology derives from '*massaï*', which means 'to detach' in Eolian, and from '*halieus*' (*fisherman*). It is said indeed that when approaching on a boat, the pilot of the Phocaean settlers, then seeing a fisherman there, asked him to 'massaï', to attach the mooring line to the land; hence the name of Massalia, a combination of 'to attach' and 'fisherman'.

The sequence of the notice of the *Epitome* can be found in the description of Eustathius, a little in disorder: the initial geographical determination first of all refers to the very words of Dionysius on the Gallic Gulf. It is given in the second part of the comment in a form close to the *Epitome*: πόλις Λιγύων περί που τὴν Κελτικήν. The foundation of the Phocaeans is mentioned at the beginning of the notice, with an additional indication (Φωκεῖς δὲ ᾤκησαν αὐτὴν, οἱ ἐκ τῆς ἕω φυγόντες τὴν τοῦ Κύρου δουλείαν). But this information originates most probably from the *Souda* as we shall see below. The etymology derived from Timaeus constitutes the end of the second part; it is almost identical to that of the *Epitome*.

If we remove the indication on the word *epistrophos* in Homer, without any direct relationship with Massalia, there remain three distinct indications. The first concerns the form of the port, the second the name of the port (the Lacydon), two indications which could be linked: we know that Stephanus of Byzantium sometimes gives other indications of geonyms close to a city, like the river Atax for Narbonne (s.v. *Narbô*). We can see there a complementary indication of the primitive notice. The third indication is precious: according to Eustathius of Thessalonica, the Marseillais are renowned for naval production. We are interested here in the very form of the name: Eustathius says τοὺς Μασσαλιεῖς, he therefore employs the form Μασσαλιεύς. Still, we have seen above that this form is indicated by Stephanus of Byzantium and him alone (going by the TLG). Given by Eustathius in a context derived from his epitome, it must originate from our author. If we stick to our Eudoxus of Cnidus hypothesis, this information would relate to the fourth century BC.

Finally, we shall call upon a third witness, the anonym text of the *Paraphrase of Dionysius the Periegete* (v. 75): "ὅπου καὶ ἡ Μασσαλία γῆ, ἤτοι πόλις, εὐλίμενος, ὅρμον περιφερῆ ἢ ἐπίδρομον ἔχουσα" (where the land or the city of Massalia is situated, fitted with a correct port, with a rounded or curved mooring post), wherein the land (in the sense of *chôra?*) of Massalia can be found.

Towards a Restitution of the Notice of Stephanus of Byzantium

After analysing in detail the comments of Eustathius of Thessalonica, we suggest, hypothetically, a less reduced notice which may be akin to the form of the first abstract of Stephanus of Byzantium. Here is the text, inserting by concatenation the comments of Eustathius of Thessalonica or the other notices of the *Epitome* (in italics in the Greek text).

Μασσαλία· [A] πόλις τῆς Λιγυστικῆς κατὰ τὴν Κελτικήν, [B] ἄποικος Φωκαέων. Ἑκαταῖος *Εὐρώπη*. Τίμαιος δέ φησιν ὅτι προσπλέων ὁ τῶν *ἀποίκων Φωκαέων* κυβερνήτης καὶ ἰδὼν *ἐκεῖ ἁλιέα ἐκέλευσε μάσσαι τὸ ἀπόγειον σχοινίον· μάσσαι γὰρ τὸ δῆσαί φασιν Αἰολεῖς· ἀπὸ γοῦν τοῦ ἁλιέως καὶ τοῦ μάσσαι ὠνόμασται. ὅρμον ἡ* Μασσαλία *ἔχει ἐπίστροφον, ὃ ἔστι περιφερῆ, περίδρομον καὶ καμπύλον, ἢ οὗ ἐπιστρέφονται οἱ ναυτιλλόμενοι. ἀγαθὸς γὰρ τοῖς* Μασσαλιώταις *λιμὴν ὁ Λακύδων. τὸ δὲ ἐπίστροφος καὶ παρ' Ὁμήρῳ κεῖται, ὅπου λέγει ὅτι καὶ Ὀδυσσεὺς ἐπίστροφος ἦν ἀνθρώπων.* [D] τὸ ἐθνικὸν Μασσαλιώτης *τὰ γὰρ εἰς ια θηλυκὰ* καὶ εἰς ιον οὐδέτερα διὰ τοῦ ωτης ποιεῖ τὰ ἐθνικά, Σικελιώτης Πηλιώτης. καὶ Μασσαλιήτης ὅπερ Ἰωνικὸν εἶναι δοκεῖ κατὰ τὸ Μασσαλιήτης, Ἀπολλωνιήτης, οἰκιήτης, ἃ κεῖνται παρὰ τῷ **Ἡρωδιανῷ**, πλεονασμὸν ἔχει τοῦ η, ὡς τὸ μυθιήτης, ὅπερ οὐδ' ἐθνικόν, καὶ τὸ Ἰουλιήτης ἀπὸ τοῦ Ἰουλίτης. τὸ δὲ Βαργυλιήτης καὶ Μασσαλιήτης τέτραπται. καὶ *Μασσαλιεύς* ·φασὶ δὲ τοὺς Μασσαλιεῖς εὐδοκιμῆσαί ποτε περί τε ὀργανοποιῖαν καὶ ναυτικὴν παρασκευήν. *[E] καὶ χώρα Μασσαλία*. καὶ Μασσαλιῶτις γυνή.

> **Massalia:** [A] city of the Ligystica at the level of the Celtic word, [B] founda-
> tion of the Phocaeans. **Hecataeus** in *Europa*. **Timaeus** says that the pilot of the
> Phocaean settlers, as he approached and saw a fisherman, asked him to attach the
> mooring line to the land; indeed, the Eolians say *'massai'* for *'désai'* (to attach).
> It takes its name therefore from *'halieus'* and *'massai'*. It should be noted that
> Massalia has an *'epistrophos'* mooring post, i.e. "rounded, circular and curved
> in" or 'where the sailors make an about turn'. The Massaliots have indeed a
> good harbour, the Lacydon. The word *'epistrophos'* can also be found in Homer,
> when he says that Ulysses is an *'epistrophos'* (visitor). [D] The ethnical form is
> *Massaliôtês;* indeed, the feminine form in -*ia* and the neutral in -*ion* have ethnical
> forms in -*ôtês*, such as *Sikeliôtês* and *Pêliôtês* And *Massaliêtês*, a form which seems
> to be Ionian going by the forms *Massaliêtês, Apollôniêtês, oikiêtês*, that can be
> seen in **Herodianus**; it has an additional êta, such as *muthiêtês*, which is not an
> ethnical form either, and *Iouliêtês* with respect to *Ioulitês*, but for *Barguliêtês* and
> *Massaliêtês* this is a letter modification. And *Massalieus;* the Marseillais are said to
> always having been renowned for the production of machines and the equipment
> of vessels. [E1] The territory is also called *Massalia*. And in the feminine form
> *Massaliôtis*.

If the form we give to this notice is voluntarily unsmoothed, it enables us nevertheless to get an idea of the more complete text that Stephanus of Byzantium had dedicated to Massalia and that Eustathius of Thessalonica read.

The Other References to Massalia in Greek and Byzantine Erudites

The in-depth researches we have conducted on all the lexica known at Byzantine time the better to understand that of Stephanus of Byzantium enable us to tackle the mentions of Massalia in these books. The first one relates to the so-called Harpocratio's lexicon, which is the oldest; the following ones can be found in the *Etymologica* in use during the Byzantine Middle Ages.

The Tradition of Harpocratio

The *Souda* mentions "Harpocratio, nicknamed Valerius" (Adler α 4014) as the author of the *Lexicon of the ten orators* (Λέξεις τῶν δέκα ῥητόρων) around the middle of the second century. A lexicon in the name of this author is known from numerous manuscripts, most of them at a later date. It has been the subject of many publications (the most complete is Keaney 1991), none of which appears totally satisfactory for research (Dickey 2007, 94). We have a long version and a more reduced version. It might be one of the rare lexica clearly dating back to Ancient times; it constitutes a testimony of the Atticising trend which accompanies the second and third quarters of the second century of the Christian era. This lexicon gives, as its name suggests, the explanation of lemmes found in the texts of the ten orators writing a "pure" Attic Greek used as a reference (Antiphon, Andocides, Demosthenes, Dinarchus, Aeschines, Hyperides, Isaeus, Isocrates, Lycurgus, Lysias). For Marseille, Hippocrates considers a text of Isocrates that we have preserved. Here is therefore the original text and the notice derived therefrom by Harpocratio.

Isocrates (*Archidamos*, 84): Ἔτι δὲ τούτου καταγελαστότερον, εἰ Φωκαεῖς μὲν, φεύγοντες τὴν βασιλέως τοῦ μεγάλου δεσποτείαν, ἐκλιπόντες τὴν Ἀσίαν εἰς *Μασσαλίαν* ἀπῴκησαν, ἡμεῖς δ᾽ εἰς τοσοῦτον μικροψυχίας ἔλθοιμεν ὥστε τὰ προστάγματα τούτων ὑπομείναιμεν ὧν ἄρχοντες ἅπαντα τὸν χρόνον διετελέσαμεν.

> It would be far more ridiculous, while the Phocaeans fleeing from the tyranny of the Great King left Asia and emigrated to Massalia, if we became so vile as to submit to the orders of people whom we have always dominated.

Harpocratio (s.v.): Μασσαλία· Ἰσοκράτης μέν φησιν ἐν *Ἀρχιδάμῳ* ὡς Φωκαεῖς φυγόντες τὴν τοῦ μεγάλου βασιλέως δεσποτείαν εἰς *Μασσαλίαν* ἀπῴκησαν· ὅτι δὲ πρὸ τούτων τῶν χρόνων ἤδη ὑπὸ Φωκαέων ᾤκιστο ἡ Μασσαλία καὶ **Ἀριστοτέλης** ἐν *τῇ Μασσαλιωτῶν πολιτείᾳ* δηλοῖ.

> **Massalia:** Isocrates says in the *Archidamos* that the Phocaeans having fled the domination of the Great King, emigrated to Massalia, but that, before that date, Massalia was colonised by the Phocaeans, as shown by Aristoteles in the *Constitution of the Massaliots*.

The lexicon adds to the mention of Isocrates, who obviously authored the notice, the indication of a Phocaean origin of the city even before the migration of the inhabitants during the destruction of Phocaea by the Persians, taking as a source the *Constitution of the Massaliots* by Aristoteles. The information which may be derived from that notice is known, and we shall not throw a new light thereon.

Harpocratio's lexicon was the source of several Byzantine lexica, in particular that of the patriarch Photius (v. 820–891), which we tend to consider as an early work, and the *Souda*, an extensive book indeed, is a lexicon of the encyclopedic type compiled around the end of the tenth century. Both texts sometimes contain minor modifications of the original text, especially testifying to a complex transmission of the oldest lexica. Here is the text of both lexica, with the translation.

Photius (*Lexicon*, s.v.): Μασσαλία· Ἰσοκράτης φησὶν ἐν *Ἀρχιδάμῳ*, ὡς Φωκαεῖς, φυγόντες τὴν τοῦ μεγάλου βασιλέως δεσποτείαν, εἰς Μασσαλίαν ἀπῴκησαν· μαρτυρεῖ δὲ τῷ λόγῳ καὶ **Ἀριστοτέλης.**

Souda **(μ 242): Μασσαλία·** Ἰσοκράτης φησὶν ἐν *Ἀρχιδάμῳ*, ὡς Φωκαεῖς φυγόντες τὴν τοῦ μεγάλου βασιλέως δεσποτείαν εἰς Μασσαλίαν ἀπῴκησαν. μαρτυρεῖ δὲ τῷ λόγῳ καὶ **Ἀριστοτέλης.**

> **Massalia:** Isocrates says in the *Archidamos* that the Phocaeans, having fled the domination of the Great King, emigrated to Massalia. Aristoteles, among others, bears witness to that.

It is probably through the text of the *Souda* that Eustathius of Thessalonica added complementary information at the beginning of his comment on Dionysius the Periegete. Indeed, we have kept a copy of this lexicon which he annotated with his own hand.

The Tradition of the Etymologicum Genuinum

We find a notice on Massalia in two Byzantine lexica, the *Etymologicum Gudianum* (Sturz 1818), compiled in Southern Italy during the tenth century (and whose primitive manuscript might have been kept) and the great compilation of the middle of the twelfth century known under the name of *Etymologicum Magnum* (Gaisford 1848). We know that both these works repeat to a vast extent the references of an older lexicon (ninth century), the *Etymologicum Genuinum*, which is only very partially published, on the basis of late and incomplete manuscripts. We cannot therefore provide the original text.

Etymologicum Gudianum (s.v., **p. 381, 52): Μασσαλία·** Φωκαεῖς καταλιπόντες τὴν Ἰωνίαν διὰ τὴν τῶν Περσῶν ἔφοδον, παρεγένοντο εἰς Γαλατίαν· καὶ ἰδόντες ἁλιέα, ἐπ' αὐτὸν ἴεσαν, ἑαυτοῖς παρακελευόμενοι *μεσσ'αλιεῖς·* οὗτος δὲ συλληφθείς, ἔδειξεν αὐτοῖς οἰκήσιμον τόπον· ὅθεν καὶ *Μεσσαλίαν* ὠνόμασαν, ἐν ᾗ καὶ ἔλαβον τὸν ἁλιέα.

Etymologicum Magnum (s.v., **p. 574, 166): Μασσαλία·** Φωκαεῖς καταλιπόντες τὴν Ἰωνίαν διὰ τὴν τῶν Περσῶν ἔφοδον παρεγένοντο εἰς Γαλατίαν, καὶ ἰδόντες ἁλιέα ἐπ' αὐτὸν ἦσαν (ἴεσαν *Sorb.*) ἑαυτοῖς παρακελευόμενοι *Μασσαλίης* (μεσσαλιεῖς *Sorb.*) οὗτος συλληφθεὶς ἔδειξεν αὐτοῖς οἰκήσιμον (τόπον *add. Sorb.*) ὅθεν *Μασσαλία* ἐκλήθη.

> **Massalia:** The Phocaeans left Ionia because of the Persian invasion and boarded in Gaul; as they caught sight of a fisherman, they walked up to him shouting "fisherman" (*'mess' alieîs'*). The man was captured and directed them to an inhabitable place; they gave the name of *Messalia*/Massalia at the place where they had captured the fisherman.

We can see in both these almost identical, a kind of mix between the information given by Harpocratio's *Lexicon* and an etymological tradition akin to that of Timaeus, but through a different transmission channel. Indeed, we know that the *Etymologicum Genuinum* has not used the *Ethnica* of Stephanus of Byzantium. For the geonyms, this lexicon rather used Oros or another unknown lexicographer, Methodios, who may be the origin of this text. The notice seems to result from a bad understanding of the text of Timaeus. This was the beginning of confusion with an African city by the name of Messalia. It is still hardly explicit there, and we may believe that this was due to simple letter copying error, that is, epsilon instead of alpha; but we shall see that the confusion with Africa gets worse in the text of the scholia.

The Scholia

The tradition that we perceive through the notices of the *Etymologica* is clearer in a scholia to Thucydides (Hude 1927).

The text of Thucydides (I, 13, 6) is as follows: Φωκαῆς τε Μασσαλίαν οἰκίζοντες Καρχηδονίους ἐνίκων ναυμαχοῦντες· δυνατώτατα γὰρ ταῦτα τῶν ναυτικῶν ἦν. (The Phocaeans on the other hand, at the time of the colonisation of Marseille, defeated the Carthaginians in a naval combat, trans. D. Roussel). The scholia explains the beginning of the sentence in the following manner:

(I, 13, 6): **Μασσαλίαν οἰκίζοντες**· Ἴωνες ὄντες οἱ Φωκαῆς καὶ πολεμούμενοι ὑπὸ Περσῶν, ἀφέντες τὴν Ἰωνίαν ἔπλευσαν ἐπὶ τὴν Ἀφρικὴν τὴν πάλαι Καρχηδόνα καλουμένην· ἀεὶ δὲ ταῖς οἰκιζομέναις αἱ πλησίον ἐναντιοῦνται. ἡ δὲ Μεσσαλία πόλις ἐστὶ τῆς Ἀφρικῆς, Καρχηδὼν δὲ ἡ νῦν Ἀφρική.

> **Founding the colony of Massalia:** The Phocaeans were Ionians and, as the Persians were at war against them, they left Ionia and sailed towards the region of Africa formerly called *Karchêdôn* (Carthage); but the neighbouring cities still oppose the foundation of a new city. *Messalia* is an African city and *Karchêdôn* is now called Africa.

Two older scholia about the *Panathenaica of* Aelius Aristides (113, 18/30) present the same confusion. They are certainly derived from the same source. The second, much shorter, repeats the information of the scholia of Thucydides and confuses *Massalia* with *Messalia*. In his text, Aelius Aristides describes the colonisation by the Greeks, from the Straits of Gibraltar to the Don: "καὶ

νῦν ἐπ' ἀμφοτέροις τοῖς πέρασι τῆς γῆς ὑμετέρων παίδων παῖδες οἰκοῦσιν, οἱ μὲν
ἄχρι Γαδείρων ἀπὸ Μασσαλίας παρήκοντες, οἱ δ' ἐπὶ τῷ Τανάϊδι καὶ τῇ λίμνη
μεμερισμένοι" (and now the children of your children live at the boundaries of
the earth on both sides, the ones extending from Massalia to the Gadeira, the
other distributed on the bank of the Tanaïs and of its marshland).

Here is the explanation according to the scholiasts:

ὑμετέρων παίδων· ἡμετέρων [ὑμετέρων C] παίδων λέγει, τῶν ἐν τῇ Μεσσαλία
[τῶν τε ἐν τῇ Ἀσίᾳ C] κατοικισθέντων καὶ τῶν ἐν ταῖς νήσοις, ὧν τινες μὲν τῶν ἐν
ταῖς νήσοις, Μιλησίων τε λέγω, καὶ ἄλλων τινῶν εἰς Μασσαλίαν [Μασσιλίαν C]
ἀπῴκησαν· κἀκεῖθεν αὖθις ἐξετάθη τούτων ἡ ἀποικία μέχρι Γαδείρων. ἐκ δὲ τῶν
ἐν τῇ Ἀσίᾳ τινὲς ἀποικίαν ἐποιήσαντο, ἔς τε τὸν Τάναϊν ποταμὸν καὶ τὴν Μαιῶτιν
λίμνην. μεμερισμένως δὲ εἶπεν, ἢ δι' ἀμφοτέρους, τούς τε ἐν τῇ Μασσαλία
[Μασσιλία C] λέγει καὶ τῇ Μαιώτιδι, ἢ διὰ τοὺς ἐν τῇ Μαιῶτιδι καὶ τῷ Τανάϊδι
μόνον, ὡς μὴ ὁμοῦ ἐγκατοικισθέντας, ἀλλὰ διῃρημένως. AC

ἀπὸ Μασσαλίας· Μασσαλία [om. D] πόλις τῆς Ἀφρικῆς· μέμνηται δὲ Θουκυδίδης
« Φωκεῖς τε Μασσαλίαν οἰκίζοντες ». κεῖται δὲ περὶ [κεῖται παρὰ D] τὸν εἴσπλουν
τοῦ πορθμοῦ τοῦ ἀπάγοντος ἐπὶ τὰς Ἡρακλείας στήλας. CD

> **Of your children:** he means 'of our children', those who settled down in *Messalia*
> as well as those who are situated in the islands. I.e., on the one hand some of
> them who emigrated to the islands, I mean the Milesians, or other to Marseille,
> and from that place, the emigration then extended to *Gadeira*. On the other
> hand, some of them who, after leaving for Asia, have founded colonies, towards
> the river Tanaïs and the Palus Meotides. He has said 'distributed', either because
> of the indication 'on both sides', thinking about those who are in Marseille on
> the one hand and in the Palus Meotides on the other, or only due to the presence
> of settlers on the one hand in the Palus Meotides and on the other hand on the
> bank of the Tanaïs, as for those who have not colonised together, but separately.

> **From Massalia:** Massalia, city of Africa; quoted by Thucydides: "the Phocaeans
> who founded Massalia". It lies at the entrance to the strait leading to the columns
> of Hercules.

There is now a great confusion around this tradition, where the city of Mas-
salia/Marseille may be confused with the African people of the *Massuloi/Massyles*
(Northeast of today's Algeria) from which the famous king Massinissa originated.

The Poleis Massalias *and the Territory of Massalie in Stephanus of Byzantium*

As we see, very careful reading through the *Epitome* provides precious information. To prolong this reflection, we may turn our gaze towards the famous
poleis Massalias which have been subjected to several studies (Clerc 1920,

242–243, Brunel 1945, Privitera 2007). Within the limits of this article, we cannot go into the detail of the arguments. However, in view of the foregoing, the word *Massalia(s)* quite probably corresponds to the meaning of 'Massalie' and not to the city properly speaking due to its presence in the part [E] of the notice of the *Epitome*. Indeed, throughout the lexicon, cities are connected to a territory, either in the form of a proper noun in the genitive form (as Σικελίας, Ἀραβίας, Θράκης, Μυσίας), or in the ktetic form (possessive) (as Φωκική, Ἰταλική, Ποντική). This determination dates back to the source-lexicon and is absolutely specific to Stephanus of Byzantium, which explains that it can be found identically for example in the scholia which are documented in a similar manner. In the case at hand, we shall translate *poleis Massalias* by 'cities of Massalie' and not 'cities of Marseille'. By 'Massalie' is meant a territory dependent of Marseille, in a form which was judged as sufficiently structured at the end of the second century BC to give rise to this type of qualification.

Let us note first of all that the cities really mentioned like *poleis Massalias* are five in number: *Alônis, Aueniôn, Kabelliôn, Kurênê* and *Rhadanousia*. Two of them (*Alônis* and *Kabelliôn*) are characterised by a reference to book I of the *Geographica* of Artemidorus. The notice of *Aueniôn* is in every particular similar to that of *Kabelliôn*, what renders the mention in Artemidorus probably. Let us also take into consideration that the notice of *Rhadanousia* belongs to book 44, situated in the most summed up part of the *Ethnica*, which explains the total absence of information; it is moreover a duplication of the notice *Rhodanousia*, which we shall see below.

These geonyms should be reconciled with the notice of the *Stoechades,* these three islands, so-called πρὸς τῇ Μασσαλίᾳ (in contact with Massalia); there may be indeed the islands of Porquerolles, Port-Cros and the Levant, which cannot be situated in contact with the very city of Marseille (they lie some 70 km away), unlike the territory that it may control.

A sixth city may have been pointed out: *Sékoanos*, called "city of the Marseillais" (πόλις Μασσαλιωτῶν) in the edition of Meineke, still with reference with book I of Artemidorus. But we are here in book 48, also quite summed up; as it has already been suggested, the word πόλις seems to be a mistake for ποταμός. The abbreviations must have been numerous in the abstracts' manuscript, which would lead to misreading when writing the most reduced part. Regardless whether it is a river visited by the Marseillais or situated on their territory, we cannot determine it but this hydronym most probably relates to the river we know under the name of Seine, or to an unknown watercourse. We shall therefore not count this geonym among the mentions of the cities of Massalia, even if the reference dates back to Artemidorus.

We shall also delete the mention of Azania. When reading through the text of the *Epitome*, it is certainly the toponym situated in Africa (today's Kenya?). It can be found in particular in Marcianus (a primary source of Stephanus of Byzantium and quoted quite abundantly throughout the *Ethnica*), but this localisation is not mentioned in the *Epitome*; still the notice of Azania is in book 2, hardly abridged. Similarly, the mention of Philon of Byblos does not correspond to anything for a so-called city 'of Massalia' and cannot be designed in his book *On the cities having generated famous men*; Αἰθιοπίας, as suggested by Berkel, should perhaps be reconciled with the confusions of uncials for a word probably modified in the original manuscript (ΑΙΘΙΟΠΙΑϹ lu ΜΑϹϹΑΛΙΑϹ, with the confusion ΑΙ/ΜΑ, ΘΙΟ/ϹϹ et Π/Λ?).

Two other cities have a slightly different reference as they are located "ἐν Μασσαλίᾳ". We have seen above (the notice of *Troizen*) that should be deleted *Troizên*, but remains *Rhodanousia*. It has long been noticed that *Rhadanousia* and *Rhodanousia* represented a single city. The duplication is explained by two different spellings and therefore two distinct transmissions, already present in the source-lexicon, which would follow the tide of a second author other than Artemidorus for the second, situated 'in Massalia' whereas the first is so-called 'from Massalia'. The source for both cities is most probably Artemidorus. *Rhodanousia* can hence be added to our list with certainty.

Without going into detail here, we shall bear in mind that Artemidorus, in the 169th Olympiad (between 104 and 101 BC), has identified a number of cities such as 'cities of Massalia', that is, situated on a territory attached to Massalia, which extended at that time up to Italy (continuously or discontinuously).

To conclude this modest review of the data associated with Marseille in the epitome of the *Ethnica* of Stephanus of Byzantium, we should bear in mind that the documentary base, and hence the geographical identification of most geonyms, dates back to a pattern already structured in the middle of the second century of the Christian era, which we call the source-lexicon without prejudging its author. The contribution of Oros of Alexandria, for authors starting from Herodianus in the middle of the fifth century, is not negligible either, in particular for the grammatical aspects. Finally, Stephanus of Byzantium adds the references derived in particular from three main geographers, Strabo, Pausanias and Marcianus, texts which admittedly have reached us for the greatest part.

The successive "work" reduction phases deprive us of an important quantity of antic authors, but reading Byzantine authors, at the forefront of whom Eustathius of Thessalonica should be placed, sometimes enables us to remedy this disappearance. This research is made easier by the digital resources (TLG) which give access to the numerous erudite texts of that time.

The detailed understanding of the *Epitome* enables us to obtain a new method for reading the text of Stephanus of Byzantium, a text which is rich and systematically structured. It is at the heart of our reflection on Western Europe. Taking into account the number of lemmes (36) kept for the South of France, no doubt it will be possible to enrich the knowledge of this geographical area in connection with the Phocaean foundation of Marseille.

Bibliography

Billerbeck, M., Gaertner, J.F., Wyss, B. & Zubler, C. (eds.), 2006–2014, Stephani Byzantii Ethnica: Einleitung, kritischer Text, Ubersetzung und Anmerkungen; I: Alpha—Gamma. Berlin/New York: Walter de Gruyter, 2006, X-64*-441 p.; II: Delta—Iota. Berlin/New York: Walter de Gruyter, 2011, IX-17*-310 p.; III: Kappa—Omicron. Berlin/New York: Walter de Gruyter, 2014, VIII-19*-454 p. (*Corpus Fontium Historiae Byzantinae* 43/1, 2 et 3).

Bouiron, M., 2012, «Du texte d'origine à l'*Épitomé* des *Ethnika*: Les différentes phases de réduction et la transmission du lexique géographique de Stéphane de Byzance», *Rursus [En ligne]*, 8 | 2012, mis en ligne le 29 novembre 2012, consulté le 12 septembre 2013. URL: http://rursus.revues.org/1027; DOI: 10.4000/rursus.1027.

Brunel, J., 1945, "Etienne de Byzance et le domaine des Marseillais", *Revue d'études anciennes*, XLVII, 1945, 122–133.

Clerc, M., 1920–1921, *Massalia; histoire de Marseille dans l'Antiquité, des origines à la fin de l'Empire romain d'occident (476 ap. J.-C.)*. Marseille: Tacussel, 1920–1921, 2 vol.

Dickey, E., 2007, *Ancient Greek Scholarship: A Guide to Finding, Reading, and Understanding Scholia, Commentaries, Lexica and Grammatical Treatises, from their Beginnings to the Byzantine Period*. Londres/New York: Oxford University Press, 2007, 368p.

Gaisford, T., 1848, *Etymologicum Magnum*. Oxford, 1848.

Gras, M., 2003, "*Antipolis* et *Nikaia*: les ambiguïtés de la frontière entre la Massalie et l'Italie". In: *Peuples et territoires en Gaule méditerranéenne. Hommage à Guy Barruol*, 2003, 241–246 (Supplément à la Revue archéologique de Narbonnaise, 35).

Honigmann, E., 1929, *Stephanos Byzantios*, in Pauly-Wissowa, III A 2 (1929), col. 2369–99.

Hude, K., 1927, Scholia in Thucydidum ad optimos codices collata, Leipzig.

Kaldellis, A., 2005, The Works and Days of Hesychios the Illoustrios of Miletos, *Greek, Roman, and Byzantine Studies*, 45, 2005, 381–403.

Keaney, J. (ed.), 1991, *Harpocration: Lexeis of the Ten Orators*. Amsterdam: Hakkert, 1991, 291p.

Meineke, A. (ed.), 1849, *Stephani Byzantii Ethnicorum quae supersunt*. Berlin 1849 (2nd ed.
    Graz 1958, Chicago 1992).

Privitera, S., 2007, "*Poleis Massalias*: da Artemidoro di Efeso a Eustazio di Tessalonica",
    Melanges de l'École française de Rome, Antiquité, 119, 1, 2007, 41–49.

Sturz, F.W., 1818, *Etymologicum Graecae Linguae Gudianum et alia, p. -grammaticorum
    scripta e codicibus manuscriptis nunc primum edita* Leipzig, 1818, 682 col.

6. Territories of the Massaliot Identity: Conservatism or Political and Moral Loosening?

SOPHIE BOUFFIER AND EMMANUÈLE CAIRE

The political and social history of Massalia has given rise to few works, if not in older times in more general syntheses, such as that of Michel Clerc (Clerc 1927–1929) or of Monique Clavel-Lévêque who sought to explain the political regime of the city by the commercial specialisation of its elites (Clavel-Lévêque 1977), or in articles centred on the specificity of the Phocaean expansion and settlements (Lepore 1970), and whose purpose was to detect a possible Phocaean identity and a socio-political link between the metropole and its colony. More recently, a few synthesis pages can be found in the monograph of Antoine Hermary, Antoinette Hesnard and Henri Tréziny (Hermary, Hesnard & Tréziny 1999), and in the *Carte Archéologique de la Gaule* (Collin Bouffier 2005). The main reason for this apparent lack of interest is the lacunar character of documentation and, consequently, without our being able to see a causal effect, the mostly archaeological orientation of research on Marseille in the twentieth and in the beginning of twenty-first century. We may quote as an example the recent comment on book 4 of the *Geography* of Strabo who does not expand on that subject in the chapter dedicated to Marseille (Thollard 2009, 209–234). The purpose of our contribution therefore in this volume will thus be to query from scratch the view offered by ancient testimonies, which insist on the specificity of the Massaliot regime and society. Contemporary historians have emphasised on several occasions the ideological orientation of these texts and in particular the partial character of Roman time documentation, which exalts good morals and the *Eunomia* regime (good organisation and distribution): these would have marked the history of Marseille (Guyot-Rougemont & Rougemont 1992; Collin Bouffier 2005). Beyond our debate, our aim here is to reintegrate this so-called Massaliot specificity in a more general cultural context, characteristic of the Greek *Koinè*, by placing in parallel the socio-political data of the Phocaean city with what we know of the other communities of the Greek world. To get a picture of the political institutions and of the social organisation of Massalia, we have a number of literary texts available which, although mostly belated, provide us with two types of information, some on the political regime, its institutions and its evolution, and others on the Massaliot society and its values. This apportionment will guide our development, which will take place in two stages: a first part will focus on the analysis of the Massaliot political regime, with emphasis on the testimony of Aristotle, and a part on the Massaliot society, to deconstruct the view offered by an ancient tradition, strongly marked by Roman ideology.

Original Institutions?

The oldest testimony in our possession on the Massaliot institutions and society is that of Aristotle in its *Politeiai*, through several disseminated fragments in his political work or transmitted by belated sources, in particular the intellectual of the second century AD, Athenaeus of Naucratis in his *Deipnosophists*.

The use of writing *Politeiai* can be traced from the fifth century BC. This literary genre, perhaps turned into fashion by the Sophists, spurred the Ionian curiosity for the diversity of the human social organisations largely illustrated by the *History* of Herodotus. Consequently, the first fragments preserved, those of the Athenian oligarch Critias, refer to Greek cities and populations (the Lacedemonians, the Thessalians, perhaps the Athenians) but also probably to non-Greeks, like this undetermined population known for wearing braies (Critias frgts. B6–15 and B31–38 [88DK]).

The usual translation of the word *politeia* is "constitution" but this term corresponds quite imperfectly to the Greek notion. Indeed, the *politeia* is not limited to political institutions: it includes the mode of education, the customs, the clothing and food habits, and the history of a given people. The *Politeia of the Lacedemonians* written by Xenophon is a perfect example. Actually the investigation on the *politeiai* undoubtedly achieved the widest development with the vast enterprise initiated by Aristotle in the context of the Lykaios. The catalogue of Diogenes Laertius attributes to Aristotle a collection of 158 *politeia*, which might include, alongside constitutions of Greek cities (among which that of Athens kept to a vast extent thanks to a papyrus found in Oxyrinchus in the nineteenth century) that of Barbarian states (Cicero, *De finibus*, V, 4, 11), unless the investigation of the latter was reserved to another collection, that of the *Nomima*, whose exact title remains uncertain, but that some authors, Varro for example, notify as *Nomima Barbarika* (Varro, *De lingua latina*, VII, 70). The old testimonies and the fragments preserved show that these studies dealt with the institutions as well as the morals, the customs and the history of the cities and peoples concerned. The 158 Aristotelian *Politeiai* certainly included a *politeia of the Massaliots.*

The **Politeia** of the *Aristotelian* **Massaliots: State of the Sources**

The Fragments

Only two fragments (frgs. 549 and 508 Rose) exist from this *"Constitution" of the Massaliots.* The first one, of a certain magnitude, was transmitted by Athenaeus.

> Τὸ ὅμοιον ἱστορεῖ γενέσθαι καὶ Ἀριστοτέλης ἐν τῇ Μασσαλιωτῶν πολιτείᾳ γράφων οὕτως· Φωκαεῖς οἱ ἐν Ἰωνίᾳ ἐμπορίᾳ χρώμενοι ἔκτισαν Μασσαλίαν. Εὔξενος δ' ὁ Φωκαεὺς Νάνῳ τῷ βασιλεῖ, τοῦτο δ' ἦν αὐτῷ ὄνομα, ἦν ξένος. Οὗτος ὁ Νάνος ἐπιτελῶν γάμους τῆς θυγατρὸς κατὰ τύχην παραγενόμενον τὸν Εὔξενον παρακέκληκεν ἐπὶ τὴν θοίνην. Ὁ δὲ γάμος ἐγίγνετο τόνδε τὸν τρόπον··ἔδει μετὰ τὸ δεῖπνον εἰσελθοῦσαν τὴν παῖδα φιάλην κεκερασμένην ᾧ βούλοιτο δοῦναι τῶν παρόντων μνηστήρων, ᾧδὲ δοίη τοῦτον εἶναι νυμφίον. Ἡ δὲ παῖς εἰσελθοῦσα δίδωσιν εἴτε ἀπὸ τύχης εἴτε καὶ δι' ἄλλην τινὰ αἰτίαν τῷ Εὐξένῳ··ὄνομα δ' ἦν τῇ παιδὶ Πέττα. Τούτου δὲ συμπεσόντος καὶ τοῦ πατρὸς ἀξιοῦντος ὡς κατὰ θεὸν γενομένης τῆς δόσεως, ἔλαβεν ὁ Εὔξενος γυναῖκα καὶ συνῴκει μεταθέμενος τοὔνομα Ἀριστοξένην. Καὶ ἔστι γένος ἐν Μασσαλίᾳ ἀπὸ τῆς ἀνθρώπου μέχρι νῦν Πρωτιάδαι καλούμενον· Πρῶτος γὰρ ἐγένετο υἱὸς Εὐξένου καὶ τῆς Ἀριστοξένης. (Ath. XIII, 576a–b)

Aristotle in his *Constitution of the Massaliotes* (fr.560) claims that something similar happened (there). He writes as follows:

> The Phocaeans who inhabit Ionia were traders and founded Massalia. Euxenus of Phocaea was a guest-friend of King Nanos—which was actually his name. Euxenus happened to be visiting when this Nanos was celebrating his daughter's wedding, and he invited him to the feast. The wedding was organized as follows: After the meal, the girl had to come in and offer a bowl full of wine mixed with water to whichever suitor there she wanted, and whoever she gave it to would be her bridegroom. When the girl entered the room, she gave the bowl, either by accident or for some other reason, to Euxenus; her name was Petta. After this happened, and her father decided that the gift had been made in accord with the god's will, so that he ought to have her, Euxenus married her and set up

housekeeping with her, although he changed her name to Aristoxene. There is still a family in Massalia today that descended from her and known as the Protiadae; because Protis was the son of Euxenus and Aristoxene. (Trad. S. Douglas Olson, Loeb)

The main merit of this fragment, for the issue at hand, is especially to testify to the existence of a *Politeia of the Massaliots* attributed to Aristotle and to be used as a *verbatim* quotation of this book. But it does not say much about the institutions, nor even about the customs or the Massaliot way of life. De facto, the *Politeia* properly speaking is not the purpose of this passage of Athenaeus whose centre of interest, in the book XIII of the *Deipnosophists*, is love. Thus, the fragment is partitioned in order to focus the narrative on the meeting and the union of Euxenos and Petta, at the origin of the foundation of Massalia[1].

The second fragment may seem even more disappointing. It is a very short notice of Harpocration, a grammarian of the second century AD and author of a *Lexicon of the ten orators*. Under the entry *Massalia*, the lexicographer reads:

Μασσαλία· Ἰσοκράτης μέν φησιν ἐν Ἀρχιδάμῳ ὡς Φωκαεῖς φυγόντες τὴν τοῦ μεγάλου βασιλέως δεσποτείαν εἰς Μασσαλίαν ἀπῴκησαν· ὅτι δὲ πρὸ τούτων τῶν χρόνων ἤδη ὑπὸ Φωκαέων ᾤκιστο ἡ Μασσαλία καὶ Ἀριστοτέλης ἐν τῇ Μασσαλιωτῶν πολιτείᾳ δηλοῖ. (Harp. *s.v.*Μασσαλία)

Massalia: Isocrates says in Archidamos that Phocaeans fleeing the tyranny of the Great King left to settle in Massalia. But the fact that, before that time, Massalia was inhabited by Phocaeans, is also emphasised by Aristotle in his *Politeia of the Massaliots*.

The words of Harpocration seem to confirm the existence of a *Politeia of the Massaliots* attributed to Aristotle. The second part of the notice shows that both traditions existed about the settlement of Phocaeans in Marseille, one linking their departure from Phocaea to the Persian domination on Ionia, the other, situating this departure in a former time, that of the legendary foundation evoked by Athenaeus. But it should not be concluded that Aristotle himself necessarily mentioned both these traditions in his *Politeia*, nor even that Harpocration had direct access to the Aristotelian text and quoted him precisely. The use of the verb δηλοῖ (he shows that) instead of γράφει (he writes that) is rather the index of a summary of the information contained in the *Politeia*, and the double settlement of the Phocaeans in Massalia could be a conclusion that the lexicographer or his source derived from the contradiction between the version of Isocrates [2] and that of Aristotle. Harpocration, just like Athenaeus, may have had only a second-hand knowledge of the *Politeia of the Massaliots* through selected pieces. Both refer to the same passage, since the sentence of Harpocration visibly reworded the first sentence transmitted in the fragment of Athenaeus, and both authors on this occasion made the only explicit mentions of the *Politeia of the Massaliots* now in our possession. This sentence transmits a piece of information reliably, always repeated then[3], that of the Phocaean (and hence Ionian) origin of the foundation of Marseille. But we shall see that the importance ascribed to that remark may not only be due to doxographical transmission.

Other Traces of the Politeia of the Massaliots?
Other authors, mentioning Massalia at times, may have used without stating so explicitly (and perhaps without knowing it) information whose first source is the Aristotelian *Politeia*. Such may be the case of another passage of Athenaeus and of a passage of Aelianus. Athenaeus, in book X of the *Deipnosophists* (X 429a) notes a number of restrictions to the usage of wine in the legislation of different cities. After mentioning the prohibition of drinking neat wine under the penalty of death in the laws of Zaleukos in Locri Epizephyrii, he notes: παρὰ δὲ Μασσαλιήταις ἄλλος νόμος τὰς γυναῖκας ὑδροποτεῖν. Ἐν δὲ Μιλήτῳ ἔτι καὶ νῦν φησι Θεόφραστος τοῦτ' εἶναι τὸ νόμιμον ("In Massalia there is a different law, which specifies that women are to drink nothing but water; this is still the custom even today in Miletus, according to Theophrastus (fr.579b Fortenbaugh)" (Trad. S. Douglas Olson, Loeb). Aelianus, for his own part, writes (*Var.Hist.* II 38): Νόμος καὶ οὗτος Μασσαλιωτικός, γυναῖκας μὴ ὁμιλεῖν οἴνῳ, ἀλλ' ὑδροποτεῖν πᾶσαν γυναικῶν ἡλικίαν. Λέγει δὲ Θεόφραστος καὶ παρὰ Μιλησίοις τὸν νόμον τοῦτον ἰσχύειν, καὶ <μὴ> πείθεσθαι αὐτῷ τὰς Ἰαδάς, ἀλλὰ τὰς Μιλησίων γυναῖκας. ("There was a law at Massalia that women should not touch wine, but drink water at all ages. Theophrastus says this law was also in force at Miletus, and while Ionian women did not adhere to it, at least the Milesians did." (Trad. N.G. Wilson, Loeb).

Both passages, quite close in substance as in form, visibly originate from the same source. This source is named, at least for Miletus. It is Theophrastus. But the presence of the demonstrative, suggesting that we are dealing with the same law in Massalia and in Miletus, an association emphasised (in the passage of Aelianus) by the adverb καί, leads us to think that Theophrastus is also the source of the first part of the notice and probably information on Locrii, also mentioned by Aelianus, just before touching upon the case of Massalia and of Miletus. Theophrastus might have been the first to see a link between the wine legislation in Massalia and in Miletus. Still, Theophrastus, a student of Aristotle, first scholarch of the Lykaios, authored a treatise on drunkenness, lost today, to which the publishers of the fragments tie the assembly of both notices (fr. 579 A and B). But he also authored a treatise on laws, which obviously used the materials derived from the investigation on the *Politeiai*.

Similarly, we can reconcile to a third passage of Athenaeus and a short article found in a collection of Alexandrine proverbs attributed to Plutarch. In both cases, the Massaliot morals are also addressed.

Ἴβηρες δέ, καίτοι ἐν τραγικαῖς στολαῖς καὶ ποικίλαις προιόντες καὶ χιτῶσι ποδήρεσι χρώμενοι, οὐδὲν ἐμποδίζονται τῆς πρὸς τοὺς πολέμους ῥώμης. Μασσαλιῶται δὲ Ἰβηρικῶς μέν εἰσιν ἐσταλμένοι, ἐθηλύνθησαν δὲ καὶ ἀσχημονοῦσι διὰ τὴν ἐν ψυχαῖς **μαλακίαν**, διὰ **τρυφὴν** γυναικοπαθοῦντες. ὅθεν καὶ ἡ παροιμία·πλεύσειας εἰς Μασσαλίαν. (Athenaeus XII 523b–c)

The Iberians in fact go out dressed in elaborate robes that resemble those worn in tragedy, and wear tunics that hang to their feet, although this has no negative effect on their strength in war. The Massaliotes, on the other hand, who wear the same costume as the Iberians, became effeminate. The weakness and addiction to luxury in their hearts, at any rate, has led to them behaving in an ugly way and allowing themselves to be treated like woman, hence the proverb "I hope you sail to Massalia!" (Trad. S. Douglas Olson, Loeb)

Εἰς Μασσαλίαν πλεύσειας: οἱ Μασσαλιῶται θηλύτερον ἔζων, καὶ στολαῖς ποικίλαις καὶ ποδήρεσι χρώμενοι, ἔτι δὲ τὰς κόμας μεμυρισμένας ἀναδεδεμένοι, καὶ διὰ ταύτην τὴν **μαλακίαν** ἀσχημονοῦντες. (Plutarch *Alexandrine Proverbs* 60)

Sail therefore towards Massalia: the Massaliots led an effeminate way of life, wearing colourful outfits down to their feet, with their hair tucked up, tied and perfumed, emphasised by an indecent behaviour due to their notorious sluggishness.

This time, both texts cannot be overlapped exactly inasmuch as each of them contains specific details (for example the comparison with the Iberians in Athenaeus, the head dress details in Plutarch), but there is no question about their common origin. In both cases, the description is associated with a proverb with obscene undertones: "Sail towards Massalia", and both of them stress the effeminacy and sluggishness exhibited by the Massaliots. Their comparison enables us to deduce that this source addressed in quite a detailed way the description of the clothing and of the outfit (*schèma*), of the way of life, which is, as we have seen, a constitutive element of the writing of the *Politeiai*. Besides, even if neither of these texts refers to the Ionian origin of the Massaliots, the judgment passed on their costume and their outfit, in blatant contradiction with what the others say about their virtue, the severity and the excellence of the Massaliot institutions, is in line with the *topos* which associates luxury, sluggishness and an effeminate way of life with Ionia. It ought to be stressed incidentally that in book X of Athenaeus, dedicated to luxury, this passage appears slightly before another notice about the Milesians who lost their virile character by indulging in sluggishness and luxury, a notice also ending with the quotation of a proverb: "there was a time when the Milesians were virile" (Πάλαι ποτ' ἦσαν ἄλκιμοι Μιλήσιοι). This time, the source is quoted explicitly: it is indeed Aristotle (Athenaeus XII 523f).

The pieces of information and the judgments passed in these texts, of different origins and times, are often clichés more than not and their use should be taken with a grain of salt. These testimonies should not be considered as backing up or negating each other, as enabling us to measure a permanence or an evolution of the Massaliot customs and ways of life, inasmuch as all of them fall within the doxographical history of the same original text, the *Politeia of the Massaliots* ascribed to Aristotle.

The Politics *of Aristotle and the Marseille Institutions*

A second source, which maintains close relations with the *Politeia of the Massaliots*, provides more accurate information on the nature of the regime. This is the major theoretical book of Aristotle on politics, composed in fact of a collection of treatises, where the philosopher bases his reflection on materials collected in the context of the investigation of the *Politeiai* of the different cities[4]. Marseille is mentioned there twice.

The first mention can be found in book V and supports an analysis on the causes and the origins of the revolutions.

Ἔχει δὲ καὶ ἡ ἐξ ἄλλων ἀρχὴ στάσεως διαφοράς. Ὀτὲ μὲν γὰρ ἐξ αὐτῶν τῶν εὐπόρων, οὐ τῶν ὄντων δ' ἐν ταῖς ἀρχαῖς, γίγνεται κατάλυσις, ὅταν ὀλίγοι σφόδρα ὦσιν οἱ ἐν ταῖς τιμαῖς, οἷον ἐν Μασσαλίᾳ καὶ ἐν Ἴστρῳ καὶ ἐν Ἡρακλείᾳ καὶ ἐν ἄλλαις πόλεσι συμβέβηκεν· οἱ γὰρ μὴ μετέχοντες τῶν ἀρχῶν ἐκίνουν, ἔως μετέλαβον οἱ πρεσβύτεροι πρότερον τῶν ἀδελφῶν, ὕστερον δ' οἱ νεώτεροι πάλιν· οὐ γὰρ ἄρχουσιν ἐνιαχοῦ μὲν ἅμα πατήρ τε καὶ υἱός, ἐνιαχοῦ δὲ ὁ πρεσβύτερος καὶ ὁ νεώτερος ἀδελφός· καὶ ἔνθα μὲν πολιτικωτέρα ἐγένετο ἡ ὀλιγαρχία, ἐν Ἴστρῳ δ' εἰς δῆμον ἀπετελεύτησεν, ἐν Ἡρακλείᾳ δ' ἐξ ἐλαττόνων εἰς ἑξακοσίους ἦλθεν. (Aristotle *Politics* V 4.2–3 1305b)

Faction originating with other people also has various ways of arising. Sometimes, when the honours of office are shared by very few, dissolution originates from the wealthy themselves, but not those who are in office, as for example, has occurred at Marseille, at Istrus, at Heraclea, and in other states; for those who did not share in the magistracies raised disturbances until as a first stage the older brothers were admitted, and later the younger ones again (for in some places a father and a son may not hold office together, and in others an elder and a younger brother may not). At Marseille the oligarchy became more constitutional, while at Istrus it ended in becoming democracy, and in Heraclea the government passed from a smaller number to six hundred. (Trad. H. Rackham, Loeb)

To understand this passage, the classification of the constitutions according to Aristotle should be reminded briefly. In book III of the *Politics* Aristotle establishes a rigorous taxonomy which leads him to distinguish the forms of

regimes by the combination of both criteria: that of the number and that of
the distinction between straight forms (those aiming at general interest) and
diverted forms (those in which the government follows a particular interest). The monarchy (government of a sole person) is thus shared between
royalty (straight form) and tyranny (diverted form): the small number
government between aristocracy (straight form) and oligarchy (diverted
form), the large number government between *politeia* (straight form) and
democracy (diverted form). The word *politeia* is used by Aristotle to designate
the straight form of the large number regime (IV.8.1293b–1294a). This word
is ambiguous since polysemic: it is first of all the generic term which is used
for designating any form of regime; it is also the one referring, as we saw, to a
particular literary genre. But Aristotle employs it deliberately, if we admit that
this name is in reality an absence of name[5], since the philosopher recognises
that *politeia* is the designation common to all regimes[6], but he justifies this
particular use by the fact that it is here *politeia* par excellence inasmuch as
the prerequisite is excellence from the largest number of people. The cities of
Sparta, Carthago and Crete, which knew neither sedition nor tyranny, were
among those which experienced such *politeia*. And as shown by the example
of certain cities governed by *politeia* before diverting it towards democracy,
Tarentus (V.3.7, 1302b), after a victory against the Iapygians at the time of
the second Medic war, and Syracuse (V.4.9, 1304a), on the day following the
victory against Athens in 413, the conservatism of institutions is one of the
keys to *politeia*.

However, the taxonomy established in book III is getting softer in other
parts of the *Politics*, when Aristotle examines the existing regimes and considers that there is a whole gradation inside each of the categories, with possible mixtures within the same regime of institutions pertaining to different
categories, or still brutal or progressive evolutions leading from one form to
another.

The text of interest mentions such an evolution in Marseille when the
regime switched from an oligarchy to a form closer to a *politeia*. The form
(or the forms) of the oligarchic regime are long examined by Aristotle but all
boil down to a common definition: Oligarchy is the diverted form of the small
number government, where the government targets the particular interest of
the rich. De facto, oligarchy, for Aristotle, can be defined as "the government
of the rich".

This single passage condenses in reality two different facts. On the one hand,
the progressive widening of the *archai* (i.e., of the exercise of magistracies)
to several representatives of the same family. Aristotle remains quite vague on
the exact conditions of such widening. The end of the text leads us to think

that two representatives of a same family could only access simultaneously to the *archai*, but the beginning of the text suggests a tighter restriction inasmuch as if they exclude rebel, probably because that access is de facto prohibited. Both interpretations are not mutually exclusive, since at the time of Strabo still, the six hundred *Timouchoi* were magistrates for life (Strabo IV 1.5). But the change in question does not modify fundamentally the nature of the regime in the thought of Aristotle. The Massaliots simply switch from a narrow oligarchy to a slightly wider oligarchy, from a situation where only one head of family may exercise a legal authority (probably to maintain a balance between the "families" dating back to the first settlers, like that of the Protiads), to an opening-up to several representatives of the same branch. But this does not justify in any way the judgment of Aristotle on the fact that in Marseille the regime came closer to a *politeia*. To understand this assertion, we need to refer to another passage of the *Politics*.

This second passage can be found in book VI, in a section dedicated to oligarchies and to the way the latter can be preserved by extending themselves:

> Τὴν δὲ μετάδοσιν γίνεσθαι τῷ πλήθει τοῦ πολιτεύματος ἤτοι καθάπερ εἴρηται πρότερον, τοῖς τὸ τίμημα κτωμένοις, ἢ καθάπερ Θηβαίοις, ἀποσχομένοις χρόνον τινὰ τῶν βαναύσων ἔργων, ἢ καθάπερ ἐν Μασσαλίᾳ κρίσιν ποιουμένους τῶν ἀξίων ἐν τῷ πολιτεύματι καὶ τῶν ἔξωθεν. (Aristotle *Politics* VI.4.5, 1321a)

> And the bestowal of a share in the government upon the multitude should either go on the lines stated before, and be made to those who acquire the property-qualification, or as at Thebes, to people after they have abstained for a time from mechanic industries, or as at Marseille, by making a selection among members of the governing classes and those outside it of persons who deserve inclusion. (Trad. H. Rackham, Loeb)

The evolution of the regime could not be summed up this time to the possibility of accessing simultaneously (or even alternately) magistracies for several members of the same family. It is indeed an extension of the *politeuma*. The *politeuma* is defined by Aristotle as the part of the city whose vocation is to participate in the government (regardless whether an individual exercises a legal authority at a given time or not, it is part of the *politeuma* if it meets the conditions to access these positions). The extension of the *politeuma* does not necessarily imply modifications of the institutional structures: the mode of designation of the magistracies, the number of Council members, and the organisation of the executive power may remain unchanged. It is the number of the potential candidates which constitutes the opening of the oligarchy. The three cases quoted by Aristotle offer as many possible modalities to extend the *politeuma*. The first one consists in fixing a census threshold, which de facto opens access to the *politeuma* to all the citizens reaching this threshold, regardless of their family origin. It is also possible to play with the height of this threshold according to the expected result. The second concerns the oligarchies in which the access conditions to the *politeuma* excluded the artisans and the merchants (which amounted in fact in reserving them to the citizens receiving a property income). Lifting the exclusion after a certain delay for those who had ceased their activity also enables mobility and possible extension of the *politeuma*. The case of Marseille is more complex: First of all because we need to understand what Aristotle means by "selection" (κρίσις), then because the nature of the "merit" of those who are chosen (τῶν ἀξίων) is not clearly explained.

On the latter point, it is impossible to analyse the collection of the criteria according to which a man was deemed worthy of belonging to the *politeuma*. They were probably as numerous as varied and were assessed according to their family situation (Strabo IV 1.5 goes on to say that "none can become a *timouchos* if he is childless and not a descendant of three generations of citizens": τιμοῦχος δ' οὐ γίνεται μὴ τέκνα ἔχων μηδὲ διὰ τριγονίας ἐκ πολιτῶν γεγονώς), but certainly included as well the compliance with laws and customs, pure morals, the observance of religious rules, as testified by the scarce allusions in Greek and Latin authors. Besides one of the most important criteria should have been certainly the level of incomes, failing which for Aristotle, Massalia would have definitely ceased to be an oligarchy. What is suggested implicitly by the Stagirite is that the personal value, the virtue (ἀρετή), with the whole complexity of the significance of this word in Greek, was the declared selection criterion of the *politeuma* in Massalia. This assertion is repeated, explicitly this time, in the judgement of Strabo: "the government under which the Massaliots live is aristocratic, and of all aristocracies theirs is the best ordered [...]" (IV.1.5: διοικοῦνται δ' ἀριστοκρατικῶς οἱ Μασσαλιῶται πάντων εὐνομώτατα).

Why then does Aristotle consider in book V that the political evolution of Massalia led the city to get closer to a *politeia* and not an aristocracy? Probably because this evolution is precisely linked with an extension of the *politeuma* and its opening to the *plethos* (the mass, the large number, the people). In several passages of the *Politics,* the philosopher admits that, in the reality of facts, the difference between aristocracy and *politeia* is highly tenuous (II 11, 1273a4; IV.8, 1294a27–29; IV.9.1294b10 and 40). As for the "selection" made among the worthy men in Massalia, two hypotheses can be envisioned. In the first hypothesis, selection enables constitution of the *politeuma*. This means that the political body liable to access government functions was screened on a regular basis, that men from the *plethos* if deemed "worthy" could be integrated thereto, but that conversely, other who had hitherto been members could be excluded because they were not deemed "worthy" to stay. This interpretation could be backed up in an anecdote reported by Lucianus, where a certain Menekrates who, for a time was rich and honoured, "had one day his personal property removed, and was at the same time deprived of his political rights by the Six Hundred for having presented an unlawful proposition" (*Toxaris or on* Friendship 24: ἀφηρέθη τὴν οὐσίαν ἐκ καταδίκης, ὅτεπερ καὶ ἄτιμος ἐγένετο ὑπὸ τῶν ἑξακοσίων ὡς ἀποφηνάμενος γνώμην παράνομον). But there is another possible hypothesis, according to which the selection mentioned by Aristotle would refer to the mode of designation of high-ranking magistrates, chosen for their merit, among those who already were part of the *politeuma* but also among the *plethos*. Cicero may well allude to this mode of designation of the magistrats when he asserts: "The Massaliots, our clients, are governed with the greatest justice by chosen and top-rank citizens" (*Republica* I 27: *Massilienses nostri clientes per delectos et principes ciues summa iustitia reguntur*). But, in any event, if the situation described by Strabo, with a Council (*synedrion*) of 600 *Timouchoi* exercising their office for life, was that already as described by Aristotle in the *Politeia of the Massaliots*, the *politeuma* should then coincide with this *synedrion* and the mention of a fixed number would then mean that opening the *politeuma* to the masses as analysed in the *Politics* does imply the admission of a greater number, by less stringent conditions to attain governmental functions.

The nature and the evolution of the regime of the Massaliots still remains difficult to apprehend and the historiography has endeavoured to identify and to date the steps of this evolution (balance, in Collin Bouffier 2005). According to Michel Clerc (1927–1929, 426–427), three, possibly four, phases should be envisioned: the magistracies would have been reserved to the older brothers first of all, then to the younger brothers in the same family whose head participated in the political decision; a third step would have integrated the sons of families excluded hitherto who met the conditions of eligibility, i.e, the selection of the most worthy among the members of the ruling class. A last step would have been completed the opening process by creating the *synedrion*, which would be posterior to Aristotle as the latter does not mention it, hence between 322 (date of the death of Aristotle) and 197 BC, date of the decree of Lampsacus who involved that *synedrion* (SIG2 591, l.45). Monique Clavel-Lévêque, for her own part, sees the evolution of the political regime as linked with the commercial activity and the political slackening resulted from expanding trade: the first step should be dated to the sixth century and would have consisted of associating the sons to the father and the younger sons to the older sons; the second step, at the turn of the sixth and of the fifth centuries, would have integrated the category of the "rich merchants", born from the business and maritime expansion of the city. A last step would have seen the birth of the *synedrion* at the end of the fourth or beginning of the third century BC, with the expansion of the city to the North and the reconstruction of the walls (Clavel-Lévêque 1977, 116–120). Finally, Ettore Lepore saw only one step of change, at the turn of the sixth–fifth centuries BC, as a consequence of the expansion of the wine-growing sector and of the ceramic fabrication in Marseille: these economic mutations would have created an agrarian and artisanal class anxious to defend its interests, rather than devoted to the exploitation and the safety of the territory (Lepore 1970). So few data make it impossible to reach the bottom of the case and the taking of Phocaea by the Persians in 546/545 probably represented a decisive stage for the political functioning of Marseille. It is also the time of arrival of the Phocaean migrants for whom room was made and who claim rights to power, and it is also probably at this time that the so-called "Ionian" aspect of the city was strengthened, as evoked by Strabo.

The Ionian Character of the Massaliot Institutions

In the wake of Aristotle, the older authors insist on the original, possibly unusual character of the Massaliot institutions. In addition to a few allusions in late Roman authors, Strabo is the most informative on this subject (IV, 1, 5).

> Διοικοῦνται δ' ἀριστοκρατικῶς οἱ Μασσαλιῶται πάντων εὐνομώτατα, ἀνδρῶν ἑξακοσίων καταστήσαντες συνέδριον διὰ βίου ταύτην ἐχόντων τὴν τιμήν, οὓς τιμούχους καλοῦσι. πεντεκαίδεκα δ' εἰσὶ τοῦ συνεδρίου προεστῶτες, τούτοις δὲ τὰ πρόχειρα διοικεῖν δέδοται. πάλιν δὲ τῶν πεντεκαίδεκα προκάθηνται τρεῖς οἱ πλεῖστον ἰσχύοντες, τούτων δὲ εἷς· τιμοῦχος δ' οὐ γίνεται μὴ τέκνα ἔχων μηδὲ διὰ τριγονίας ἐκ πολιτῶν γεγονώς. οἱ δὲ νόμοι Ἰωνικοί, πρόκεινται δὲ δημοσίᾳ.

> The government under which the Massaliots live is aristocratic, and of all aristocracies theirs is the best ordered, since they have established an Assembly of six hundred men, who hold the honour of that office for life; these they call Timouchoi. Over the Assembly are set fifteen of its number, and to these fifteen it is given to carry on the immediate business of the government. And in turn, three, holding the chief power, preside over the fifteen. However a Timouchos cannot become one of these three unless he has children or is a descendant of persons who have been citizens for three generations. Their laws are ionic, and are published to the people. (Trad. H. Leonard. Jones, Loeb)

Strabo confirms the Aristotelian presentation of an oligarchic regime, whose structure he defines: a pyramidal hierarchy where all the offices are filled by people from the same pool of talent: a *synedrion* of councillors chosen according to their *timè*, who as we know were in charge of external affairs and justice

(Valerius Maximus, *Memorable Facts and Words*, II, 6–7; Lucien, *Toxaris or Friendship*, 24); the college of the fifteen magistrates and the triumvirate in charge of the executive power are also recruited among these councillors and their representativeness seems analogous to that of the Athenian prytanes. The *Timouchoi* are not specific to Massalia, but they seem to exist in the Ionian cities such as Lebedos, Teos, and its Abdera colony, Priene, Thasos, going by the epigraphical study dedicated by Gunther Gottlieb to this institution (Gottlieb 1967). The magistracy is old and its attributions and functions vary according to the regimes: the recurring factor is that the *Timouchoi* are still endowed with important powers, like the proposition of decrees or the management of public money. In Marseille, the *timè* of these magistrates is associated with the quality of *axios* evoked in the text of Aristotle: one had to prove worthy to attain magistracies and as emphasised above, the word encompasses moral attitudes that should not be understood in a modern sense. The examination of candidates to joining magistracy, but also to being relieved from an office, is a traditional exercise in Greek, especially Ionian cities: It is well known in Athens (Aristotle, *Constitution of the Athenians*, 55) and it is not an investigation of morality conducted by the police authorities, but a verification of the criteria annexed to the citizen's condition by the Boulè: in Athens, from the middle of the fifth century BC, date of Pericles' decree, one must prove that one is the son of an Athenian citizen and of an Athenian lady from the citizens' family to claim this status; since the citizenship gives access not only to the political life but also to justice and to certain financial and economic advantages, notably the distributions of cereals in case of severe shortage, or certain indemnities. Such is the case here, but whereas in Athens only one generation of citizens among the ascendants was required, three generations were necessary in Marseille, and this limit of three levels of heredity seems to be a threshold of official and symbolic recognition, which can be observed in other Greek cities, through the cult of the Tritopatores, great great grandfathers, known in older cities like Athens or Delos (Würst 1939, Bendlin 2014, Philochoros, FGrH 328 F 182), or in Greek colonies like Selinunte, where a Sacred Law rules the religious practices as regards the Tritopatores, or great great grandfathers, pure and impure, while the latter may play a positive or negative role in the political and social life of the city (Jameson, Jordan & Kotansky 1993, Iannucci et al. 2016). The cult attested of Zeus Patrôos (lastly Hermary, Tréziny 2000, 149) and the existence of a Massaliot ceremony of the *Apaturia*, a celebration which gathered those with the same fathers and which integrated the adolescents old enough to join officially the socio-political categories of the city (Salviat 2000), confirm the importance of the family links for structuring political and religious life.

Besides, like the Athenian strategy, reserved to the sole citizens who are family fathers, the necessity of a descendance determines the quality of *Timouchos*. Paradoxically, it may thus be noted that, in a harbour city, marked by the circulation of people and whose sources emphasise their mixed origins, the genealogical transmission and the parenthood links structure the society and its political institutions. It is probable that this orientation of the Massaliot laws, qualified as Ionian by Strabo, froze at the arrival of the second wave of Phocaean migration, after 546. As did Thucydides, who integrated the Siciliot foundations in a syngeneic, an ethnic parenthood, regardless whether it was political and cultural, Dorian and Chalcidian (Thuc. VI.3), Strabo shows a unique interest in this type of political heritage. In other fields, the religious and cultural similarities between Marseille and Ionia were emphasised (Salviat 2000, 1992). Henri Tréziny queries the above urban filiations. From a political viewpoint, can we say that Marseille is a Ionian city? The basic structuration of the Marseillais civic body is unknown, but the existence of the *Apaturia* seems to point to a distribution between the four traditional tribes of the Geleontes, Aigicoreis, Argadeis, Hopletes, attested in other Ionian cities like Athens before the reforms of Clisthenes, or Miletus. Perhaps due to the collegial character of the main magistracies, which implies the main offices to alternate, like the head of the leading trio. Conversely, the number fifteen, which constitutes the executive power is not a so-called Ionian figure, unlike the figure twelve, whose ancient as well as modern tradition tends to see the structuring role in the Ionian political, social and religious institutions (Lévêque & Vidal-Naquet 1992, 97–98). Fifteen is not a canonical figure in the Greek world and if the civic body is effectively structured in four tribes, the fifteen and three figures are not dividers thereof. Besides, Strabo (XII, 8, 11) integrates the political form of Marseille in a wider background:

> ἔστι δ' ἐνάμιλλος ταῖς πρώταις τῶν κατὰ τὴν Ἀσίαν ἡ πόλις μεγέθει τε καὶ κάλλει καὶ εὐνομίᾳ πρός τε εἰρήνην καὶ πόλεμον· ἔοικέ τε τῷ παραπλησίῳ τύπῳ κοσμεῖσθαι ὥσπερ ἡ τῶν Ῥοδίων καὶ Μασσαλιωτῶν καὶ Καρχηδονίων τῶν πάλαι.

> This city [Cyzicus] rivals the foremost of the cities of Asia in size, in beauty and in its excellent administration of affairs both in peace and in war. And its adornment appears to be of a type similar to that of Rhodes and Massalia and ancient Carthage. (Trad. H. Leonard. Jones, Loeb)

We may note first of all the same positive appreciation as in Aristotle, correlated to the antiquity of these *politeiai*: a regime is wise when it has proved efficient from ancient times, which suggests the conservatism of institutions in question. It can also be observed that these are cities of different origin and hence kinships a priori: two Ionian cities, Cyzicus, Milesian foundation, and Massalia, but also a so-called Dorian city and a Phoenician city. Their sole common feature is that all of them are colonial foundations. Thus, apparently and comparatively to other colonial cities, Massalia had to set up a mixed regime, born from the influences experienced during the successive collective migrations, in particular the exile of many Phocaeans in the second half of the sixth century BC; a regime which then froze around a closed oligarchy, reserved to the families arrived or formed during the first two centuries of life of the city.

Sumptuary Laws Intended for Correcting the Tryphe of the Massaliots and Regulating Their Lifestyles

The historiographical tradition has, for a long time, emphasised the oriented vision of authors of Roman time on the city of Marseille (Guyot-Rougemont & Rougemont 1992): we should also note the dichotomy between the Greek and Roman perceptions of the Massaliot society. On the other hand, they depict a city lost by its *tryphe*, its *malakia*, words which are more or less synonyms and which designate the sluggishness, the lack of energy of its constitution, of its morals and of its life; on the other hand, they exalt a community having kept the purity of its morals and of its regime through time.

Giuseppe Nenci, in a still fundamental article (1983), noted the features of the *tryphe*, a relatively vague and approximate notion, difficult to translate into our languages with a single vocable, and which takes on a more precise meaning in the contexts of use. Thus we are dealing with a collective phenomenon, which moves people (the Persians and the Lydians, as well as the Etruscans, the Messapians, the Samnites and the Italiot populations in contact with them) and the cities they would have contaminated by their contact, the Ionians, and in particular the Milesians in the East and the Italiot populations in the West. *Tryphe* also designates a social status, that of elites who would have abandoned themselves to an effeminate way of life, ascribed by Herodotus, Theopompus or Poseidonius to their clothing or their food habits. As a constant of Ionian cities, this way of life is also attested in the Athenian aristocracy of the Archaic time, as they tie their long hair with golden and cricket-shaped clasps (Thuc. 1.6.1–3). Thus, the Massaliots cover themselves with long colourful clothes, called ποικίλαις and wear their hair tied and perfumed, like sissies (*supra*). Marseille asserts thereby its Ionian origin, but from the vantage point of ancient tradition it can also be traced back to Iberic Barbarians, the furthest from the Greek centres, by distance as well as by frequency. This way of life develops in reality in prosperous cities, which are well integrated in the Mediterranean trade so that it reflects the economic wealth of the societies in question. The cities supposedly subjected to that *tryphe*, Athens, Miletus, Sybaris, Syracuse, Marseille, are also those most involved in maritime commerce, whereas that economic power benefits first and foremost the local aristocracies.

To fight against that *tryphe*, presented as the testimony to the debauchery and to the decline of the societies in question, many cities, from Athens to Syracuse, have edicted sumptuary laws, not so much intended to prohibit this way of life but rather to supervise it and to delineate ostentatious manifestations. In Marseille, a number of measures known by late texts enable us to put in evidence an analogous policy to reduce luxury. Without seeking to repeat here in detail the measures listed in the rather subjective text of Valerius Maximus, and supposedly respecting the ancient morals, it will be noted that the control of the city is exercised in particular on weddings and funerals, some of the most important events of the social and family life, as well as the symposion, the essential framework of the aristocratic life in the archaic time. Thus, according to Strabo (IV.1.5), "the largest dowry represents one hundred gold coins, as well as the value of five gold coins in clothes and five more in golden jewels; it is forbidden to give a bigger one". According to the Latin historian of the first century AD, Valerius Maximus (*Memorable facts and words*, II, 6–7),

> *Duae etiam ante portas eorum arcae iacent, altera qua liberorum, altera qua seruorum corpora ad sepulturae locum plaustro deuehuntur sine lamentatione, sine planctu. luctus funeris die domestico sacrificio adhibitoque necessariorum conuiuio finitur.*

"Two coffins can be found outside their doors, one for free men, one for slaves, used for transporting the dead to their sepulchre on a cart, without lament nor complaint. The grieving only lasts the day of the funeral, with a sacrifice". Similarly, as in Miletus, the way of life of ladies comes across as regulated, especially by a law prohibiting wine. (Athenaeus and Aelianus, *supra*)

The texts mentioned do not enable us to date these measures which are presented as atemporal laws. Valerius Maximus places the same importance on the respect of the Marseillais for their ancient morals and their sympathy for Rome (Valerius Maximus, II.6), which already raises doubt about this testimony: "This explains that the inhabitants of Massilia are still showing today the seriousness of their discipline, since the respect of the ancient morals as well as their sympathy for Rome made them particularly remarkable." We can understand these customs and conclude that the Phocaean city was not isolated by integrating Marseille in a political and cultural environment. To dwell on the three fields evoked supra, wedding, funeral, commensal practices, various laws are known in cities in the Aegean world and the Western area, which govern ostentatious abuses (Ampolo 1984a, 1984b). In Athens, the law of Solon, which limits the manifestations of pain to the family only and restricts the expenses made for the dead (no more than three pieces of clothing), regulates the public times for the funeral rites, that is, *ekphora*, the mortuary party, by limiting the number of participants, in particular women, by suppressing the sacrifice of an ox, and by prohibiting strangers from visiting the tomb. But the legislator, deemed by the Athenians as responsible for all the good laws edicted throughout their history, would also have reduced to three the number of pieces of clothing worn in public or brought as dowry (Plutarch, *Solon*, 12.8). In Mytilene, Pittacos would also have moderated the luxury of funerals (Sappho, Frgt 98 Voigt) and punished more severely the crimes committed under the influence of alcohol (Aristotle, *Pol.* II.12.1274b; Diogenes Laertius, I.76). In Sparta, the *Rhetra* introduced by Lycurgus would also have limited the manifestations of grief (Plutarch, *Lycurgus*, 27.1–4). The epigraphy finally informs us on analogous dispositions, notably on the number pieces of clothing worn by the dead (law of Keos, fifth century BC, *IG* XII, 5, 593 = Sokolowski 1969, 97, 188–191; law of Gortyn, III.1.37). All these regulations have spread between the sixth and the fifth century BC, a period during which civic bodies and political institutions were implemented.

In the West, the same type of legislation is adopted in Rhegion, where a funeral legislation is attributed to Charondas (Hense 1958, IV.2.24 = Meineke 44.40); in Syracuse, where Gelon revives an older law limiting the sumptuary funeral parties and reducing the usual expenses made for a mourning (Diod. Sic., XI.38.1–5). The rules for restricting feminine luxury are also known in Locrii Epizephyrii, where Zaleucos obliged free women to wear white clothes for religious and funerary ceremonies, against colourful clothing which became the exclusive prerogative of non-free women (the Suda, s.v. Zaleucos). The same would apply to Syracuse, where they were forbidden to wear ornamental golden jewels, colourful garments or any other purple-girded clothes, unless they displayed their status of public hetairs. They did not have the right any longer to go out after sunset, and even during the day, they required the permission of the *gynaikonomoi* and had to be accompanied by a single slave under the penalty of being accused of adultery. An analogous law would have forbidden men to wear too ostentatious garments or to wear make-up, failing which they would be declared adulterous and effeminate (Phylarchus, in: Ath. XII.521b–c; Brugnone 1992).

We have emphasised the similarities, possibly the assimilations between all these texts, written in the wake of the Pythagorean school, implanted in Crotona and in Magna Graecia of the second half of the sixth century BC with Pythagoras, up to Archytas of Tarentum in the fourth century BC, and who regularly advocated the prohibition of luxury and of *tryphe*, deemed as responsible for the decline of the cities; in these cities, the respect of a certain behavioural and dress temperance, integrated in health hygiene, was intended for stamping out civil dissensions between the aristocrats and the people, or for facing the threats from the Italic populations who had become organised and structured under their influence and affirmed themselves as opponents of the same calibre. The historian Phylarchus, to whom we owe a portion of this information, was also an admirer of the Spartan constitution and of the Lacedemonian reformer, Cleomenes III, in the third century BC, and he could only depict these societies, which he considered as corrupt, in an unfavourable light. What Antonietta Brugnone had already stressed was these laws directly concerned the circulation of objects, in particular the garments and cloths from Ionia, of high quality (in particular by the usage of purple) and hence expensive; this trade route, starting in the Ionian cities and probably Phocaea, and which involved the civic elites, consumers of luxury products, might represent a threat to the social and political balance of the city. This is incidentally what caused the loss of Sybaris, completely wallowing in its *tryphe*, since it was destroyed by Crotona, the Pythagorean city that Pythagoras rectified with severe discipline: to the best of our knowledge, nobody depicted a law against luxury and loosened morals, but rather a forbidding of outrageous behaviours.

The close link between Rome and Marseille, as revealed by our sources, may also have played a role in emphasising the typically Roman virtue of the Massaliot society: the Roman city itself adopts laws both on the funerary rites and the dress behaviours, in particular of women, like the law of the XII Tables, which would have taken its source in the reforms of Solon (Cic. *Laws*, 2, 23), then the sumptuary laws of the third century BC: the lex Metilia, in 217, proscribing the usage of certain types of cloth dyeing; the Lex Oppia, in 215 BC, forbidding Roman women to wear golden jewels of more than half a pound in weight, garments of variegated colours (we can see here the 'poikilai' cloths of the Greek cities), to drive a chariot in town and in the outskirt except for religious ceremonies (Livius, XXXIV.1; Ampolo 1984a; 1984b). If the Roman sumptuary laws are presented as directed against the bad influences from Greek cities in Italy, they especially reflect the intention to slow down the ostentatious luxury of the elites and meet the same objectives as promulgated in the sixth and the beginning of the fifth century BC by the Greek cities: in a time of crisis of the regime and of society, they contributed to rebalancing of civic forces by addressing a relatively minor aspect of the local aristocracies, their ostentatious way of life, whereas the people demanded access to magistracies and put their powers and privileges into question. How can they be interpreted and dated in Marseille? The influx of Western products, put in evidence by these sumptuary laws, must have been as plentiful in Marseille as in Sicily or in Magna Graecia, up to the taking of Phocaea in 546 BC. The second half of the sixth century is marked both by the arrival of Phocaeans in the West and by the beginning of hostilities between Greeks and local populations, which could be observed both in the field and in texts. The probable installation of a new wave of settlement in the Massaliot city could both generalise this *tryphe* that the Phocaeans knew so well or applied in Ionia, and cause the rejection of this way of life that the Massaliots logically associated with a universe which had not been there for one, possibly two generations. The reapportionment of the Western trade networks around Marseille and the political evolution that, after others, we have suggested situating in this key-moment of the Massaliot history, may have led the city to query the practices of its fathers and to claim a kind of local identity, born from the Phocaean *syngeneia* and anchored in a cultural Gaul territory.

Notes

1. On this fragment and the founding legends of Marseille, see Pralon 1992.
2. The remark of Isocrates is in fact a memory of Thucydides (I 14.1) when the latter describes the development of the Greek maritime powers, successively mentions the Ionian naval power at the time of Cyrus and Cambyses, that of Samos at the time of Cambyses, then the naval victory of the Phocaeans over the Carthaginians "as they were founding Marseille" (Φωκαῆς τε Μασσαλίαν οἰκίζοντες Καρχηδονίους ἐνίκων ναυμαχοῦντες).
3. The notice of Harpocration is repeated as such in the major Byzantine lexica (*The Suda, the Ethnika* of Stephanus of Byzantium, *the Etymologicum Magnum...*).
4. This does not mean that the *Politeia* des *Massaliotes* was written before the passages of the *Politeiai*. Weil (1960, 291) considers that *Politics* is older, but that Aristotle uses in both passages of the *Politeiais* the same preparatory sheet.
5. The absence of name for this regime was already stressed by Plato in the *Republic* (302d. The foreigner noted there that democracy "must be considered as twofold... even if it does not have a double name" (νῦν δ᾽ αὖ καὶ ταύτην ἡμῖν θετέον ἐστὶ διπλῆν [...] οὐδ᾽ εἰ τοὔνομα ἤδη διπλοῦν ἐστι ταύτης). The demonstration of the *Republic* did not require however venturing a name for this regime.
6. Arist. *Pol.* 3.7.1279a38–39: καλεῖται τὸ κοινὸν ὄνομα πασῶν τῶν πολιτειῶν, πολιτεία.

Bibliography

Ampolo, C., 1984a, Il lusso nelle società arcaiche: note preliminari sulla posizione del problema. IN: *Opus*, 1984. 3 (2), 469–476.

Ampolo, C., 1984b, Il lusso funerario e la città antica. *AION*, VI, 71–102.

Bendlin, A.E., 2014, Tritopatores. In: H. Cancik & H. Schneider (eds.), *Brill's New Pauly. Antiquity Volumes*. Brill on line.

Brugnone, A., 1992, Le leggi suntuarie di Siracusa. *Parola del Passato*, XLVII, 5–24.

Clavel-Lévêque, M., 1977, *Marseille grecque. La dynamique d'un impérialisme marchand*, Marseille, Jeanne Laffitte, 209p.

Clerc, M., 1927–1929, *Massalia. Histoire de Marseille dans l'Antiquité, des origines à la fin de l'empire romain d'occident*, (476 apr. J.-C.), Marseille, 480p. et 489p.

Collin Bouffier, S., 2005, Marseille pendant l'Antiquité grecque et romaine. In: M.P. Rothé & H. Tréziny (dir.), *Carte Archéologique de la Gaule. Marseille et ses alentours, 13/3*, Académie des Inscriptions et Belles-Lettres, Paris, 217–224.

Fortenbaugh, W.W. et al., 1992, *Theophrastus of Eresus. Sources for His Life, Writings, Thought and Influence*. Part Two, Brill; Leyde-New-York-Cologne, 465p.

Gottlieb, G., 1967, *Timuchen. Ein Betrag zum griechischen Staatsrecht. Vorlgelegt am 15. Juli 1967 von Hermann Strasburger*. Heidelberg, Carl Winter, 52p.

Guyot-Rougemont, Cl. & Rougemont, G., 1992, Marseille antique: les textes littéraires grecs et latins. In: M. Bats, G. Bertucchi, G. Congès & H. Tréziny (eds.), *Marseille grecque et la Gaule, Actes des colloques de Marseille*, 18–23 novembre 1990. Lattes-Aix-en-Provence, 45–50. (*Etudes Massaliètes* 3).

Hense, O., 1958, *Ioannis Stobaei Anthologii*, livre 4, Berlin, Weidmann.

Hermary, A., Hesnard, A. & Tréziny, H., 1999, *Marseille grecque. La cité phocéenne: 600–49 av. J.-C.* Paris, Errance, 181p.

Hermary, A. & Tréziny, H., 2000, Les cultes massaliètes: documentation épigraphique et onomastique. In: *Les cultes des cités phocéennes. Actes du colloque international organisé par le Centre Camille Jullian*, Aix-en-Provence/Marseille, 1999. Aix-en-Provence, Edisud,147–157. (Etudes Massaliètes, 6).

Iannucci, A., Muccioli, FM.,& Zaccarini, M., La città inquieta. Selinunte tra Lex sacra e defixiones, Milan, 2015, Mimesis-Diadema 2, 354p.

Jameson, M.H., Jordan, D.R. & Kotansky, R.D., 1993, *A lex sacra from Selinous. Greek, Roman and Byzantine Monographs* 11, Durham, 171p.

Lepore, E., 1970, Strutture della colonizzazione focea in Occidente. *Nuovi Studi su Velia, Parola del Passato*, 19–54.

Lévêque, P. & Vidal-Naquet, P., 1992, *Clisthène l'Athénien*. Paris, Macula, 1992 (1964), 163p.

Nenci, G., 1983, Tryphé e colonizzazione. In: *Modes de contacts et processus de transformation dans les sociétés antiques. Actes du colloque de Cortone (24–30 mai 1981) organisé par la Scuola Normale Superiore et l'École française de Rome*. Pise-Rome, *Scuola Normale Superiore- École française de Rome*, 1019–1031.

Pralon, D., 1992, La légende de la fondation de Marseille. In: M. Bats, G. Bertucchi, G. Congès & H. Tréziny, *Marseille grecque et la Gaule,* Aix-en-Provence, Edisud, 141–150. *(Etudes Massaliètes* 3).

Rose, V., 1887, *Aristotelis qui ferebantur librorum fragmenta.* Leipzig.

Salviat, Fr., 1992, Sur la religion de Marseille grecque. In: M. Bats, G. Bertucchi, G. Congès & H Tréziny (eds.), *Marseille grecque et la Gaule.* Aix-en-Provence, Edisud, 141–150. (Etudes Massaliètes 3).

Salviat, Fr., 2000, La source ionienne: Apatouria, Apollon Delphinios et l'oracle, l'Aristarchéion. In: *Les cultes des cités phocéennes.* Actes du colloque international organisé par le Centre Camille Jullian, Aix-en-Provence/Marseille, 1999. Aix-en-Provence, Edisud, 25–31. (Etudes Massaliètes, 6).

Sokolowski, Fr., 1969, *Lois sacrées des cités grecques.* Paris, de Boccard, 368p.

Thollard, P., 2009, *La Gaule selon Strabon. Du texte à l'archéologie. Géographie, livre IV.* Traduction et études. Paris/Aix-en-Provence, Centre Camille Jullian, BiAMA, 2, 261p.

Voigt, E.M., 1971, *Sappho et Alcaeus. Fragmenta.* Amsterdam, Athenaeum, Polak and Van Gennep, 507p.

Weil, R., 1960, *Aristote et l'histoire.* Essai sur la «Politique» (Collection: Études et Commentaires, XXXI). Paris, Klincksieck, 1960, 466p.

Würst, E., 1939, Tritopatores. *Pauly Realencyclopädie des classischen AltertumsWissenschaft*, sv. Tritopatores, Stuttgart, Band VII, A1, 324–327.

7. *Marseille: An Ionian City in the Greek West*

Henri Tréziny

The Foundation

The founders of Marseille are, according to the written sources, Greeks who arrived around 600 from Phocaea, a city of Southern Aeolis, in the North of Smyrna[1]. A second contingent might have arrived around 545–540, at the time of the taking of Phocaea by the Persians. No other literary source mentions another metropolis for Massalia. However, Strabo, when he evokes the cult of Artemis of Ephesus, so present in Marseille and the Massaliot colonies in the West, reminds us that this cult was introduced by an Ephesian woman, Aristarcha, who becomes in Marseille the priestess of Artemis. Although Strabo does not specify at which time the episode of Aristarcha is situated (around 600 or around 540), it has been suggested that the "pan-Ionian" character of the Artemis of Ephesus in Marseille could only be explained after the conquest of Ephesus by the Lydians and the takeover of the sanctuary by Cresus (Malkin 1990). It is exact if Aristarcha is considered a real character, but not necessarily if he is admittedly an 'etiological' character, intended for translating a phenomenon, that is, the importance of an Ephesian cult in Marseille that had become incomprehensible. In one of his latest publications, Irad Malkin (2011, 197–204) interprets the development of the cult of Artemis of Ephesus as an emanation of the "Phocaean networks" in the West. He sees Emporion as a Phocaean site, which at least should be discussed since the Massaliot influence seems so strong, anyway after the foundation of Neapolis, but omits to specify also that Artemis of Ephesus is attested neither in Alalia nor in Velia which are, for their own part, without any possible argument, purely Phocaean foundations. The Artemis of Ephesus is therefore more connected to Marseille than to the Phocaean world.

The cult of Artemis of Ephesus is known by the literary sources in Marseille, in Spain in Emporion, Rhoda or Hemeroskopeion and in the delta of the Rhône. We therefore wondered (Dominguez 2000) whether Ephesus had not played a part in the colonisation of the Western Mediterranean region. Another detail which has been little emphasised is the presence in Marseille, when the Greeks arrived, of two leaders of the fleet (*duces classis*, according to Justin), Protis and Simos. The disappearance of Simos from the narrative of Aristoteles and generally from the bulk of the tradition after the wedding of Protis and of the daughter of the indigenous king should not obliterate its presence in an account, which might be more ancient, even if the tradition at its origin is more recent. Still, in the bulk of the foundation accounts of the Greek colonies, the existence of several leaders (*oecists*) is generally the symptom of the presence of several contingents of settlers of diverse origins. The exclusion of Aristarcha and the disappearance of Simos would consist in re-writing the foundation myths in a strictly Phocaean perspective, maybe at the initiative of the family of the Protiads, after the strengthening of the Phocaean contingent who followed the taking of Phocaea by the Persians and (perhaps) the battle of Alalia.

De facto, in a clarification on the religion of Marseille, F. Salviat (1992) insisted on the Pan-Ionian character of the Massaliot cults: Artemis of Ephesus, but also Apollo Delphinios honoured in the Greek trading post of Naucratis, and other minor divinities. But it should not be forgotten that if the sanctuary of Artemis occupies in Ephesus, at the foot of the acropolis of Aya Soluk, a position of choice at the bottom of the Gulf and of the port area, that of Apollo Delphinios is placed analogously behind the Lions port of Miletus. Rather than a meeting of pan-Ionian cults, the "pan-Ionian" religion of Massalia therefore gathers diverse Ionian cults which each have a strongly marked origin.

If the texts are not explicit, it is very difficult to characterize this ethnical variation through archaeological arguments. The easiest would be to examine the imports to Marseille of ceramics from Eastern Greece in the first half of the sixth century and to see whether such or such a region of Ionia is particularly represented. But it is only simple from a theoretical viewpoint: the archaic ceramics of Marseille are still too poorly known and too little published, and the comparison files lack the Phocaean files especially. And even should we be able to characterise these imports, they would first of all testify to commercial flows the interpretation of which in ethnical terms might be at least dangerous.

We shall therefore limit ourselves to that quite general overview of Marseille as an "Ionian" city, which considers more specifically Phocaean characteristics from the second half of the sixth century (Fig. 1). We shall first study it from the town planning scheme, which has been relatively well documented to this day[2].

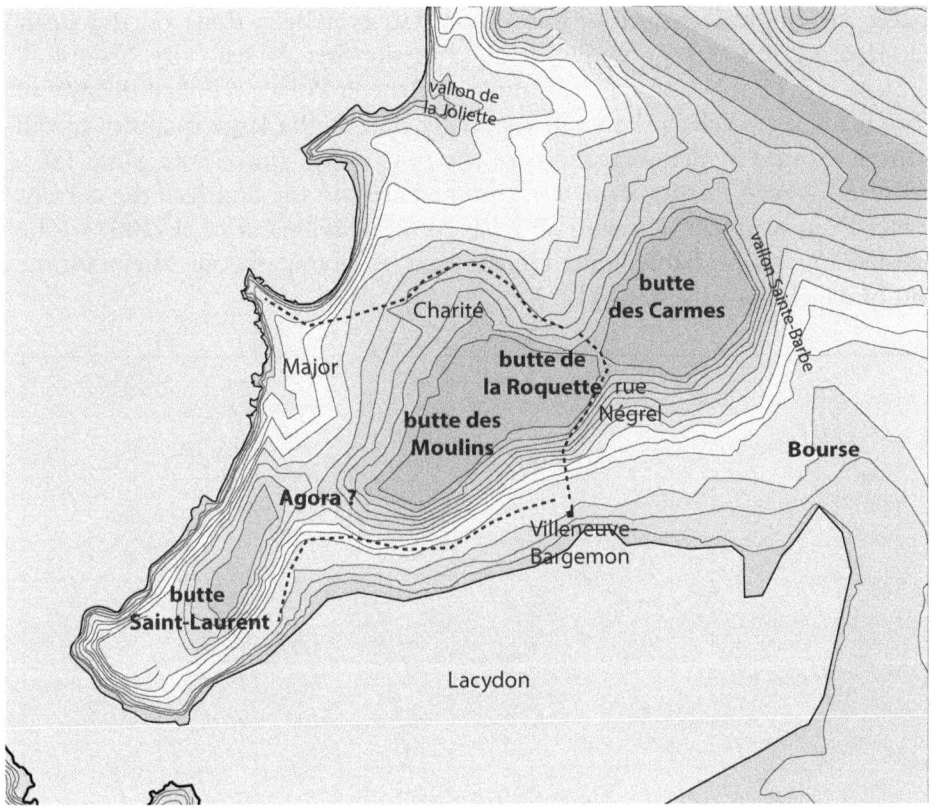

Figure 1. Topographical layout of Marseille around 520 BC.

The Town Planning Scheme

The oldest residential districts excavated in Marseille date back from the first quarter of the sixth century and can be situated on *Butte Saint-Laurent*: at the summit, under the forecourt of the Saint-Laurent church, on the South-eastern slopes (*Collège Vieux-Port*), on the Northern slope. Although they present in detail a regular aspect (quadrangular rooms), these residential sectors do not form a homogeneous assembly, but they rather seem to be organised around terrace walls following substantially the level curves. But the excavated areas are so confined that we would think twice before suggesting a layout of that first installation. The habitat seems to be restricted by the ditch by the *rue Four-du-Chapitre*. Beyond that, in the sector of the Major (Cathedral), the traces of occupancy are less clear and the presence of an incineration tomb could be the clue of a funerary area in the suburban space. Although no extensive excavation had ever been done on the *Butte des Moulins*, it was supposedly included in the first Archaic city, first of all because it probably housed the temple of Athena Polias, a Poliad divinity of Phocaea and of Velia[3], then and especially due to the large quantity of old potteries found in the excavations of the port (*place Jules-Verne, place Ville-neuve-Bargemon, Espace Bargemon*), immediately in the South of the current Hôtel-Dieu hospital (*Parcours de ville*, 24–25; Mellinand et al. 2007). The first habitat was probably limited in the East by a rampart, only the maritime end of which has subsisted (Fig. 1)[4].

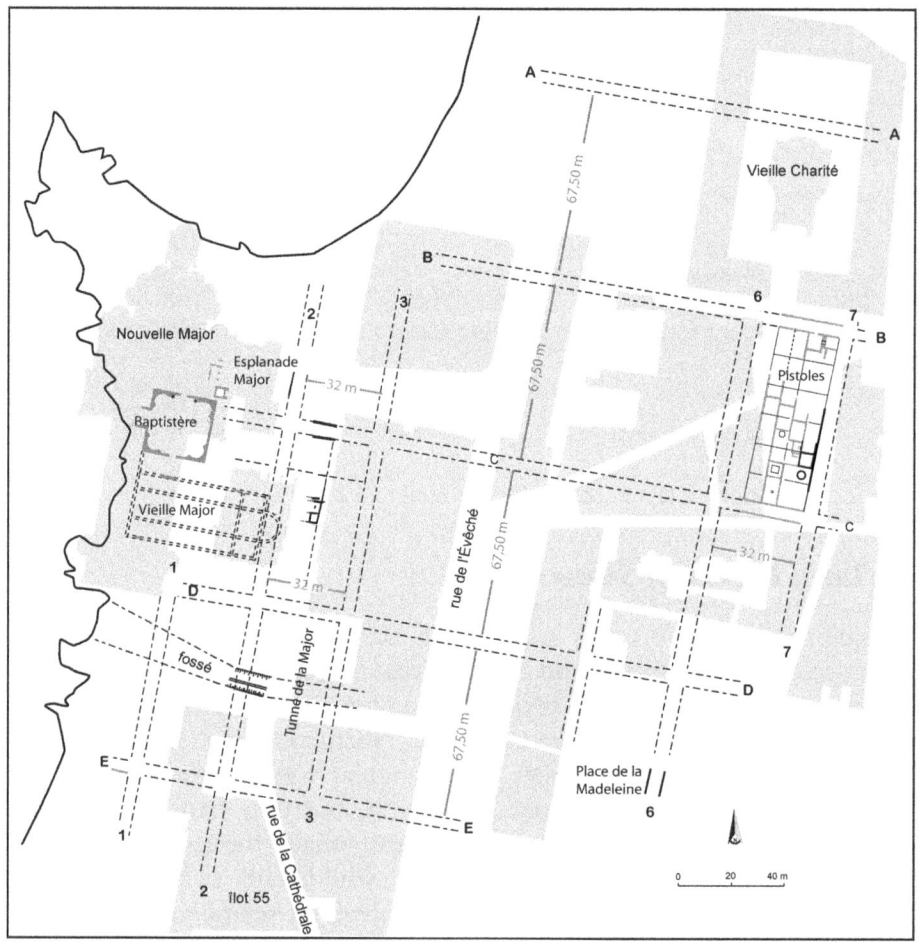

Figure 2. The district of the Panier: Orthogonal layout of the Archaic city as of approx. 570 BC.

A new orthogonal district, covering the whole sector from the Panier to the Vieille Charité in the North seems to have been built around 570–560 in the North of the primitive city (Fig. 2). This new urban orientation seems to cover hitherto non-urbanised sectors, but also a part of the previous habitat as on the excavation of the *Rue de la Cathédrale*. Recent works carried out at the foot of the Hôtel-Dieu have led scholars to assume that this regular plan also extended over the Southern slopes of the *Butte des Moulins* (Mellinand 2013). Conversely, it never seems to have covered the whole of Saint-Laurent Hill. The orthogonal district was first put in evidence in the excavation of the *Place des Pistoles*, in the South of the Vieille-Charité, with two East-West streets substantially corresponding to the *Rue de la Charité* (street B) and the *Rue du Panier* (street C, now found more in the West during the excavation of the *tunnel de la Major*). Another East-West street was identified more in the North, in the courtyard of the Charité (street A), a fifth in the South, in the *avenue Vaudoyer* (street E). The dimension of the blocks is almost certain in the North-South direction, between the A-B-C-D-E streets. It is assessed by L.-Fr. Gantès at 67.50m [5]. Street C is more than 4m in width, and the average interaxial distance can be calculated at approx. 71.50m (assuming that the width of the streets is constant, which is not certain as we shall see).

A North-South street, called 1, had long been assumed as facing the South entrance of the Vieille-Major; it was found at the South end of the excavation of the *Tunnel de La Major* (*CAG Marseille*, 436, 440). Street 2 appeared in the excavations of the *Tunnel de La Major* and *Esplanade de La Major* (Paone 2013), and can be found more in the South, for the Roman time, in the excavation of the *Rue de la Cathédrale* or *Ilot 55*. The existence under the former *Rue Rouge* of a street 3 can be deduced from the presence in the excavation of the *Tunnel de La Major* of a medial block axis. Streets 4 and 5 have not been found, but street 6, 7m wide, appeared in a recent excavation on *Place de la Madeleine* (Gantès 2013). Finally, street 7 was excavated on the Eastern rim of the Pistoles block, under the former *Rue des Pistoles*. The framework thus defined remains quite partial and still contains many uncertainties.

The date of the streets unearthed is sometimes uncertain. Only street 7 is dated with certainty from the sixth century BC. Street C is dated around the Cathedral at the fifth century and *Place des Pistoles* at the Hellenistic time, streets E and 2 in Roman times. We should not be disturbed: the network of the streets is certainly archaic, even if the preserved states are generally the most recent.

The spacing of the North-South streets is more difficult to appreciate. I suggested a few years ago that the blocks *Place des Pistoles* were approx. 22m in width (Tréziny 2001b, 141), but this measure today seems improbable, the spacing of the street allegedly in the West of the block being in fact covered with a mosaic of Roman time (*CAG Marseille*, 484). The single sector where a precise assessment can be made today is that of the Cathedral de La Major. There is indeed a distance of approx. 16.40m between street 2 found in the excavation of the *Esplanade de La Major* (Paone 2013, 27) and the medial axis of the Eastern block more Eastward (*CAG Marseille*, 431–432), which implies a block width of approximately 32.80m between streets 2 and 3 and an average interaxial distance of 36.80m (assuming a constant width for the streets). Towards the West, this dimension is more or less valid for the spacing of streets 1 and 2.

The new North-South *rue* (called 6 by me) excavated on *Place de la Madeleine* has an atypical width of approx. 7m, only the Western part of which was dedicated to road traffic. The Eastern half seems to have had a cultural use, but the Eastern wall would lie 32m away from street 7 (Gantès 2013, 24–25), which corresponds to the previous module. Between both these sectors, the distance between streets 2 and 7 (approx. 200m, streets included) might correspond to 5 interaxial distance of approx. 40m (for 4m wide streets), 5 blocks of 36m, which appears excessive. We must therefore imagine that one of streets 3 to 5 was much wider, probably the *Rue de l'Evêché* which plays a particular role between the *Place de Lenche* (ancient agora?) and the future *Porte Galle*.

We shall add that these assessments are always difficult. First of all because, if the system is undoubtedly regular and orthogonal in its principle, it might be less so when considering the detail of its layout on a rather undulating and sometimes craggy landscape; then because it is only known by very limited excavations between which extrapolations are delicate; finally because we know street layouts of quite variable dates and the facade realignments may have modified the street layout slightly with the course of time. We shall therefore not try to specify the dimension of the plots which occupy half a block each, even less to propose a metrological interpretation. But we shall observe that the ratio between the North-South length of the blocks (67.50m) and their width (around 32/32.80m) is quite close to 2, which implies that they are extremely stocky.

In the Greek West, the blocks of the archaic cities are quite elongated, *per strigas* to use the traditional language. The dimensions are quite variable according to the sites and the periods, but have variable widths, between 22/25m for the oldest (Syracuse, Megara Hyblaea around the end of the eighth century) and some forty metres (Syracuse in the fourth century), and lengths which are also variable but generally quite significant. The ratio between length and width oscillates between 4 and 8. Particularly charac-teristic are the layouts of cities founded during the sixth century, such as Poseidonia, an Achean colony founded around 600 (8:1); Agrigento, a sub-colony of Gela, founded around 580 (7:1); Neaples founded around 500 (ratio 5:1). To find ratios comparable to those of Marseille, we had to wait for the fifth century and the construction of Thourioi whose layout is attributed to Hippodamos of Miletus (a ratio around 1.5:1) and the fourth century with the foundation of Tyndaris on the Northern coast of Sicily (2.5:1).

I have therefore suggested (Tréziny 2006a, Tréziny 2006b), and shall not come back to it in detail, that the archaic layout of Marseille might be an illustration of the town-planning of the archaic Ionian cities (Phocaea, Miletus, Ephesus) still quite poorly known, which would explain the apparent coincidence between the module of Marseille and that of Thourioi.

Managing Public Areas

Another peculiarity of the Marseille town planning is the rarity, if not the absence, of public edifices and notably of sanctuaries. We shall set aside the place of worship of the *Rue Négrel*, with its *naïskoi* with feminine representa-tions whose significance has long been debated (*infra*, 184). We are dealing anyway with a suburban sanctuary, outside the first city-wall. We only have literary mentions from the sanctuaries properly speaking, as well as a few hardly explicit and votive objects or deposits and a great limestone capital[6]. The existence of ancient places of worship below the medieval churches, often postulated by the *Antiquaires*, is not demonstrated.

Still, the recent excavations have put in evidence complex situations which can be recovered, I think, in this direction. It is first of all the excavation of the forecourt of the Saint-Laurent church which has delivered remnants of houses with the elevation of adobes of the first quarter of the sixth century. These relatively well preserved houses seemed abandoned from the second quarter of the century and backfilled. In Roman times, a large retaining wall perhaps supported the podium of a temple replaced in the twelfth century by the current church. Although no particularly votive object has been found in the embankments, we shall assume that a small place of worship was situated in the North of the habitat of the first quarter of the sixth century. The latter is enlarged during the sixth century as the result of large earthworks which have protected the oldest remains (Fig. 3a).

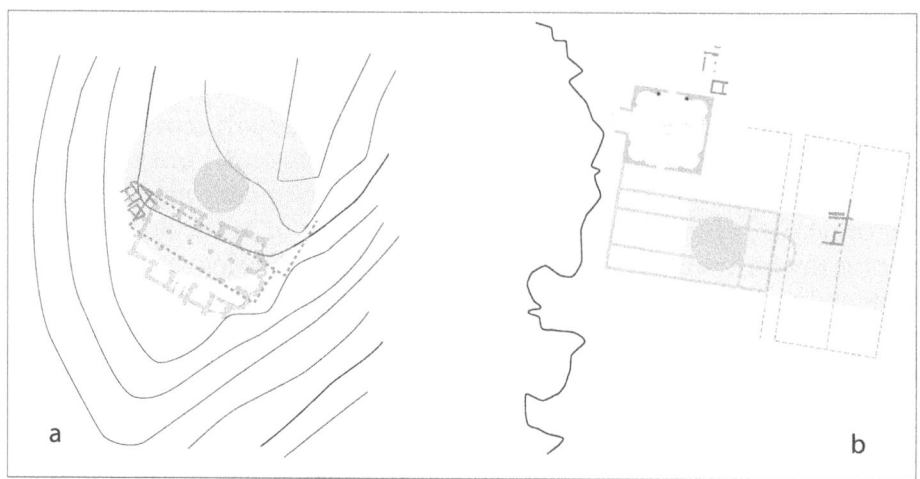

Figure 3. Hypothetical development of the sanctuaries of the sixth century BC (a) below the Saint-Laurent church; (b) below the church de La Major. In white, paleo-Christian or medieval structures; in black, Archaic walls; in grey, Roman walls; extension of sanctuaries in flat dark and light grey.

A comparable situation can be found below the cathedral of La Major, in the light of the excavations of the *Tunnel de La Major*. The block situated in the East of the church, on the highest spot of the relief, has preserved a habitat of the second quarter of the sixth century apparently abandoned before the end of the century. The most recent remains, if they existed, have been completely razed. In the North and in the South, in lower coasts, remains of Classic, then Hellenistic and especially Roman times rest on the substrate, but the Archaic levels have disappeared. The sole logical explanation for this astonishing observation is that this part of the habitation pocket has been expropriated to leave room for an extension of the temenos which was probably situated below the Vieille Major, for instance at the time of the construction of a new temple and/or of a new altar which were more monumental (Fig. 3b).

These are only hypotheses, but they find support in the situation of Velia at the end of the Archaic time. We know that the oldest sanctuaries of the acropolis of Velia (probably dedicated to Hera and Athena Polias) had a relatively limited extension, immediately in the North of the habitat, so-called polygonal village. It is at the beginning of the fifth century around 480 that the polygonal village was abandoned and backfilled, as the same time as the construction of a long retaining wall with large rectangular stones which enables the widening of the temenos. Extension of the temenos and abandonment of a dwelling quarter are contemporary, in Velia as in Marseille, of a considerable enlargement of the urban space.

This type of development of the urban space constitutes an analogy between Velia and Marseille, which opposes these "Ionian" cities to the Achaean cities of the Magna Graecia (Metaponto, Poseidonia), wherein the public space occupies all at once a very important position in the centre of the city. Of course, the extension of public space at the expense of private space can be also found in Sicilian colonies of Doric origin, such as Megara Hyblaea, in the South of the agora, or Syracuse, in the sector of the Ionian temple, but in lesser proportions.

Emporion or apoikia?

Compared to its sister (or daughter) Empuries, Marseille at the beginning was often designated as an emporion, which was to become a city only around the end of the sixth century[7]. In a voluntarily polemic formulation, Fr. Villard proposed a few years later to consider Massalia as a conventional colonial foundation, an *apoikia*, which only from the middle of the sixth century adjoined to the city "a high-class *emporion*". Everything is obviously a question of definition, and if the economy of Marseille is based on the *emporia* without any mistake, it seems difficult to consider it as an *emporion* on a par with Naucratis, Gravisca or the *emporion* of the Palaiapolis of Empuries[8]. If an *emporion* is a small-sized site, with a limited population, installed on the edge of an "indigenous" habitat (regardless whether Egyptian, Etruscan or Iberian), deprived of its own territory, then Greek Marseille, extending as soon as at the beginning of the sixth century over some twenty hectares cannot be qualified thus. This does not prevent the prosperity of the city from being founded to a vast extent on the maritime exchanges and on the *emporia*; there might have been a port space in the city, which could be called an *emporion*. But the town itself is first of all a city, a colony, an *apoikia*, three vocables which are diversely fashionable, but which express for me more or less the same thing.

We could add today to François Villard's argument a better knowledge of the town-planning of Archaic Marseille. The delimitation in the urban space of Marseille of an orthogonal registered space probably assumes, here as somewhere else in the colonial world, a urban building process, even if it is still difficult to put these blocks in evidence. This plot was made available for the delimitation of urban blocks, *oikopeda* whose surface area should not exceed 100 to 200m², the space necessary for the construction of a house, also probably implies, as admitted by most commentators, the land division of a rural space around the city. Reduced at first, this territory extends quite rapidly, obviously to the detriment of the indigenous populations, which causes conflicts echoed by the literary tradition (Justin, XLIII, 4: Livy, V, 34), and the archaeological documentation starts to provide evidence thereof [9]

As an "Ionian" thus, probably in the beginning, then "Phocaean" city, Marseille comes across as a colonial city of the Western Mediterranean region, which does not disown its Western origins nor its trading vocation, but is integrated perfectly in the *koine* of the colonial Western Greek world.

Notes

1. Aristote, *Constitution of the Massaliots* (= Athenaeus, XIII, 576); Strabo, IV, 1, 4; Justin, 43, 3–5. The ancient texts of the origins of Marseille have often been gathered, for example (in translation) in the appendix to the volume *Marseille grecque* (1999, 167–178) or the chapter IVB of the *CAG Marseille* (2005, 145–159). Among the numerous discussions, let us quote Pralon 1992, Bats 1994, Gras 1995, Morel 2006, Malkin 2011, Garcia, Bouffier, *supra*, 53–74.
2. For the topography of the city, we shall refer systematically to volume 13/3 of the *Carte archéologique de la Gaule* (*CAG Marseille*) by completing it with other references for the discoveries after 2004.
3. On Athena in Marseille, Tréziny 2000, 85; Hermary 2000.
4. About this construction, Hesnard et al. 2001 (quay), Tréziny 2001a (rampart).
5. Gantès 1992, 8; measure taken on the excavation of the Pistoles between streets B and C. For street A, *CAG Marseille*, p. 485.
6. On the cults of Marseille in general, cf Hermary, Tréziny 2000, Hermary, *infra*, 181–190.
7. Arcelin 1986, 47: "the ancient *emporion* became a *polis* as of the end of the 6th century".
8. On the definition of the *emporion*, cf. Bresson, Rouillard 1993.
9. The site of *Marseilleveyre* in the South might have been abandoned as soon as in the middle of the sixth century, then construction of the rampart of the Baou de Saint-Marcel in the East (second quarter of the sixth century?), construction in the North (around 530?) of the fortification of the Mayans, soon to be abandoned.

Bibliography

Arcelin, P., 1986, Le territoire de Marseille grecque dans son contexte indigène. In: M. Bats & H. Tréziny (eds.), *Le territoire de Marseille grecque*. Aix-en-Provence, Université de Provence, 43–104 (Et. Massa., 1).

Bats, M., 1994, Les silences d'Hérodote ou Marseille, Alalia et les Phocéens en Occident jusqu'à la fondation de Vélia. In: B. D'Agostino & D. Ridgway (eds.), *APOIKIAI. I più antichi insediamenti greci in Occidente*. Naples, 133–148.

Bouiron, M. & Mellinand, Ph., 2013, *Quand les archéologues redécouvrent Marseille*. Paris, Gallimard/Inrap, 2013, 174p.

Bresson, A. & Rouillard, P. (eds.), 1993, *L'Emporion*. Bordeaux, Centre Pierre Paris, 1993, 248p.

Dominguez, A.J., 2000, Phocaeans and the Ionians in Western Mediterranean. In: F.Krinzinger (ed.), Die Ägäis und das westliche Mittelmeer. Beziehungen und Wechselwirkungen 8. bis 5. Jh. v. Chr., actes du colloque de Vienne, 1999. Vienne, 2000, 507–513.

Gantès, L.-Fr., 1992, La topographie de Marseille grecque. Bilan des recherches. In: M. Bats, G. Bertucchi, G. Congès & H. Tréziny (eds.), *Marseille grecque et la Gaule*. Lattes-Aix-en-Provence, Adam éditions, 71–88 (Et. Massa., 3).

Gantès, L.-Fr., 2013, Les fouilles de la place de l'îlot Madeleine, *Archéothéma* 29, juillet–août 2013, 24–25.

Gras, M., 1995, L'arrivée d'immigrés à Marseille au milieu du VIe s. av. J.-C. In: P. Arcelin et al. (eds.), *Sur les pas des Grecs en Occident*. Lattes-Paris, Adam éditions, 363–366 (Et. Massa., 4).

Hermary, A., 2000, De la mère des dieux à Cybèle et Artémis: les ambiguïtés de l'iconographie grecque archaïque. In: *Agathos daimon. Mythes et cultes. Études d'iconographie en l'honneur de Lily Kahil*. Athènes, EFA, 193–203 (*BCH,* suppl. 38).

Hermary, A. & Tréziny, H. (eds.), 2000, *Les cultes des cités phocéennes*. Lattes/Aix-en-Provence, Adam éditions, 220p. (Et. Massa., 4).

Hesnard, A., Bernardi, Ph. & Maurel, Chr., 2001, La topographie du port de Marseille de la fondation de la cité à la fin du Moyen Âge. In: M. Bouiron et al., *Marseille: trames et paysages urbains de Gyptis au Roi René*. Lattes/Aix-en-Provence, Adam éditions, 159–202 (Et. Massa., 7).

Malkin, I., 1990, Missionnaires païens dans la Gaule grecque. In: I. Malkin (ed.), *La France et la Méditerranée. Vingt-sept siècles d'interdépendance*. Leyde, 40–42.

Malkin, I., 2011, *A Small Greek World. Networks in the Ancient Mediterranean*. Oxford, 304p.

Mellinand, Ph., Sillano, B., Tréziny, H. & Weydert, N., 2007, Marseille grecque. Découverte de nouveaux vestiges emblématiques, *Archéopages*, 20, 20–25.

Mellinand, Ph., 2013, Le bâtiment romain de l'Hôtel-Dieu, *Archéothéma* 29, juillet–août 2013, 24–25.

Morel, J.-P., 2006, Phocaean colonization. In: G. Tsetskhladze (ed.), *Greek Colonization: An Account of Greek Colonies and Other Settlements Overseas*. Leyde, 358–328.

Paone, Fr., 2013, Les découvertes antiques sur le site de l'Esplanade Major, *Archéothéma,* 29, juillet–août 2013, 26–27.

Parcours de ville: A. Hesnard, M. Moliner, F. Conche & M. Bouiron, 1999, *Parcours de villes. Marseille: 10 ans d'archéologie, 2600 ans d'histoire*. Marseille, Musées de Marseille, 178p.

Pralon, D., 1992, La légende de la fondation de Marseille. In: M. Bats, G. Bertucchi, G. Congès & H. Tréziny (eds.), *Marseille grecque et la Gaule*. Lattes-Aix-en-Provence, Adam éditions, 51–56 (Et. Massa., 3).

Rothé, M.-P. & Tréziny, H. (eds.), 2005, *Carte Archéologique de la Gaule*, vol. 13/3, *Marseille et ses environs*. Paris, AIBL, 925p.

Salviat, Fr., 1992, Sur la religion de Marseille grecque. In: M. Bats, G. Bertucchi, G. Congès & H. Tréziny (eds.), *Marseille grecque et la Gaule*. Lattes-Aix-en-Provence, Adam éditions, 141–150 (Et. Massa., 3).

Tréziny, H., 2000, Les lieux de culte dans Marseille grecque. In: A. Hermary & H. Tréziny (eds.), *Les cultes des cités phocéennes*. Lattes/Aix-en-Provence, Adam éditions, 81–99 (Et. Massa., 4).

Tréziny, H., 2001a, Les fortifications de Marseille dans l'Antiquité. In: M. Bouiron et al., *Marseille: trames et paysages urbains de Gyptis au Roi René*. Lattes/Aix-en-Provence, Adam éditions, 41–57 (Et. Massa., 7).

Tréziny, H., 2001b, Trames et orientations dans la ville antique: lots et îlots. In: M. Bouiron et al., *Marseille: trames et paysages urbains de Gyptis au Roi René*. Lattes/Aix-en-Provence, Adam éditions, 137–147 (Et. Massa., 7).

Tréziny, H., 2006a, Marseille et Vélia, villes ioniennes. In: *Velia. Atti del 45° Convegno di Studi sulla Magna Grecia, Sett. 2005*. Tarente, 507–531.

Tréziny, H., 2006b, L'urbanisme archaïque des villes ioniennes: un point de vue occidental. In: O. Mariaud (ed.), *L'Ionie pré-classique: territoire et organisation de l'espace*. Bordeaux, 225–247 (= *REA* 108).

Villard, Fr., 1992, La céramique archaïque de Marseille. In: M. Bats, G. Bertucchi, G. Congès & H. Tréziny (eds.), *Marseille grecque et la Gaule*. Lattes-Aix-en-Provence, Adam éditions, 163–170 (Et. Massa., 3).

8. At the Frontiers of Massalian Territory: Greek and Indigenous Rhythms from the Seventh to Second Century BC

Loup Bernard, Sophie Bouffier and Delphine Isoardi

The cove of *Vieux Port*, where the Phocaeans settled in the late seventh century BC, is inserted into a coastal plain of 180Km², watered by the Huveaune, descending from the plain of Aubagne to the East, and its tributary the Jarret, and by the course of the Aygalades descending from the North of the basin. The peculiarity of this relatively fertile alluvial plain lies in that it is fairly closed and protected from within, because it is surrounded by hilly mountains, that of Nerthe in the North, of l'Etoile and the Garlaban in the Northeast, of Carpiagne, of St. Cyr and of Marseilleveyre in the South. Its only easy opening towards the hinterland lies in the East at the Penne sur-Huveaune, towards the plain of Aubagne, the natural receptacle of the Huveaune (Fig. 1), and point of outlet towards the Inland communities. This territory represents the natural area of Marseille, which can be operated according to the economic guidelines of the Greek city.

The birth of Marseille had the opportunity but also the misfortune to have a legend of foundation that has guided or permanently blinded historiography (few Greek colonial foundations are in this case) by focusing on this key moment that could have been represented by the arrival of the Phocaeans in the cove of *Vieux Port*. To sum up, chaos reigned before Protis and the arrival of the Greeks would be the starting point of a political, social, economic and cultural structuring of the plain of the Huveaune. Without denying the contribution of the founding texts of Marseille, the passages of Aristotle (in Athenaeus *Deipnosophists*, XIII 576) or of Justin (XLIII. 3–4) who have already been the subject of many analyses and interpretations (see *supra* Bouffier & Garcia), we chose to give up this angle of attack to focus on the results of

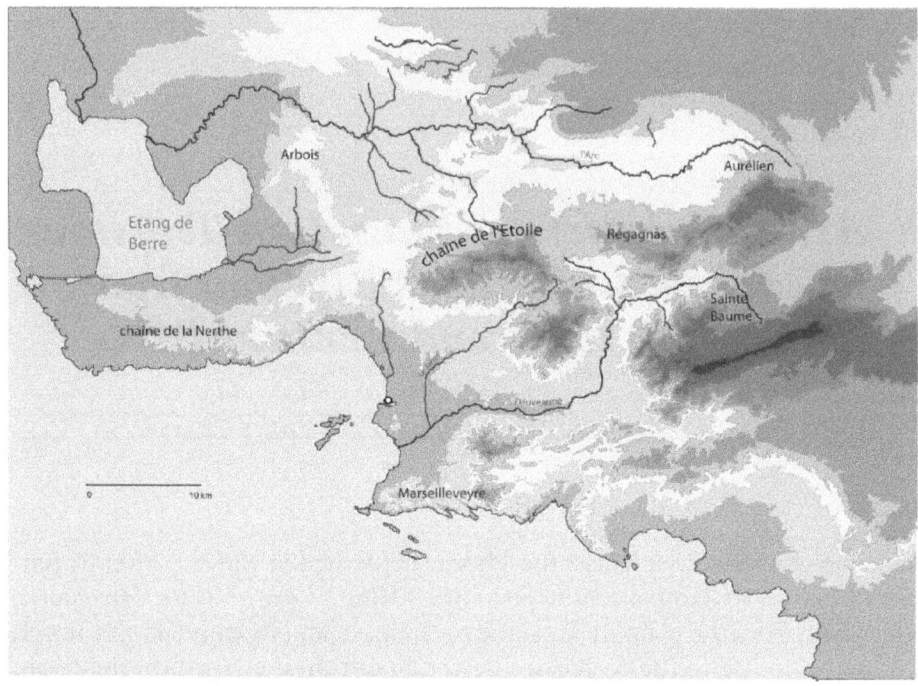

Figure 1. Marseille basin (H. Tréziny).

archaeological research for more than ten years on the Marseille basin and
to propose an updated reading of the terroir of the Phocaean city since its
foundation until the first century BC. To do this, the recent excavations of
Roc de la Croix and of *Marseilleveyre,* of *La Tourette,* the surveys of the massifs of Marseilleveyre and Carpiagne, and the study of their furniture were
incorporated into a broader, historical, and archaeo-demographic framework
associated with a territorial and geographic analysis.

Methodological and Epistemological Questions: How to Apprehend the Knowledge of the Marseille Territory

Although the Marseille area was one of the longest addressed thanks to
inventories and surveys of the nineteenth century (Villeneuve-Bargemon
1829; Gilles 1876 Saurel 1877–1878;), sites of local excavations discovered at the same time (Clastrier 1910; Vasseur 1914; Bout de Charlemont
1913; Gérin-Ricard 1934), it stayed away from major debates and scientific
programs that spurred research on the Greek territories in the twentieth
century (see the synthesis of the Taranto Symposium 2000: *Problemi* 2001)

and the historiography of the Phocaean city suffers in comparison with that of other colonial cities, particularly in southern Italy and in the Black Sea, while Marseille has played an important role in the history of Greek expansion in the Mediterranean as well as in the construction of the French or Provençal identity.

The first synthesis was erected in 1985 at the symposium "Le territoire de Marseille" *(Etudes Massaliètes* 1, 1986) before the effort focused on the excavation of Celtic sites and of the Greek city itself that produce new inventories after the year 2000. The publication of the volume of the *Carte Archéologique de la Gaule,* devoted to Marseille and its surroundings in 2005 (Rothé & Tréziny 2005) provides researchers with a reasoned catalogue of the sites listed on this date, but especially the interpretations of P. Boissinot on the ancient vineyard (Boissinot 2001; 2005; 2010) have enabled progress concretely on the issues of *chôra.* The recent survey campaigns as well as the samplings conducted on sites that may be known but never investigated, resulted in a first synthesis on the expansion of the Phocaeans from the cove of *Vieux Port* and their relationships with the surrounding populations in 2010 (Bernard, Collin Bouffier & Tréziny 2010). We plan to update it in light of the work that we have carried out in the basin of Huveaune in recent years.

To reflect on the identification of Marseille soils and of the native soils over time, and how they can meet or mingle, different approaches have been tried, but the scarcity of archaeological markers limits our analysis attempts. The state of the documentation of the Marseille basin, including its modern acceptance, is indeed very incomplete due to the dense urbanisation and has seen rare preventive operations. Thus, the *chôra* appears only through a few windows opened by recent excavations on the work of expressways, tram or subway. Older research on the hilltop site had focused on topics related to the presence of indigenous people and their settlement patterns: we have particularly sought, possibly inventoried, grouped fortified dwellings. Only certain sectors have been the subject of further research, generally related to the activity of a researcher as was the case around the Baou-Roux and the work of P. Boissinot (Boissinot 1993) or it is the prominence of a site which stimulated research into its surroundings, as is the case for *Saint-Marcel* (Gantès 2014). We should also mention here the old knowledge of the so-called cultual caves of the massif of Marseilleveyre and the work of P. Vasseur (Vasseur 1914) and P. Agostini (Agostini 1965, 1967). These areas are generally over-represented compared to other areas, some of which had never been the subject of systematic research hitherto. The archaeological documentation considered here essentially comprises the sites listed in the

Carte Archéologique de Marseille, published in 2005; we added the results of surveys and excavations conducted since 2000 (2000–2008: Collin Bouffier 2009; Bernard, Collin Bouffier et al. 2006, 2007, 2008, 2010, 2011; D'Ovidio 2014; Bouffier, Bernard & Isoardi 2015). Le *Projet Collectif de Recherches,* funded by the Archaeological Service of Provence-Alpes—Côte d'Azur has tried to target the margins of the current city: lower slopes and nearby hills, best preserved but inaccessible. The prospection could not be systematic since legibility is variable and generally poor in the scrubland. This research raises questions relating to erosion and is currently being studied. They were then focused on the hills, located a little further back, even though we were aware that the investigation of the plain itself would have informed us better about the modes of territorial occupation and exploitation of the Phocaeans. We have tried to grasp the concept of spatial rhythm of the occupation of Marseille basin, through the maps offered here and which represent a first cumulative state of maps generated at the end of the last century and over the last decade. These should indeed be understood as a stock-taking of the state of research and the reading proposals on the territories of the Massaliots and of the Celtic-Ligurians. These materials highlight the strengths (at least those we identify as such)—and the questions that remain unanswered.

Birth of a Greek Chôra

The emergence of a Greek city, in the Aegean world and in the Mediterranean regions gradually occupied by the Greeks, is accompanied by the acquisition of a geographic space, designed to accommodate both human and civic community, but also to ensure its supplies, as modelled by the political theorists in the fifth and fourth century BC (Plato, *Laws,* 745b Aristotle, *Politics,* 1326b, VII.5; 1330a, VII. 7–8). The demarcation of this area resulted in many border wars between the eighth and the sixth century BC (thus between Argos and the different cities of the Argolid that it eventually absorbed or between Corinth and Megara: De Polignac, 1995, 64–78) forcing the defeated cities to look for other ways to ensure the survival of their population, including through recourse to emigration overseas. Although the phenomenon of Greek expansion is more complex than a simple transfer of individuals seeking to solve problems of *stenochoria*—narrowness of land—of the original community, the foundation of an *apoikia* (contingent situated away from the house) involves installing in a geographical area that historiography, following the model of the metropolitan city, distinguished into two areas, separated in a second stage by fortifications:

the urban space, which becomes the centre of main political bodies and territory, the *chôra*. The latter can be defined or confined by markers, whether religious, extra-urban sanctuaries for printing the presence of the Greek community in the landscape (as the sanctuary of the *Tavole Palatine* in Metaponto or the Olympieion in Syracuse) or to mark the border of this *chôra* (as the Heraion of Sele in Poseidonia); military, forts or *phrouria* evoked by the texts but seldom identified for colonial areas (e.g., Sicily, see Collin Bouffier 2011, 79). The definition of the territory also distinguished between near territory and area of influence. The first is the survival soil, generally understood as a work area, accessible on foot or using transport animals within a time that allows round-trip between the place of residence and the field. It is generally dedicated to food polyculture as highlighted by recent work (Brunet 2001): cereals, fruit trees (including olive trees and vines), and legumes. Under the colonial foundations, this zoning calls for placing at the heart of the debate the relationships between Greeks and local populations, relationships whose peaceful or conflictual character may structure the geopolitical evolution of a region.

In the case of Marseille, historiography, based on the texts of Strabo or Justin, considered non-operative this definition of territorial space and emphasised the maritime expansion of the Massaliots (Bats 2001). Indeed, both authors of the Roman epoch highlight the maritime and commercial vocation of the Phocaeans. According to Justin (43.3), "The Phocaeans, forced by the aridity of their territory to engage in activities rather on sea than on land, lived off fishing and trade and even piracy which at that time was held glorious" and their descendants, "The Massaliots occupy an area planted with olive trees and covered with vines but poor in cereals because of its aridity, to the extent they relied more on sea than on land. They preferred to benefit from their gifts for navigation-related trades" (Strabo, *Geography, IV,* 1.5). The city would even have given birth to more or less mythical explorers such as Pytheas and its predecessor Euthymenes. The ancient texts have thus shaped a canvass of territorial organisation, marked by milestones: the founding of a city by the Greeks on a space allocated by a native king Nanos, a limited *chôra*, planted with vines and olive at least in the first century BC, rich and often troubled relationships with the surrounding Celts in the second half of the sixth century BC, first with the war against the successor of King Nanos and in the fourth century BC, the conflict with King Catumandus, only known events of these conflicts which would have punctuated the history of the Greek city going by the statements of ancient historians. But these relations especially emphasise the value ascribed by the Massaliots, yet considered first as seamen, to the possession of the fostering and wealth-producing land.

The Major Times of the Massaliot Space

Before the Founding of Marseille
(Late Bronze Age, from 725 to 600)

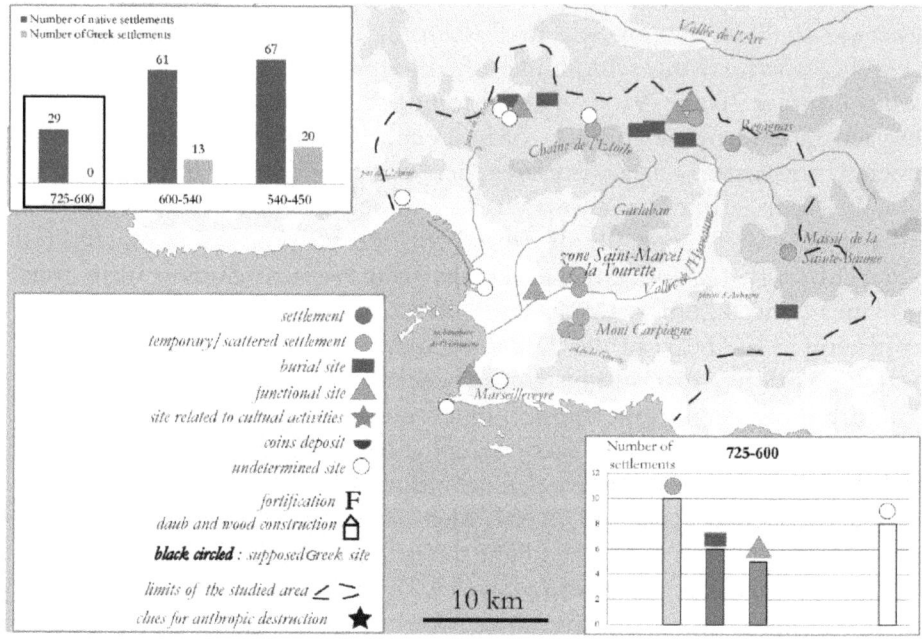

Figure 2. Greek and Native settlements in Marseille basin during 725–600 BC (D. Isoardi).

The date of the end of the seventh century BC, if widely attested by archaeology (including through the datings in the ancient levels of the first port, ceramics facies which are related or not shown) permeates the minds of the researchers who tend to see therein a *terminus ante quem,* where local populations would then switch from a status of "primitive" societies characteristic of a Final Bronze Age or a *facies suspendien* which remain poorly defined for the Marseille region from those of "chiefdoms" which remain to be defined more precisely (Garcia 2014, 51).

This first phase raises many problems of readability to archaeologists, who lack characterisations for dwellings not searched or searched too far away in time, the dating of sites is loose and the state of the research limited. In fact, this pivotal phase between the end of the Bronze Age and the full Iron Age was ignored by research in recent decades. If the Mailhacian facies is now well known for the Languedoc, and the fields of urns or the Hallstatt C are the subject of much Northern work, the Marseille Provence in particular and the Provençal research in general still hesitate to recognise this period. The habitat, which does not use stone building techniques, also leaves few traces in the landscape and can be spotted by search only; ceramics can be easily confused with other forms of dating which can vary from late prehistory to the Middle Ages; finally, metal furniture has been approached recently only (Beylier 2012). The corollary of this fact is that even with a wide range time (125 years instead of half-centuries usually considered) we argue here about twenty small representative sites. The best studied site is that of the Baou-Roux which was. Boissinot's Phd subject (Boissinot 1993): it is characterised for that period by an unfortified construction of perishable materials, but it is probably more representative of Provençal than coastal villages.

The question of a settlement or of a native habitat just before the arrival of the Greeks on the future site of Massalia remains open. Apart from the discovery of a fossilised shore of the period during preventive operations, very few pieces are known: a wristband from the end of the seventh century to the first quarter of the sixth century BC from the excavations carried out on the *Place Villeneuve-Bargemon* (Arcelin 1999, 20; Bernard, Collin Bouffier & Tréziny 2010); a few vases prior to 600 BC on the Place Villeneuve-Bargemon (Rothé & Tréziny 2005, 375). The digging of the tunnel of the Major has allowed archaeologists to uncover post holes, but which have not been studied and therefore are not datable. A grave, dated by radiocarbon between the beginning of the eighth century and the third quarter of the seventh century BC (Rothé & Tréziny 2005, 432) was discovered in the same area, but the possibility of a Greek protocolonial tomb cannot be excluded. In all cases, Marseille does not seem to have been an important site before the arrival of the Phocaeans.

On the study area that interests us in this section (Fig. 2), the sites are very rare. The surveys and samples of recent years have revealed a set of small habitats, not very distant from each other around the future site of *Saint-Marcel* and of *La Tourette* (Gantès 2014). Traces of human impact or culture(?) are also recognised, particularly at the source of *Saint-Jean-du-Désert* where a moated network of the late Bronze Age or the early Iron Age was observed (Rothé & Tréziny 2005, 719–720) and interpreted as a trace of deforestation. Some habitats situated in the reliefs bordering Marseille *(L'Étoile,* Regagnas, *Sainte-Baume)* were researched but the earliest levels are difficult to read. Tombs are also reported, but these are old excavations.

The important sites in the area are just as difficult to grasp: *Saint-Blaise* seems to have exerted an influence during this phase of the first direct contacts between Greeks and local populations. It is interesting to note here that this meeting phase is hardly reflected in Southern furnishings: where are diplomatic gifts offered in the context of hospitality and friendship links established by the Phocaeans? These various "leaders" do not seem to differ fundamentally in terms of equipment and social level from those of the Alps or the rest of Europe (Beylier 2012 for weapons; Bernard & Roure 2010) as shown e.g. by furniture mounds, from the Luberon to the *Sainte-Victoire* or the *Sainte-Baume*. Note that they are set back from the coast and deliver more Etruscan than Greek furniture (*oinochoai*, pearled basins: cf. Bouloumié 1990a, 1990b, 1990c; Bouloumié & Lagrand 1977).

The littoral area does not seem attractive to natives before the foundation of Marseille. In the present state of research, the sites are rather on the hill tops and located inland (like the Baou Roux in the North for example), the need for grouping or fortification is not blatant, which obviously does not contribute to the recognition of the sites by archaeologists. On the location of Marseille, occupancy seems sporadic at best and sites such as those of the *Roc de la Croix* or Caronte (Gateau, Trément & Verdin 1996, 226) enable us to get an idea of the habitat at these periods.

The fact that we have a limited overview of the forms of habitat should not encourage us to see in this period a primitive golden age, in which egalitarian Segobriges would have led a peaceful life. The tombs reflect a hierarchy and a strong social stratification: some of them contain weapons (Beylier 2012) and are integrated into the world of Celtic Hallstatt C, although largely in the periphery of the phenomenon. In the Hallstattian world as in Provence, the following period is better known to archaeologists.

The foundation of Marseille by Phocaeans is attested archaeologically by many elements. Without wishing to list an inventory specifically, the development of sites can be observed in connection with this new settlement in the coastal plain (thirteen sites in total). Are we dealing with small habitats or already agricultural structures? The question remains open. We must also mention here the occupancy of some caves of the massif of Marseilleveyre: The shelters of the *Font de Voire* and the Cave of *L'Ours* might have been occupied, but these are old excavations and the furniture is poorly characterised in spite of the work of A. Marsolat in 2005 (Bouffier, Bernard & Isoardi 2015).

The Foundation of Greek Marseille and the Installation of the Phocaeans (600–540/530): What Impact on the Natives?

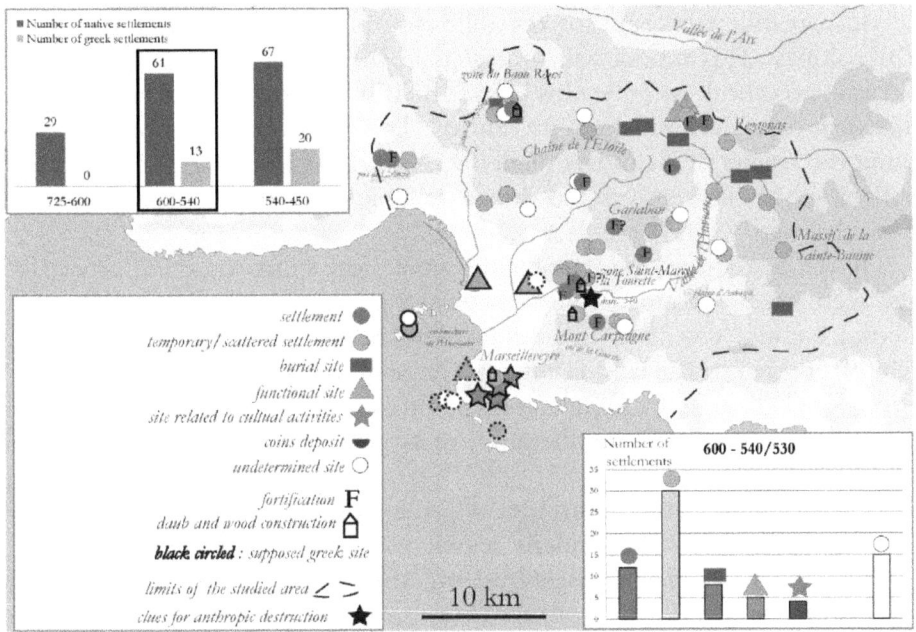

Figure 3. Greek and Native settlements in Marseille basin during 600–540 BC (D. Isoardi).

Regarding intramural Marseille, two elements are noteworthy: the construction techniques that have been observed in the islet of the *Cathédrale* during a rescue show a first phase dating back to around 600–580 on a field void of any anterior implantation. The habitat is implanted as a loose frame in two small buildings on structural columns, with a rectangular plane (6.70 × 5 m, oriented North-South and East-West) identified. This is a domestic site that has produced hearths as ashy lenses, metallurgical activities as well as wells (lastly, Bouiron et al. 2001). We note, in Marseille, the joint use of construction techniques of perishable materials with solid buildings at that time, without the possibility to propose a differentiation between the function and the occupants of these buildings—we could consider Celtic-Ligurians in buildings on posts, or else barns in connection with Greek solid habitats, even a temporary habitat stage pending a permanent structure.

The other notable element is the rapid clogging of the port that has allowed the preservation of the very first levels. This phenomenon has been the subject of precise and innovative work under the direction of Chr. Morhange

(Morhange et al. 1998) and clearly indicates the human impact on the environment. Indeed, the clearing and the erection of a city of several dozen hectares and turning its *chôra* into vineyards (also attested by excavations at the *Alcazar*, but especially for the following period) led to strong erosion of the slopes. This model will be tested in the future in the watershed of Huveaune to check whether this impact is visible in the plain of Marseille or whether it only concerns the "city centre". This work can be realised by combining the results of diagnoses made by the Institut National de Recherches Archéologiques Préventives and the geographic data and by linking them to known habitats.

On the Segobrige side, habitats become more numerous, and especially they seem to be grouped. Nevertheless, a population increase cannot be inferred because you have to bear in mind that the development of stone architecture tied to the land facilitates a reading in surveys as well as in excavations of these sites by archaeologists and it should not be seen as a systematic link between the proliferation of known sites and the expansion of settlements.

How to interpret the occurrence of grouped settlement sites, surrounded by small satellite sites, particularly legible on the "lock of the Huveaune" (D'Ovidio 2014)? The *Saint-Marcel* site thus seems to crystallise several "indigenous farms". The reasons for these groupings/travels/installations of Celtic populations at the fringes of the city have not been proven yet. Are we dealing with day labourers approaching the city, wine merchants serving as relays to the hinterland, or farmers seeking an outlet for their surplus? In all cases, the choice of implanting sites on the heights raises a number of questions that should not make us forget, however, that the current extension of Marseille certainly masks lowland sites.

These Celtic-Ligurian habitats are built using mixed techniques, the stone appeared, but as *Saint Marcel* as well as *Marseilleveyre*, houses on structural columns are attested (D'Ovidio & Rothé 2005, 699–716). On the site of Tamaris for example, the first brick and mortar houses follow the double apse plan known for the prior brick and mortar period over a short contemporary phase (Duval 1998). Nevertheless, the oldest levels, especially for older excavations, are difficult to date precisely in the sixth century BC.

In the present state of research, at least four settlements can be assumed around the Phocaean city (Fig. 3): the *château des Aygalades* and *Collet-Redon* in the North, sectors poorly identified by older work; the zone of the *Baou-Roux* in the North-West and the sector of *La Cloche* to the West; in the East, the

Tourette—Saint-Marcel, the massif of Saint-Cyr—Carpiagne and in the South, the massif of Marseilleveyre. Some of them disappeared in the next period.

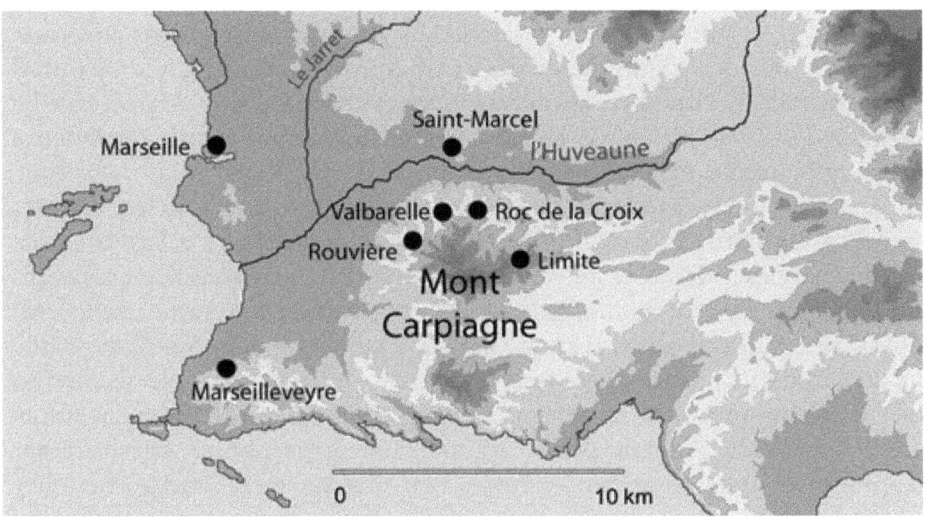

Figure 4. Settlements of the south-eastern zone of the Marseille basin (H. Tréziny).

At the entrance of Huveaune, in the coastal plain, the site on the ridge lines *(Roc de la Croix, Valbarelle)* seem all to overlook the river (Fig. 4 and D'Ovidio 2014; Gantès 2014): should this be seen as a desire for political or territorial claim? The monitoring of herds or the need to seek a natural protection could also explain this choice of perching. On the left bank of the Huveaune and upstream of *Saint-Marcel* in the massif of *Saint-Cyr*, the traces identified by the prospections at the *Mt Rouvière*, at the *Valbarelle*, at the pass of the *Limite* reveal an occupancy still difficult to interpret.

Only the *Roc de la Croix* (Collin Bouffier 2008; Bernard & Garcia 2012; Bernard, Collin Bouffier & Tréziny 2010) and the site of *Marseilleveyre* have been subject to excavations and traces of occupancy attested therein indicate the presence of small habitats, limited in size, nonfortified with constructions of perishable materials, mixed furniture of native ceramic and imported pottery, presence of pebbles that one could interpret as sling bullets, but that may have served for hunting as well as for waging war.

The *Roc de la Croix* site was occupied for half a century at the beginning of the sixth century, and if it has not delivered any structures, the furniture consists of Etruscan and Punic amphorae, of decorated CNT (urns). Imports are mainly Etruscan; counts highlight 75% of CNT out of the total number of fragments, the remainder being composed of imports. The absence of Massaliot productions dates the site in the early sixth century BC. Agricultural activities can be guessed by the presence of grindstone fragments and large containers. The other sites mentioned are hardly datable but could be linked to this period. Eventually, a Gallic synoecism towards Saint Marcel can be considered in a sector that will remain strategic throughout the independence period of Marseille.

The site of *Marseilleveyre* has been the subject of work in recent years (Bouffier, Bernard & Isoardi 2015). Long interpreted as a relatively large oppidum, it has today been re-evaluated and its extension has been reduced. Indeed, what had been interpreted as a bulwark seems rather to correspond to a modern path, resting on a dry stone terrace. Similarly, while the repeated pickups for more than a century on the whole field seemed to refer to a site on a scale of several hectares, and offered a dating window ranging from the Archaic period to the Hellenistic period, the different samplings, conducted at key locations that may have received a sedentary habitat or have captured erosion sediments, have, for now, not confirmed a long-term occupancy, unless these levels are eroded today. In the current situation, the items unearthed allow us to offer an occupancy dated from the sixth century BC mainly by the shards of Etruscan amphora (datable between the late seventh and the early sixth centuries). In terms of unturned ceramic, we note that the identified forms are already present in the Late Bronze Age. We were able to excavate a portion of a house characterised by trenches for palisaded walls and posts with wedging stones to support the roofing. The soil is hardly finished, mud was used extensively, for the walls optionally, bulkheads and possibly the roofing. As the final plan is not yet available, we shall confine ourselves here to clarify that it is an oval plane oriented according to the prevailing wind and implanted on a small plateau of about 1.5 hectares, overlooking the plain of the Huveaune. The presence of two crushed vases (one of them made of cob) and the distribution of ceramic remains have led us to consider the existence of a storage area and differentiated spaces near this oval structure. Thus in one of the search areas, large clusters and alignments of shards, as well as different axes materialised by post holes define placeholders. Finally, in some shards but especially in the reserved areas, at the last scraping, mud plates appeared: are we dealing with large containers collapsed there? With bases for amphoras and dishes? Here we have various external structures that housed domestic activities (CNT or mud dishes, whorl, grinder), and containers for storage, mainly in amphora. The state of conservation of artifacts, crushed, interspersed and burned (without our being able to certify whether it is arson) may demonstrate a destruction layer. These amphorae illustrate the varied panel of trade with the Mediterranean traders in the Archaic period, and probably via Marseille (Fig. 5): Etruscan amphora, probably the Punic and Greek Oriental (Samos-Miletus, Chios and perhaps Clazomenae) sphere, a mortar probably of Phocaean origin and not local, a handle made of *bucchero nero*. In the end, the house being excavated appears to have been built in a period of up to three generations after the foundation of Massalia and instead almost contemporary with the foundation of the city or even slightly earlier, in the Southern limit of its supposed territory and one has to wonder whether it should not be part of a dispersed settlement that our limited investigations could not highlight. Indeed, given the amount of pickups made for more than a century on the plateau, and the number of grindstone fragments, we can venture the hypothesis that many of these houses were located there, in a socio-economic model where the need to regroup, agglomerate or fortify the perimeter was not that pressing. The issue of sedendarity also arises: to what extent are these dwellings sustainable? The absence of animal remains and of analyses currently does not allow us to argue. Testifying to a very likely indigenous occupation, this property stands out by its characteristics (sparsely populated and built with perishable materials), the combination of grouping and fortification then in full swing on contemporary sites such as *St. Blaise* or *Tamaris,* nearby. In fact, rather datable to the early sixth century, the site of *Marseilleveyre* does not differ that much from the overall evolution of habitats in unconsolidated perishable materials. Contemporary of the implementation period of the Phocaean colony around 600 BC and abandoned during the sixth century BC, it can be traced to a transition time, generally speaking, for the protohistorical world. Finally, we may question its purpose: installed at the border of the plain and of the massif, was it facing the plain and its operation? Or was it incorporated in a pastoral form of economy on the hills, because when considering the geographical and hydrological conditions of this coastal massif, the assumption of cereal or even tree farming proves difficult, if not impossible on small plots.

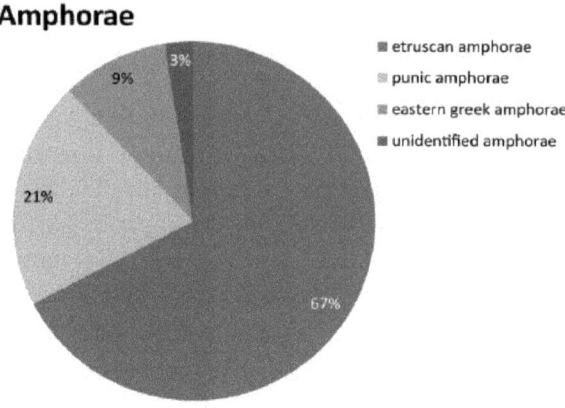

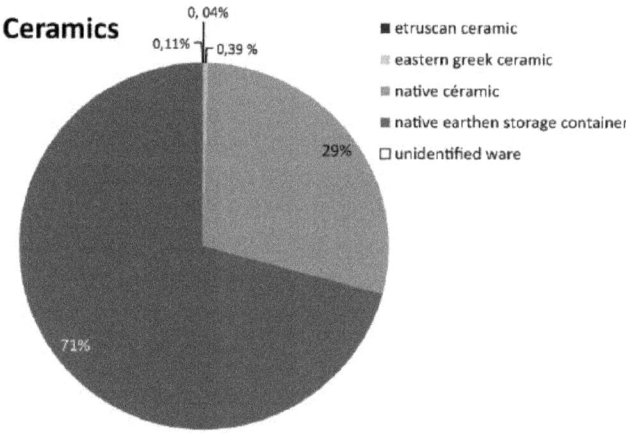

Figure 5. Marseilleveyre ceramics (D. Isoardi).

The *Marseilleveyre* site integrates indeed into a massif which saw some occupancy from the Neolithic, and especially from the sixth century BC. (Bouffier, Bernard & Isoardi 2015), especially in certain caves identified and probed from the late nineteenth and the early twentieth century. The areas around the excavated site confirmed the attendance of the entire area, including the traffic lanes leading to the *Pas de la Selle* and the *Puits du Lierre*, that is to say towards the inside of the massif. In the current state of the literature, we cannot know whether the sites have experienced recovery phases. The ceramics of the caves of the *Cirque du Puits du Lierre* are not characterised with sufficient precision to enable fine dating. If the caves are contemporary with the site of *Marseilleveyre,* this situation can give the impression that Greeks and Celts shared this massif, whereas occupancy seems to have been rather Greek, while the native habitats appear to have been native (Vidal et al. 2000). This would seem to confirm the legendary harmony with local settlers during the early days of implantation. Again work of archaeological geography should enable us to clarify the density of human occupancy and its impact on the massif (breeding or agriculture? deforestation? fires?).

In this first phase of the existence of Marseille, the importance of import furniture, including Etruscan, on sites and the absence of ceramic production in Marseille (particularly amphorae, attested only from the second half of the sixth century BC) seem to attribute to the Phocaean city the role of relay in the emporic wine trade, a wine that its vineyards do not seem to have produced before the next phase.

540/530 to 450—Massaliot Economic Expansion / Marseille at the Head of Its Own Economic Territory... What Impact?

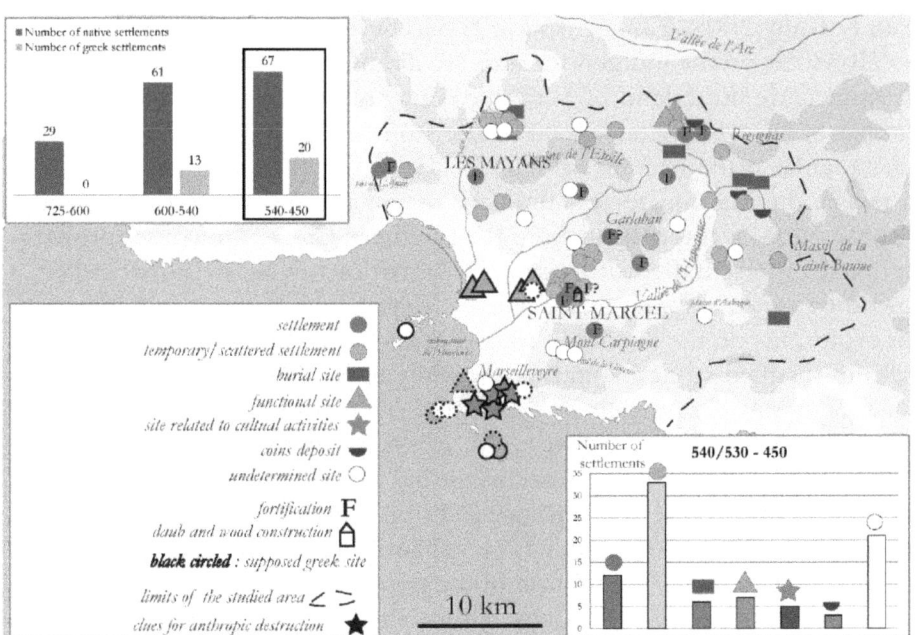

Figure 6. Greek and Native settlements in Marseille basin 540–450 BC (D. Isoardi).

The main change is economic since Marseille produces its own wine, an export object and it sets up its own economic territory (Bertucchi 1992).

The number of amphorae on the sites is decreasing, and one finds almost only Massaliot amphorae, testifying to the economic monopoly of Marseille in the South. This phenomenon has often been explained by the taking of Phocaea by the Persians in 546, the foundation of Aleria and the defeat of the Phocaean exiles before an Etruscan-Carthaginian coalition which pretexted of acts of piracy by the Greeks to get rid of these maritime rivals. We have already remarked that, despite the silence of the ancient tradition, following the defeat of Alalia, some of these Phocaeans had to take refuge in Marseille (Gras 1995), as the city took on a new socio-economic turn, visible in its urban and perhaps political expansion. It became the only Greek power in the Western Mediterranean and reorganised the maritime traffic around its port, probably reconsidering and expanding its trade to the hinterland.

This is also the period for which the Mediterranean imports should be related with the development of the Celtic princely phenomenon, but the latter does not seem to concern Provence, probably too close to the places of production and distribution of such *exotica* and *keimalia* (Rolley 2013; Brun & Ruby 2008, 72–76; Isoardi & Sacchetti, to be published).

However, on the indigenous side, we did not notice any great change in the immediate hinterland of Marseille compared to the previous phase: the number of known habitats is stable, the stone building related to land with a rectangular plane becomes the norm. However, the proliferation of ramparts, like the Mayans, for example, may seem to indicate a greater concern for protection or ostentation from the Southern Gauls. This site is probably the most representative of these transformations in lifestyle that reflect a downturn or a combination of natives (depending on how one interprets this evolution) on the border of Marseille (some ten kilometers, two hours,' walk) in fortified stone habitats. Following ancient discoveries, H. Tréziny could carry out excavations in the 1990s. The towers are rectangular, the imposing walls (triple cladding) and access to the site is via an overlapping cart door. A trapezoidal enclosure has been noticed in the North, in the highest part of the site but its condition has failed to specify the function thereof. In the furniture, whose exhaustive study remains to be done, nothing indicates a differentiation of the population or specific sectors. The site seems occupied by the Celts, although the percentages of unturned ceramic and monochrome gray ceramic are lower than those of *Saint Marcel* for example. But it was abandoned very quickly, attesting to a period of existence of only half a century (525–475), probably under Massaliot pressure; the Greeks could hardly accept the presence of an independent fortified site at such short distance from the city, as some of us have suggested (Bernard, Collin Bouffier & Tréziny 2010).

Should we see in the abandonment of the site the first signs of tension, even conflict between Greeks and natives, as they encourage the literary sources? The good relationships initiated with King Nanos would soon deteriorate from its succession and the texts attest to the existence of episodic conflicts that were only completed with the taking of Marseille by Caesar in 49 BC. Thus, as recalled by Justin (43.4–5): "On the death of Nannus, King of Segobriges, who had given the Phocaeans a place to build their city, his son Comanus who took his place, a wren asserted to him that one day Massilia would cause the ruin of neighbouring peoples and that it had to be crushed at its very birth, lest later then oppressed it. He adds this fable: "One day a pregnant dog begged a shepherd where it could deliver her puppies. Having obtained it, it still asked permission to raise its young there. At the end, once its young had grown up, leaning on its home garrison, it arrogated to itself the ownership of the place. Similarly these Massilians, who now seemed to be tenants, would become masters of the country one day. Excited by this advice, the king set a trap to the Massilians. On the day of the festival of Floralia [Anthesteria], he sent him to the city, as hosts, a large number of brave and intrepid men and actually had a larger number still transported on carts where they remained hidden under reeds and foliage. He himself is hiding with an army in the nearby hills, so that when the doors would be opened at night by the emissaries, as I said, he can participate in time in the ambush and conquer the city buried in sleep and in wine. But a woman, a relative of the king, betrayed the conspiracy. She had a young Greek lover. Touched by the beauty of the young man, she told him in a hug, the secret of the ambush, nudging him to evade the danger. The latter immediately reported the matter to the magistrates, and the trap thus discovered, all Ligurians were arrested and those hiding under the reeds were removed. All of them had their throats slit and the king's trap was opposed another trap: he perished himself with seven thousands of his tribe. Since then, the Massilians closed their doors on the festival days, stood guard on the ramparts, inspected foreigners, remained vigilant and keep the city in peace time, as if they were at war. Thus the good institutions were preserved, less from necessity than the use of doing one's duty. Then there were great wars with the Ligurians and the Gauls. These wars, where they won many victories, elevated the glory of the city and reflected the courage of the Greeks among their illustrious neighbours." A text that is supported by the testimony of Strabo (4, 1, 5): "Later, however, their courage enabled them to consolidate their power by seizing a part of the land around them, and the same vigour allowed them to found cities, or rather fortresses, those of Iberia to protect the Iberians (to whom they transmitted their ancestral cult of Artemis of Ephesus, and how to perform a sacrifice the Greek way), Rhoe Agathé [or, according to a correction, Rhodanousia Agathea] to protect against the barbarians who live around the Rhône, Tauroention, Olbia, Nikaia and Antipolis against Salyens and the Ligurians inhabiting the Alps."

One may also venture the hypothesis of a brutal destruction at the *Roc de la Croix* could testify to a Greek-type arrow tip or a spear tip (made of iron) discovered at the surface during surveys, and a set of calibrated rollers (throwing pebbles?) and traces of fire on the mud fragments could testify; but the state of the documentation on the site, the argument remains tenuous. The destruction of *Saint Marcel* around 540 in the sector III for phase I has generated more elements: a spear tip of Hellenic type with two fins and a lateral barb; Hellenic arrow type fragment with three fins. Following this episode, the thickening and the extension of the curtain wall have been implemented. It was probably at that time that can be attributed the small deposit of metal objects found outside the rampart, in a bank backed against the curtain wall, at the very foot of the perimeter wall. This deposit (bronze weapons and ornaments with a small batch of weapons and iron tools) is interpreted as a foundryman hideout, buried around the second half of the sixth century BC and which contains among others a pin dating from the Bronze Age.

Finally, the fire of the habitat of *Marseilleveyre,* as seen as the time of the excavation, can be dated to this period. Is it an accidental fire or a military episode? There is nothing to argue at the moment about the archaeological documentation. This may be evidence of the massif itself which will give us the solution. From the middle of the sixth century BC, the settlement of *Marseilleveyre* seems abandoned and the caves of the *Cirque du Puits du Lierre* have their own existence.

If one seeks to identify the actors involved in this traffic from the facies of the furniture found in caves, we must recognise that their profile is very different on the site itself and in the mountains. Among the small dozen of known caves, some located close to the settlement of the sixth century BC (in the *Cirque du Puits du Lierre*) were subject to a cult between the sixth and the third/second centuries BC, with peak activity between 525 and 450. And as Anne-Lise Marsolat had studied it (2005), non-turned pottery is very little represented, unlike the Greek furniture, essentially consisting of clear paste of Massaliot manufacture, banquet vases (olpai, oinochoai, cups and crateriscs), hydriae and lamps, sometimes miniaturised, but also some terracotta figurines (bearded male head and female head headdress with a crown in the cave of *l'Argile*) suggesting the religious function of these meeting places. These caves that surround one of the few industry sources, the fountain of the *Puits du Lierre*, are kind of dead end because they are not located on passageways, but basically at the bottom of a circus leading nowhere. However, other shelters situated nearby, in the valley of the *Font de Voyre*, had to be frequented when traveling between the outside and inside of the massif, as suggested by the uncovered furniture, predominantly consisting of unturned kitchen ceramic (edge of *lopas* or *caccabe)*, cups or bowls, and urns: furniture that does not seem to have a votive destination and that also certify an occupancy from the second half of the sixth century and during the fifth century BC. The large attendance of this sector of the massif between the second half of the sixth and the end of the second century BC is supported by the furniture formerly found in the massif of Marseilleveyre, but not located with accuracy.

The rise of all cultual caves of the massif, at a time when the establishment of the site of *Marseilleveyre* disappears, can be read in two ways. Either the Celto-Ligurians could extend, by offerings from the Greek city, a cult initiated by their ancestors from the late Bronze Age or the early Iron Age. These objects also testify to trade relations which were woven between each other, but in the state of publications and given the age of the excavation, it is difficult or impossible to propose Celtic cults in these caves. The Celtic sites in relation to caves are poorly studied in our Mediterranean regions in the Metal Ages. To mention only one, the Aven Plerimond (Var), the former presents quite specific furniture facies, very remote from the deposits of Marseilleveyre representing Greek rather than Celtic rites (Boyer et al. 2006). The only exception, but without any certainty, the existence of a bronze sword fragment of the first Iron Age, with a possible origin from Marseilleveyre could prove the existence of a cult or the presence of a burial (Rothé & Tréziny 2005, 691). Massaliots in these caves may have developed an extra-urban worship and the aim will be to understand its meaning. Since the now classic work of Pierre Vidal-Naquet on the *ephebeia* (1991) and François de Polignac (1995, ch. 2–3), emphasis was laid on the importance of borders in the appropriation of the procurement area, the *chôra*, and the symbolic representations of the territory. In the archaic and classical periods, the spatial advance of the *polis* and the agrarian exploitation of the territory have been marked by the establishment of sanctuaries for marking the border and the extremity of the *eschatia*, ultimate areas of the civic space. The community usually leaves fallow these border fringes, due to the risk of border conflicts. In the areas of Greek expansion, especially in Sicily and Magna Graecia, the

Greeks settled sanctuaries that can ensure the link with local communities or on the contrary officialise the possession of space by the new city. This is the case, for example, of the Heraion of Sele, of the Heraion of the Cap Colonna or of the sanctuaries of Demeter in Sicily. The defense of the territory and its boundaries is then a priority for civic and military policy of the city and is generally entrusted to young people undergoing training, *ephebes* or age classes that are no longer fit to serve outside. Whether the Spartan *krypteia* or the Attic *ephebeia*, emblematic of education of future citizen, but that are found in other Greek cities, the training of the future *Hoplite* requires a stay in the wild areas of the *chôra* where, by a process of symmetrical inversion, the young leads a life contrary to that characterising his civil existence, that is, rough and austere living conditions marked by isolation and disorder. The gods attested in these initiation rites, besides Apollo or Artemis, include Dionysus. In Marseille, the cultual destination of the caves of Marseilleveyre could therefore be linked with the initiation rites of young Massaliot citizens. They are difficult to access, either because they are hidden from view, or because they are open in the cliffs, and require strong physical training and endurance characteristic of the athletic and military training schemes. This sanctification of the caves could also be linked with the gradual exploitation of the plain and the cultivation of the vine—which would strengthen the hypothesis of L.-Fr. Gantès on the consecration of at least some of them to Dionysus. Wine-growing is now better documented, as shown in the overview of Philippe Boissinot on the plots of Marseille (Boissinot *infra*). From the second half of the sixth century BC, the Massaliots took possession of the entire plain of the Huveaune that they dedicate to wine-growing, as evidenced by the vineyard plantations in Saint Jean du Désert, Station Louis Armand. The boundaries of the territory were then driven back to the hills bordering the plain. Monumental shrines in the Massaliot territory have not been found for the time being either on the plain of the Huveaune or at its limits. The cult caves of *Le Draiou*, of *l'Argile* and *Puits du Lierre* may have allowed the political centre to embrace the whole country by delegating to young citizens the control of areas considered wild or dangerous, all the more so since their greatest period of occupancy corresponds precisely to the time of appropriation of the plain and of establishment of the wine-growing operation, between 540 and 450. This period seems to correspond to a stabilisation of the *chôra* towards the Valley of the Huveaune (no vineyard is attested close to the Estaque for now), and the beginning of more conflictual relationships between Greeks and Celts.

Hellenistic Pulses

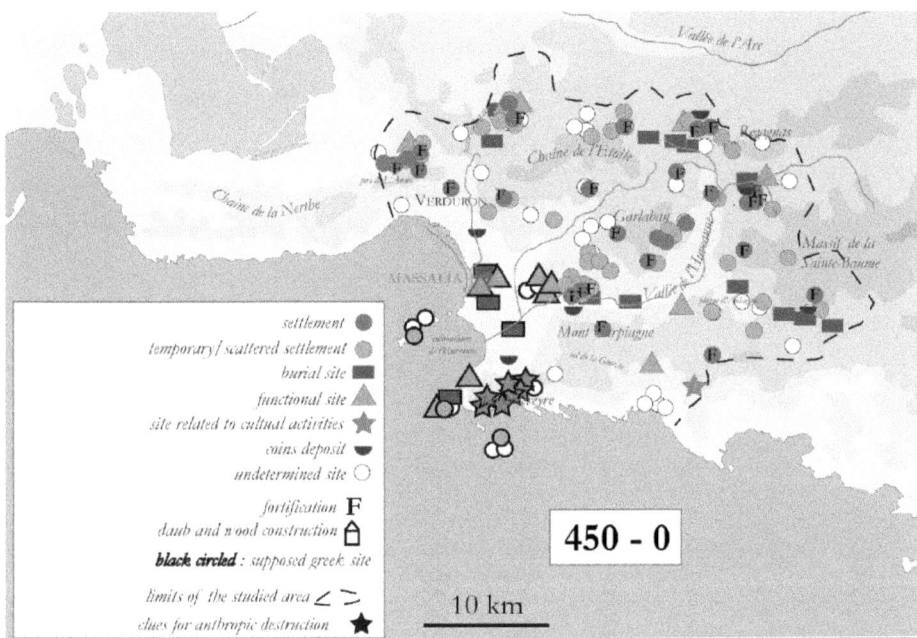

Figure 7. Greek and Native settlements in Marseille basin during 450–0 BC (D. Isoardi).

The development of the Massaliot agriculture seems to continue throughout the Marseille basin. Despite tenuous knowledge, the extension of land registries in the valley of the Huveaune is proven, at least within a ¾ km radius from the fortification. Besides the well-known example of *Saint-Jean-du-Désert,* agrarian traces were also highlighted in the district of *la Fourragère* (Rothé & Tréziny 2005, No. 299), at the metro station *Louis Armand* (Bernard et al. 2006), to the East of ancient Marseille, in the enclosure of the *Parc Chanot,* in the South (Rothé & Tréziny 2005, No. 222), and around the station *Saint-Charles,* to the North (Rothé & Tréziny 2005, No. 145). These agrarian traces (Fig. 8), sometimes with artifacts suggestive of agricultural establishments, seem at present the most reliable marker for the development of the Massaliot *chôra.*

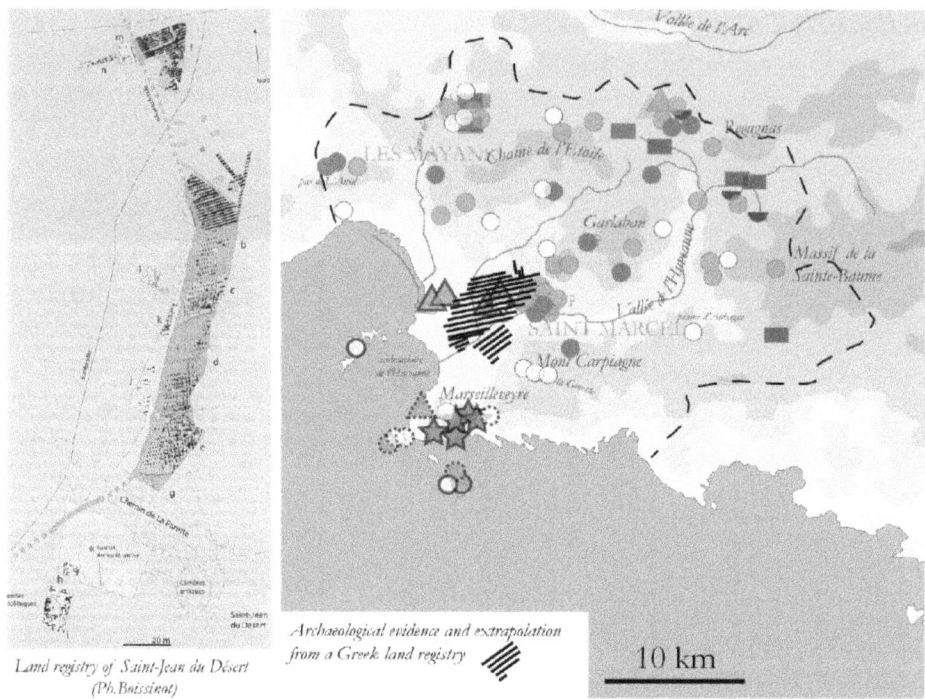

Land registry of Saint-Jean du Désert (Ph.Boissinot)

Archaeological evidence and extrapolation from a Greek land registry

10 km

Figure 8. Archaeological evidence and extrapolation from a Greek land registry (D. Isoardi, P. Boissinot).

Some of the habitats known for earlier periods disappear between the third century and the end of the second century like the *Baou of Saint-Marcel*, which seems no longer occupied between about 330 and 180, and finally disappears around 110/100 (Rothé & Tréziny 2005, No. 277), or the *Tourette* in the *Petit-Saint-Marcel*, which no longer offers any testimony after the second century BC, after a low occupancy at the third century (Rothé & Tréziny 2005, No. 274–275). The disappearance of these sites was generally linked to the Roman victory over the Salyans in 123/122 BC, which put an end to fighting between Greeks and natives. This destruction would confirm the indications given by Justin and Strabo. The Massaliots have therefore established over the Salyan and Ligurian populations a domination that they resented and from which they might have sought to break free.

However, other institutions appear, at least in the Southeast and in the North of the city. In the Southeast of Marseille, near the aforementioned sites, bordering the swampy areas of the Huveaune, a site of the second century is attested at the Valentine. Its agricultural function seems established by the presence of grindstone fragments. In the Northeast sector of the

Marseille basin, surveys have suggested a poorly known presence in *Château-Gombert* and in Allauch, in the same places that delivered some fragments of Ionio-Massaliot and Massaliot amphorae. Some samples of Greco-Italic amphorae attest to the continuity of occupancy.

But the best known site for this period is today that of the Verduron. This pre-Roman settlement, located in the North of *Marseille,* overlooking the Greek city from which it is remote only by 9 km as the crow flies. The view encompasses the entire harbor, the harbor entrance, the islands and the communication routes. The location of the site, facing the sea, confers on it a probable strategic role. Since its discovery, the oppidum overlooking the Phocaean city raises the question of the relationships between Greeks and natives while fueling the debate on the territory of the oppida and the operating modes of the territory of Greek Marseille. Early work in the early twentieth century was complemented by an extensive excavation between 1999 and 2006, which has been directed by Loup Bernard.

The Verduron is a site on a steep slope and with a low extension (less than 1,500m²), which has a regular plan organised around an "axial wall". The enclosure wall—are we dealing here with a rampart?—is not imposing (1m wide). The internal architecture, earthbound stones, is typical of pre-Roman habitats of the period: the rock on which the settlement is located has been systematically hacked and the cuttings were used to build drains to the outside. Only four cells are installed on top of the oppidum and the rest of the habitat slopes down to the sea: a central islet, a lane on both sides side of the latter, the other cells being backed to the rampart. The map of this property is very regular and enables us to work on emulation relationships between Greek and Celtic societies. The very type of implantation refers to a normality of pre-Roman habitat, if it exists. The regularity of the site (in terms of islets, lanes, walls widths) allowed to propose a comparison with a Celtic-Ligurian module spotted on the first phase of the Oppidum of the Entremont (Badie & Bernard 2008). Recent excavations have clearly shown the violent destruction of the site around 200 BC (levels of ceramics batches in place, weapons, trampled vases, spears in some *dolia*).The latter probably resulted from an organised army with artillery; some tenuous signs suggest looting. This destruction, which is most likely the result of Marseille, excludes good relationships with the Phocaean city and the role of *phrourion* that could be previously proposed for the site. The ceramics unearthed are commonplace for the pre-Roman habitats of the region. Most of the furniture (85%) consists of local unturned ceramics, mainly urns of various sizes, as well as bowls, cups and a crater made of unturned ceramic. The turned crockery consists mainly of clear Massaliot ceramics (especially cups, a few jugs and mortars) and black varnished Italic ceramics of the third century. Massaliot

Amphorae (type 9) are rare and the presence in stratigraphy of an isolated Ibe-ro-Punic amphora Maña D is one of the director fossils regarding chronology. Storage is attested by the presence of *dolia* and mud as well as by the presence of earthen containers. The site is however not an attic: the volumes stored correspond to the consumption of a small number of people, not to reserves intended for trade or storage for sowing purposes.

The metal furniture is exclusively of Celtic type. Several possible ritual installations have been uncovered. The comprehensive studies of residual household in Celtic habitats tend to show the frequency of exposure of the dead (Brunaux et al. 1997). In addition to the famous heads cut, many other human bones can be found on the other Celtic sites of the period. We are therefore clearly dealing with a Celtic-Ligurian settlement just outside Greek Marseille and guarding the accesses to the city by sea as well as by land. The relationships of the inhabitants with their Greek neighbours seem limited: the site activities are difficult to perceive. Agriculturally, the lack of stables or stockyards excludes any livestock. The low value of land but above all the lack of speculative storage space such as silos or battery of *dolia* excludes an attic function that would have fed Marseille (Strabo IV, 1.4). No craft pro-duction could be detected. Finally, despite the proximity of the Phocaean city, imports are low and trade exchanges seem underdeveloped. The Verduron can be linked with similar sized sites unearthed in the Massif de la Nerthe as *Teste-Nègre* or the oppidum of *La Cloche,* located about ten kilometers away. Many other Provence sites destroyed at this same time, even in the Alps (*St-Martin-de-Brômes* for example), even if a synchronous destruction is not yet proven. It is tempting to reconcile these elements of Celtic pressure on Marseille as described by Strabo (4, 6, 3) and that the Romans would have eradicated: "Sextius, who after his victory over the Salyens, founded near Mas-salia a city to which he gave his name and that of the warm waters it has [...], establishes there a Roman garrison and fended off the Barbarians from the coastal area leading from Massalia to Italy, what the Massaliotes had not fully succeeded in doing. However, he obtained only from the Barbarians that they receded twelve stadia from the sea near the ports and eight stadia in rocky areas; and the abandoned territories were handed to the Massaliotes." It is likely that the inhabitants of the sites of the Nerthe created an outpost during a period for which Marseille did not have sufficient troops to venture outside the walls; the Massaliots, aided by their Roman allies would then have destroyed the site (Bernard 2003; Bernard to be published). In the process, the sites of *Teste-Nègre* or the first village of Entremont would also have been destroyed.

The site of the Verduron is representative of the Celtic-Ligurian "boom" preceding the conquest of the Narbonne region. The number of high fortified sites listed for the departments of the *Bouches-du-Rhône* and Vaucluse (Bernard 2003) increases from 40 sites for the period 400–250 BC to 86 for the phase between 250 and 125 BC. This important increase in the number of habitats corresponds to periods in which the relationships between Greeks and Celto-Ligurians become confrontational. For now it is still impossible to refine the time ranges to understand the details of these conflicts and to differentiate quarrels which could have existed between Celts or between Celts and Marseillais and the precise role of the latter, if not in rare cases, such as the Hellenistic ramparts of *Saint-Blaise.*

From the second century BC, Marseille calling upon Roman armies changed significantly the regional map. Marseille, which had until then relatively limited territories, received large areas from Rome in the lower valley of the Rhône and the Mediterranean coast (Bernard 2003). The relationships with the indigenous populations remain ambiguous and are not confined to conflicts and to destruction sites, but they rely mostly on economic or cultural exchange that we do not intend to detail here (Collin Bouffier 2009; Tréziny 2010b; 2010c). There are influences, probably reciprocal, in the areas of hydraulic and agricultural techniques, in the adoption of the currency by some indigenous towns (such as Glanon) and the Greek alphabet to write the Gaul language.

Conclusion

If we can no longer speak of "Marseille, a city without territory", as suggested by the ancient texts emphasising the maritime vocation of Marseille, the latest research seems to reinforce the vision transmitted by these ancient texts on the relationships between the Phocaeans and the local populations. Starting from friendly relationships and matrimonial ties noticeable in the topographical and architectural traces of the various settlements, the relations appear to have gradually degraded, with the exclusively Greek occupancy of the plain of Marseille and the implantation of perennial crops disrupting previous operations which have remained poorly characterised so far. The evolution of relationships between each other then varies according to the interests they may have in the exchange. Thus, the evolution of storage facilities outside the plain of the Huveaune (Garcia, *infra*) and the discovery of vineyards in this same plain show that two types of production were related, as shown by D. Garcia and D. Isoardi (Garcia & Isoardi, 2010). With the increased Phocaean demand for cereals from the sixth century BC, the indigenous communities in the hinterland, mostly from Provence and Languedoc, would have been induced to produce more: this is highlighted by the increase in size of silos with a view to marketing, or the gradual adoption of storage structures from the Greek world, such as *pithos*, attics in airy atmosphere, to the detriment of simple proto silos used for centuries. This marketing of cereals, as evidenced for example by the farm granary of Coudounèu-Provence (fifth century BC) (Verdin 1997; 2000) would have increased the Greek pressure on the plain of Marseille where the Phocaeans produced wine, the currency for trading their imports, at the expense of local populations. This movement would have resulted in a political and economic domination of the Provençal habitats whose brutal demographic decline during the fifth and fourth centuries as underlined by D. Isoardi, to the benefit of the Greek population of Marseille (Isoardi 2008). These ongoing discussions will have to be confronted with the expected results of further research on the massif of Marseilleveyre, and integrated in a new environmental project, centred on the issues of the human impact on the Huveaune Valley, which will combine archaeological and soil data.

Bibliography

Agostini, P., 1965, Contribution à la connaissance du peuplement du massif de Marseilleveyre. *Provincia*, V, 268, mai 1965, 205–207.

Agostini, P., 1967, Le massif de Marseilleveyre. *Provence Historique*, XVII, 70, 333–359.

Arcelin, P., 1999, Bracelet en bronze. In: A. Hesnard, M. Moliner, F. Conche et al., *Parcours de villes. Marseille: 10 ans d'archéologie, 2600 ans d'histoire*. Catalogue d'exposition, Aix-en-Provence, Edisud, 20.

Badie, A. & Bernard, L., 2008, Organisation modulaire du site du Verduron à Marseille (Bouches-du-Rhône), habitat gaulois du IIIe siècle avant notre ère. In: *Archéologie de Provence et d'ailleurs, Mélanges offerts à Gaëtan Congès et Gérard Sauzade, Bulletin Archéologique de Provence*, Supplément 5, Editions de l¹APA, 291–299.

Bats, M., 1986, Le territoire de Marseille grecque: réflexions et problèmes. In: M. Bats & H. Tréziny (dir.), *Le territoire de Marseille grecque. Actes de la table ronde d'Aix en Provence (16 mars 1985)*. Etudes Massaliètes, 1, Publications de l'université de Provence, 17–42.

Bats, M., 2001, La *chôra* de Massalia? In: *Problemi della chora coloniale dall'Occidente al Mar Nero. Atti del Quarantesimo Convegno di Studi sulla Magna Grecia, Taranto 2000*. Tarente, Istituto per la storia e l'archeologia della Magna Grecia, 491–512.

Bernard, L., 2003, *Confrontation de deux régions de l'Europe celtique à l'âge du fer: les cas de la Provence et du Baden-Württemberg*, Thèse de doctorat sous la direction de D. Garcia, Université de Provence, Aix-Marseille 1, Aix-en-Provence 2003, 321p.

Bernard, L. & Garcia, D., 2012, Die Anfänge der Urbanisierung in der Region von Marseille und in Südostfrankreich am Ende des 7. und im 6. Jahrhundert v. Chr. In:

M. Schönfelder & S. Sievers (eds.), *Die Frage der Protourbanisation in der Eisenzeit. La question de la proto-urbanisation à l'âge du Fer, (actes 34e coll. AFEAF Aschaffenburg, mai 2010—Thème spécialisé)*, 211–220.

Bernard, L., Chevillot, P. Lachenal, T., Sargiano, J.P., Senepart, I., & Vasselin, B., 2006, Rapport final d'opération: Fouille préventive. Station Louis Armand à Marseille (BdR), 98p.

Bernard, L., Collin Bouffier, S., Copetti, A., D'Ovidio, A.M. & Dumas, V., 2006, *Sondages sur le site du Roc de la Croix*. Novembre 2006. Aix-en-Provence, DRAC PACA.

Bernard, L., Collin Bouffier, S. & Copetti, A., 2007, *Sondages sur le site du Roc de la Croix*. Septembre 2007. Aix-en-Provence, DRAC PACA.

Bernard, L., Collin Bouffier, S. & D'Ovidio, A.M., 2008, *Sondages sur le site de Marseilleveyre*. Aix-en-Provence, SRA PACA.

Bernard, L., Collin Bouffier, S. & Isoardi, D., 2010, *Sondages sur le site de Marseilleveyre*. Aix-en-Provence, SRA PACA.

Bernard, L., Collin Bouffier, S. & Tréziny, H., 2010, Grecs et indigènes dans le territoire de Marseille. In: H. Tréziny (ed.), *Grecs et indigènes de la Catalogne à la mer Noire*. Paris/Aix, Errance/CCJ, BiAMA 3, 2010, 131–145.

Bernard, L., Bouffier, S., Copetti, A. et al., 2011, *Oppidum de Marseilleveyre. Campagne 2011*. Aix-en-Provence, SRA PACA.

Bernard, L. & Roure, R., 2010, Naissance de la Protohistoire méridionale. In: S. de Beaune (ed.), *Écrire le passé. La fabrique de la préhistoire et de l'histoire à travers les siècles*, Paris, CNRS, 2010, 351–362.

Bertucchi, G., 1992, *Les amphores et le vin de Marseille: VIe s. avant J.-C. -IIe s. après J.-C.* Paris, Ed. du CNRS, 250p.

Beylier, A., 2012, *L'armement et le guerrier en Méditerranée nord-occidentale au premier âge du fer*, Lattes, Edition de l'Association pour le Développement de l'Archéologie en Languedoc-Roussillon, 2012. Coll. Monographies d'Archéologie Méditerranéenne (MAM), 31, 500p.

Boissinot, P., 1993, *Archéologie de l'habitat protohistorique: quelques points méthodologiques (historiographie et épistémologie) examinés à partir de la fouille d'une agglomération de la périphérie Marseillaise*. Thèse de Doctorat, Toulouse, EHESS, 1993, 738p.

Boissinot, P., 1998, Un lot de DSP dans le faubourg de Saint-Barnabé à Marseille. Les données stratigraphiques. In: M. Bonifay, M.B. Carre & Y. Rigoir (dir.), *Fouilles à Marseille: les mobiliers (Ier–VIIe siècles ap. J.-C.). (Etudes Massaliètes*, 5). Lattes-Aix-en-Provence, ADAM-Errance, 283–285.

Boissinot, P., 2001, Land Allotment and Ancient Vineyards around Marseille. In: *Problemi della chora coloniale dall'Occidente al Mar Nero. Atti del quarantesimo convegno di studi sulla Magna Grecia: Taranto 29 settembre–3 ottobre 2000*, Tarente, 491–513.

Boissinot, P., 2005, Le pays des Ségobriges? B-La Protohistoire du Bassin de Marseille. In: M.P. Rothé & H. Tréziny (dir.), *Marseille et ses alentours. 13/3. Carte archéologique de la Gaule*, Paris, Académie des Inscriptions et des Belles Lettres, 2005, 117–140.

Boissinot, P., 2010, Des vignobles de Saint-Jean Du Désert aux cadastres antiques de Marseille. In: H. Tréziny (ed.), *Grecs et indigènes de la Catalogne à la Mer Noire*. Paris/Aix, Errance/CCJ, BiAMA 3, 2010, 147–154.

Boissinot, P., Infra, Viticulture in Marseille Territory. In: S. Bouffier & D. Garcia, *Greek Marseille and Mediterranean Celtic Region*, Peter Lang, New-York.

Bouffier, S., Bernard, L. & Isoardi, D., 2015, Le site de Marseilleveyre entre Grecs et indigènes: état de la question, recherches récentes et nouvelles approches». In: R. Roure (dir.), *Contacts et acculturations en Méditerranée Occidentale. Hommages à Michel Bats,* Hyères [2011], Aix-en-Provence, BiAMA 15, 2015, 17–26.

Bouiron, M., Tréziny, H., Bizot, B., Guilcher, A., Guyon, J. & Pagni, M. (dir.), 2001, *Marseille. Trames et paysages urbains de Gyptis au Roi René.* Actes du colloque international d'archéologie. Marseille, 3–5 Novembre 1999. (*Etudes Massaliètes,* 7). Aix-en-Provence, Edisud, 459p.

Bouloumié, B., 1990a, Les tumuli de Vauvenargues. In: *Voyage en Massalie. 100 ans d'archéologie en Gaule du Sud. Musées de Marseille.* Marseille, Musées de Marseille/Edisud, 135–137.

Bouloumié, B., 1990b, Nécropoles. Rites de l'âge du Fer, inhumation et incinération. Le mobilier funéraire. In: *Voyage en Massalie. 100 ans d'archéologie en Gaule du Sud. Musées de Marseille.* Marseille, Musées de Marseille/Edisud, 126–129.

Bouloumié, B., 1990c, Les tumuli de Pertuis. In: *Voyage en Massalie. 100 ans d'archéologie en Gaule du Sud. Musées de Marseille.* Marseille, Musées de Marseille/Edisud, 130–133.

Bouloumié, B. & Lagrand, Ch., 1977, Les bassins à rebord perlé et autres bassins de Provence. *RANArb,* 10, 1–31.

Bout de Charlemont, H., 1913, Inventaire sommaire de mes fouilles et recherches à Marseilleveyre. *Bulletin Société Archéologique de Provence,* 19, 282–283.

Boyer, R., Dedet, B. & Marchand, G., 2006, L'aven sépulcral de Plérimond à Aups, Var (VIe s. av. J.-C.). *Gallia,* 63, 171–209.

Brun, P. & Ruby, P., 2008, *L'âge du Fer en France. Premières villes, premiers Etats celtiques.* Paris, La découverte, 177p.

Brunaux, (J.-L.), Meniel, (P.) & Boulestin, (B.), 1997, La résidence aristocratique de Montmartin (Oise) du IIIe au IIe s. av. J.-C. Paris, 270p.

Brunet, M., 2001, À propos des recherches sur les territoires ruraux en Grèce égéenne: un bilan critique. In: *Problemi della chora coloniale dall'Occidente al Mar Nero, XL Convegno di Studi sulla Magna Grecia. Taranto, 29 settembre-3 ottobre 2000,* Tarente, 27–46.

Clastrier, S., 1910, Fouille d'un habitat liguro-celto-grec. *A.F.A.S., 39ᵉ session Toulouse,* 1910 (1911), 849–850.

Clavel-Leveque, M., 1977, *Marseille grecque. La dynamique d'un impérialisme marchand,* Marseille, Jeanne Laffitte, 209p.

Clerc, M., 1927–1929, *Massalia. Histoire de Marseille dans l'Antiquité, des origines à la fin de l'Empire romain d'Occident (476 apr. J.-C.).* Marseille, Laffitte, 480p. et 489p.

Collin Bouffier, S. (dir.), 2002, *Rapport de prospection thématique. Zone 13: occupation du sol dans le bassin de Marseille de la Préhistoire à l'époque moderne. Allauch, Château-Gombert, l'Estaque, Marseilleveyre*. Aix-en-Provence, SRA PACA.

Collin Bouffier, S. (dir.), 2008, L'occupation du sol dans le bassin de Marseille: de la Préhistoire à l'époque moderne. *Bilan Scientifique 2007*. Aix-en-Provence, Service Régional de l'Archéologie, Direction Régionale des Affaires Culturelles Provence-Alpes-Côte d'Azur, 146.

Collin Bouffier, S. (dir.), 2009, *L'occupation du sol dans le bassin de Marseille: de la Préhistoire à l'époque moderne. Document final de Synthèse 2007–2009.* Aix-en-Provence, SRA PACA, 2009.

Collin Bouffier, S., 2009, Marseille et la Gaule méditerranéenne avant la conquête romaine, in: B. Cabouret, J.P. Guilhembet & Y. Roman (éd.), *Rome et l'Occident, du IIe siècle av. J.-C au IIe siècle apr. J.-C.*, Colloque de la SOPHAU, [15–16 mai 2009], *Pallas*, 80, 35–60.

Collin Bouffier, S., 2011, Diodore de Sicile, témoin du Ve siècle av. J.-C.: un âge d'or pour la Sicile? In: S. Collin Bouffier (dir.), Diodore d'Agyrion et l'histoire de la Sicile, journée d'étude Lyon 2, Lyon avril 2009. *Dialogues d'Histoire Ancienne*, Suppl.6, 70–112.

De Polignac, F., 1995, *La naissance de la cité grecque: cultes, espace et sociétés, VIIIe–VIIe siècles*, Ed. La Découverte, Paris, 230p.

D'Ovidio, A.M., 2010, *Marseille. Zones incendiées ouest Saint Cyr/Carpiagne*. Bilan scientifique. Aix-en-Provence, DRAC PACA, 2010.

D'Ovidio, A.M., 2014, L'occupation gauloise du massif de Saint-Cyr-Carpiagne à la fin de l'âge du Bronze, premier âge du Fer: étude préliminaire. In: S. Bouffier & D. Garcia (dir.), *Les territoires de Marseille*, Arles, Errance-Actes Sud, 2014, 99–110.

D'Ovidio, A.M. & Rothé, M.P., 2005, Notice les Baou de Saint-Marcel. In: M.P. Rothé & H. Tréziny (dir.), *Carte Archéologique de la Gaule. Marseille et ses alentours, 13/3*, Académie des Inscriptions et Belles-Lettres, Paris, 699–716.

Duval, S., 1998, L'habitat côtier de Tamaris (13). *DocAMérid*, 21, 133–180.

Gantès, L.F., 1990, *Marseilleveyre*. In: *Voyage en Massalie. 100 ans d'archéologie en Gaule du Sud. Musées de Marseille*. Marseille, Musées de Marseille/Edisud, 156–161.

Gantès, L.F., 2014, Un habitat de hauteur de l'âge du Fer aux portes de Marseille: le site de la Tourette Quartier du Petit Saint-Marcel. In: S. Bouffier & D. Garcia (dir.), *Les territoires de Marseille,* Arles, Errance-Actes Sud, 2014, 111–120.

Gantès, L.F. & Rothé, M.P., 2005, Notice 232. In: M.P. Rothé & H. Tréziny (dir.), *Carte Archéologique de la Gaule. Marseille et ses alentours, 13/3,* Académie des Inscriptions et Belles-Lettres, Paris, 685–691.

Garcia, D., 1997, Les structures de conservation des céréales en Méditerranée nord-occidentale au premier millénaire avant J.-C.; innovations techniques et rôle économique. In: D. Garcia & D. Meeks (eds.), *Techniques et économie antiques et médiévales. Le temps de l'innovation,* Paris, Errance, 88–95.

Garcia, D., 2014, *La Celtique méditerranéenne. Habitats et sociétés en Languedoc et en Provence du VIIIe au IIe siècle av. J.-C.* Arles, Actes Sud /Errance, 250p. (2nd edition edited and improved, 2004).

Garcia, D. & Isoardi, D., 2010, Variations démographiques et production de céréales en Celtique méditerranéenne: le rôle de Marseille grecque? In: H. Tréziny (ed.), *Grecs et indigènes de la Catalogne à la mer Noire.* Paris/Aix, Errance/CCJ, BiAMA 3, 2010, 403–424.

Garnier, J.L., 2010, *Notice sur l'oppidum de Marseilleveyre.* Aix-en-Provence, SRA PACA, octobre 2000.

Gateau, F., Trément, F. & Verdin, Fl., 1996, *Carte Archéologique de la Gaule. L'étang de Berre. 13–1,* Paris, Académie des Inscriptions et Belles-Lettres 226.

Gérin-Ricard, H. de, 1934, Les oppida autour de Marseille. *Comptes Rendus de l'Académie des Inscriptions et des Belles Lettres,* 68–69.

Gilles, I., 1876, *Marseille depuis 3000 ans, celtique, grecque et chrétienne.* Draguignan, 1876, 64p.

Gras, M., 1995, L'arrivée d'immigrés à Marseille au milieu du VIe s. av. J.-C. In: *Sur les pas des Grecs en Occident. Etudes Massaliètes* 4, Adam-Errance, Lattes-Paris, 363–366.

Hermary, A., Hesnard, A. & Tréziny, H. (dir.), 1999, *Marseille grecque: la cité phocéenne (600–49 av. J.-C.),* Paris, Hauts lieux de l'histoire, Errance, 181p.

Isoardi, D., 2008, *Les populations protohistoriques du Sud-Est de la France: essai d'approche démographique.* Thèse de doctorat d'Archéologie de l'Université de Provence (Aix-Marseille I), 4 vol. (I et II: texte, 365p.; III et IV: annexes).

Isoardi, D. & Sacchetti, F., Commerce méditerranéen et occupation du territoire au premier âge du Fer, du Sud de la Gaule à l'Europe Centrale: nouvelles données d'analyse spatiale et essai d'approche interdisciplinaire, colloque AFEAF Nancy 2015, à paraître.

Marsolat, A.L., 2005, *Les grottes de Marseilleveyre. Inventaire et étude de matériel.* Université de Provence, Aix-en-Provence, 1 vol. 118p et 1 vol. d'annexes, mémoire de DEA.

Morhange, C., Provansal, M., Vella, C. et al., 1998, Montée relative du niveau de la mer et mouvements du sol à l'Holocène en basse Provence (France, Méditerranée). *Annales de géographie,* n°600, 139–159.

Problemi della chora coloniale dall'Occidente al Mar Nero. Atti del quarantesimo convegno di studi sulla Magna Grecia: Taranto 29 settembre–3 ottobre 2000, Tarente, 2001, 1065 p.

Rolley, C. (ed.), 2013, *La tombe princière de Vix.* Paris, Picard, 2 vol.: 383, 135 p.

Rothé, M.P. & Tréziny, H. (dir.), 2005, *Carte archéologique de la Gaule. Marseille et ses alentours. 13/3.* Paris, Académie des Inscriptions et Belles-Lettres, 925p.

Saurel, A., 1877–1878, *Dictionnaire des villes, villages et hameaux du département des Bouches du Rhône,* Marseille, 2 vol., 389 p et 416p.

Tréziny, H. (ed.), 2010a, *Grecs et indigènes de la Catalogne à la mer Noire.* Paris/Aix, Errance/CCJ, BiAMA 3, 2010, 726p.

Tréziny, H., 2010b, Note sur les céramiques indigènes présentes à Marseille, In: H. Tréziny 2010a, 509.

Tréziny, H., 2010c, Fortifications grecques et fortifications indigènes dans l'Occident grec. In: H. Tréziny 2010a, 557–566.

Vasseur, G., 1914, *L'origine de Marseille. Fondation des premiers comptoirs ioniens de Massalia vers le milieu du VIIe siècle. Résultats des fouilles archéologiques exécutées à Marseille dans le Fort Saint-Jean.* Marseille, 284p.

Verdin, F., 1997, Coudounèu (Lançon-de-Provence, Bouches-du-Rhône): une ferme-grenier et son terroir au Ve s. av. J.-C. *DocAMérid*, 19–20, 1996–1997, 165–198.

Verdin, F., 2000, La ferme-grenier de Coudounèu. In: J. Chausserie-Laprée (dir.), *Le temps des Gaulois en Provence.* Martigues, Musée Ziem, 147–150.

Vidal, M., Vernhet, A. & Pujol, J., 2000, Les grottes sanctuaires: à propos des exemples aveyronnais, première approche d'une étude comparative étendue au sud de la France et à la péninsule ibérique. In: B. Dedet, P. Gruat, G. Marchand, M. Py & M. Schwaller, *Aspects de l'Âge du Fer dans le Suc de Massif Central. Actes du XXIe colloque international de l'Association française pour l'étude de l'Âge du fer, Conques-Montrozier 8–11 mai 1997.* Lattes: Association pour la recherche archéologique en Languedoc oriental, 65–80. (M.A.M, 6).

Vidal-Naquet, P., 1991, *Le Chasseur noir: Formes de pensée et formes de société dans le monde,* Paris, La Découverte [1981], 490p.

Villeneuve-Bargemon, Comte Chr. De, 1829, *Statistique du département des Bouches du Rhône,* Marseille, 1821, 1824, 1826 et 1829, 4 vol., avec atlas, 1826, 1834, 17 pl. et 8 plans.

9. The Cults of Greek Marseille

Antoine Hermary

In spite of the important discoveries of the last decades, Marseille is still one of the rare ancient Greek cities where no place of worship is localised with certainty. Indeed, excavations have not yet enabled scholars to identify the sanctuaries mentioned by the ancient authors, and the different votive objects unearthed since the nineteenth century cannot be attributed to precise divinities, for want of inscribed dedications or a significant architectural context.

Written and Numismatic Testimonies

The *akra* ("summit" or "headland") on which according to Strabo (4.1.4) the sanctuary of Ephesian Artemis and that of Apollo Delphinios were situated,[1] corresponds either to the *Butte Saint-Laurent* or to the La Major church area (Tréziny 2012; Hermary & Tréziny forthcoming), and the "citadel of Minerva" (the hill on which the sanctuary of Athena was situated), mentioned by Justin (43.5), should be the current *Butte des Moulins* "Mound of Windmills", but no remains provide evidence to that effect. These literary texts, not prior to the first century BC, testify to the transfer towards Marseille of cults characteristic of three Ionian cities of the Minor Asia coast: the Phocaean metropolis for Athena (the main female divinity of Aeolis and Northern Ionia), Miletus for Apollo Delphinios (although Strabo goes on to say that the god is common to all the Ionians) and Ephesus for Artemis, and Strabo, in the text mentioned previously, describes the transfer of her cult by priestess Aristarcha and its diffusion into the Massaliot foundations. Association of these different cults has led some to think that, when the city was founded (or shortly after), Greeks from Ephesus and Miletus had joined forces with the Phocaeans, considered by the bulk of the literary tradition as the founders of *Massalia* (Domínguez 2012, with previous bibliography).

The head of these three divinities was regularly featured from the fourth century on the Massaliot coins, in a casual iconographic form (Richard 2000). Contrary to what can be seen in other Greek cities (especially in the imperial time), no monetary image reproduces the appearance of one of the cult statues, alluded to by Strabo (13.1.41) for the case of Athena, who remarks on the other hand (4.1.4) "how carefully the small Massaliot cities respected the traditional aspect of the Ephesian Artemis". One has often thought—relying on the indication by the same Strabo (4.1.5) that "the Romans had given to the cult statue of Artemis on the Aventine the same aspect as that of the statue of Massalia"—that the image of this "Massaliot-Roman" Artemis was reproduced on a denarius struck in Rome 48 BC by L. Hostilius Saserna, but this identification has been contested (Bats 2014; Hermary & Tréziny forthcoming). Apart from a very small helmeted terracotta head from the excavation of the *Parc des Phocéens*, the interpretation of which is in fact uncertain, Athena is represented only by a long lost statuette and by a small marble bust bearing the aegis, dating from the imperial time (Bouiron & Mellinand 2013, 72). A marble torso, smaller than nature, found close to the beach of the Catalans, represents a "Severe Style" Apollo of the "Tiber type", which is not prior to the first century BC (Rothé & Tréziny 2005, 674–675 fig. 990; Long & Hermary 2007, 121–125), and the Ephesian Artemis is only represented by a so-called polymast (with multiple breasts) marble statuette, whose provenance is in fact uncertain (Rothé & Tréziny 2005, 753 fig. 1125).

To these testimonies should be added that of coins from the second half of the fifth century BC, showing on the front face a juvenile head with the inscription "Lakydon" and on the reverse a helmeted head (Hermary 2012). According to two later texts (Pomponius Mela (2.5.77) and Eustathius (*comment on Dionysius Periegetes* 75), the Lakydon was the name of the port of Marseille, and the horned head with dishevelled hair quite probably linked "Lakydon" to the aquatic world: We may think of a god or a local hero adopted by the Greeks of Marseille.

The other divinities whose worship is attested by literary or epigraphic sources are as follows (Hermary 2012).

Dionysos

According to Justin (43.4), the Gauls had attempted to sneak into the city at the time of the *Floralia*, a celebration of Dionysos which probably corresponds to the Greek *Anthesteria*. Diverse objects of almost certainly votive character could have a connection with the cult of Dionysos,[2] but a fragmentary inscription from the first half of the fifth century BC should also be taken into account, an inscription unearthed on the site of *La Bourse*, which may have featured the name of the god (Decourt 2004, 7 no. 2; Rothé & Tréziny 2005, 177 fig. 40).

Leucothea

The sole attestation in our possession in Marseille is late (beginning of the third century AD) and indirect, since it relates to a prominent figure, T. Porcius Cornelianus, who was a priest of this marine goddess (Decourt 2004, 14–16 no. 8; Rothé & Tréziny 2005, 179 no. 8.). This cult, also attested in Velia, admittedly belonged to an ancient Phocaean tradition. The importance of water-related divinities is confirmed by various discoveries in the region of the harbour (see below).

Zeus

An inscribed altar, dated from the end of the Hellenistic period or from the beginning of the imperial time testifies to a cult to Zeus Patroos (i.e., "ancestral") of the *Kasinetoi* family. The block, of relatively significant size (100 cm long × 77 cm wide), supposedly originates from the *Butte des Carmes*, but its context is totally unknown (Decourt 2004, 11–12 no. 5; Rothé & Tréziny 2005, 178 no. 5). It may be a private edifice as well as a public space or a sanctuary in which this family group would have worshipped their ancestral god. A long lost statue, unearthed in *Rue des Consuls*, and a fragment of relief from the excavation of the Roman docks seem to represent Zeus, upstanding in the first case, sitting upon his throne and holding his sceptre in the other (Rothé & Tréziny 2005, 357 fig. 316 (relief)). It is impossible to say whether they are objects consecrated to the god in a sanctuary.

Votive Objects Suggesting the Proximity of a Place of Worship

An ionic capital from the end of the Archaic period is the sole architectural element ascribable to a temple of *Massalia,* but it was found outside its original context (Theodorescu & Tréziny 2000). However, a few offerings deposits enable us to assume the close presence of a sanctuary and to venture a few hypotheses on the cult worshipped there. Based on the number and the nature of the objects, we shall distinguish three main groups, those of the *Rue Négrel,* of the area of the harbour and of the area of *La Bourse.* Let us add however that Archaic structures discovered during the excavation of the *Pistoles* have provided plenty of ceramic objects, among which quality imported vases, associated with a "lantern" of exceptional type and with a few fragments of terracotta figurines (Moliner 2000). The presence of fauna remains and shellfish suggested the practice of ritual banquets in the vicinity of a cult place. It is difficult to draw accurate conclusions, but it can be noted that during a more recent occupancy phase of the site, towards the end of the Classical era and the beginning of the Hellenistic period, other objects seem to have a cultic function, like a terracotta antefix decorated with a Silen's head, which probably was part of a sacred edifice, as well as a fragment of a large earthen basin, whose rim is decorated with an embossed chariot race (Rothé & Tréziny 2005, 492 fig. 567–568). A few fragments of terracotta figurines might also belong to votive objects, but their small number and the disparate character of the representations do not enable us to assess the possible beneficiary of the worship. The absence of continuity between the Archaic and the end of the Classical periods remains problematic.

The Rue Négrel

Some fifty limestone shrines, which ought to be called *naiskoi* ("chapels") rather than "stelae", were found in that area, 47 in 1863 (only 41 entered the museum) and three in 1946. They were probably sculpted between the middle of the sixth and the beginning (?) of the fifth century BC. They represent a woman seated facing us in a small edifice, clothed in the way of the Ionian Archaic statues (Fig. 1). In one case at least, the person is carrying a small lion on his knees. A study underway[3] has enabled us to locate remains of painted decoration and to notice that some of these *naiskoi* had not been completed. If we agree to interpret women as divinities, their frequently discussed identity remains difficult to establish from the monuments properly speaking: The identification with the Anatolian goddess Cybele, often proposed, is quite hypothetical. We do not have reliable indications for the excavations of 1863, but in 1946–1947 Fernand Benoit unearthed in the immediate proximity of the three fragmentary *naiskoi*, associated with Attic ceramic shards, some fragments of terracotta figurines and of plastic vases also dating from the end of the Archaic period. As established by H. Tréziny, the same Benoit had discovered a short distance away in the North-West, at the foot of the *Butte de la Roquette*, a cave in which a spring flew, which had been channelled in Roman times. A connection therefore between this spring and the votive *naiskoi* cannot be ruled out, and we may be dealing in this case with the cult of a Nymph or another water-related divinity (Tréziny 2000, 96–98). On the other hand, Benoit found in the same area two heads of Silenic aspect which belonged to a type of vase attested in the excavations of the harbour, downhill from the *Rue Négrel* (Collin Bouffier 2000, 75 fig. 11).

Figure 1. Limestone stele from the Rue Négrel. Musée d'Histoire de Marseille, inv. 1544. © Musée d'Histoire de Marseille (Almodovar/Vialle).

The Area of the Harbour

In the 1990s, the excavations of the *Places Jules-Verne* and *Villeneuve-Bargemon* unearthed a considerable quantity of pottery of the Archaic period and a number of objects whose votive function seems indisputable: A miniature *naiskos* of the same type as those of the Rue Négrel, and elements belonging to some ten plastic vases of *askos* type made of local clear clay, one of them having been reconstructed (Fig. 2).[4] It features a pot-bellied monster, resting on three small feet in the form of lugs and fitted with a moulded horned head of Silenic aspect, as well as a folded tail at the rear of the vase. The presence of horns and the bovine tail remind one of the representations of the god-river Acheloos, an identification which could be strengthened by the comparison with a plastic vase of the necropolis of Ampurias (Collin Bouffier 2000, 75 fig. 11). The painted decoration of the *askos* found at the *Place Villeneuve-Bargemon* emphasises the originality of the vases produced in Marseille: A wing is painted rather clumsily on the main face (towards which the Silen's head is turned), a water type bird is engraved and painted on the other. This first series of plastic vases therefore associates with a bull's body (marked by its tail and its horns) a head related to the Dionysiac world and a decoration of aquatic birds. Other fragments of *askoi* from this area belong to at least one different type, since one of the ends is formed of a modelled bird's head and fragments of a fanned tail seem to belong to a bird rather than a fish. Thus, the importance of the theme of the bird asserts itself in this series of objects whose cultic function is hardly questionable.

Figure 2. Askos from the harbour's excavations. Musée d'Histoire de Marseille. © Centre Camille Jullian.

In the current state of the study, the following remarks can be made:

- The *askoi* with a Silenic head and the small limestone *naiskos* enable us to establish quite an accurate link between the votive objects of the *Rue Négrel* and those of the area of the harbour;
- These objects mainly relate to a feminine cult, to which the theme of the bird could allude, as well as a fragment of lamp (unpublished), an end of which features a frog's head. However, the *askoi*, taking

inspiration both from the images of Acheloos and of the Dionysiac world, rather allude originally to a masculine cult of fecundity: A fragment of a big earthen phallus found in the excavation of the *Place Jules-Verne* goes along the same line;

- As well as, in the rest of the Greek world, the cult of Nymphs is associated with caves, springs and the god-river Acheloos, the women sitting in the *naiskoi* and the *askoi* of the *Rue Négrel* and harbour area could relate to a cult linked with the spring discovered by F. Benoit and, possibly, a stream flowing towards the harbour;
- The enigmatic Lakydon represented on some coins from the second part of the fifth century could also relate with a cult of waters, perhaps of pre-Greek origin.

The presence of one or several water-based cults in the area of the harbour would not be astonishing when compared to the topography of Phocaea where beneath a major archaic sanctuary (dedicated to Athena?), several niches have been dug into the rock, close to the harbour, perhaps for accommodating stelae comparable to those of the *Rue Négrel*. On the other hand, the existence of a cult of Nymphs called Gennaids (Pausanias 1.1.5) and of local coins featuring the head of Acheloos close to Phocaea will be mentioned. In the neighbouring city of Kyme, *naiskoi* of the type of the *Rue Négrel* were found close to a spring, and a dedication to the Nymphs is engraved on a statue of a sitting woman unearthed close to a spring between Miletus and Didymoi. However, association to Dionysiac elements could be characteristic of Marseille.

It will be noted finally that all the objects which may be related to this cult (*Rue Négrel* and excavations of the harbour) are anterior to the Classical era. Would this sanctuary have disappeared towards the end of the Archaic period? Would this disappearance be connected to the extension of the city at the same time? It is currently impossible to reach a conclusion.

La Bourse

The excavations of this site, in particular in its Northern part, have delivered a number of objects to which a votive function can be attributed, but contrary to what we have just seen for the area of the harbour, very few are anterior to the Classical period. We have to mention a small wooden *kouros* of the third quarter of the sixth century (Hermary 1997), and especially two fragments of *askoi*, akin to those of the area of the harbour, one of them in the form of a bird, which were associated with an imported high quality Archaic pottery (Rothé & Tréziny 2005, 536–537 fig. 673). It cannot be ruled out that these objects were originally part of the same votive assembly as those of the *Rue Négrel* and of the area of the harbour. Some ten terracotta fragments belonging to seated female figurines date back from the Classical time, or possibly from the beginning of the Hellenistic period (Fig. 3). As two fragments of *kernoi* and a pig figurine were found in the same area, identification with the goddess Demeter of these female characters wearing a high crown (*polos*) and sitting upon a richly decorated throne could be proposed (Tréziny 2000, 89–91; Hermary 2015, 302–303 figs. 4–5). A graffito incised into the bottom of an Attic cup-skyphos from the end of the fifth century can be mentioned. It is difficult to read, but the hypothesis of a dedication to "Kleia Genethlios", a character who would be associated with procreation and birth, is undoubtedly the most certain (Hermary & Tréziny 2000, 151–152).

Figure 3. Terracotta head from La Bourse's excavations. Musée d'Histoire de Marseille, inv. B 604. © Centre Camille Jullian (C. Durand).

These cult places, without any architectural remains, were situated just outside of the town, near its Eastern entrance and close to late Classical tombs.

Notes

1. "It is in the headland (*akra*), however, that the Ephesium and also the temple of the temple of the Delphinian Apollo are situated. The latter is shared in common by all Ionians, whereas the Ephesium is a temple dedicated solely to the Ephesian Artemis".
2. See below for the Dionysiac aspect of certain *askoi* found in Rue Négrel and in the excavations of the harbour.
3. PhD thesis of Laura Rohaut, Université d'Aix-Marseille/Centre Camille Jullian. See previously Hermary 2000, with the bibliography.
4. *Ibid.*, 74–75 fig. 10; Rothé and Tréziny 2005, 377 fig. 347.

Bibliography

Bats, M., 2014, L'Artémis de Marseille et la Diane de l'Aventin. In: S. Bouffier & D. Garcia (eds.), *Les territoires de Marseille antique*. Arles et Paris, Errance, 133–142.

Bouiron, M. & Mellinand, P., 2013, *Quand les archéologues redécouvrent Marseille*. Paris, Inrap and Gallimard, 174p.

Collin Bouffier, S., 2000, Sources et fleuves dans les cultes phocéens: les exemples de Marseille et Vélia. In: Hermary & Tréziny 2000, 69–80.

Decourt, J.-C., 2004, *Inscriptions grecques de la France (IGF)*. Lyon, Maison de l'Orient et de la Méditerranée, 364p.

Domínguez, A.J., 2012, The First Century of Massalia: Foundation, Arrival of Migrants and Consolidation of a Civic Identity. In: Hermary & Tsetskhladze 2012, 61–82.

Hermary, A., 1997, Un petit kouros en bois de Marseille (fouilles de la Bourse). *Revue archéologique*, 227–242.

Hermary, A., 2000, Les naïskoi votifs de Marseille. In: Hermary & Tréziny 2000, 119–133.

Hermary, A., 2012, Lakydôn, dieu ou héros indigène dans Marseille grecque. In: Hermary & Tsetskhladze 2012, 109–124.

Hermary, A., 2015, Les figurines en terre cuite dans le Sud de la Gaule (VI^c–Ier s. av. J.-C.). In: R. Roure (ed.), *Contacts et acculturations en Méditerranée occidentale. Hommages à Michel Bats. Actes du colloque de Hyères, 15–18 septembre 2011*, 299–308. Arles, Éditions Errance, 299–308.

Hermary, A. & Tréziny, H. (eds.), 2000, *Les Cultes des cités phocéennes. Actes du colloque international Aix-en-Provence / Marseille, 4–5 juin 1999*. Aix-en-Provence, Édisud and Centre Camille Jullian, 202p.

Hermary, A. & Tréziny, H., forthcoming, Artémis d'Éphèse, de Marseille à Arles. In: E. Okan & C. Atila (eds.), *Festschrift in Honour of Ömer Özyiğit*, forthcoming.

Hermary, A. & Tsetskhladze, G.R. (eds.), 2012, *From the Pillars of Hercules to the Footsteps of the Argonauts*. Leuven, Paris and Walpole (MA), Peeters, 384p.

Long, L. & Hermary, A., 2007, Étude préliminaire de deux fragments de statues en marbre et d'une statuette en bronze trouvés au large des Catalans à Marseille. *Cahiers d'archéologie subaquatique* 16, 117–130.

Moliner, M., 2000, Les niveaux archaïques de la place des Pistoles à Marseille: un espace cultuel?. In: Hermary & Tréziny 2000, 101–117.

Richard, J.-C., 2000, Les divinités sur les monnaies de Marseille (IVe–Ier s. av. J.-C.). In: Hermary & Tréziny 2000, 191–196.

Rothé, M.-P. & Tréziny, H., 2005, *Carte archéologique de la Gaule. Marseille et ses alentours 13/3*. Paris, Académie des Inscriptions et Belles-Lettres, 925p.

Theodorescu, D. & Tréziny, H., 2000, Le chapiteau ionique archaïque de Marseille. In: Hermary & Tréziny 2000, 135–146.

Tréziny, H., 2000, Les lieux de culte dans Marseille grecque. In: Hermary & Tréziny 2000, 81–99.

Tréziny, H., 2012, Topography and Town Planning in Ancient Marseille. In: Hermary & Tsetskhladze 2012, 83–107.

10. *The Territories In-between: Marseille, Rome and the Gauls*

Rachel Feig Vishnia

Introduction

I was first intrigued by Marseille's relationship with Rome when writing about
the period between the First and the Second Punic Wars (241–218 BC) (Feig
Vishnia 1996, 1–9). Our main and practically only source for this otherwise
undocumented period the first two books of the Greek historian Polybius
which provide valuable information, not only on the incidents that eventually led to the Second Punic War, but also on Rome's conquest of the Po
Valley and her first intervention in the Greek mainland. However, an essential
shortcoming impairs Polybius' account: he is predisposed to believe that the
Second Punic War was inevitable after Rome's unlawful seizure of Sardinia in
238 (Polyb. 1.88.8–12; 3.10.3; 3.13.1–2; 3.15.10; 3.27.7; 3.28.2–3; 3.30.4).
Accordingly, all important matters that occurred between the years 241 and
218 BC are interpreted in the light of the forthcoming and crucial conflict
between the two Mediterranean powers (Polyb. 1.88.12; 2.13; 2.36.5–7).

Polybius' preconception, however, is misleading, and it obscures the fact
that Rome neither anticipated nor planned another war with Carthage. As
I see it, Rome's interest at that period lay far elsewhere; her eyes were turned
to a much closer arena, to northern Italy, her main efforts being concentrated
towards the conquest of the Po Valley (Feig Vishnia 1996, 13–25).

And yet, I had had one problem with this assessment, that is, how can one
explain the Ebro treaty signed between Rome and Carthage in 226, evidently
in view of the Carthaginian advance eastward on the Spanish Mediterranean
coast, a treaty according to which, as Polybius (3.27.10) relates in one sentence " the Carthaginians are not to cross the Ebro in arms".[1] On one hand,
as I have already argued, everything points to the fact that Rome had no

interest whatsoever in Spain at that specific point of time,[2] and yet, a formal treaty laying a clear cut dividing line was signed. Why then was such a treaty necessary if Rome had no interest in Spain? I could not but conclude that the treaty was signed for the benefit of a third party (as was the case with the Mamertines on the eve of the First Punic War [Polyb.1.10–11]) and that the only part who might have been threatened by the Carthaginian advance on the Spanish Mediterranean coast eastward were Marseille's Spanish colonies.[3] This is both intriguing and impressive. Rome would not render such a significant service to any ally—unless it was an important one—and certainly not without asking something in return. The only logical inference that can be drawn when surveying the problem in its historical context seems to indicate that Rome needed Marseille's watchful eyes on the movement of the Gallic mercenaries who penetrated Italy across the Alps at a crucial time, the eve of the planned and massive assault of the Romans on the Gauls in the Po Valley which began in 225 BC and ended with the conquest of this important region in 222 (Feig Vishnia 1996, 9–25).

The Romano-Massaliot connection was a very minor issue in my book written in 1996, but it stimulated a drive to learn more about Greek Marseille, about which—I must admit—I knew practically nothing. Eventually, I undertook to conduct fuller research on the relationship between the two cities—relations that have been described ubiquitously as unique—from about 600 BC, the supposed date of the beginning of the rapport, until 49 BC, when Greek Marseille chose to support what turned out to be the losing party in the civil war between Caesar and Pompey, and was consequently deprived of its political independence and prominence.

Current State of Research

The history of Greek Marseille is usually studied within a much larger subject matter—that of Greek colonization in general, and Greek colonization in the Western Mediterranean in particular, especially in light of the new and exciting archaeological finds dug under both land and sea in Marseille and its surroundings.[4] From the point of view of Roman historians, Marseille holds little interest, and its story is generally deemed unrelated to the course of Roman history during the period under discussion. Marseille raises some interest in modern scholarship only when Rome becomes involved in southern Gaul in the course of the second century BC (Clemente 1974; Hermon 1983).

Giuseppe Nenci, in an original and incisive study (1958) was perhaps the first to analyze the role that Rome's relations with Marseille played in Roman foreign policy. Nenci was the first to sketch the interactions between

Romans, Massilians, Etruscans Carthaginians, Syracusans and Italiots in the western Mediterranean and to stress their importance. However, he confined his study to the years 600–264 BC, and did not really question the credibility of his rather problematic sources. In fact, he claims that throughout this whole period we are dealing with a trio ('un colloquio a tre'): Rome, Marseille and Carthage. This is a rather problematic interpretation that raises more problems than it solves. Frank Kramer (1948) attempted to appreciate the role that Marseille played in Roman politics as well. However, he too confined his study to the years that preceded the Second Punic War (226–218), and sought the solution in the domestic arena, that is, in Roman factional rivalries as was the fashion in the post WWII years.[5] Therefore, from all perspectives, it seems to me that a comprehensive and methodical analysis of this subject is in order, hoping that the effort will yield valuable results.

It is not an easy task. First, because the ancient literary source material is extremely scanty and diffused among many and diverse authors. Secondly, because much of the evidence is archeological and pertain mostly for the first period of the relationship between the two, that is the sixth and fifth centuries BC.

Particularities and Goals

The distinctiveness of the relations between the two cities is rather striking. No other known contacts between Rome and a foreign state feature both such friendliness and such a long and uninterrupted duration. The only other long term known association is that between Rome and Carthage which lasted from 509 to 264 BC. Furthermore, the relations between Rome and Marseille offer a unique and singular view of Roman, and—to a much lesser degree unfortunately—of Massilian history. It is rather evident that Rome held Marseille in high esteem and treated the Greek city as an equal partner well into the second century BC after the Mediterranean basin had come under her rule, when it came to the Greek's city's help time and again and even increased its territories. Thus, if we make good use of the abundant archaeological material that has accumulated during the past few decades and continues to flow regularly, and if we ask straightforward questions—free, as much as possible, from hindsight—, then the ancient and well-known ancient sources could yield new, intriguing and wide-ranging insights concerning the two cities in particular, and the western Mediterranean in general during the period under discussion.

The Beginning of a Beautiful Friendship

The first question that needs to be addressed concerns the date of the begin-ning of the relationship. Two testimonies point to a very early date. First, we have the story about the Phocaeans who, on route to Gaul, visited Rome sometime during the reign of its fifth king, Tarquinius Priscus (616–579 BC), and concluded some kind of a treaty with the Romans (Justin 43.3). This alleged visit serves as yet another piece of evidence to establish the much debated question of Marseille's foundation date. To some Roman archaeol-ogists, who assume that the Phocaeans landed in Ostia, it provides further proof that the city was indeed founded in the seventh century by Rome's fourth king, Ancus Marcius (646–616), as recounted by Livy, and not in the fourth century as the archaeological finds suggest (Zevi 2000). Yet is this account true? The only source that tells about the encounter around 600 BC is Pompeius Trogus whose work is partially preserved in the summaries of Justin. Due to Justin's rather incompetent work, Trogus' sources are dif-ficult to trace (Alonso-Núñez 1987, 1994; Syme 1988; Yardley 2003). Since Trogus' ancestors were Gallic in origin (Vocontii), he may have repeated local anecdotes or sources which have left no other trace and whose veracity is questionable.

One cannot of course rule out completely the historicity of such a visit, the Phocaeans were, after all, superb and inquisitive sailors. Nonetheless, the notion of a formal treaty at such an early stage seems implausible. The idea may have sprung from the knowledge about the archaic practice common among Greeks, Etruscans and Carthaginians to sign commercial treaties—an example of which is probably the first treaty between Rome and Carthage traditionally dated to the first years of the Republic (508–507 BC).

Further proof to show that the friendship was struck around 600 BC is invoked from Strabo 4.1.5 who relates that there were many indications of the good relationship between the two cities, one of which was the fact that the *xoanon* of Diana on the Aventine was constructed by the Romans in the same artistic design as that of Marseille's Ephesian Artemis. The cult of Diana on the Aventine was founded by Servius Tullius Rome's sixth king (575–535 BC) and, relying on Strabo's testimony it has been often argued, without any contemporaneous evidence, that the cult was imported from Marseille where it had been set up, so it is assumed, shortly before. Yet Rome did not have to turn to Marseille for this. She could have copied the cult from the many Greeks in Italy and in Rome itself. Livy (1.45) clearly implies that it was copied from Asia and that its purpose was to promote the greatness of Rome and to make it supreme among the Latin communities. The temple it should be stressed was built by the nations of Latium conjointly with the Roman people.[6] And one can surely draw further conclusions from the fact that it was built on the Aventine, outside the *pomerium* at that period.

The credibility of the sources can be questioned and the evidence is circumstantial, yet, the general historical background against which they are set implies that during the regal period, perhaps even before the rise of the 'Etruscan' kings, expansion towards the sea was a manifest Roman policy (Camous 2004), and that Rome was influenced by and involved in the burgeoning Mediterranean liaisons during the Archaic period.

I would like to argue, therefore, that although one cannot completely rule out that some sort of insignificant contacts between Phocaean and Romans did in fact occur during the reign of Tarquinius Priscus—the relations between Rome and Marseille were not established in 600 BC. The sources thus implying are either unreliable or anachronistic. Nonetheless, these accounts are indicative of Rome's situation at that period and its relations vis à vis Etruscans, Latins and Carthaginians.

So when did the relations actually begin? Formal relations between states are usually formed on the basis of mutual interests; notably, such interests were totally absent around 600 BCE. It is therefore necessary to establish the approximate date in which the friendship was actually struck and to trace the background against which it was launched.

I believe that Rome began to show interest in Marseille only after the Gallic sack of the city (ca. 390 BC) and that the intermediary between Marseille and Rome was the Etruscan city of Caere—which had special and well attested connections to the Phocaeans (Hdt. 1.167). Caere, it should be noted, was Rome's closest ally at that period and it gave refuge to the Vestal Virgins and to Rome's holiest objects during the Gallic occupation (Liv. 5.40). I would conjecture therefore that the Etruscan city was probably a party to the treaty as well. The original treaty was hence between three and not two cities.[7]

Both Rome and Caere had suffered gravely from the new factor that had entered the Italian scene in the beginning of the fourth century, the Gauls. They had settled in the Po Valley and on the Adriatic coast and gradually drove the Etruscans out of Cisalpine Gaul and then began to meddle, mostly as mercenaries, in Italian rivalries. Caere, which had virtually saved Rome from the Gauls around 390 BC, suffered too at their hands when several years later Dionysius I, the tyrant of Syracuse, sacked the sanctuary at Pyrgi, Caere's port in 384 BC, with the help of Gallic mercenaries (Diod. Sic. 15.14).

While Rome had barely survived the Celtic attack, and the sanctuary of Caere's port was pillaged, Marseille, as was apparently well known, had successfully withstood its Celto-Ligurian neighbors for over two hundred years and had managed to establish many colonies in their midst (Liv. 5.34). It is probably under these circumstances that Caere and Rome sought out Marseille's friendship (and not vice versa), and it is in the Gallic context that Marseille's friendship proved most beneficial. Cicero specifically and repeatedly maintains that Marseille's greatest service to Rome was rendered during the wars against the Gauls. In his speech on behalf of Fonteius (13), Cicero declares: '…there is also the city of Massilia, to which we have already alluded, inhabited by brave and faithful allies, who have found in the resources of the Roman people a recompense for the dangers that they have run in our Gallic Wars'. In the *Philippics* (8.18), Cicero speaks in the same vein: '…that city, without whose help our ancestors never triumphed over the Transalpine tribes.…'

What was the nature of Marseille's assistance to Rome from about 380 to the second half of the third century BC? Presumably, Marseille's attested ties with some Celto-Ligurian tribes, the position of her colonies at the feet of the Maritime Alps, whom Michel Bats rightly compares to the Roman maritime colonies (Bats 2004), the information that traders going up and down the Rhône and the Durance brought with them, and Marseille's connections with tribes that controlled the passages in the Alps—all these allowed the city to gather information on the movements of the Gallic mercenaries that passed into Northern Italy. Mapping out the possible ways and means in which Marseille gathered information and passed it to Rome could be deciphered with the aid of Barruol's monumental work (1969 revised edition 1999). Much can be also assumed from the contacts between the cities in later periods.

What did Marseille receive in return? Marseille probably received exemption from taxes and other substantial benefits as suggested by Justin (34.5), the nature of which need to be further investigated, and other honors as well. It may well be that the treaty had a mutual help clause against common enemies.

The formal relations between the two cities began, as I would suggest, only after the Gallic Invasion (ca. 390) and were established through the mediation of Caere, Rome's stronger ally at that period who was also a party to the pact. Both cities, having suffered at the hands of Transalpine Gallic mercenaries, approached the Greek city that had firmly withstood its Celto-Ligurian neighbors. In this context an interesting question arises to which as yet I have found no answer. What happened to Caere's treasury at Delphi[8] after she had lost territories to Rome in 353 and her independence in 253? Did Caere continue to keep it? Is it possible Roman donations to Delphi had been first stored in Caere's treasury and only later moved to the Massilian treasury where they have been witnessed?[9] And another question to which there is no answer, was the original treaty ever renewed? We know of at least three treaties between Rome and Carthage; are we to suppose that the Romano-Massaliot treaties were renewed from time to time? I believe that the original treaty was renewed—yet I have no proof for it. Unless we can deduce something from the various appellations by which Marseille was addressed (by Cicero and Justin)—I shall return to this later.

Their Finest Hour—The Gallic Wars and the Second Punic War (225–201 BC)

This period denotes the zenith of the relations between the two cities, when Rome, now the suzerain of peninsular Italy, and Marseille, a Western Mediterranean power, cooperated as close equal allies, rendering services to each other. The fact that Caere had fallen under full Roman control in 253 BC does not seem to have affected the original treaty. On the contrary, as I will argue, the relations seem to have become closer as Rome most probably transferred her donations to Delphi, from Caere's treasury to that of Marseille.

We have nothing to prove that Marseille was in any way somehow involved in the First Punic War (264–241 BC). It would have been only natural for Rome—who had no experience in naval warfare, to turn to Marseille, who had had many clashes with Carthage, for guidance—but, if Rome indeed did ask for assistance, we know nothing of it.

After the end of the First Punic War, in 241, Rome set out to conquer the Po valley, in order to do away with the Gallic threat once and for all. The logistics and the military operations were meticulously planned[10] and Marseille doubtless helped in the strategic preparations as may be deduced from Cicero's praise. But the relations, it should be stressed, were not one-sided and Rome had to fill her part in the bargain as well. The Ebro treaty of 226 BC, as I have already argued, makes little sense unless considered from a Massilian point of view. Consequently it can be deduced that the treaty was not signed in order to draw a line between Rome and Carthage's respective spheres of influence in Spain, but rather to protect Marseille's interests and colonies on the eastern Spanish coast in view of Carthage's advent in southern Spain. This treaty and its interpretation were to become later a major contributory factor to the outbreak of the second Punic War.

It is difficult to establish whether Rome took a calculated risk in 226 BC, or whether the senate was aware of the possible future complications. I believe that Rome had no inkling of what the Carthaginians had in store. In any case, Marseille's prominence in Roman politics at that period is clearly manifested.

Marseille's massive assistance to Rome during the Second Punic War and in the first two decades of the second century BC, when Rome had to virtually recapture the Po Valley, is well attested, and we may reasonably assume that the she had rendered more services than those recorded by the ancient authors. The nature of Marseille's assistance, at first, consisted mainly of information on the movements of Gallic mercenaries across the Alps, hence intelligence on the Punic forces and active aid as well. Another point which should be perhaps further explored is the role that Ampurias played during the second Punic War and during the second century BC when Rome was constantly fighting in the two new Spanish provinces created in 196.[11]

From Preeminence to Dependence 200–49 BC

Theoretically, Marseille stood to gain from the expulsion of Carthage, an old and bitter commercial rival, from Spain, but ironically enough, the situation that consequently evolved proved to be detrimental to Marseille. Rome preferred to transport her forces to the problematic two new Spanish provinces through southern Gaul. The frequent Roman military presence in the region together with internal problems between the Celto-Ligurian tribes themselves resulted in many attacks on Roman armies and on Massilian territories and colonies. Marseille, unlike in earlier centuries, was unable to cope with the new situation on her own, and called on Rome repeatedly for help, and Rome, forever grateful, always complied and even enlarged Marseille territories, hoping that she would thus be better equipped to guard the road to Spain. It took Rome quite a long while to understand that there was little left of Marseille's past abilities and that Rome's old ally was unable to deal with the situation on her own. In 118 BC, Rome finally took things in hand; to properly defend the region which has become strategically imperative; Rome founded a province, Gallia Narbonensis and constructed the *Via Domitia*, the road that led from Italy over the Alps and through the south of France to Spain (Barruol 2004).

The upheaval caused by the invasion of the Germanic tribes at the end of the second century BC did not improve the situation. During the first century BC, Marseille managed not to get involved in the civil wars that tore Rome apart, although nearby Spain constituted a main conflict area, housing the Marians that had escaped Sulla headed by Sertorius in the seventies of the first century BC. But in 49 BC, after serious deliberations, Marseille decided to side with Pompey, who represented, it should be remembered, Roman legal authority, and paid a heavy price for this decision. Ironically Rome's expansion in Cisalpine Gaul and in Spain, made possible in many ways due to Marseille's help, was to become detrimental to Marseille's interests, standing and commercial interest.

The Nature of the Relations: What Sort of an Ally?

Since the relations between the two cities lasted for centuries, it is of utmost importance to examine them closely and to survey their evolution throughout the centuries. This point has never been investigated before and it is not an easy task since the character of the relationship is nowhere clearly outlined. In Justin's *Epitome* of book 43 of Pompeius Trogus the association is described as *amicitia* (43.3.4) and several lines later as *foedus* (43.5.3), two obviously different terms to anyone familiar with Roman political vocabulary regarding its allies; both are completely anachronistic (Badian 1958). About 70 BC, in his speech on behalf of Fonteius (13), Cicero refers to the Massilians as 'very brave and most faithful allies' *fortissimorum fidelissimorumque sociorum*, definitely an unequal relation. In his essay *De Republica* (1. 57) probably written before 49 BC, he refers to the Massilians "our clients" (*nostri clientes*) a term which suggests some sort of dependence or someone to whom some sort of protection is offered—a term which probably reflects Marseille needs at that period.[12] The nature of the relations, it seems, underwent changes in the course of the years, reflecting the changing positions of both parties to the original pact (just as did the various treaties between Rome and Carthage (Scardigli 1991). The changing statuses, as I have suggested earlier, were with all probability defined and registered in renewed treaties.

Wrap-up

I first thought of entitling my study surveying the relations between the two cities "A Mediterranean Liaison" based mainly on their geographical position vis à vis the Mediterranean. As the study gradually burgeoned, I realized that what strongly connected them was not the sea in-between, but rather the territories in-between, modern southern France stretching from the western Mediterranean coast to the Alps, which were settled by various Gallic tribes. Although not a consolidated power, the Gallic tribes, those who first invaded Cisalpine Gaul, and later those beyond the Alps who crossed the Alps to serve as mercenaries in Italian rivalries in the fifth and fourth centuries BC, pose a long standing and acute problem to Rome until the Po valley was finally sub-jected and pacified in the first quarter of the second century BC. Yet, at the very same time, as a result of the Second Punic War, Rome was drawn into

Spain and the path that led from Italy to the new Spanish provinces passed through territories of certain hostile Gallic tribes who clashed periodically with Roman forces. Marseille played a significant role in all these events.

Gaul was finally pacified by Julius Caesar towards 50 BC after quelling the revolt of Vercingetorix. Ironically, however, Marseille, who would have doubtless greatly profited from the pacification of Gaul, made a risky choice which turned out to be the wrong one and as a result lost her independence and prominence.

Notes

1. For various interpretations of the Ebro treaty, other than mine, see: Erdkamp 2009; Eckstein 2012. On the contract in general see Scardigli 1991.
2. See also Badian 1958, p. 47; Sumner 1986.
3. See Kramer (1948) and n. 2 above.
4. Bats 1992; 1998; Hermary, Hesnard & Tréziny 1999; Rothé & Tréziny 2005.
5. On factional rivalries in domestic Roman politics at the third and early second centuries BC see Cassola 1962 and Scullard 1972.
6. On this issue see: Gordon 1932; Momigliano 1968; Ampolo 1970; Gras 1987; Paribeni 1981. On the cult of Diana of Aricia and its relation to Diana on the Aventine see Green 2012.
7. On Caere's special relations with Rome see Sordi 1960; 1993.
8. On the treasury see Strabo 5.2.3. See also Salviat 1981; Briquel 1998; D'Agostino 2000.
9. Namely the golden bowl offered after the victory over Veii in 396 BC: Liv. 5.25.7–10; 5.28.1–5; App. *Ital.* frag. 8.3.
10. Polyb. 2.23.2–12. See also Feig Vishnia 1996.
11. Liv. 21.60.1–2; 21.61.5; 26.19.11; 28.42.3; 34.9.1–12; 34.11–16.
12. Cf. Also Liv. 28.42.3 in which Marseille is referred to as....*urbem sociorum*. The relevant date is 205 BC.

Bibliography

Alonso-Núñez, M., 1987, An Augustan World History: The 'Historiae Philippicae' of Pompeius Trogus. *G&R* 34.1, 56–72.

Alonso-Núñez, M., 1994, Trogue Pompée et Massalia. *Latomus* 53 110–117.

Ampolo, C., 1970, L'Artemide di Marsiglia e la Diana dell'Aventino. *PP* 25, 200–210.

Badian, E., 1958, *Foreign Clientelae*. Oxford, Clarendon Press, 342p.

Barruol, G., 1969/1999, *Les peuples préromains du sud-est de la Gaule: étude de géographie historique*. Paris, Second revised edition, Suppl. RAN, 410p.

Barruol, G., 2004, *La Via Domitia: Provence—Alpes du Sud: itinéraire de Tarascon au col du Mont-Genèvre*. Montpellier, Alpes de Lumière, 11p.

Bats, M., Bertucchi, G., Congès, G., & Tréziny, H. (dir.), 1992, *Marseille grecque et la Gaule*. Lattes-Aix en Provence, ADAM/PUP, 497p.

Bats, M., 1998, Marseille archaïque—Etrusques et Phocéens en Méditerranée nord-occidentale, *MEFRA* 110 2, 609–633.

Bats, M., 2000, Marseille et Rome des Tarquins à César. In: *Les dossiers d'archéologie: Marseille dans le monde antique*, 154, 80–87.

Bats, M., 2004, Les colonies massaliètes de Gaule méridionales: sources et modèles d'un urbanisme militaire aux IVe-IIIe s. av. J.-C. In: S. Agusta-Boularot & X. Lafon (dir.), *Des Ibères aux Vénètes*. Rome, École française de Rome, 51–64.

Briquel, D., 1998, Le città etrusche e Delfi: dati d'archeologia delfica. In: G. Pugliese Caratelli (dir.), *Annali della fondazione per il Museo C. Faina* 5, Rome, Quasar, 143–169.

Camous, Th., 2004, *Le roi et le fleuve: Ancus Marcius Rex aux origines de la puissance romaine*, Paris, Les Belles Lettres, 381p.

Cassola, F., 1968, *I gruppi politici romani nel III secolo A.C.* Rome, L'Erma di Bretschneider, 436p.

Clemente, G., 1974, *I Romani nella Gallia meridionale (II-I sec. a.C.): politica ed economia nell'età dell'imperialismo*, Bologna, Pàtron, 209p.

D'Agostino, B., 2000, Delfi e l'Italia tirrenica: dalla protostoria alla fine del periodo arcaico. In: A. Jacquemin (dir.), *Delphes cent ans après la grande fouille*, Athènes, École française d'Athènes, vol. I, 79–86.

Eckstein, A.M., 2012, Polybius, the Gallic Crisis, and the Ebro Treaty, *CPh*, 107/3, 206–229.

Erdkam, P., 2009, Polybius, the Ebro Treaty, and the Gallic Invasion of 225 B.C.E., *CPh*, 104/4, 495–510.

Feig Vishnia, R., 1996, *State, Society and Popular Leaders in Mid-Republican Rome 241–167 BC*. London, Routledge, 264p.

Gordon, A.E., 1932, On the Origin of Diana, *TAPHA* 63, 177–192.

Gras, M., 1987, Le temple de Diane sur l'Aventin, *REL*, 89, 47–61.

Green, C.M.C., 2007, *Roman Religion and the Cult of Diana at Aricia*, Cambridge UK and New York, Cambridge Univ. Press, 359p.

Hermary, A., Hesnard, A. & Tréziny, H. (dir.), 1999, *Marseille grecque: la cité phocéenne (600–49 av. J.-C.)*, Paris, Errance, 181p.

Hermon, E., 1983, *Rome et la Gaule Transalpine avant César (125–59 av. J.-C.)*, Napoli, Joven Editore, 363p.

Kramer, F.R., 1948, Massilian Diplomacy before the Second Punic War, *AJPh*, 69.1, 1–26.

Momigliano, A., 1962, Sul dies natalis del santuario federale di Diana sull'Aventino, *Rendiconti della classe dell'Accademia dei Lincei* 7, 387–392.

Nenci, G., 1958, Le relazioni con Marsiglia nella politica estera romana, dalle origini alla prima guerra punica, *RELig*, 24, 24–97.

Paribeni, E., 1981, Di Diana Nemorensis e di Artemide Efesia, *Dialogui di Archeologia*, n.s. 3, 41–48.

Paterson, J., 1978, Transalpinae Gentes: Cicero, De Re Publica 3.16, *CQ*, n.s 28.2, 452–458.

Rothé, M.-P. & Tréziny, H., 2005, *Carte archéologique de la Gaule. Marseille et ses alentours 13/3*. Paris, Académie des Inscriptions et Belles-Lettres, 925p.

Salviat, F., 1981, Le trésor de Marseille à Delphes et sa dédicace, *Archéologie du Midi méditerranéen*, 3, 7–16.

Scardigli, B., 1991, *I Trattati Romano-Cartaginesi: introduzione, edizione critica, traduzione, commento e indici*. Pisa, Scuola Normale Superiore, 373p.

Scullard, H.H., 1972, *Roman Politics 220–150 B.C.* Oxford, Clarendon Press, 325p.

Sordi, M., 1960, *I Rapporti Romano-Ceriti e l'origine della civitas sine suffragio*. Roma, "L'Erma" di Bretschneider, 188p.

Sordi, M., 1993, I rapporti fra Roma e Delfi e la decima. In: A. Mastrocinque (dir.), *I grandi santuari della Grecia e l'occidente*. Trento, Università degli studi Dipartimento di scienze filologiche e storiche, 158p.

Sumner, G.V., 1968, Roman Policy in Spain before the Hannibalic War, *HSCH*, 72, 205–246.

Syme, R., 1988, The Date of Justin and the Discovery of Trogus, *Historia*, 37, 358–71.

Yardley, J.C., 2003, *Justin and Pompeius Trogus: A Study of the Language of Justin's "Epitome" of Trogus*. Toronto-London, Buffalo, University of Toronto Press, 284p.

Zevi, F., 2000, Roma arcaica e Ostia. Una riconsiderazione del problema. In: I. Berlingo, H. Blank, F. Cordano et al. (dir.), *Damarato. Studi di antichita classica offerti a P. Pelagatti*, Milano, Electa, 233–243.

11. Marseille Territories of Exchanges

Marie-Brigitte Carre

Marseille before Rome

The first centuries of the Mediterranean exchanges of the Phocaean city can be summed up in a few lines, a subject quite well-treated by Michel Bats (in particular: 1992; 2012). The *emporia* developed by the people of Marseille right from the foundation of the city is an alternative to the poverty of their territory. This commercial vocation, through it would become the main economic power of the Gallic coasts as of the second half of the 6th century BC, is confirmed by the literary sources, in particular Strabo (IV, 1,5, transl. Loeb): "They [the Massaliots] possess a country which, although planted with olive-trees and vines, is, on account of its ruggedness, too poor for grain; so that, trusting the sea rather than the land, they preferred their natural fitness for a seafaring life" as well as by archaeology. Marseille plays the part of a transit and redistribution harbour. As a harbour dedicated to tin, gold, silver and iron in the West at the Archaic period thanks to its relationships with Spain and inner Gaul, the route leading to the Cornouaille in Brittany, the city is an intermediate (intermediary?) between the Greeks and the natives to whom it has secured commercial outlets since the sixth century BC.

However, this commercial vocation did not prevent it from searching for its own resources. Recent emphasis on the development of the wine-growing sector (Bernard, Collin Bouffier & Tréziny 2010, 138) has reinforced the evidence of amphorae which show the diffusion of Marseille wine throughout the Mediterranean basin since the sixth century BC (Bats 1990). The traces of cultivation are especially obvious since the Hellenistic period: the archaeological material collected in the sector of St Jean du Désert enables us to date that phase from the fourth century BC at the earliest. The land registries defined in the wake of this study and the excavations of the city centre mention a previous Greek planning system (Boissinot 2010). It has been suggested to date it from a possible arrival of Phocaeans in the middle of the sixth century BC, which would have had as a consequence an increased pressure of the inhabitants of Marseille on the cultivable lands close to the city. Around 540–530, the city which hitherto imported its wine from Etruria and from Greece (Sourisseau 2011, 219) starts to produce the amphorae which can be used for exporting its wine, in particular on the Italic markets (Bertucchi 1992).

This distribution was probably secured by the people of Marseille themselves. Even if it cannot be excluded that ships from other nationalities had come to Marseille to fetch the local produce (wine certainly, oil? *salsamenta?*), the crews, the ships and the merchants were arguably natives of Marseille. This is anyway what the inscriptions reveal, which do not mention other nationalities (Hermary, Hesnard & Tréziny 1999, 91–95). With the production of ceramics, especially clear paste ceramics, the diffusion of the Massaliot productions on all the sites of Southern Gaul testifies to a true redistribution monopoly by the merchants of the Phocaean city.

Marseille and the Roman Expansion in the Mediterranean Basin

As of the beginning of the fourth century BC, the Roman expansion, first in Italy, then in the Western Mediterranean region, imposes political mutations which generate a new commercial policy: Marseille, cut off from the Eastern Greek world, develops what Michel Bats (2012, 152) calls "a Massaliot *colonial network*". The foundation of its colonies in Gaul, Agathè (end of the fifth century or beginning of the fourth century BC), Olbia (around 325), Tauroeis (beginning of the third century), Antipolis and Nikaia (probably around the middle of the third century BC), forms a protective glaze for the city. Marseille thus ensures the control of its coastline and of the maritime routes towards Spain and Italy and still holds a quasi-monopoly. So, in Genoa, the Massaliot amphorae and clear ceramics predominate in the fourth–third centuries BC (Bats 1992, 273).

The Sources

Over the last decades, the excavations of the sites in the south of Gaul, especially in the Languedoc, have provided data to specify the presence of amphorae and of ceramics. However the discoveries have not enabled us to retrieve in Marseille the structures corresponding to the economic activity of the Hellenistic time (Hesnard, Bernardi & Maurel 2001). With the reorganisation of Augustean time, the harbour was cleaned thoroughly and all the sediments of Greek time were removed from the basin. Primarily, the data of the material derived from the ancient excavations, those of the Hellenistic backfill of La Bourse (Bertucchi & Marangou 1989) and of the shipwrecks, give us our understanding of the evolution of commerce at the Hellenistic time in Marseille. It is almost guaranteed indeed that the ships that sank in the natural harbour of Marseille were heading for the city, since the maritime route linking the Gallic Western coast to Italy is situated further in the south. From the fifty shipwrecks or so sunk between the Estaque, the Marseilleveyre archipelago and Planier island, several of them date back to the beginning of the city, but none of them is attributed to the third century BC. Conversely, six of them are dated between the end of the third century and the middle of the second century BC (Hesnard 1992).

The Evolution of Commerce in Marseille

In the first half of the third century BC, the production of clear paste ceramics from Marseille still account for the major part of table pottery (between 75 and 60%) (Bats 2005). Their presence remains identical to those of the fourth century BC, whether it is in Marseille or on the sites of Southern Gaul or of Catalonia. The imports of Attic ceramics decrease and disappear towards the beginning of the third century. They are replaced little by little, from the end of the fourth century BC, with black-varnished ceramics from Central and Southern Italy. This period sees the steady diffusion of the wine from Marseille, still dominating quantitatively the imports of wines from Greece, Sicily and Magna Grecia, especially in Languedoc and in the Iberic peninsula (Py 1990). The middle of this century sees the emerging competition of wines from Sicily and Magna Grecia alongside Greek wines, in particular Rhodian (Bats 1992, 274–275). The oldest levels of the backfill of the Bourse, dated between 200 and 180, still show the equivalent presence of Massaliot and Greco-Italic amphorae, while the shipwrecks reveal the arrival of Italian and Aegean products. The Grand Congloué 1 shipwreck, sunk between 210 and 180, contained 400 Greco-Italic wine amphorae from Campania and Sicily and more than 7000 pieces of A Campanian ceramic; some thirty Greek amphorae from Rhodes and Cnide made up the rest of the cargo. There again, Greco-Italic amphorae are transported by the shipwrecks Ecueil de Miet 4 at the beginning of the second century BC, Ecueil de Miet 5 around 175, and Mont Rose, middle of the second century BC. The most recent backfill of the Bourse contains archaeological material which can be dated between circa 170 and 140. A single amphora from Marseille comes from there, against 33 Greco-Italic amphorae. The Marseille ceramic (clear paste and other workshops of the region) decreases from 47% in the lower backfill to 27.5% in the upper backfill while at the same time, the proportion of common Italic ceramic (like the Campanian) increases from 24 to 67%. The recent study of the material of the site of rue J.-Fr. Leca (Tchesnakoff 2013) reinforces these first researches. Said material has been divided into the following chronological sequences (1: first quarter of the second century; 2: second quarter of the second century; 3: third quarter of the second century, insignificant; 4: last quarter of the second century and first quarter of the first century BC). The rapid decrease in Massaliot amphorae to the benefit of Italic imports can be observed: from 59% for sequence 1 to 26% for the following quarter century. The portion of the other imports remains relatively stable (between 5 and 10%). We can see during the same period a similar evolution in table crockery. The local production decreases from 44% to 21% of the total, while Campanian production increases from 48 to 65%.

In Eastern Languedoc, the Greco-Italic amphorae arrive in large numbers as soon as in the first quarter of the second century, and especially in Lattes where it accounts for more than 20% of amphora shards (Py, Adroher-Auroux & Sanchez 2001, 45). The calculation of the proportion of amphorae with respect to all pottery (Bats 1986, 404; Py 1990, 77) shows a multiplication of the imports of Italian wines by approximately ten during the second half of the second century. The phenomenon speeds up even more after the Transalpine conquest.

Between 125 and the Fall of Massalia

The Roman allies are again called upon by the Massaliots to cope with the aggression of the Ligurians, the Voconces and the Salyens. If Marseille recovers the bodies of its enemies after 122, in particular the lands pacified by the Romans, that is, the coastal strip of 12 *stadia*, close to the harbours (i.e., between 2 and 2.5 km), 8 *stadia* (1600m) on the rocky coasts, the strip is in fact quite limited. The expedition of Cn. Domitius Ahenobarbus against the Allobroges and the Arvenes in 122 and the foundation of Narbonne, the capital of the new Transalpine province in 118, seem to comfort Marseille in its role of privileged ally by granting illusory control over the Eastern Provence. In 109–102, the invasion of the Cimbres, Ambrons and Teutons stopped by Marius on the banks of the river Arc does not seem to reach Marseille. It proves profitable to him since the city recovers the control of the *Fossae Marianae* that

Marius had dug by his legions, for the sake of occupying them pending the attack (Vella, Leveau & Provansal 1999). This channel, intended to remedy the obstacles of the delta of the Rhône, which had represented an obstacle since the beginning of the traffic between the valley of the Rhône and of the Mediterranean region, is part of an economic as well as military strategy. Thus, Plutarch (*Life of Marius*, 15) explains that "transporting by sea all what the army needed was then slow and costly" since the alluvia of the Rhône and the bar which prevented the ships of a certain tonnage from running up the water made the upriver travel long and tedious. "Marius, later, seeing that, in consequence of the silting, its mouths were becoming stopped up and difficult of entrance, cut a new channel, and, upon admitting the greater part of the river here, presented it to the Massiliotes as a meed of their valour in the war against the Ambrones and Toygeni." The text of Strabo (IV, 1, 8) insists on the advantages supposedly gained by the Massaliots; Marius donates them this canal "and the wealth they carried off from this source was considerable, because they exacted tolls from all who sailed up an all who sailed down it". But this is probably here a gift marking the end of the pre-eminence of the trade of Marseille: since Marseille is increasingly dependent on its ally and the Roman traders rapidly get the control of its commercial circuits towards the hinterland and internal Gaul. Moreover, according to a hypothesis by Patrice Arcelin, it is then that the Massaliot merchants could start losing the monopoly of the contacts with the populations of the riverbanks. Since these privileged relationships, ensured by the community of Arles-Théliné, under Massaliot domination, could be transferred to the Roman *negotiatores* in a booming period of the Italian traffic towards Gaul and towards the emporion of Lyon, while Arles left quickly the stronghold of Marseille for that of the Italian merchants (Arcelin 2008, 112–114).

The Shipwrecks and the Excavation Data

Between 150 and 50 BC, the multiplication of shipwrecks suggests an intensified traffic between Marseille and Italy: seventeen ships were identified, often with large dimensions, all from Italy, transporting a cargo of wine, sometimes completed by ceramics or other products (Hesnard 1992). On the site of the rue Leca (Tchesnakoff 2013), in its last session dated between 125 and 75, the Massaliot amphorae account for only 14% of the containers against 75% of Italic amphorae, the local table ceramic 10% of objects against 71% in A Campanian.

These observations enable us to mention two recurrent problems in the historiography of Marseille.

The Prominence of the Merchants of Marseille in Commerce in Gaul and the Competition of the Italian Traders

We have seen that from the third century BC, the Italic amphorae appear in Marseille and from the second century, they rival the Massaliot amphorae until they finally prevail around 175.

The conquest of Iberia had opened up the Western route to the Roman *negotiatores* towards Western Languedoc and the Aude-Garonne axis (opening up of the internal market of Toulouse where not a single Massaliot amphora can be found at the beginning of the second century BC whereas thousands of Greco-Italic amphorae can be found). The Italic merchants bypassed the Massaliot positions and settled on the coast of the Roussillon and of the Languedoc, in Pech Maho and in Lattes in particular. As from the first half of the second century BC indeed, the Italian merchants had settled along the major natural communication pathways, for instance the Aude-Garonne axis. In Toulouse, most imported objects come from Italy (wine amphorae from the Latium and from Northern Campania, Campanian black varnish ceramic), with the first Rhodian amphorae and still a few more *lopades* from Marseille. Several Greco-Italic amphorae, dated at the latest from the middle of the second century BC, bear Italian names transcribed into Iberic letters. The persons mentioned could be interpreted as Italian merchants settled in Narbonne or in the surroundings, whose agents took delivery of the amphorae before diffusing them to the Vieille-Toulouse by the road which later became the Roman Aquitaine route (Domergue, Hesnard & Passelac 2002).

Conversely, the sites from Provence open up more slowly to Italy trade even if the conquest of Transalpine translates into increased business competition between Italian *negotiatores* and Massaliot merchants. Even so, as long as the Roman military and economic circuits are not consolidated, Rome needs the Massaliot forces to pacify the region, economically as well as militarily, a recurrent pattern in ancient texts.

The date of the end of the role of Marseille in Gaul's commerce to the benefit of the Italian traders is not clearly established and is still debated.

Patrice Arcelin (2008, 112–114) who bases himself on the example of Arles, sees the switchover of the Southern commerce into the hands of the *negotiatores* from the beginning of the second century BC. In *quartier des cryptoportiques* from the years around 225, the Italic products account for 44% of the ceramic furniture, the other half consisting of Massaliot and local productions. From 175, the imports from Italy were largely predominant and we could observe the still discrete occurrence of the productions of Romanised Catalonia; around 150, 94% of amphorae and 80% of the table pottery are of Italic origin. In the Jardin d'Hiver excavations, conversely, the amphorae and the local and Massaliot ceramics are largely predominant, from the second quarter of the second century BC, and they still represent some 90% of the total of the archaeological material. These distinctions have been interpreted as the consequences of cultural and economic breaks separating the different communities of Arles, whereas the local elites adopted more quickly the lifestyles in vogue in the metropoles. The Marseille trade is still present in the Camargue in the second century BC, but the Italian merchants henceforth ensure the redistribution of their products towards Arles and Central Gaul.

Michel Bats (1986, 391–404), in an article still providing a fundamental documentary base, has examined the distribution of Italian wine in Gaul in the second and first centuries BC, an approach which enables us to grasp the evolution of the role of Marseille in the trade of Southern Gaul. He observes indeed that the Italian amphorae cover, in Southern Gaul, a zone which is superimposed exactly on that of the great diffusion of the Massaliot productions, where during the second century BC, we can see a switchover from a majority to an exclusivity of Italic amphorae. This phenomenon is completed in the last quarter of the century. It would seem that the successive distribution of the Massaliot, then Italic, amphorae is done by the same network, that of Marseille and its agents, then at least from the conquest of the Transalpine, where that zone is entirely absorbed, the Italian go-betweens have gained in strength, then conquered the whole marketplace (Bats 2005, 272). For Michel Bats, the role of the Massaliot merchants benefiting from a long-time organised network should persist and there may be middlemen for the distribution of the Italic products at least to the end of the second century BC as testified by the presence of the ceramics of Marseille in Lattes, Narbonne or Toulouse. He also sees the evidence of the use of Gallo-Greek in writing, in spite of the creation of the province of Narbonne. The fact that the Gauls of the South of the hexagon started to use the Greek alphabet to transcribe their language and not the Latin alphabet, which was rather short-lived and limited in extent, while the Italian products were diffused in large quantities from 175, back up this hypothesis. The elimination of the Greek traffickers must thus be modulated and had to unfold gradually during the second century BC.

For Antoinette Hesnard (1992), this part of Marseille could even have lasted to the taking of the city in 49 BC. The archaeologist bases the conclusion on the data of the shipwrecks of Marseille and of the amphorae that they transport, which moderate this sensation of brutal collapse of the exchanges with Gaul by the merchants from Marseille. Since the routes of the amphorae that arrived in

Marseille or in the gulf of Fos can be followed by their stamps: that of Sestius, a landowner in Cosa, and found in the shipwreck of the Grand Congloué 2 is widespread in Gaul; same as amphorae of the shipwrecks of Plane 1 and 4, Planier 3, and Riou 3 can also be found in the gulf of Fos and on the sites of Gaul. These shipwrecks would suggest that these amphorae arrived in Marseille before going back to Fos (Via the *Fossae Marianae?*) to reach internal Gaul via the Rhône. We may wonder whether it means that the Massaliots were still the organisers of this trade or whether they did not content themselves with collecting the tax paid by the Italian traders for going through the canal of Marius.

The text sources themselves do not mention merchants from Marseille. In his correspondence, Cicero, for instance, only evokes the Italian traders. Similarly in 69 BC in the *Pro Fonteio,* a plea recanting the process against the governor of Cisalpine M. Fonteius where he is a lawyer for the defending party, he asserts that the inhabitants of Massalia, like the Roman citizens, the merchants and or the Roman publicans stand together with Fonteius. But he does not evoke the possible role played by the people of Marseille in this trade.

As for the vectors of this trade, the ships themselves, it is almost impossible, as in the previous time, to determine their origin. A few clues may however evoke the presence of sailors of such or such origin on board the ships. Thus, on board the shipwreck Pointe Lequin 2 (Porquerolles), dated from the turn of the second century BC, we find Massaliot clear paste ceramics as the same time as Greco-Italic and Campanian amphorae. The presence of Massaliot board material could be interpreted as a clue of the citizenship of the ship's occupiers (Collin Bouffier 2009, 39); conversely, almost a century later, on the shipwreck of the Grand Congloué 2 which transports Dressel 1A type amphorae from Cosa, the board material essentially consists of fine and common pottery, which suggests an Italian crew.

What Happened with the Wine from Marseille?

The massive fall of the distribution of wine amphorae from Marseille from 125, not only in Southern Gaul but also on the sites of the immediate periphery of Marseille, as in the village of La Cloche or in Olbia, raises the problem of continuous wine production in the Massaliot territory. This reduction in the number of the Massaliot amphorae is accompanied by the general decrease in the number of amphorae with respect to the total number of ceramics and of the parallel increasing arrival of especially Italic but also Aegean amphorae. This first observation can be opposed by the quantity increase in consumed ceramics which mechanically diminishes the proportion of amphorae, and that of the cultivation of local vineyards in the Languedoc (Py 1990, 82). In the Marseille territory, Plutarch (*Life of Marius*, 21) recants that after the victory of Marius on the Cimbres and the Teutons, the Massaliots fenced off their vineyards with edges built up with the bones of their dead enemies, which suggests that their vineyards must have extended almost to the valley of the river Arc still at the end of the second century BC. How then was the wine transported from these vineyards? Probably not in amphorae, although Guy Bertucchi mitigates this disappearance by noting the presence of a few rims of amphorae imitating the Greco-Italic and Dressel 1A amphorae from a local paste (Bertucchi & Marangou 1989, 83). The observations of Michel Bats show that the few imitations in micaceous paste of Greco-Italic type amphorae belong to the period 225–175 while those of Dressel 1B type seem totally anecdotal.

The resurgence of a new form of flat bottom amphorae, around the middle of the first century BC, should prompt us to reassess an old interpretation of that eclipse, which suggests that in the face of the growing indigenous demand, the increase in the Marseille population and its standard of living, self-consumption was sufficient to absorb the production and that this wine was transported in containers, such as wine skins and barrels which leave few archaeological traces (Bats 1990, 291; Brun & Laubenheimer 2004, 213). This hypothesis still remains to be backed up.

Thus, during the second and first centuries BC in Marseille as in the whole of Mediterranean Gaul, the Roman domination imposed itself little by little, indirectly, via trade and the disposal of Italian products.

After 49, Roman Marseille

It is still difficult to provide a global vision of the economy of the city after its fall before the legions of Caesar in 49 BC and the sanctions which hit it, especially the confiscation of the greatest part of its territory (Carre 2005). The first effect of the defeat of Marseille was indeed a modification of the territorial limits in Basse Provence, even if these adjustments are poorly known. Arles would have been granted the greatest part of the territory of Marseille; the latter remains indeed limited to the basin of Marseille and its steep crags (Leveau 1998, 80).

The tradition of the studies has long led to oppose to the economic vibrancy of the Greek city a significant decline in Roman times, caused by the competing colonies of Fréjus and especially of Arles whose position at the exit of the Rhône secures an advantage for exchanges with Gaul. Its maritime domination is restricted to the possession of Nice and of the Stoechad islands.

Moreover, our information for this period is rather sketchy: no or few habitat sites have been excavated and there is no artisanal site with the exception of the Butte des Carmes.

However the continuous developments and enlargements of the harbour basin, the dredging works which can be traced in the sludge of the harbour up to the fourth century, the modifications and reconstructions of warehouses in the third and fourth centuries show that the essential infrastructures of the commercial activities are attentively maintained (Hesnard, Bernardi & Maurel 2001).

The discovery in the excavations of place Jules-Verne, of a *tabella cerata* dated from the third century enables us to reconsider the prominence of Marseille in the economic life of the South of Gaul (France & Hesnard 1995). It indeed reveals the existence in Marseille of a *statio* of *quadragesima Galliarum*, that is, a 2.5% tax (1/40th) on the goods which were loaded or unloaded there. Before the discovery of this document, the nearest customs station (CIL XII, 717 and 724) was that of Arles whose role in the commercial traffic in Roman times was thus emphasised. In addition to the issues of the relationship between imperial taxation and the status of Marseille under the Empire and of the date when said tax was established, the discovery confirms the harbour importance of a site when a 2.5% tax must have been a major source of income for the State. If as proposed by Jérôme France (1999, 106–108) a second *tabella* discovered at the same place seems to mention a *vectigal terrestre maritimumque*, a municipal tax on goods, we are this time in the presence of an appreciable profit for the city, on a par with the taxes on the canal offered by Marius at the end of the second century BC.

The Resurgence of the Wine from Marseille

The export of wine reappears among the economic activities of Marseille in the second half of the first century BC after an interruption of almost one century. As soon as the Augustean period, the workshop at the Butte des Carmes produces flat-bottom amphorae whose several variations (Bertucchi 1992, forms 6 and 7, 217) are still attested in the second century AD. This production, forerunner of a generalising phenomenon throughout the region of Narbonne, represents the earliest evidence of the flat bottom containers which became the standard of wine amphorae in the following decades. Among the reasons invoked for such a radical change of form, we assume an improved relationship between the weight of the container and that of the contained, far more favourable than for the previous amphorae.

We have also admitted that their form made them more suitable for river navigation or coasting trade small units. It is difficult to measure the scope and the precise chronology of Marseille exports, since the very little micaceous paste of the variant 7 of Guy Bertucchi makes bringing them to light difficult among the other Gaul products. They can be found on the coasts of Provence (Bertucchi 1992, 110), on the sites of Lyon as from the very beginning of the Augustan times (Desbat & Martin Kilcher 1989, 343), on the sites of the North and the East of the Gauls (Strasbourg, Titelberg), always in very small quantities (Baudoux 1998; Laubenheimer & Hénon 1998); a few amphorae are still attested in Carthage (Martin Kilcher 1993, 284) and Ostia (Widemann & Naciri 1989, 295).

The consumption of wine from Marseille in Rome is attested several times by Martial who mocks its taste and its price *(Epigrams,* III, 82; X, 36; XIII, 123; XIV, 118). Still, this wine is quoted by Plinius *(NH,* XIV, 68) as the best of the Mediterranean coast between the Alps and the Pyrenees. Two mentions on an *ostrakon* and a papyrus still show that it could be found in Egypt in the second century AD (Bertucchi 1992, 208–209).

The role of the harbour in Marseille in the commerce of wine is confirmed by the presence of warehouses with *dolia* used between the first and the middle of the second century AD and which occupy more than 150m of shoreline (Hesnard 1997). These jars, intended for wine storage, containing between 1000 and 2500 l iters each, should be related to a type of specialised maritime transport of bulk wine in cistern ships provided with fixed post *dolia.* The excavation of several shipwrecks has enabled scholars to specify the chronology and the operating modalities of this traffic which appeared at the time of Augustus, around 10 BC (Hesnard 1992). Inasmuch as space and containers are needed to empty the *dolia,* upon arrival, this kind of cargo requires specific arrangements. These cargos are hence intended for major consumption or redistribution centres, where wine can be transhipped into the *dolia* of the warehouses: in addition, these *horrea* have only been located in Ostia, Lattes (Garcia & Vallet 2002, 26–35), Narbonne (Ginouvez 2010), and probably Lyon (Carre 2004). We consider that the need for very large quantities of wine for supplying troops may have been the origin of this mode of transport which appeared at the same time of the military operations on the Germanic frontier (Tchernia 1997).

Nevertheless, we do not know how this configuration integrates the production of wine from Marseille, especially if it has enabled filling up the *dolia* bound for Rome or whether these warehouses have been mostly used for storing the wine from somewhere else pending its redistribution. Only the shipwreck of the Petit Congloué could have transported, alongside the *dolia* and amphorae from the Tarraconensis, flat bottom amphorae from Marseille, as suggested by Guy Bertucchi (1992, 113) reviewing the proposition of Martine Corsi-Sciallano and Bernard Liou (1985, 35 sv.) who consider them productions from the workshop of Corneilhan. The discovery in Fos of an inscription *MASSICVM* written in full (Liou 1987, 74, F108) seems to strengthen our assumption of Massaliot amphorae. Indeed, the *tituli picti* MASS on amphorae from Marseille found in Fos, Lyon and Vindonissa had been developed *Mass(iliense uinum)* up to the discovery of this *titulus pictus* in Fos. The meaning to give to these inscriptions is however not completely clear; are we dealing with the wine of the Mont Massique, one of the "crus classés" of Plinius (*NH*, XIV, 61–66) situated close to Naples, transported in *dolia* and transhipped at its arrival in Marseille in a local container? Bernard Liou, who wondered about the transport in amphorae of a "grand cru classé", proposed that there was rather an abusive designation for wine produced and bottled in amphorae in the Narbonne region, baptised by the name of prestigious Italian "cru" (1988, 173); while Guy Bertucchi (1992, 182) prefers to maintain the development *Mass(iliense)* or *Mass(alioticum uinum)* in all the cases when the mention is not explicit.

The *dolia* warehouses of the place Jules-Verne are levelled around the middle of the second century AD at the time when the testimonies of shipwrecks disappeared, to be replaced with other types of warehouses (France & Hesnard 1995, 79). The latter, composed of juxtaposed longitudinal cells, are more extended than the previous *dolia* warehouses, confirming the maintained activity of the harbour at that time. They operated up to the fourth century, when a general fire of the buildings of the area led to their abandonment.

The other productive or artisanal activities have left practically no traces. At the most, we may mention the colouring agents of the shipwreck Planier 3 (Tchernia 1969–1970) and the alum transported in the Liparot amphorae of the shipwreck of Cassidaigne (cargos which evoke for the first century BC the presence of *fullonicae*. These tenuous remains should be reconciled with the mention in the second century of a college of *centonarii* (*CIL* XII, 410), manufacturers of rough wool fabrics.

The transformation of the fish caught around Marseille, especially tuna in the mouth of the Rhône (Oppian, *Halieutica*, III, 625–648), is attested by the collection of skeletons in the excavations of the place Jules-Verne (Sternberg 2005) and perhaps during the first century AD in the site of the Ile Verte, in La Ciotat and in Riou (Vasselin 2003, 102–103). If this activity went further than on-site consumption, it may have given rise to marketing from which we can find only a few traces: Imitations of Hispanic amphorae Dressel 7–11 for salted fish are produced on the Butte des Carmes (Bertucchi 1992, 134 sv) and rare testimonies have been retrieved on the Rhône-Rhine axis, in Lyon (Burnouf & Laubenheimer 1998, 202) or in the Titelberg (Laubenheimer & Hénon 1998, 110).

The Imports

It is not possible to date with precision the contexts found in Marseille since current studies tend, purely by chance, to favour the levels at the junction of the second and third centuries (Bonifay, Carre & Rigoir 1998, 353), especially that of the shipwreck of the Bourse in the horn of the harbour.

However, during the centuries after the city went under Roman domination, the examination of the furniture found in the excavations and the cargoes of the shipwrecks in the bay of Marseille unsurprisingly shows a city integrated in the major currents of Mediterranean exchanges (Bonifay, Carre & Rigoir 1998, 55–101): to the best of our knowledge, the origins, especially for the pottery, reflect in essence those registered by Clementina Panella in Ostia in the levels of the North-East area of the Terme del Nuotatore, dated between 160 and 190/200 (Panella 1991, 293), for example the absolute predominance, among the fine ceramics, of the African sigillata A over all the other types of production. In the contexts of the shipwreck of the Bourse, it is at the detriment of the terra sigillata of the valley of the Rhône, among which only closed shapes can be found, not represented in the ceramics of African origin. Half the amphorae are of Gallic origin, in compliance with the percentages found on the Tyrrhenian coast (18% in Ostia, 50% in Settefinestre). Among the other imports, Adriatic, Eastern, Hispanic amphorae and even a few African are amphora, premises of massive imports of the following centuries.

The economic life of Marseille, if it is not glaring, seems to remain unchanged after entering the Roman orbit. During the long peaceful period marking the first centuries of the empire, its merchant harbour was arguably the main cause for its prosperity, the quantitative significance of the sole production observable being that of wine, is difficult to be assessed since it appears to be diluted, on the external markets, in the other productions of the Narbonne region. Conversely, the commercial tradition inherited from the Greek time has probably contributed to preserving the role of merchant stronghold of this city, still less favourably situated than Arles and Fos, for the redistribution trade towards Gaul.

Bibliography

Arcelin, P., 2008, Arles protohistorique. De l'implantation coloniale grecque à l'agglomération portuaire indigène. In: M.P. Rothé & M. Heijmans (dir.), *Arles, Crau, Camargue, Carte Archéologique de la Gaule 13/5*. Paris, Académie des Inscriptions et Belles-Lettres, 97–114.

Bats, M., 1986, Le vin italien en Gaule au IIe–Ier s. av. J.-C.: problèmes de chronologie et de distribution, *DHA* 12, 391–430.

Bats, M. (dir.), 1990, *Les amphores de Marseille grecque. Chronologie et diffusion (VIe–Ier s. av. J.-C.)*, Actes de la table-ronde de Lattes [11 mars 1989]. Lattes-Aix-en-Provence, A.D.A.M.—PUP, 294p. (*Études Massaliètes*, 2).

Bats, M., 1992, Marseille, ses colonies et les relais indigènes du commerce massaliète en Gaule méridionale. In: *Marseille grecque et la Gaule*. Actes des colloques de Marseille (1990). Lattes-Aix-en-Provence, 263–278 (*Études Massaliètes*, 3).

Bats, M., 2005, Regards sur l'économie de Marseille antique, 2. La période hellénistique (350–50 av. J.-C.). In: M.-P Rothé & H. Tréziny (dir.), *Marseille et ses environs, Carte Archéologique de la Gaule* 13/3. Paris, 2005, Académie des Inscriptions et Belles-Lettres, 271–272.

Bats, M., 2012, Les Phocéens, Marseille et la Gaule (VIIe–IIIe s. av. J.-C.), *Pallas*, 89, 145–156.

Baudoux, J., 1998, Les amphores à Strasbourg, fouilles récentes du tramway (Homme de Fer) et de la rue. In: F. Laubenheimer (dir.), *Les Amphores en Gaule II. Production et circulation*. Besançon, Presses universitaires franc-comtoises, 91–105.

Bernard, L., Collin Bouffier, S. & Tréziny, H., 2010, Grecs et indigènes dans le territoire de Marseille. In: H. Tréziny (ed.), *Grecs et indigènes de la Catalogne à la mer Noire*, Paris/Aix, Errance/CCJ, BiAMA 3, 2010, 131–145.

Bertucchi, G., 1992, *Les amphores et le vin de Marseille: VIe s. avant J.-C. -IIe s. après J.-C.* Paris, Ed. du CNRS, 250p.

Bertucchi, G. & Marangou, A., 1989, Le remblai hellénistique de la Bourse à Marseille. Résultats d'un sondage, *Revue archéologique de Narbonnaise*, 2, 47–84.

Boissinot, Ph., 2010, Des vignobles de Saint Jean du désert aux cadastres antiques de Marseille. In: H. Tréziny (ed.), *Grecs et indigènes de la Catalogne à la mer Noire*, Paris/Aix, Errance/CCJ, BiAMA 3, 2010, 147–154 (BiAMA 10).

Bonifay, M., Carre, M.-B. & Rigoir, Y. (dir.) 1998, *Fouilles à Marseille. Les mobiliers (I–VIIe siècles)*, Paris-Lattes, Errance-A.D.A.M., 433 p. (Etudes massaliètes 5).

Brun, J.-P. & Laubenheimer, F., 2004, Le vignoble gaulois. In: J.P. Brun, M. Poux & A. Tchernia (dir.), *Le Vin. Nectar des Dieux, Génie des Hommes*, Gollion, Infolio éditions, 210–223.

Burnouf, J. & Laubenheimer, F., 1998, Des vides sanitaires, Place Bellecour à Lyon. In: F. Laubenheimer (dir.), *Les Amphores en Gaule II. Production et circulation*. Besançon, Presses universitaires franc-comtoises, 175–192.

Carre, M.-B., 2004, Transport en vrac. In: J.P. Brun, M. Poux & A. Tchernia (dir.), *Le Vin. Nectar des Dieux, Génie des Hommes*. Gollion, Infolio éditions, 276–277.

Carre, M.-B., 2005, Regards sur l'économie de Marseille antique, 3. Période romaine. In: M.-P. Rothé & H. Tréziny (dir.), *Marseille et ses environs, Carte Archéologique de la Gaule 13/3*. Paris, Académie des Inscriptions et Belles-Lettres, 272–274.

Collin Bouffier, S., 2009, Marseille et la Gaule méditerranéenne avant la conquête romaine. In: B. Cabouret, J.P. Guilhembet & Y. Roman (eds.), *Rome et l'Occident, du IIe siècle av. J.-C au IIe siècle apr. J.-C.,* Colloque de la SOPHAU, [15–16 mai 2009], *Pallas*, 80, 35–60.

Corsi-Sciallano, M. & Liou, B., 1985, *Les épaves de Tarraconaise à chargement d'amphores Dressel 2–4*. Paris, CNRS. (Archaeonautica 5) 178p.

Desbat, A. & Martin Kilcher, S., 1989, Les amphores sur l'axe Rhône-Rhin. In: *Amphores romaines et Histoire économique*. Rome, 339–365. (Coll. École Française de Rome, n°114).

Domergue, Cl., Hesnard, A. & Passelac, M., 2002, Les échanges commerciaux dans le Toulousain: l'exemple de Vieille-Toulouse. In: J.M. Pailler, *Tolosa: nouvelles recherches sur Toulouse et son territoire dans l'Antiquité*, Rome, 193–197. (Coll. École Française de Rome, 223).

France, J. & Hesnard, A., 1995, Une *statio* inédite du Quarantième des Gaules et les opérations commerciales dans le port romain de Marseille (place Jules-Verne), *JRA*, 8, 78–93.

France, J., 1999, Les revenus douaniers des communautés municipales dans le monde romain (République et Haut-Empire). In: *Il capitolo delle entrate nelle finanze municipali in Occidente ed in Oriente*, Actes de la Xe rencontre franco-italienne sur l'épigraphie du monde romain [Rome, mai 1996], Rome, 95–113 (Coll. École Française de Rome, 256).

Garcia D., & Vallet, L., *L'espace portuaire de Lattes antique*. Lattara 15, Lattes, Ed. Association pour le développement de l'archéologie en Languedoc-Roussillon, 223p.

Ginouvez, O., 2010, Port-la-Nautique, les entrepôts. In: *Bilan Scientifique Languedoc-Roussillon*, 42–43.

Hermary, A., Hesnard, A. & Tréziny, H., 1999, *Marseille Grecque, la cité phocéenne (600–49 av. J.-C.)*, Paris, Errance, 181p.

Hesnard, A., 1992, Nouvelles recherches sur les épaves préromaines en baie de Marseille. In: *Marseille grecque et la Gaule*. Actes des colloques de Marseille (1990), Lattes-Aix-en-Provence, A.D.A.M.—PUP, 235–243 (*Études Massaliètes*, 3).

Hesnard, A., Bernardi, Ph., Maurel, Chr., 2001, La topographie du port de Marseille de la fondation de la cité à la fin du Moyen Age. In: M. Bouiron & H. Tréziny (eds.), *Marseille. Trames et paysages urbains de Gyptis au Roi René, Actes du colloque international d'archéologie*, Marseille 1999, Aix-en-Provence, Edisud, 159–202. (Études Massaliètes 7).

Hesnard, A., 1997, Entrepôts et navires à dolia: l'invention du transport de vin en vrac. In: D. Garcia & D. Meeks (eds.), *Techniques et économie antique et médiévale: Le temps de l'innovation.* Actes du Colloque d'Aix en Provence [mai 1996]. Paris, Errance, 130–131.

Laubenheimer, F. & Hénon, B. 1998, Les amphores du Titelberg (Luxembourg). In: F. Laubenheimer (dir.), *Les Amphores en Gaule II. Production et circulation.* Besançon, Presses universitaires franc-comtoises, 107–142.

Leveau, P., 1998, Introduction. In: F. Gateau (dir.), *L'Etang de Berre.* Carte Archéologique de la Gaule 13/1. Paris, Académie des Inscriptions et Belles-Lettres, 67–147.

Leveau, P. & Trousset, P., 2000, Les sources écrites gréco-romaines et l'histoire naturelle des littoraux. *Méditerranée,* 7–14.

Liou, B., 1987, Inscriptions peintes sur amphores, *Archaeonautica,* 7, 55–139.

Liou, B., 1988, Le contenu des amphores, typologie et épigraphie: quelques cas aberrants ou embarrassants, *SFECAG,* Marseille, 171–177.

Martin Kilcher, S., 1993, Amphoren der späten Republik und der frühen Kaiserzeit in Karthago. Zu den Lebensmittelimporten der Colonia Iulia Concordia, *RM,* 100, 269–320.

Panella, C., 1991, Un contesto di età antonina dalle Terme del Nuotatore di Ostia. *StMisc,* 28, 283–297.

Py, M., 1990, La diffusion des amphores massaliètes sur le littoral du Languedoc Oriental. In: M. Bats (dir.), *Les amphores de Marseille grecque. Chronologie et diffusion (VIe-Ier s. av. J.-C.),* Actes de la table-ronde de Lattes [11 mars 1989], Lattes-Aix-en-Provence, A.D.A.M.—PUP, 73–86. (*Études Massaliètes,* 2).

Py, M., Adroher-Auroux, A. & Sanchez, C., 2001, *Dicocer 2, Corpus des céramiques de l'âge du Fer de Lattes* (fouilles 1963–1999), Lattara 14, Lattes, Association pour le développement de l'archéologie en Languedoc-Roussillon, 1306p.

Sourisseau, J.-C., 2011, La diffusion des vins grecs d'Occident du VIIIe au IVe s. av. J.-C., sources écrites et documents archéologiques. In: *La vigna di Dioniso: vite, vino e culti in Magna Grecia,* Atti del quarantanovesimo convegno di studi sulla Magna Grecia, Taranto 24–28 settembre 2009, Tarente, 143–253.

Sternberg, M., 2005, La pêche. In: M.-P Rothé & H. Tréziny (dir.), *Marseille et ses environs.* Carte Archéologique de la Gaule 13/3. Paris, 2005, Académie des Inscriptions et Belles-Lettres, 245–247.

Tchernia, A., 1969–1970, Premiers résultats des fouilles de juin 1968 sur l'épave 3 de Planier. *Études Classiques,* III, 51–82.

Tchernia, A., 1997, Le tonneau, de la bière au vin. In: D. Garcia & D. Meeks (eds.), *Techniques et économie antique et médiévale: Le temps de l'innovation.* Actes du Colloque d'Aix en Provence [mai 1996]. Paris, Errance, 121–129.

Tchesnakoff, A., 2013, Un faciès de consommation à Marseille à l'époque tardo-hellénistique. La céramique et les amphores d'un ensemble stratifié du site de la rue J.-F. Leca (IIᵉ– Iᵉʳ s. av. J.-C.). In: *SFECAG,* Actes du Congrès d'Amiens [9–12 mai 2013], Marseille, 351–363.

Vasselin, B., 2003, L'île Verte (La Ciotat, Bouches du Rhône). In: M. Pasqualini, P. Arnaud, & C. Varaldo (dir.), *Des îles côte à côte. Histoire du peuplement des îles de l'Antiquité au Moyen-Age*, Actes de la table ronde de Bordighera [12–13 décembre 1997], Aix-en-Provence—Bordighera, Association Provence Archéologie-Istituto di studi liguri, 89–109. (Supplément au *Bulletin Archéologique de Provence*, 1).

Vella, C., Leveau, P. & Provansal, M., 1999, Le canal de Marius et les dynamiques littorales du golfe de Fos. In: Gallia, 56, 131–139.

Widemann, F. & Naciri, A., 1989, Analisi delle anfore galliche d'Ostia. In: *Amphores romaines et Histoire économique*, Rome, 285–296 (Coll. École Française de Rome 114).

12. Greek Marseille and the Gauls of the South: Quite Different Funeral Practices (Fifth–Second Centuries BC)

Bernard Dedet

Introduction

The issue of the relations between Greek settlers and indigenous populations of Southern Gaul is usually addressed in terms of commercial exchanges and of their repercussions on the economy and the lifestyle of the autochthonous, including their access to writing. The funeral usages, for their own part, which reflect the collective representations of death and of the Hereafter, and which also express social dispositions, are only rarely taken into account. Still, they undeniably provide a marker of cultural identity. The comparison of the funeral practices of the inhabitants in Marseille with those of the Natives of Southern Gaul enables us to query the depth of the relations between both populations and the limits of the assimilation processes (Dedet 2011a). This comparison has only been possible of late, since satisfactory documentation became available on both sides, in sufficient quantity and in particular including the analysis of human bone remains.

For Marseille, the necropolis of Sainte-Barbe, excavated recently, provides a sound base to know the funeral usages of its inhabitants, or at least of a sample of them, with a series of 96 tombs ranging between 400 and 150 BC (Moliner et al. 2003). Several sepultures discovered recently can be added: rue Tapis-Vert, cours Julien, district of Saint-Mauront, basin Le Carénage, Le Pharo and more or less sketchy clues on the funeral terraces of La Bourse (Bertucchi 1992, 132–134; Rothé & Tréziny 2005, 599–600, 676–679), as well as the recent excavation, carried out in 2012 and under study, of some thirty sepultures datable from the fourth to the third centuries BC in Le Lazaret d'Arenc (Fig. 1).

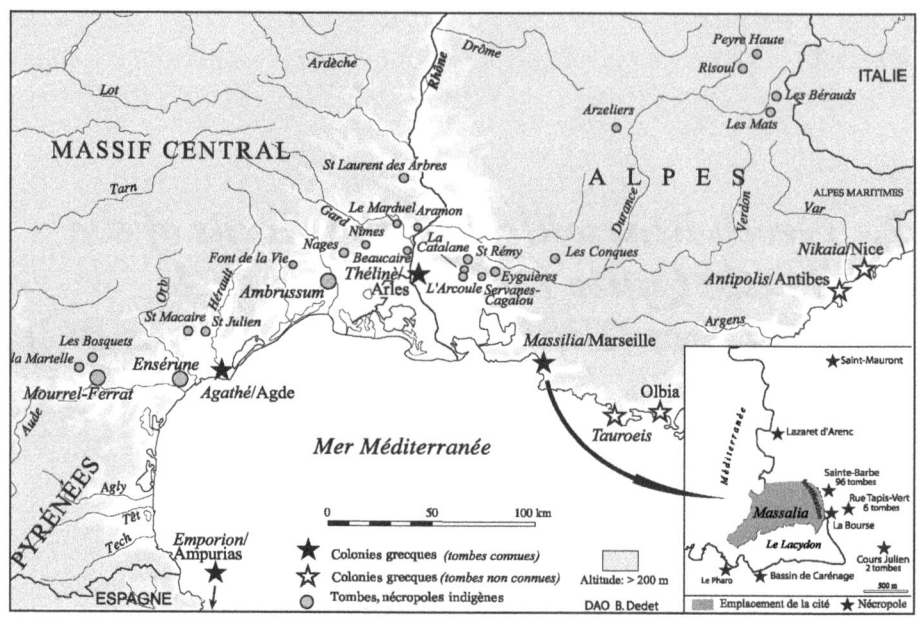

Figure 1. Cemeteries or tombs in South France (end of the fifth century BC/beginning first century BC); at the bottom, on the right, Greek Marseille cemeteries or tombs. (DAO B. Dedet, CNRS)

By contrast, as regards the regional native world of the second Iron Age, three sites mainly are available today: the necropolis of Ensérune (Hérault) with a pyre and approx. 120 tombs, whose bones have been studied, ranging between 500 and 200 BC (Dedet & Schwaller 2010), and two recent discoveries, 13 tombs of the last quarter of the fourth century BC of the necropolis of Mourrel-Ferrat in Olonzac in Western Languedoc as well (Janin et al. 2000) and a district of the necropolis of *Ambrussum*, in eastern Languedoc, including 25 tombs and a pyre of the third century BC (Dedet 2012). A sector recently excavated, and under study, of the necropolis of Le Sizen-Vigne in Beaucaire (Gard), with some hundred tombs, most of them dated from the second half of the fourth century and from the first half of the following century, should shortly provide quite a significant documentation in this respect. They can include the tomb of the middle of the fifth century BC of Font de la Vie in Saint-Bauzille-de-Montmel (Hérault), and a few tombs of the second and first centuries BC in Beaucaire, also, in Nîmes and in Aramon in the Gard, as well as in the Alpilles in Provence (Dedet & Schwaller 2010) (Fig. 1).

This comparative analysis is organised around four major themes: the age breakdown of the population of the deceased admitted into the cemetery; the processing of corpses; the accompaniment material; the pyres and the aerial portion of the tombstones. Eventually, we shall query the results of the comparison of the Massaliot and native funeral practices.

The Distribution of the Deceased in the Necropolis According to the Age at Death

Quite a significant difference between the cemeteries of *Massalia*/Marseille and those of the native world can be noted in the distribution of the deceased according to the age at death (Fig. 2). It mainly concerns the very young children, stillbirths, newborns and toddlers, that is, the under one-year old class.

These deaths, at an age characterised by a very high mortality rate in an ancient-type demography, are completely absent from the native necropolis in the South of Gaul, with the exception of those discovered in the same sepulture as a feminine connotated adult, and which must point to the deaths of pregnant women or in childbirth. This absence for this age class is particularly significant in the three necropoles for which data are abundant: Ensérune, Mourrel-Ferrat and *Ambrussum* (Fig. 2 A, B and C).

Conversely, in Marseille/Sainte-Barbe, these very young deaths are well attested and their presence perfectly complies with the mortality expected from a pre-Jennerian society: for the bulk of the Greek portion of the necropolis, the mortality quotient of the under one-year old is 312%, which matches the reference quotients calculated by demographers for life expectancies at birth ranging between 25 and 35 years (Ledermann 1969) (Fig. 2, A, B and C).

The following class, that of the young children from 1 to 4 years-old, is well marked in Marseille, but it also appears in the necropolis of the native world. However, in both cases, it is more or less under-represented, with quotients of 45% to 61% in Marseille-Sainte-Barbe and 95% in *Ambrussum* (Fig. 2 B and C). Conversely, from the 5–9 years-old, in Marseille as well in the indigenous world, the archaic mortality pattern is respected.

The result is an important conclusion pertaining to the age of admission in the cemetery. In Marseille, the 0–1-year old class is normally buried in the cemetery. Such a custom is quite common in the Greek world from the Archaic period and during the Classic and Hellenistic periods. Moreover, it is well attested in both other Phoacean colonies in the region, in *Agathé*/ Adge (study underway of B. Dedet, G. Marchand and M. Schwaller) and in *Emporion*/Ampurias (Almagro i Basch 1953), even if, in the latter case, the absence of anthropological study does not enable us to measure whether the proportion of these defaults corresponds precisely to the expected mortality.

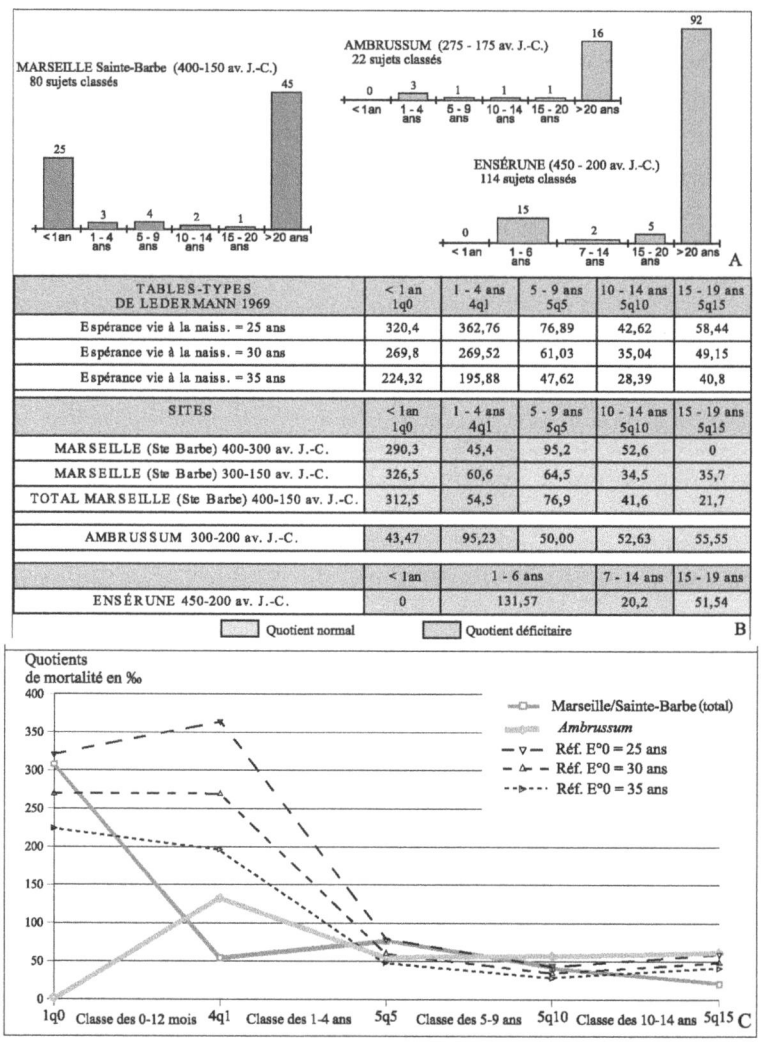

Figure 2. (A) Proportions of deceased from an identified age class of Cemeteries in Marseille/Sainte Barbe, Ambrussum and Ensérune. (B) Comparison of probabilities of dying (in percentage) for immature deceased in the Greek Marseille/Sainte Barbe Cemetery and indigenous Ambrussum and Ensérune Cemeteries. For comparison, Ledermann model life tables (1969, 86–88) about life expectancy from birth to 25 years, 30 years, and 35 years. (C) Comparison of the curve of probabilities of dying (in percentage) for immature deceased in the Greek Marseille/Sainte Barbe Cemetery and indigenous Ambrussum Cemetery as three benchmark populations, who show life expectancy from birth (E0) to 25 years, 30 years and 35 years (from Ledermann model life tables (1969, 86-88)) (DAO : B. Dedet, CNRS).

The situation is quite different in the native communities of the second Iron Age where the toddlers are not entitled to the community cemetery, with the exception of foetuses of dead pregnant women or of women who died during delivery. Accession of children came only later and gradually, first of all for a portion of the 1–4 year-old then, apparently, normally from the 5–9 year-old. It is a traditional process since it can be noted in all the necropolis of the region from at least the end of the Bronze Age (Dedet 2008; 2011b).

What is the fate of these very young deceased in the native world? We find many children dead in perinatal phase, buried inside the agglomerations of the living, in houses or in domestic courtyards. At the moment, more than one hundred and fifty individuals have been recognised in some thirty habitats of Southern France, in Roussillon, in Languedoc, in the South of the Massif Central in Provence, from the beginning of the first Iron Age and throughout the second Iron Age (Fig. 3 A).

This totally contrasts with Marseille: the excavations of dwellings of Greek time carried out to this day in the Massaliot city, as in other Greek trade offices of the Gaul coastline, in Olbia of Provence or *Agathé*/Agde in Languedoc, have not exposed any tomb nor any remains of toddlers' skeletons. It may be useful to outline that the Marseille usage completely contrasts with that of the neighbouring dwellings: newborns buried in the native way in houses can be found all around Marseille, in Saint-Blaise, in Roquepertuse, in Entremont, and even, less than eight kilometres away from the walls of the Greek colony, in Le Baou de Saint-Marcel.

The Treatment of the Deceased in Marseille and in the Native World

The Usages for Under One-Year-Old Children

For foetuses and subjects deceased in perinatal phase found in the dwellings of the native world, the norm is individual primary inhumation, in a little dug pit, fitting with the sizes of the body, in the habitation house or in the adjoining domestic courtyard. In this respect, the case of the *oppidum* of Gailhan, in the Gard, is exemplary, for the fifth and fourth centuries BC (Fig. 3 A and B) (Dedet, Duday & Tillier 1991). This is in total contrast with older dead who have access to the cemetery and who were all cremated at that time.

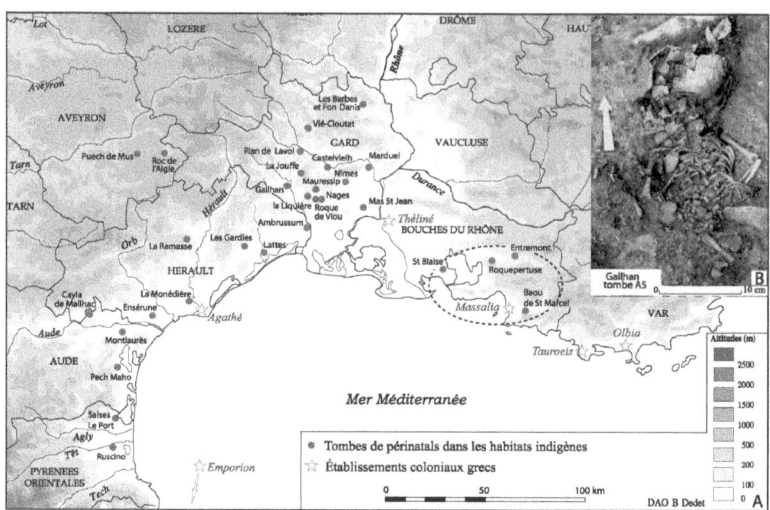

Figure 3. Protohistorical habitats of South Mediterranean Gaul which delivered tombs or rests of perinatal individuals and/or infants. The dashed line shows particularly Gallic oppida near Massalia (DAO B. Dedet, CNRS). At the top, on the right, is an example of perinatal deceased tomb in Gailhan Gallic oppidum around 400 BC (photo B. Dedet, CNRS).

According to observations made on the position of the members, these children were apparently not swaddled before burial. They are deprived of any piece of garment or of adornment. In fact, from the Late Bronze Age to the first half of the first century BC, there was in the South of Gaul a well-defined custom or cultural model of burial in dwellings reserved for toddlers (Dedet 2008, 79–138; Dedet 2011b, 141–142). And its specificity seems all the more obvious as the usages attested for that age in Greek Marseille are quite different. In fact, all the dead foetuses and perinatal babies deposited in the Marseille/Sainte-Barbe necropolis are buried but in so doing, and contrary to the native world, they do not differentiate from other, older children, but under ten-years old, who are all buried as well, nor from the very large number of adults, indeed a majority of them, who were not cremated either. The tombs of these toddlers are distributed among those of the older deceased. However, the treatment of their corpse, i.e. no cremation, seems to induce a preferential location in the Western sector of the cemetery, predominantly occupied by buried adults, whereas the Eastern portion mostly includes cremated adults (Fig. 4) (Moliner et al. 2003, 237–238). In the necropolis of the Greek world, since the Classical period these newborns, likewise not cremated, have also been set aside from cremated adults and, on the contrary, associated with no cremated adults, although the reasons for such an arrangement remain unknown (Michalaki-Kollia 2010, 164).

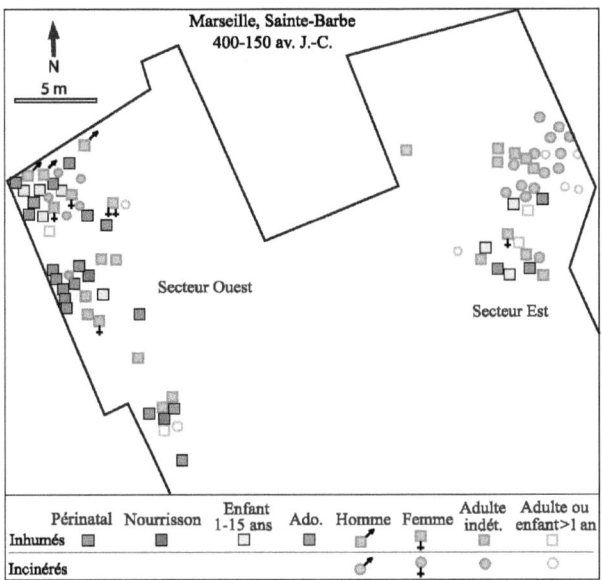

Figure 4. Spatial distribution of the deceased from the Greek Marseille/Sainte Barbe Cemetery depending on the age at the death (DAO B. Dedet, CNRS).

The ways the body is laid in Marseille/Sainte-Barbe can be quite different. The newborns can sometimes be deposited in open ground, but only for a minority of them (8 out of 23). Exceptionally, the body may lie in a wooden coffin (1 case). But in fact, the vast majority, 14 out of 23, are placed in a vase, the *enchytrismos* of the archaeologists, a custom well-known in Greece and which can be found in the other colonies of the Western Mediterranean region, in *Agathé*/Agde and in *Emporion*/Ampurias (Fig. 5 A).

Here, this receptacle is most often a Massaliot amphora, scooped to the body through (Fig. 5 B), and sometimes a hydria or an œnochoe (fig. 5 C). And the "foetus" is also buried in a small urn, signalled in one of the enclosures of La Bourse. In these Massaliot *enchytrismos*, the body position is quite symbolical, the head towards the exit, to follow the comparison between uterus and vase, which can be found in the fifth century BC already, in the treatises of the Hippocratic Corpus.

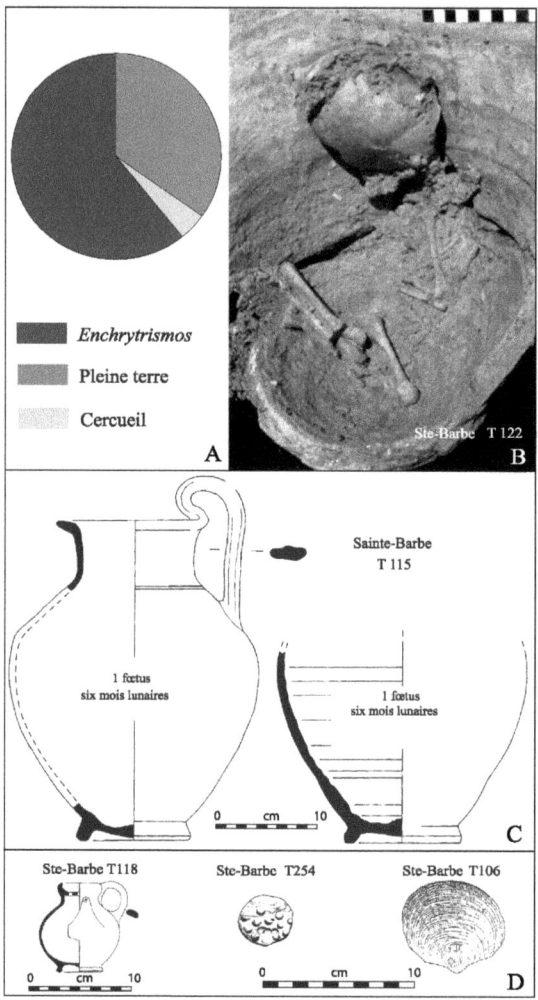

Figure 5. Treatment of the perinatal individuals in the Greek Marseille/Sainte Barbe Cemetery: (A) Proportions of methods of corpse's deposits (DAO B. Dedet, CNRS). (B) An example of *enchytrismos* in a Massaliot amphora, Tomb 122 (photo S. Bien et F. Cognard, INRAP). (C) *Enchytrimos* in clear paste jug for 2 foetus in Tomb 115. (D) Material placed in Tombs 118 (massaliot *guttus in* clear paste), 254 (*corymbus*) and 106 (shell) (from Moliner et al. 2003).

In Marseille/Sainte-Barbe, for the oldest of the age class, the few toddlers between two and twelve months of existence, the vase-receptacle is not used any longer. Their bodies are buried in open ground or in a casing. In the native world, there are a very small number of cases of buried babies within the household sphere, and they show exactly the same practice as perinatals. But little is known about the treatment of most of these toddlers since they were too few to be found in dwellings as well as in necropoles, in view of the expected mortality since, in a pre-Jennerian society, as many children die at birth and in the first month of life as well as in the following eleven months. This also marks a change in attitude in the Indigens, after the first month of life (Dedet 2008, 139–156).

The Indigens do not place any objects with the bodies of the perinatals and the same goes for the few babies deposited in the dwellings. In the Massaliot necropolis, a number of these deceased is admittedly deprived of any material, but such is not the case for all of them. One third of these under-one-year olds is fitted with objects or offerings, most often shellfish valves, especially scallop shells, more rarely a ceramic jug or an *œnochoe* (3 cases), a *guttus* (which may have been used as a feeding-bottle) in one case, and in another case, a *corymbus,* an earthen floral element from a mortuary crown in the Greek fashion (Fig. 5 D).

The Treatment of the Bodies of the Deceased after the First Year of Existence

In the southern native world of the second Iron Age, all the deceased admitted in the cemeteries are cremated. The sole exception relates to the Southern Alps with the persisting usage of interment, at least up to the third century BC. This is the culmination of a very clear progression of cremation that can be traced since the beginning of the last millennium BC (Fig. 6). In the Late Bronze Age III, in the tenth–ninth centuries BC, cremation is the rule West of the Hérault river and of the Western edge of the Massif Central, whereas burial is exclusive East of the Hérault river. Then, with the passing of time, cremation spread towards the East and became exclusive everywhere from the middle of the fifth century BC, except for the Southern Alps (Dedet 2004). This concerns at least the "normal" deceased, by excluding the perinatals, as we have seen, and the adults and adolescents whose unburnt remains are deposited in cultural premises, such as for example that of the Cailar in the Gard, in the third century BC (Roure et al. 2011). There are other notable exceptions to this "systematic cremation" in the South of France in the second Iron Age, the Greek colonies for which necropolis are known, Marseille and Agde (Fig. 6).

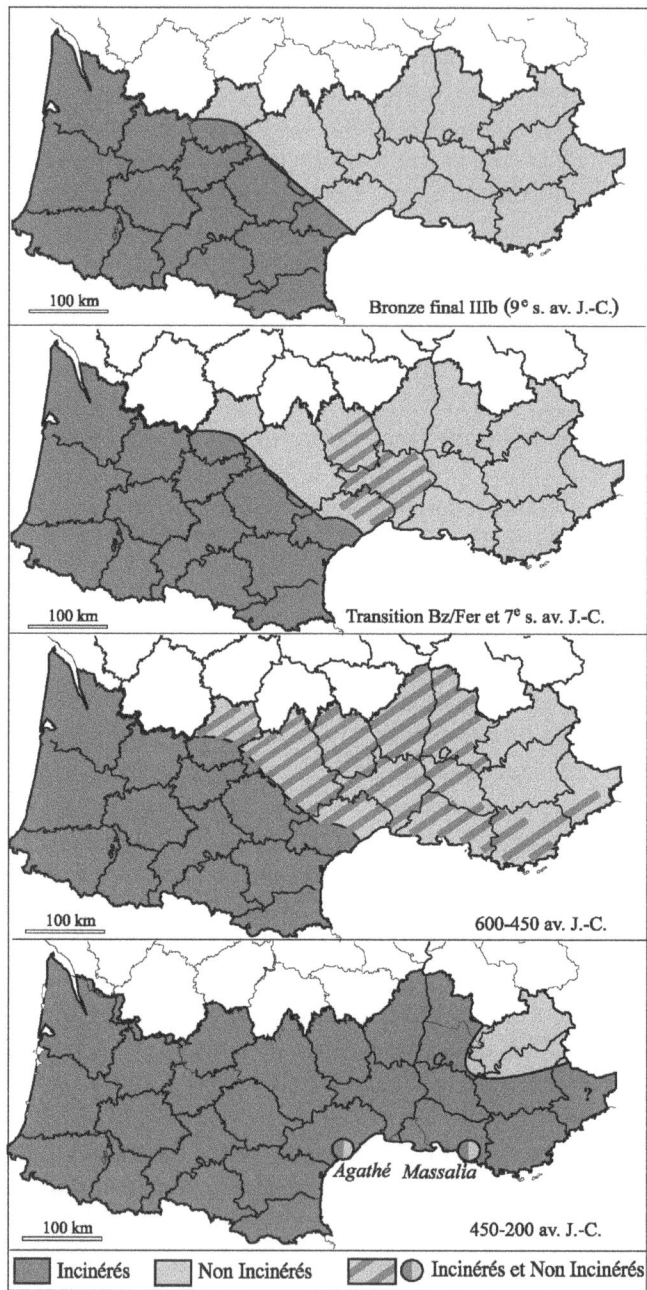

Figure 6. Schematic comparative distribution of cremated deceased and non-burnt deceased in tombs of the cemeteries and funeral groups in South France, from Final Bronze Age IIIb unto the end of Second Iron Age (DAO B. Dedet, CNRS).

In Marseille, indeed, cremated and non cremated deceased were present generally. More precisely in Sainte-Barbe, both practices in force are the primary interment and the secondary deposition of cremation (Fig. 7). The portions of Marseille necropolis of the Tapis-Vert and of Saint-Mauront also show this duality of treatment, whereas cremation is the rule in the Bourse in the fourth–third centuries BC except for the buried "foetus" noted.

MONDE INDIGENE			MARSEILLE / SAINTE-BARBE		
Classes d'âge	Inhumation	Incinération	Classes d'âge	Inhumation	Incinération
< 1 an	en habitat		< 1 an		
1-10 ans		en nécropole	1-10 ans		
grands enfants adolescents adultes		en nécropole	grands enfants adolescents adultes	56 %	44 %

Figure 7. Report between burial and incineration according to the age at the moment of death in indigenous World and in the Greek Marseille/Sainte Barbe Cemetery (DAO: B. Dedet, CNRS).

The necropolis of Sainte-Barbe also provides several interesting complementary observations of this variety of practices. On the one hand, it can be noted that the cremation is not performed for children below ten–twelve-years old. The eight children of this necropolis aged between one and ten–twelve years are all buried and it is also the treatment used for the two young children attested on the *Rue du Tapis-Vert* and the *Cours Julien*. On the other hand, the adults and the adolescents of Sainte-Barbe are distributed more or less regularly among both processes, twenty cremated and twenty-seven unburned individuals (i.e., respectively 43% and 57%). Finally, there has not been any evolution in the relative frequency of both types of treatment of the body, between the beginning and the end of the usage of the site of Sainte-Barbe, between the fourth century and the middle of the second century BC.

For these adults, we cannot observe in Sainte-Barbe any preference for one or the other usage in function of the sex. Admittedly, the biological sex of the subjects cremated can almost never be determined, but conversely, the study of bones of the unburned individuals shows that among them there are men (four) and women (six). The cremation therefore does not seem to be reserved to either sex.

The age, for the adults, does not seem to play a role in this choice. In Sainte-Barbe, among the four young adults detected three were buried and one was cremated, and the six elderly adults reported were all cremated. In the Tapis-Vert, the sole three adults buried are all between 40–45 and 55–60 year old.

This mix of cremated and not cremated deceased can be found in the necropolis of the Greek colony of *Agathé*/Agde, dated between the middle of the fourth century and the beginning of the second century BC. It includes twenty-four cremations (among whom a number of perinatals) and four cremations (Dedet, Marchand & Schwaller, study underway). There is a similar situation in the other Phocaean colonies of the Western Mediterranean region in *Alalia*/Aleria in Corsica (77% burials and 23% cremations; Jehasse & Jehasse 1973, 26) as in *Emporion*/Ampurias in Catalonia (Almagro i Basch 1953, 29–213). It is well known in Greece properly speaking, for example in Athens in the fifth–fourth centuries BC (Étienne, Müller, Prost 2006, 159), and if the necropoles of Phocaea, the metropolis of Marseille, are unknown for the time being, it will be emphasised that this duality between burial and cremation is fully attested in Clazomènes (Hürmüzlü 2004, 80–81), so close to Phocée from a geographical viewpoint as well as, according to Herodotus (*History*, I, 142), from the language viewpoint.

In the Greek world, this juxtaposition does not reflect the combination of different populations or ethnic groups. The same certainly goes in Marseille since the cremated and buried are accompanied by quite a similar type of furniture and this equipment strongly differs from that of the "Indigenous" of Southern Gaul.

About the Material Accompanying the Deceased
Adults and Adolescents

The comparison between Marseille and the native world is also quite instructive as regards the material placed in the tombs of the adults and of the adolescents, at both quantitative and qualitative levels.

In Marseille, the deceased adult is not always accompanied with objects. If one believes the excavations of Sainte-Barbe, which are the only reliable sources on this matter, a very high population of adults, almost one out of two (19 out of 44, i.e., 43%) is deprived of any accompaniment. And these are especially the buried who are affected by this absence, 75% of them have no accompaniment, against only 20% of the cremated. Conversely, in the native world, practically all the tombs of adults and of adolescents are accompanied with pieces of equipment.

On the other hand in Marseille, when they are present, the objects are few in number in every tomb. The vast majority of the deposits only account one or two elements and the maximum observed is six. The cremated are those most often accompanied by objects and also better provided.

In the native world, the quantities of material deposited by the dead are quite variable. They can be very small in so-called tombes *à simple ossuaire:* only a few personal objects and remains from an animal offering are then placed by the deceased. And this deposit can be even smaller as in the sepulture of *La Roussillonne,* near Nîmes, around 300 BC, whereas a sole cup is deposited, inserted into the ossuary vase. But quite often, this equipment is abundant, with up to 18 objects, as for example in tomb 163 of Ensérune.

These deviations in the proportion of adults accompanied or not with objects and in the quantity of these parts form a significant difference between both cultural domains. But there is another difference, probably stronger, which relates to the very nature of these objects.

In Marseille, when the dead have an accompaniment material, the deposit of personal objects is quite seldom: a fibula (Sainte-Barbe T 99 and 198), a loop (Sainte-Barbe T43), a ring (Sainte-Barbe T 96, 245 and 247) or a scalptorium (Cours Julien). The presence of remains of fauna is also hardly frequent (Sainte-Barbe T 41, 49, 53, 102 and 198), bones of horse or ox, which we do not know whether they were burnt with the dead or whether these are refuse of funeral meals consumed by the survivors, and collected with the human bone remains. In fact, the most frequent objects refer to the cleaning of the corpse or a symbolic tribute (Fig. 8).

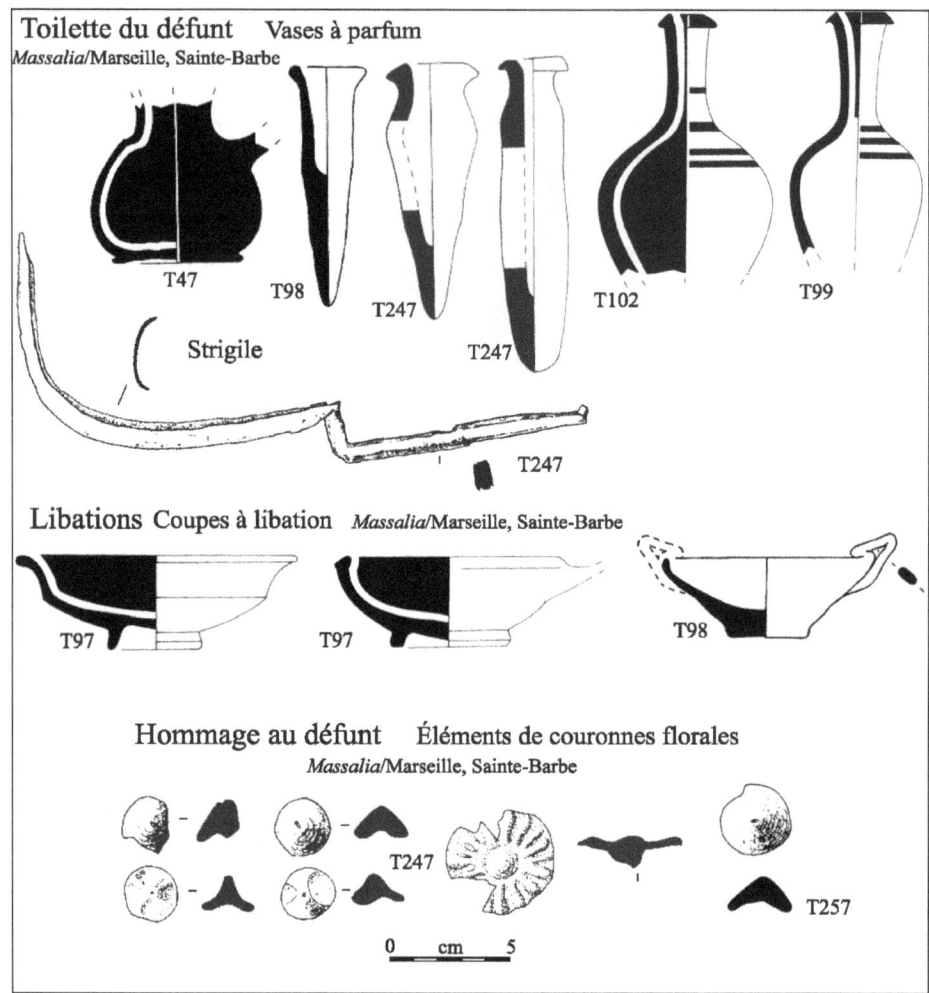

Figure 8. Objects placed in the tombs in the Greek Marseille/Sainte Barbe Cemetery, according to their function, the deceased's toilet (perfume vases, strigil), libations (cups), symbolic tributes (corymbus, floral elements of floral crowns) (from Moliner et al. 2003, modified).

As regards this mortuary cleaning, the perfume vases, lekythoi, aryballic lekythoi, alabastres, unguentaria, ceramic jugs appear in many adult tombs fitted with material (Sainte-Barbe T47, 60, 96, 98, 102, 198 and 245; Tapis-Vert T2 and sarcophagus 3; Cours Julien Tomb of adult; Saint-Mauront T5, 8 and 14). Useful in this operation, strigils can be encountered in several sepultures (Sainte-Barbe T235, 242 and 247; Tapis-Vert sarcophagus 3; Cours Julien Tomb of adult) (Fig. 9).

Other items evoke, for their own part, symbolic tributes. Cups of various sizes which can be used in libations are present in numerous tombs in Sainte-Barbe (T41, 43, 47, 96, 97, 98 and 257) and in the sarcophagus 3 of Tapis-Vert. The same goes with elements of floral crowns in ceramic, flowers in the form of small cones or corymbus, drilled with a hole to be threaded, in four sepultures of Sainte-Barbe (T90, 192, 247 and 257), in one of Tapis-Vert (urn of lead 1) and sometimes "golden on top" as in Carénage (Fig. 9).

| ☐ Inhumation | ▨ Incinération |

TOMBES D'ADULTES		Vase à parfum	Coupe Coupelle	Cruche Urne	Couronne florale	Strigile	Bague	Fibule	Scalpt.	Fuseau & peson	Coquille	Faune
Ste-Barbe	T 47	☐										
	T 41		☐									▨
	T 257			☐								
	T 56											▨
	T 98	▨	▨									
	T 96	▨						▨				
	T 60	▨		▨								
	T 102	▨										▨
	T 235	▨				▨						
	T 198	▨						▨				
	T 245	▨										▨
	T 97		▨									
	T 43						▨					
	T 247				▨							
	T 90				▨							
	T 192				▨							
	T 242				▨							
	T 53										▨	
Rue Tapis Vert	Tombe 2	☐										
	Sarco. 3 (2 sujets)	☐			☐							
	Urne plomb 1	☐										
Cours Julien	Tombe adulte	☐				☐			☐			
St-Mauront	Sépulture 5	☐										
	Sépulture 8	☐										
	Sépulture 14	☐									☐	
	Sépulture 7	☐		☐								

Figure 9. Summary table of material associations in the Greek Marseille/Sainte Barbe Cemeteries according to the method of body's treatment (DAO : B. Dedet, CNRS).

All this material concerns cremated as well as buried people; these are exactly the same objects or types of objects that can be found in both cases (Fig. 9). On the other hand, they never indicate whether it's a man or a woman. The comparison examination of the objects associated with the buried in Sainte-Barbe whose biological sex is known does not reveal any specific object distinguishing the sex.

Ultimately, therefore, it is essentially a material of Hellenic culture that takes place in the tomb in Marseille, objects used for cleaning the dead, to honour him or make libations. The Greek written sources testify widely, and it is the same with many Attic white lekythoi where these parts are figured on the tomb (Fig. 10). And these are also the same objects which are deposited at the same time in many other Greek necropolis, such as for example that of Kalfata in Apollonia-du-Pont, in present Bulgaria (Hermary 2010, 143–145). Conversely, the accompaniment of the adults of the Indigenous world of Southern Gaul is quite different.

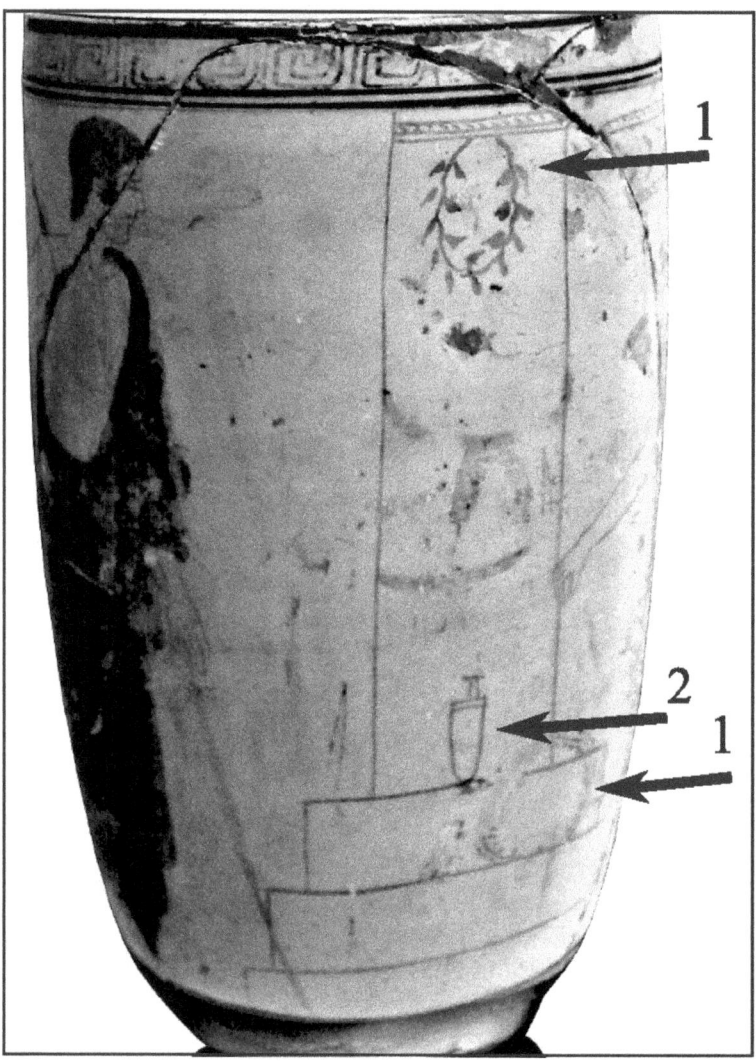

Figure 10. White-ground Attic lekythos by the Sabouroff Painter, around 450 BC, which represents a funeral monument where we can see (1) floral crowns and (2) perfume vase (cliché : B. Dedet, CNRS).

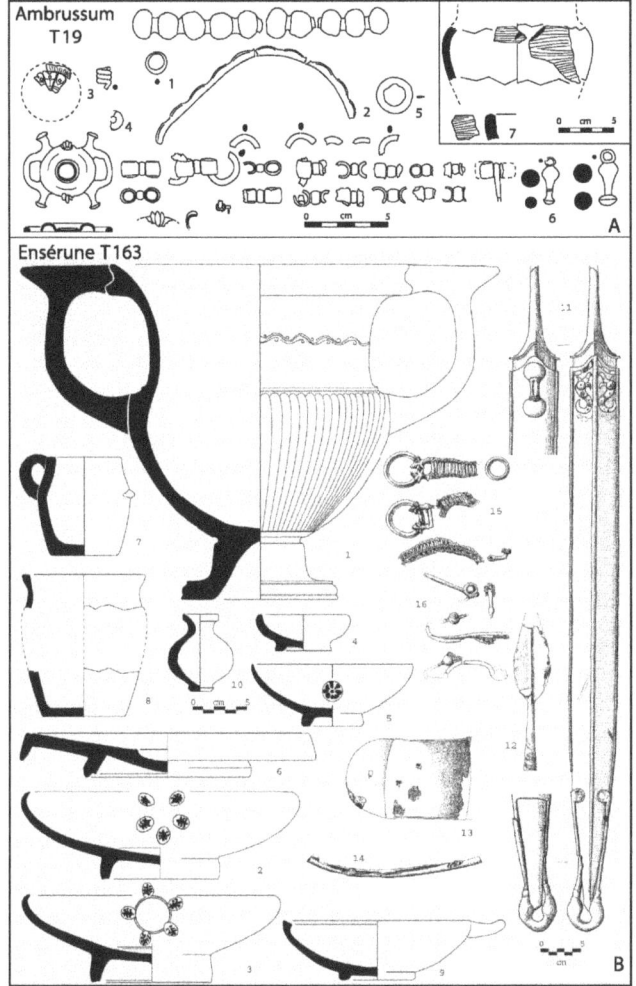

Figure 11. Two examples of tombs from indigenous world. (A) Ambrussum, Tomb 19 [1: silver ear-ring; 2: bronze bracelet; 3: fibula, bronze and coral; 4: glass paste; 5: bronze ring; 6: elements of bronze chain-belt; 7–8; shards of urns and unturned cups] (drawing: B.Dedet, CNRS). (B) Ensérune, Tomb 163 (1-6: black glaze vases; 7–8: unturned vases; 9–10: clear paste vases; 11: iron sword in its sheath; 12: iron lance tip; 13–14: elements of iron shield; iron sword and its suspension; fragments of 4 iron *fibulae* (from Rapin & Schwaller).

Among the indigenous people, the deposit generally consists of different assemblies (Fig. 11).

These are especially personal objects of the dead, pieces of clothing and of adornment, objects of daily life activities or not, often with a sexual connotation clearly announced. Spindle whorls, chain-belt with double links, ear pendants, sets of two bracelets or more, pearl necklace made of glass paste or of coral are deposited with women. Such is the case for example for five of the sixteen tombs of adults or of adolescents of *Ambrussum* (T2, T6, T11, T19 and T23) (Dedet 2012). Sharp objects, such as knives and arms, refer to men, and it is often the complete armament panoply, lance tip and heel, sword and its suspension and metal elements of the shield, which is attested. In Ensérune, out of thirty-four tombs discovered between 1954 and 1988, eleven contain presumably masculine objects, mainly weapons (tombs GS 146, 150/151, 157, 158, 163, 170, 171, 175 and 178 and tombs SCH 2 and 3), and three of the presumably feminine parts, spindle whorl or ear-rings (tombs GS 147 and 172 and tomb SCH 6) (Gallet de Santerre 1968, 73–83; Schwaller et al. 1995).

Tombs with weapons account for approximately one third of the adult tombs in Ensérune and in *Ambrussum*: as in both cases, presumably masculine and feminine adults are balanced and such a proportion could signify that all the men who can fight take their weapons with them into their tomb, whereas conversely, no tomb in Marseille of Greek time provided any weapons.

Another quite frequent custom among the Natives and rare in Marseille is that of placing animal remains in the sepulture. All the sepultures of *Ambrussum* include an isolated bone or, more rarely, a portion of skeleton. Both these formulae illustrate two different gestures, perhaps remains of meals shared by the survivors near the pyre or of the tomb in the first case. And in the second, an unconsumed food for the deceased person (Dedet 2012). Most of the tombs in Mourrel-Ferrat contain isolated animal bones (Janin et al. 2000). These are also extensively present in the sepultures in Ensérune in the third century BC, but this necropolis also shows another custom constituted by the deposition of full poultries and of quarters of unburnt caprines and pigs. Here, prepared and non-consumed meat has accompanied the deceased in his tomb (Schwaller et al. 1995).

On the other hand, vases are deposited in a few tombs of the native world, which may be ascribed to a fringe of the population in contact with foreign merchants, that is, vases referring to the collective and social consumption of wine, with the usage of vases borrowed from the Greek culture, the banquet, but sometimes to provide another usage than the Greeks: first of all solely drinking vases made with a lap, accompanied from around 300 BC, by the imported crater which is also used as an ossuary, as well as symbolic animal offerings. This form of "Greek style" banquet that the native tombs reflect, with the foreign accessories for the service of wine, these are all borrowings from the Greek culture, but not to their funeral practices.

Thus, in this indigenous world, unlike Greek Marseille, the deposits in the tombs reflect the characteristics of the deceased, age, sex, activities or position and social significance.

On a Few Other Aspects of Funeral Practices

The comparison can be extended to other dispositions of the funeral practices, which add other elements in terms of differences.

About Cremated Deceased

If in Marseille-Sainte-Barbe as in the three best known native necropoles, Mourrel Ferrat, Ensérune and *Ambrussum*, there is no sector reserved for the cremation of the deceased and another for the burial of their remains, tombs being installed near the pyres, a few differences seem to exist in this field between both cultural domains, but the small number of cases known dictates prudence.

Among the Natives, these pyres are generally installed on a platform arranged with rubble and added soil. In particular in *Ambrussum*, this base is formed with residues from the dwellings of the living, perhaps with a symbolic purpose. Conversely in Marseille, the bonfires are placed directly on the ground, barely leaving the trace of a rubefacient surface area, without an arranged base.

The individual or shared character of those structures is probably more significant. In autochthonous necropolis, these pyres were used for several successive cremations, as indicated by the quantity of human bones discovered. For example, the pyre B1 of *Ambrussum* has operated to burn five to seven deceased, clothed and adorned, accompanied by their personal objects adapted to their age and/or their sexual category (Dedet 2012, 99–142). Conversely in Sainte-Barbe, the only necropolis in Marseille where these structures have been studied, each of them has only included a small quantity of human bones and this might indicate that they are individual and not collective…but with the proviso of course that they have not been cleaned.

In Marseille, the burnt bone remains can be deposited in an ossuary, as is the most frequent case in Sainte-Barbe, or directly in the pit, or still according to a mixed process associating both previous modalities, a mixed process particularly present in the terraces of La Bourse where these deposits are placed in stone craters. Apart from these craters, only represented in the region of the Bas-Rhône and at a later stage, in the first century BC, these three formulae, ossuary, absence of ossuary and mixed, can also be found in Southern Gaul, in variable proportions according to the necropolis, but in this native world, these are three quite traditional practices, used long before the arrival of the Greeks since they were acknowledged as soon as in the late Bronze Age.

In Marseille as in the Natives, the ossuary is quite often a current vase in daily life, but the use of specific vessels, such as lead urns, is attested there, contrary to the autochthonous world. On the other hand, in this latter case, certain vases or rare categories of vases in the habitats are quite clearly

employed in this funerary usage. Such is the case in Ensérune, with the Greek
black-glazed cantharuses serving as an ossuary in two thirds of the tombs of
the second half of the fourth century and the beginning of the third century
BC, whereas these vases are on the contrary quite rare in the houses of this
oppidum. This is still the case at the same time with non-lathed fully smoothed
vases, with fumigated cooking, in the necropolis of Beaucaire.

The Vision of the Tomb

There is in Marseille a category of dead for whom the vision of the tomb
is of great significance for the survivors. Such is evidently the case, in the
fourth century BC, of those who benefit from two monumental terraces in
La Bourse, quite close to the western gate of the rampart of the Phocaean
city, carefully built in the Greek fashion, with large stones, and decorated with
bosses or triglyphs on the face hugging the path securing access to the city.
But for all the others, the visible portion of the sepulture remains very modest
and only marks the landscape discretely, and the same applies to the second
Iron Age in the native world.

   In *Ambrussum*, the pit having received the funerary deposition and its immediate surroundings where vases or portions of vases have been placed, are covered
with only a very light mound of earth including bone and furniture element
from the pyre, which form a device altogether modest. This signalling of the
tomb in Ensérune is more significant: the loculus is covered with a small accumulation of rough stones and sometimes completed by an oblong rough stone,
erected like a stele. For the average person, in Marseille, a heaping up of stones,
of amphora shards and of reclaimed materials, or still lying slabs, close and cover
the pit ; and many of these tombs are indicated on the surface by a planted stone,
of rough work, often trimmed into a pyramid shape. In both cultural domains,
this discrete marking and signalling of the tomb is quite independent from the
distinctive characters of the deceased and of its funerals, his age and his sex, the
type of treatment of his body and of his remains, and the material placed in the
sepulchral pit. It shows that the important thing is not so much where are placed
the remains of the dead but the future that awaits them elsewhere.

Two Different Conceptions of the Hereafter

In the second Iron Age, the Mediterranean Southern part of France provides two sets of funeral practices quite different from each other, that of the
Natives and that of the Marseille Greeks, without notable mutual influence
(Fig. 12). Admittedly, it may be objected that the corpus of usable sepultures
is relatively small, especially for Marseille where only 104 sepultures, distri-

buted over two centuries approximately, can be accounted for at the moment. But, in the Phocaean colony, these tombs appear in several necropolis, each time exhibiting the same practices, even if Cours-Julien and Tapis-Vert only include a few units, while Sainte-Barbe is much larger in number. And additionally, the necropolis of La Bourse offers an eminently Greek architecture. This sampling therefore enables us to put forward a number of conclusions.

	INDIGÈNES, IXᵉ-VIᵉ s. av. J.-C.	INDIGÈNES, Vᵉ-IIᵉ s. av. J.-C.	MARSEILLE, Vᵉ-IIᵉ s. av. J.-C.
Périnatals	Maison Tous inhumés Fosse Pas d'objets	Maison Tous inhumés Fosse Pas d'objets	Cimetière Tous inhumés Enchytrismos ou fosse Objets pour 1/3 d'entre eux
Enfants < 10 ans	Accès progressif au cimetière Languedoc occidental : Tous incinérés Languedoc oriental / Provence : Tous inhumés avant VIe s., Incinérés ou inhumés au VIe s.	Accès progressif au cimetière Tout Languedoc / Provence : Tous incinérés	Cimetière Tous inhumés
Grands enfants Adolescents Adultes	Languedoc occidental : Tous incinérés Languedoc oriental / Provence : Tous inhumés avant VIe s., Incinérés ou inhumés au VIe s. Mobilier - plus ou moins abondant - personnalité du défunt (sexe, importance sociale) - présence d'armes (rares ou fréquentes)	Tous incinérés Mobilier - plus ou moins abondant - personnalité du défunt (sexe, importance sociale) - armes fréquentes	Inhumés ou Incinérés avec même type de mobilier Pas de mobilier dans 40% des tombes Si mobilier, peu d'objets : - toilette du mort - libations - hommage Pas d'armes

Figure 12. Comparative table of funeral practices in the indigenous world and in the Greek city of Marseille. It shows both the continuity between the First and the Second Iron Age practices for the Southern Gauls, in spite of the evolutions caused by the internal dynamics of the indigenous world, and the impermeability between natives and Greeks.

The Massaliot rites rather reflect the Greek customs of the time, accommodating the perinatal dead in the cemetery of the city, quite often inside a vase, using the interment for children and some adults, cremating other adults, only placing in the tomb a very small quantity of material, often nothing at all, and generally simply the soiled objects used for cleaning the dead, for the actions linked with the farewell ceremony, libations or offerings of flower crowns. This simplicity shown by the remains corresponds to the impression conveyed by Valerius Maximus on funeral of Marseille (*Facts and memorable sayings*, II, 6–7): "the dead are led to their sepulture, transported on a cart, without laments nor complaints. The mourning only lasts the day of the funeral, with a sacrifice attended by the members of the household, followed by a banquet with all the relatives".

No influence of the native customs in that matter seems to shine through in the tombs of the city of *Massalia*. This underlines somehow the image given by classical Latin authors to Greek Marseille, that of a community strongly attached to its customs and original traditions, although isolated at the end of the world, surrounded by many autochthones, described as dangerous, bathed by "the waves of the Barbarity", to repeat the phrase of Cicero in the *Pro Flacco* (XXVI, 63). Nothing in the tombs currently known in the Marseille colony evokes the presence of individuals who would have been treated "as natives".

For their own part, the native funeral usages are traditional, whether it be the rules relating to the age of acceptance in the village cemetery, of the progressive accession of the children to that location, of the material outlining the personality of the deceased, often insisting on any belonging to the masculine or feminine world, often as well on his/her social significance and/or his/her power, with the presence of weapons and vessels attesting a form of "banquet". And if the perinatals and the babies have no accompaniment, it is because they are not considered as yet as beings truly born to the society. These native practices are in line with those known in the region since the end of the Bronze Age and throughout the first Iron Age. They do not appear either transformed or solely modified in contact with the Greek settlers, regardless of the geographical proximity or distance with respect to the colonial establishments, in spite of the commercial penetration of those and the transformations caused by the latter in the economy, in certain lifestyles and the form of the habitat (Fig. 12).

This impermeability between both spheres, in this field, can be explained because we are dealing with the most intimate human concerns and that it undoubtedly reflects two conceptions of death which are fundamentally different. Moreover, the ethnologists have emphasised many times a similar phenomenon regarding the European colonisation of modern time. For example, Louis-Vincent Thomas wrote about Black Africa: "The funeral rites seem to be the stronghold best resisting acculturation" (Thomas 1982, 251).

For the natives of the South of protohistorical France, death in itself is not an end of the existence, but a Hereafter where the deceased can enter to survive under different conditions and somehow escape from death to some extent. It opens the door to another place where the body-double of the deceased will survive with the double of the objects which symbolised his terrestrial existence. In the text on a lead medium deposited in a tomb of the necropolis of L'Hospitalet-du-Larzac in Averyon, we find allusions in Gaul language to the visible world (*vodercos*), to death (*nepos*) and to the invisible world of the Hereafter (*antumnos*) (Lambert 1994, 160–172). It is indeed a document dated from the first century AD, but it supplies native religious terms and notions, and derived from a country remote from urban centres, the plateau of the Larzac, it relates to an autochthonous environment, a direct heir from the local past. Not only do the dead have another life in this hereafter, but in addition "the newly dead" can transmit messages to older dead and to divinities, through the passage of material objects on the pyre. And moreover Diodorus of Sicily, describing the customs of the Southern Gauls in the first half of the first century BC, leaves no doubt on the subject: "during the funerals, they (the Gauls) throw into the fire letters written to parents already dead, as if the latter could read them" (Diodorus of Sicily, *Historical Library*, V, 28, 6).

For their own part, for the Massaliots of the fourth, third and second centuries BC, as for the average person of Greece at the time, outside the intellectual or philosophical circles, death is first of all the end of life's pleasures and also a vague sojourn in the kingdom of shadows, the Hades, without any landmarks or hopes of any accomplishment, a death without horizon (Rudhardt 1992; Mikalson 2009). In that Hereafter, the fate of the souls and the nature of their survival remain rather confused and in fact are predominant in the idea of a non-existence after death. Most of the Attic epitaphs of that period are silent on the matter, whereas some content themselves with evoking the gods of the Hades, others the heavens, the "ether"; but most often they express the nostalgia of the past life and of its pleasures. Besides, when Diodorus of Sicily reports this native custom of placing on the newly dead letters addressed to those who had passed away before, the expression he uses, "as if the latter could read them", might point out that he does not believe in such survival after life.

To say the least, the observation of such a tightness between both cultures of the Mediterranean Southern region of France in the second Iron Age is not exclusive to the sole domain of tomb. It has already been formulated about other aspects of the religious sphere and of certain customs. This is the case of the cultural areas and of the native "ritual" deposits, in Languedoc as well as in Provence, which do not contain any material borrowed from the Greek world (Arcelin, Dedet & Schwaller 1992; Golosetti 2009) unlike, for instance, to places of indigenous cults in Sicily or Southern Italy in contact with the Greek settlers established in these countries (Osanna 2010). Quite significant in this respect is the Gaul custom to cut off the head of the vanquished enemies and to expose these trophies on the rampart of the *oppidum* or in porticos, including quite close to Marseille, as on the habitat of Le Baou de Saint-Marcel, only one hour and a half away on foot from the Greek colony, and which is still in force at the beginning of the first century BC, as at the entrance of the *oppidum* of La Cloche less than fifteen kilometres away (Chabot 1983, 51).

Conclusion

The funeral customs hence come across as a privileged criterion for cultural identification. The two large human groups of the protohistorical South of France, that of the Natives and that of the Greeks in the colonies settled on the coastline show no exception. No tomb after the "native fashion" is attested in *Massalia*/Marseille, no more than in *Agathé*/Agde; similarly, no sepulture after the "Greek fashion" transpires in the necropoles of the native *oppida*, as Ensérune, *Ambrussum* or Mourrel-Ferrat. From this lack of exchanges in mortuary practices we may derive and suspect some of the behaviours then in force in a number of concrete situations.

1. The case of mixed marriages in Marseille. At the death of the indigenous spouse of a Greek settler, either her body would be sent back into her village of origin, or most probably, she would be buried after the Greek fashion, thereby reflecting a kind of assimilation by marriage. And, in any case, for the deaths of the descendants of these mixed marriages, the Greek fashion would prevail.
2. In Marseille also, the case of the "Barbarians" of the Marseille periphery working in the colony. When they died, the bodies of these natives would be transferred to their village of origin.
3. Finally, the case of the Greeks who could live in the native world. Going by the example of Ensérune, of *Ambrussum* or still of Mourrel-Ferrat, if there are Greeks in these *oppida*, they do not stay there until they die or else their bodies would be repatriated to the colony from which they originate. But the absence of tombs "according to the Greek rite" raises doubt that these Gaul agglomerations had even hosted many Greeks. Therefore, it would appear that the undeniable Greek contribution in the economic and social changes of the Iron Age of the Mediterranean Southern France would be mostly the produce of native intermediates.

Bibliography

Almagro i Basch, M., 1953, *Las necrópolis de Ampurias. I. Introducción y necrópolis griegas.* Barcelona, Diputación provincial de Barcelona-Consejo superior de investigaciones científicas 399p. et XVIII pl. HT (coll. *Monografías Ampuritanas* III).

Arcelin, P., Dedet, B. & Schwaller, M., 1992, Espaces publics, espaces religieux protohistoriques en Gaule méridionale. *Documents d'Archéologie Méridionale*, 15, 181–242.

Bertucchi, G., 1992, Nécropoles et terrasses funéraires à l'époque grecque. Bilan sommaire des recherches. In: M. Bats, G. Bertucchi, G. Congès & H. Tréziny (dir.), *Marseille grecque et la Gaule, actes du Colloque international d'Histoire et d'Archéologie et du Ve*

Congrès archéologique de Gaule méridionale, Marseille, 1990, Lattes/Aix-en-Provence, ADAM éditions/Université de Provence, 123–137 (Études Massaliètes, 3).

Chabot, L., 1983, L'oppidum de La Cloche aux Pennes-Mirabeau (Bouches-du-Rhône) (synthèse des travaux effectués de 1967 à 1982). *Revue Archéologique de Narbonnaise,* XVI, 39–80.

Dedet, B., 2004, Variabilité des pratiques funéraires protohistoriques dans le sud de la France: défunts incinérés, défunts non brûlés. *Gallia,* 61, 193–222.

Dedet, B., 2008, *Les enfants dans la société protohistorique. L'exemple du Sud de la France.* Rome, École française de Rome, 400p. (coll. de l'École française de Rome, 396).

Dedet, B., 2011a, Les Gaulois du Midi et Marseille grecque: deux mondes funéraires. *Gallia,* 68-2, 2011, 1–45.

Dedet, B., 2011b, Changements de traitement funéraire des enfants selon l'âge au décès en France méridionale durant la Protohistoire. In: D. Castex, P. Courtaud, H. Duday, F. Le Mort & A.M. Tillier (dir.), *Le regroupement des morts. Genèse et diversité archéologique,* éd. Ausonius, Bordeaux, 135–159 (Thanat'Os 1).

Dedet, B., 2012, *Une nécropole du second Âge du Fer à Ambrussum, Hérault.* Paris/Aix-en-Provence, éd. Errance/Centre Camille Jullian, 288p. (Bibliothèque d'Archéologie Méditerranéenne et Africaine, 11).

Dedet, B., 2015, Pratiques funéraires et identité culturelle: Marseille grecque et les Indigènes du Sud de la Gaule (IV⁵–II⁵ s. av. J.-C.). In: R. Roure (ed.), *Contacts et acculturations en Méditerranée occidentale. Hommages à Michel Bats,* Paris/Aix-en-Provence, éd. Errance/Centre Camille Jullian, 267–283 (Bibliothèque d'Archéologie Méditerranéenne et Africaine 15).

Dedet, B. & Schwaller, M., 2010, Les pratiques funéraires en Languedoc et en Provence du V⁵ au milieu du II⁵ s. av. J.-C. In: P. Barral, B. Dedet, F. Delrieu, P. Giraud, I. Le Goff, S. Marion & A. Villard-Le Tiec (dir.), *Gestes funéraires en Gaule au Second Âge du Fer.* Actes du 33⁵ colloque de l'AFEAF, Caen 2009, thème spécialisé. Besançon, Presses universitaires de Franche-Comté, 269–290 (Annales littéraires, n° 883; Série « Environnement, sociétés et archéologie », n° 14).

Étienne, R., Müller, C., Prost, F., 2006, *Archéologie historique de la Grèce antique.* Paris, Ellipses, 2ⁿᵈ edition, 399p.

Gallet de Santerre, H., 1968, Fouilles dans le quartier ouest d'Ensérune (Insula n°X). *Revue Archéologique de Narbonnaise,* I, 39–83.

Golosetti, R., 2009, Dépôts rituels de la Protohistoire récente en Gaule méditerranéenne: définition et questions méthodologiques. In: S. Bonnardin, C. Hamon, M. Lauwers & B. Quilliec (dir.), *Du matériel au spirituel. Réalités archéologiques et historiques des « dépôts » de la Préhistoire à nos jours.* Actes des XXIX⁵ rencontres internationales d'Archéologie et d'Histoire d'Antibes. Antibes, Éditions APDCA, 293–302.

Hermary, A. (dir.) 2010, *Apollonia du Pont (Sozopol). La nécropole de Kalfata (V⁵–III⁵ s. av. J.-C.). Fouilles franco-bulgares (2002–2004).* Paris/Aix-en-Provence, Errance/ Centre Camille Jullian, 200p., 129pl. h.-t. (Bibliothèque d'Archéologie Méditerranéenne et Africaine, 5).

Hürmüzlü, B., 2004, Burial Grounds at Klazomenai: Geometric through Hellenistic Periods. In: A. Moustaka, E. Skarlatidou, M.C. Tzannes & Y.E. Ersoy (eds.), *Klazomenai, Téos and Abdera: Metropoleis and Colony*. Proceedings of the International Symposium held at the Archaeological Museum of Abdera, 20–21 October 2001. Thessaloniki, 77–96.

Janin, T., De Bouby, J., Boisson, H., Chardenon, N., Gardeisen, A., Marchand, G., Montecinos, A., Séjalon, P., 2000, La nécropole du second âge du Fer de Mourrel-Ferrat à Olonzac (Hérault). *Documents d'Archéologie Méridionale*, 23, 219–248.

Jehasse, J. & Jehasse, L., 1973, *La nécropole préromaine d'Aléria, 1960–1968*. Paris, éd. du CNRS, 632p., V et 184pl. ht. (supplement to *Gallia*, XXV).

Lambert, P.-Y., 1994, *La langue gauloise*. Paris, Errance, 240p.

Ledermann, S., 1969, *Nouvelles tables-types de mortalité*. Paris, INED, 260p. (Travaux et documents, cahier n° 53).

Michalaki-Kollia, M., 2010, Un ensemble exceptionnel d'enchytrismes de nouveau-nés, de fœtus et de nourrissons découvert dans l'île d'Astypalée, en Grèce: Cimetière de bébés ou sanctuaire ? In: A.M. Guimier-Sorbets & Y. Morizot (eds.), *L'enfant et la mort dans l'Antiquité I. Nouvelles recherches dans les nécropoles grecques. Le signalement des tombes d'enfants*. Actes de la table-ronde d'Athènes, 2008. Paris, De Boccard, 161–205 (Travaux de la Maison René Ginouvès, 12).

Mikalson, J.D., 2009, *La religion populaire à Athènes*. Paris, Perrin, 261p.

Moliner, M., Mellinand, P., Naggiar, L., Richier, A. & Villemeur, I., 2003, *La nécropole de Sainte-Barbe à Marseille (IVᵉ s. av. J.-C.–IIᵉ s. ap. J.-C.)*. Aix-en-Provence, Édisud/Centre Camille Jullian, 491p. (Études Massaliètes, 8).

Osanna, M., 2010, Greci ed indigeni nei santuari della Magna Grecia: i casi di Timmari e Garaguso. In: H. Tréziny (ed.), *Grecs et indigènes de la Catalogne à la mer Noire*, Paris/Aix, Errance/CCJ, BiAMA 3, 131–145 (*Bibliothèque d'Archéologie Méditerranéenne et Africaine*, 3).

Rothé M.-P. & Tréziny, H., 2005, *Marseille et ses alentours*. Paris, Maison des Sciences de l'Homme, 925p. (coll. *Carte Archéologique de la Gaule, 13/3*).

Roure, R., Girard, B., Ciesielski, E., Duday, H., Gardeisen, A., Creuzieux, A. & Py, M., 2011, Le Cailar, Gard, France. In: R. Roure & L. Pernet (dir.), *Des rites et des Hommes. Les pratiques symboliques des Celtes, des Ibères et des Grecs en Provence, Languedoc et Catalogne*. Catalogue d'exposition. Paris, Errance, 146–151.

Rudhardt, J., 1992, *Notions fondamentales de la pensée religieuse et actes constitutifs du culte dans la Grèce classique*. Paris, Picard, 344p.

Schwaller, M., Duday, H., Janin, T. & Marchand, G., 1995, Cinq tombes à incinération du deuxième âge du Fer à Ensérune (Nissan-lez-Ensérune, Hérault). In: P. Arcelin, M. Bats, D. Garcia, G. Marchand & M. Schwaller (eds.), *Sur les pas des Grecs en Occident. Hommages à André Nickels*. Paris/Lattes, Errance/ADAM éditions, 205–230 (*Études massaliètes* 4).

Thomas, L.-V., 1982, *La mort africaine. Idéologie funéraire en Afrique Noire*. Paris, Payot, 272p.

13. Land Allotment and Ancient Vineyards around Marseille

Philippe Boissinot

The Discoveries of Saint-Jean du Désert

The plains surrounding the historical core of Marseille have been amply urbanised since the nineteenth century and are therefore poorly known in archaeology. For the contemporary periods of the Greek occupation, we could only note a few necropolis (Saint-Mauront, Cours Julien), a few monetary discoveries (Mazargues) and a potter's furnace (Pointe Rouge). The road network and the layout of the aqueducts, even for a period extended to the end of the Antiquity, had hardly given rise to far-reaching research, in spite of the observation of a few sections, if only a few lopsided speculations. With the ring road construction project (L2) at the very heart of the East suburb, the first preventive research started in a sector situated some 4 kilometres away from the gates of the ancient city (Fig. 1). Among the discoveries carried out in the years 1993–1994, we shall note the presence of fossil plots in a small dale of the district of Saint-Jean du Désert which cuts into the small reliefs between Huveaune and Jarret, the two main water currents of the basin of Marseille. This is a collection of fields among which only the parts where the subsoil was wrought in-depth have been kept (Fig. 2); the distribution and the nature of the remains, in the form of trenches (Fig. 3) or of isolated pits, all arranged along lines parallel and sometimes accompanied by ditches, suggest that we are dealing here with traces of the ancient wine-growing sector, agricultural techniques now well known by Southern archaeology (Boissinot 1995, 2001). It is known moreover that the local wine production was one of the wealth sources of the Phocaean colony since the end of the sixth century BC (Bats 1990; Bertucchi 1992) and not surprisingly, traces thereof could be found at that distance from the city. The furniture collected, certainly originating from the compost laid in the plant holes, enables us to date to the fourth century BC at the earliest, in a vineyard area which already seems to have been operated (but under what form?) for at least two centuries. After the implementation phases, numerous transformations can be observed in fields up to the Roman era, which nevertheless does not shatter the general organisation of the plots in the least. During the High Empire, this assembly was partially buried under the silts from the closest river overflown; although, in spite of these important accretion phenomena, later still (sixth–seventh centuries AD), the same orientations can be found within the wall of a small rural settlement. The implementation of modern day fortified towns thoroughly modified the rural landscape. Only the plots of the Hellenistic period near a small, now fossil, brook have been excavated, whose overflow has just been signalled. We therefore know only one of their dimensions, their width most probably. If they demonstrably extended further along a direction perpendicular to the watercourse, this land fragmentation could be designated as a lanyard. We may suggest moreover that access to the vineyards was provided by one or several path(s) situated further East, in a sector which has not been operated to this day on the hillside. The orientations of the agrarian remains located on the field show slight variations, which is not so surprising since only the breakdown of the fields, at best, is available to us, and not the breakdown of the intermediate structures of a possible land registry which, for its own part, would probably be far more regular; it should be reminded that the intermediate structures, according to the definition given by E. Sereni, form in the agrarian morphology the intermediate level of organisation between the fields and the territory (Chouquer & Favory 1991, 69–71); in Greek context, they may correspond in particular to the *klèroi*, plots of land chosen by lot and ascribed to settlers. Besides, the different measures carried out, among the plantations properly speaking as well as from one plot to the other, have not enabled to us outline a coherent metrological system. Even if a foot close to 31 cm seems to have been used in some cases, it accounts only for a portion of the distances, and certainly not for the dimensions of the plots; we have proposed to interpret this variability as related to the ways of planting proper to every wine-grower, within (probable) divisions in excess of the surface excavated (Boissinot 2003). Thanks to the agrarian excavations of Saint-Jean du Désert, we now have a relatively well dated window within a certainly regular land fragmentation; it remains to know whether said land fragmentation can be extended to far greater spaces around. The sample studied enables us incidentally to assume long durability of the fragmentary limits with time, which is particularly encouraging for a regressive study of the vineyard area in Marseille. Other preventive excavations also took place in the same sector at a later stage. They have also unearthed other portions of ditches, new ancient agrarian traces also containing clues of layering or bowing (Fig. 4), which is a specific reproduction technique of the vineyard by layering a buried vine shoot (sites of the Pavillon d'Agrément, Chemin de La Parette, Line 1 of the Tramway La Fourragère). More upstream in the same valley, traces of a site (a rural allotment?) from the fifth century BC have been acknowledged in the South sector of the so-called German Campaign property, but unfortunately without any information on the related growing practices. In other contexts of the basin of Marseille, the discoveries of wine-growing traces, all of them ancient, have multiplied since then, in the curtilage of the Parc Chanot, in the Saint-Pierre district, and closer still to the ancient city, of the location of the former Alcazar (Fig. 5) and on the Western flank of the Saint-Charles mound (lastly, for all of the sites: Rothé & Tréziny 2005). They provide as many bearings for reconstructing the agrarian landscapes of ancient *Massalia*.

Figure 1. Location of the site of Saint-Jean du Désert (1) on an aerial photo of 1944 (Aérophotothèque, Centre Camille Jullian, Aix-en-Provence). Other sites mentioned: Campagne Lallemand (2), the ancient city of Massalia (3), the indigenous oppidum of the Baou de Saint-Marcel (4).

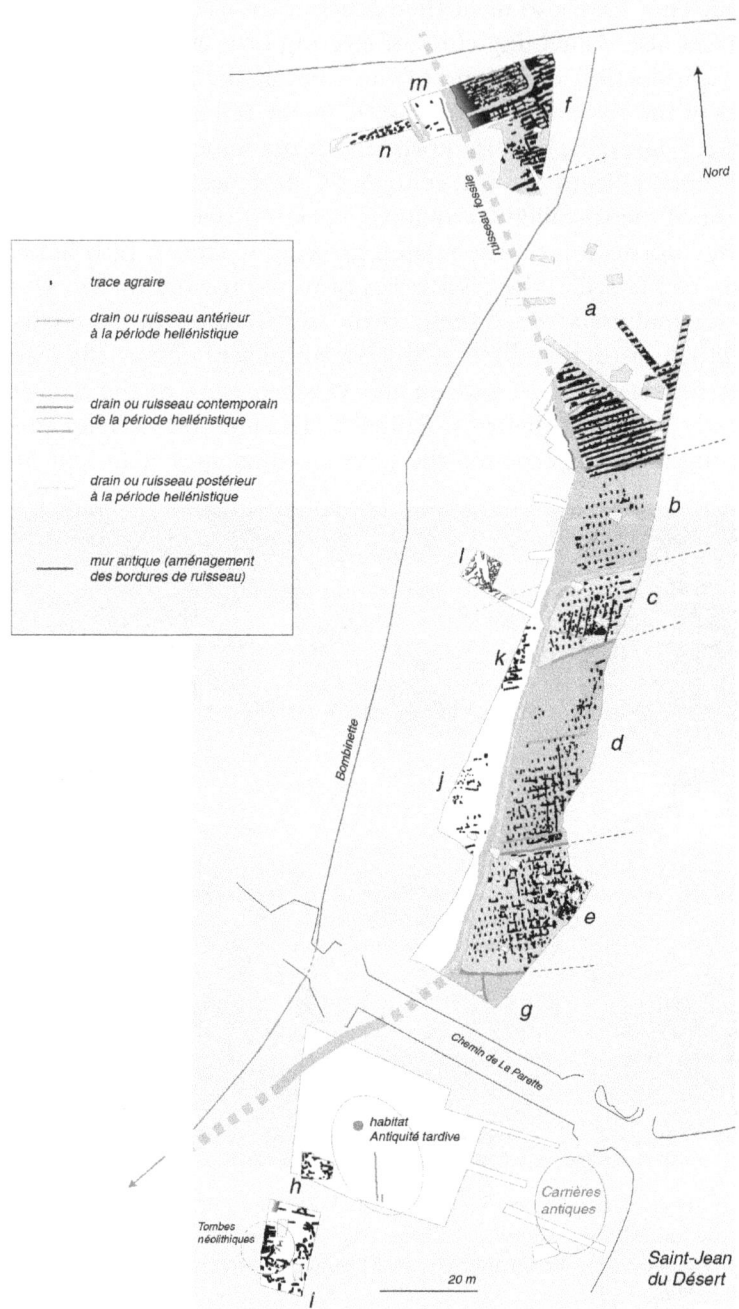

Figure 2. The land fragmentation of Saint-Jean du Désert in diachrony.

Figure 3. View of a vineyard, constituted of parallel trenches, in Saint-Jean du Désert (fourth century BC).

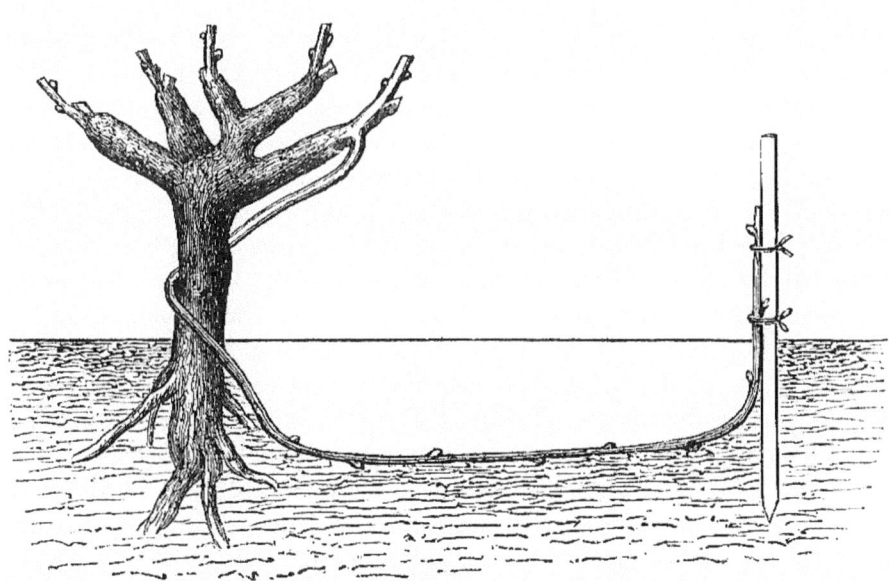

Figure 4. The technique of bowing (or layering), according to an agronomic treatise in the beginning of the twentieth century. (Chauzit & Chapelle, 1902)

Figure 5. Layout of the vineyard of the Alcazar (phase 1D), according to M. Bouiron in Rothé & Tréziny 2005, 581.

From Agrarian Traces to Ancient Land Fragmentations

The approach to ancient land fragmentations in a sector thus transformed by urbanisation and industrialisation is quite an awesome task. The aerial photographs and their possible fossil revelations, performed too late in the twentieth century, are here sadly inadequate; the investigation must then be started from the oldest mapped out land registries, in that particular instance those carried out at the beginning of the twentieth century at a time when Saint-Jean du Désert was still only a hamlet surrounded with fields and fortified towns. These documents, unfortunately poorly preserved in the sectors where they have been looked up extensively (town centre), have been scanned recently by the office of Departmental Archives of the Bouches-du-Rhône. From these images, it has been possible to obtain a vectorised version and to put together different selected sheets (Les Olives, Saint-Julien, Saint-Pierre, and partially, Notre-Dame de la Garde and Saint-Cyr) (Fig. 6). As might be expected from these imperfect land surveys, splicing among the different layers raises a few problems, but does not compromise at all a study of general orientations. If now we highlight on this modern land registry all the limits having the same orientations as those located during excavations in Saint-Jean du Désert, that is, more or less two main orientations, neither regularity nor significant concentration can be noted over the whole assembly studied, mostly between Huveaune and Jarret (Fig. 7).

Figure 6. Location of the sheets studied and scanned of the so-called Napolean land registry of Marseille (in grey).

But during this step, we could observe that axes with neighbouring orientations clearly appeared in that sector with rigorous equidistance (398) as well as precise parallelism. On the so-called Napoleon land registry, they are mainly materialised by pathways and plot curtilages. The orientation axes, approximately NL—80° West, go through without discontinuity the river Jarret, but cut short near the alluvial plain of the Huveaune, leaving room to another structuration of the space on the left bank. One of these major axes might even have taken its rise at the "*Porte d'Italie*" of the ancient harbour of Marseille, leaving parallel thereto on its left, but a few metres therefrom, the enclosed plot unearthed on the site of the Alcazar by the team directed by M. Bouiron, which strongly supports an ancient dating, possibly as early as the fifth century BC (Rothé & Tréziny 2005, 583) (Fig. 8).

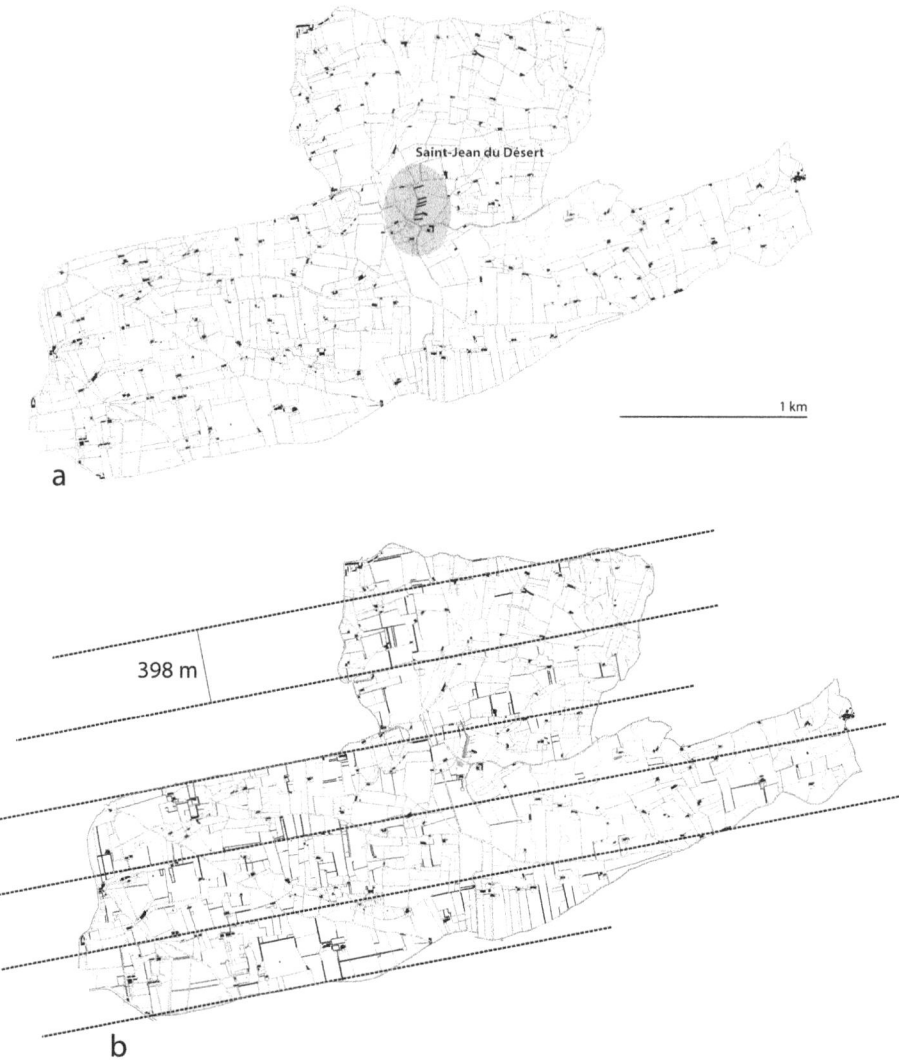

Figure 7. (a) Projection of the main archaeological structures of Saint-Jean du Désert on the sheets of the surrounding so-called *Cadastre Napoléon* land registry; (b) Location (in black and grey) on the same collection of the plot curtilages, parallel or orthogonal to the assemblies put in evidence in Saint-Jean du Désert. The structuring axes are highlighted in black (system A).

Figure 8. Analysis proposition of the modern land fragmentations in the East of Marseille. System A, of Greek origin, is in black.

Assuming that the land fragmentation sought mirrors that put in evidence around the Greek colony of Metaponto in Magna Graecia, formed of long parallel axes (but without looking for a strict orthogonality in the way plots were cut out, and locally without regular periodicity), one of which is connected directly to the city (Adamesteanu & Vatin 1976; Adamesteanu 1978; Carter 1981, 2006), Marseille does provide a sound starting point for further research. In the absence of axes more or less perpendicular to the previous ones, we shall abstain from suggesting in this instance a more regular pattern still, that of a chequer board, or of an organisation into perfectly rectangular plots as can be observed on large portions of territories in the Greek cities of Crimea (Chtcheglov 1992; Carter et al. 2000).

The fact that the plot curtilages put in evidence in the scrapings in Saint-Jean du Désert are not exactly parallel to these major axes does not undermine the pattern at all: we know that there is a certain play in the breakdown of the fields within intermediate structures, as we could see on the site of Girardes, in Vaucluse, although of Roman time (Early Roman Empire), with vineyard limits which are not systematically parallel or orthogonal to the kardo and to the *decumanus* of land registry B of Orange, i.e. the intermediate structures of this territory divided into hundreds of units (Boissinot & Roger 2004).

If however the hypothesis is correct, it can be noted that the archaeological window studied here is situated at the end of the "regular sector", the modern plot curtilages located further East do not refer to any extension of the axes; not surprisingly in these cases, the datings obtained for Saint-Jean de Désert are so low, whereas the colonisation of the land only took place after the operation of the vineyard area closest to the city.

A Greek Planning System?

During this analysis, we have gathered a number of clues which may qualify as sound, on the issue of the (probable) ancient land registries of Marseille: there are parallel and equidistant lines in the land fragmentations of the modern era, whereas they do not seem to link any settlement cluster effectively attested in the medieval era or later; one of these lines leads directly to one of the gates of the ancient city ("Porte d'Italie to La Bourse"), along an identical slope to that assumed from the analysis of the archaeological documentation of this peri-urban sector (Bouiron 2001; Bouiron & Tréziny 2001, fig. 2); well-dated archaeological sets, at the earliest to the fifth century BC at Alcazar and in the fourth century BC in Saint-Jean du Désert, seem to be located between these parallel lines and they relate off-scratch from the wine-growing sector, along a progression from near the city to far away from the city, apparently stopping halfway to the first protohistorical agglomeration of the basin (Saint-Marcel/La Tourette). All these elements concur to suggest the existence of an agrarian planning system of Greek era throughout this Eastern sector of the city. The orientation selected is obviously not that of a route through the bulk of the basin of Marseille and to lead eventually to the maritime itinerary to Italy since, if it had been the case, it would have bumped against the mountain range of Allauch farther East. It is therefore to contemplate other oblique axes to bring communications towards the South-east, in the direction of the valley of Huveaune; such lines are not absent from the so-called Napoleon land registry, but we do not have any argument to date them. Should we, to understand this selected orientation, evoke the river which has become emblematic of the modern city, the *Cannebière*, which could have flowed in that direction in the Saint-Bauzile valley, probably channelised and associated with land reclamation works of the archaic time? (Bouiron 2001, 322).

Now that a frame (system A) has been proposed, we must attempt to validate it by suggesting excavations at significant points, notably along strong axes located; there is here a decisive argument to remain strong in supporting preventive excavations in the suburb of Marseille, so long forgotten from archaeological research. However, taking into account what we have stated about the possibilities of circulation within the basin of Marseille, we may expect to find oblique axes, and plots at the junction of frames which are not orthonormal; these cases, if they crop up in emergency excavations, will not weaken the pattern. Finally, it will remain to confirm the orthogonal overlapping of the major axes to generate the different agrarian settlements, as it appears in the rectangular plot excavated in the Alcazar—but not documented so far in Saint-Jean du Désert; since other methods that might have been used, as in Metaponto, have materialised, in particular through parallelograms.

As regards the extent of this planning system (system A), our information is not distributed uniformly. We have prioritised for this research the surroundings of Saint-Jean du Désert, and the link between that sector and the ancient city. The vectorisation of the modern land registry has also encompassed a few portions on the left bank of the Huveaune which show quite a different configuration, perhaps with equidistant axes, but different orientations as well. In the sector of Saint-Giniez/Prado, on the right bank and close to the beach of the same name, regularities appear, with diverging lines from those of system A, closer at any rate; we shall note that the contact area is characterised by a lesser deviation between the axes of the easternmost set (Fig. 8). For all the other sectors of the basin of Marseille, only a few boards have been vectorised, without proceeding to their assembly for the time being. Consequently, we cannot offer for the North and Northeast portions any accurate agrarian system; however, the few attempt to provide an explanation for system A have proven fruitless, which would seem to indicate that the planning put in evidence in this study continues in the North of the city, and in particular on right bank of the Jarret, before this river follows an elbow to join the Huveaune. Conversely, serious clues of a SW-NE oriented frame can be deduced from the archaeological observations in the town centre, rue Leca, where a portion of the route has been unearthed, in a sector which should be close to the city at the Archaic time and which urbanised only later, at the Hellenistic time (Conche 2001; Tréziny 2001). And in the modern land registry, similar orientations can be read further North, suggesting a development far beyond ancient fortifications. Outside this probable case, it goes without saying that all possible systems different from the one denominated A have not been dated yet and could belong to a period subsequent to the Greek occupation. If, conversely, all of them should be situated before the Roman time, we could see in Marseille a device comparable to that of Metaponto, where rivers form limits between differentiated organisations.

The historical reasons for such an agrarian planning system can be situated in literature. In the ancient world, operations are generally associated with the allotment of new settlers, indirectly (and more or less partially) to the stranglehold on terrains taken away from "indigens". If the installation of system A is dated at the latest to the period when the first agrarian plot of the Alcazar was implemented, i.e. the middle of the fifth century BC (Rothé & Tréziny 2005: State 1C) which previous episode of the history of the city should be adopted? If the time of foundation is brushed aside, there still remains the possibility of an arrival of Phocaean emigrants in the middle of the sixth century BC, after they had been hunted away from Phocaea by the Persians, following the interpretation proposed by I. Malkin and M. Gras to go beyond the ambiguity of the texts of Herodotus and of Strabo together (Gras 1995). Regardless of the historical reality, archaeology demonstrates that this phase (540/530 BC) corresponds to the first production of wine amphorae in Marseille, that is, the creation of a vineyard close to the city, overwhelmingly intended for wine export (Bats 1990). It is by no means irrelevant to note that both peri-urban sites to which we have referred, the Alcazar and Saint-Jean du Désert, were first planted as vineyards before experiencing mixed fortunes. These plantations are admittedly posterior to the creation of the first "export vineyard", by almost a century in the first case, much later in the second, and they undoubtedly provided benchmarks in the progressive implementation of cash crops within a land registry frame probably set up to meet the inflow of new Greek emigrants.

Marseille is not the sole Greek city in Gaul which experienced agrarian planning. Some of its colonies implanted on the coastline the better to control the circulation of people and of goods, such as Olbia and Agde, and more or less conclusive clues of structuration of their territory have been disseminated. The environment of the Var establishment lends itself best to the exploitation of aerial snapshots. Looking for an orthonormal land registry, J. Benoit (1985) has reconstructed a well-developed set in the North of the city, oriented following the curtilages of the city itself, with elongated plots measuring 105 m × 52.5. The morphological agrarian work, relying to a vast extent on the search for metric constants, could not until now be tested by archaeology; it leads to a result which can only be characterised by chronological speculations. The case of the city on the banks of the Hérault, Agde, seems more complex. The formal analyses of A. Nickels (1981) seem to show a succession of urban and peri-urban planning systems which ought to be reviewed by querying the dynamics and the degradation of the land fragmentations; since, by camping on formal and metric positions too much, the result is that a protohistorical necropole (Le Peyrou) vastly anterior to the Greek implantation settled within a land registered set (Guy 1995), whose socio-historical conditions are difficult to grasp. Finally, the Greek Marseille case is not as hopeless as it appeared initially!

Bibliography

Adamesteanu, D., 1978, Le subdivisioni di terra nel Metapontino. In: M. Finley (dir.), *Problèmes de la terre en Grèce ancienne*, Paris, Mouton, 49–61.

Adamesteanu, D. & Vatin, C., 1976, L'arrière-pays de Métaponte. *CRAI*, janvier-mars, 110–123.

Bats, M. (dir.), 1990, *Les amphores de Marseille grecque*. Lattes-Aix-en-Provence, ADAM-Université de Provence (Etudes Massaliètes 2), 294p.

Benoit, J., 1985, L'étude des cadastres antiques: à propos d'*Olbia* de Provence. *Documents d'Archéologie Méridionale*, 8, 25–48.

Bertucchi, G., 1992, *Les amphores et le vin de Marseille, VIe s. av. J.-C.—IIe s. ap. J.-C.* Paris, CNRS (25ᵉ suppl. à la RAN), 250p.

Boissinot, P., 1995, L'empreinte des paysages hellénistiques dans les formations holocènes de Saint-Jean-du-Désert (Marseille). *Méditerranée*, 82, 33–40.

Boissinot, P., 2001a, Archéologie des vignobles antiques du sud de la Gaule. *Gallia*, 58, 513–544.

Boissinot, P., 2003, Métrologie de l'arboriculture antique dans le Midi de la France. In: F. Favory (dir.) *Métrologie agraire antique et médiévale*, Presses Universitaires Franc-Comtoises, 37–58.

Boissinot, P. & Roger, K., 2002, Le domaine viticole des Girardes à Lapalud. In: F. Favory & A. Vignot (dir.), *Actualité de la recherche en histoire et archéologie agraire* (colloque AGER V, Besançon 2000), Besançon, Presses Universitaires Franc-Comtoises, 225–240.

Bouiron, M., 2001, Les espaces suburbains. In: M. Bouiron, H. Tréziny, B. Bizot, A. Guilcher, J. Guyon & M. Pagni (dirs.), *Marseille. Trames et paysages urbains de Gyptis au Roi René*, Lattes-Aix-en-Provence, ADAM-Université de Provence (Etudes Massaliètes 7), 319–335.

Bouiron, M. & Tréziny, H., 2001, Une porte antique sous la rue Colbert? In: M. Bouiron, H. Tréziny, B. Bizot, A. Guilcher, J. Guyon & M. Pagni (dirs.), *Marseille. Trames et paysages urbains de Gyptis au Roi René*, Lattes-Aix-en-Provence, ADAM-Université de Provence (Etudes Massaliètes 7), 63–73.

Carter, J.C., 1981, Rural Settlement at Metaponto. In: *Archaeology and Italian Society*, BAR Int. Series, 102, 167–178.

Carter, J.C., 2006, *Discovering the Greek countryside at Metaponto*. Ann Arbor, The University of Michigan Press, 287p.

Carter, J.C., Crawford, M., Lehman, P., Nikolaenko, G. & Trelogan, J., 2000, The Chora of Chersonesos in Crimea, Ukraine. *American Journal of Archaeology*, 104, 707–741.

Chauzit, B. & Chapelle, J.-B., 1902, *Traité d'agronomie méridionale*, Paris, Masson, 378 p.

Chouquer, G. & Favory, F., 1991, *Les paysages de l'Antiquité*. Paris, Errance, 239p.

Chtcheglov, A., 1992, *Polis et chora*. Paris, Annales littéraires de l'Université de Besançon, 304p.

Conche, F., 2001, Les fouilles du 9 rue Jean-François Leca. In: M. Bouiron, H. Tréziny et al. (eds.), *Marseille. Trames et paysages urbains de Gyptis au Roi René*, Aix-en-Provence, Edisud (Etudes Massaliètes 7), 131–136.

Gras, M., 1995, L'arrivée d'émigrés à Marseille au milieu du VIe s. av. J.-C. In: P. Arcelin, M. Bats, D. Garcia, G. Marchand & M. Schwaller (dirs.), *Sur les pas des Grecs en Occident. Hommages à André Nickels*, Lattes-Aix-en-Provence, ADAM-Université de Provence (Etudes Massaliètes 4), 363–366.

Guy, M., 1995, Cadastres en bandes de Métaponte à Agde. Questions et méthodes, In: P. Arcelin, M. Bats, D. Garcia, G. Marchand & M. Schwaller (dirs.), *Sur les pas des Grecs en Occident. Hommages à André Nickels*, Lattes-Aix-en-Provence, ADAM-Université de Provence (Etudes Massaliètes 4), 427–444.

Nickels, A., 1981, Recherches sur la topographie de la ville antique d'Agde. *Documents d'Archéologie Méridionale*, 4, 29–50.

Rothé, M.P. & Tréziny, H. (dirs.), 2005, *Marseille et alentours*. 13/3 (Carte Archéologique de la Gaule), Paris, MSH, 925p.

Tréziny, H., 2001, Trames et orientations dans la ville antique: lots et îlots. In: M. Bouiron and H. Tréziny et al. (eds.), *Marseille. Trames et paysages urbains de Gyptis au Roi René*, Aix-en-Provence, Edisud (Etudes Massaliètes 7), 137–145.

14. The Greco-Massaliot Shipwrecks in the Place Jules-Verne in Marseille and the Evolution of Greek Ship Construction from the Sixth to the Fourth Century BC

Patrice Pomey

The Greco-Massaliot Shipwrecks in the Place Jules-Verne in Marseille

In 1992–1993, the preventive excavations of the Place Jules-Verne, situated in immediate vicinity of the Vieux-Port (Old Harbour) of Marseille, brought to light a portion of the ancient harbour dating back to the Greek and Roman periods (Hesnard 1994) and no fewer than seven ancient shipwrecks: among which two were Greek and five Roman (Pomey 1995) (Fig. 1). Both Greek shipwrecks, *Jules-Verne 7* and *Jules-Verne 9*, were discovered close to the ancient shore, resting against each other, after they were voluntarily abandoned at the end of the sixth century BC (Fig. 2). The construction of ships by the shipyards of Marseille, dates back to the middle of the century, that is, two generations only after the foundation of the city, around 600 BC, by Greek settlers from Phocaea. Rather well preserved, the shipwrecks testify to ships in use at the times of the foundation of the city and illustrate in an exemplary manner the techniques of naval construction of the Archaic time practised on the Massaliot shipyards and directly inherited from Phocaeans (Pomey 1998, 2001). The excavation and the study of the shipwrecks were entrusted to the team of naval archaeology of the Jullian Centre, a laboratory of Mediterranean archaeology (Aix-Marseille University, CNRS, MCC, INRAP), which after long reconstruction work succeeded in proposing their complete reconstruction. In parallel, both shipwrecks were deposited upon completion of their excavation to be the subject of a preservation and restoration treatment in the ARC-Nucléart laboratory of Grenoble (Bernard-Maugiron 2007). They are now exhibited, alongside four other Roman shipwrecks originating from the Place Jules-Verne (*Jules-Verne 3, 4* and *8*) and from La Bourse, in the Musée d'Histoire of Marseille, which thus provides a unique set of ancient shipwrecks in the Mediterranean region.

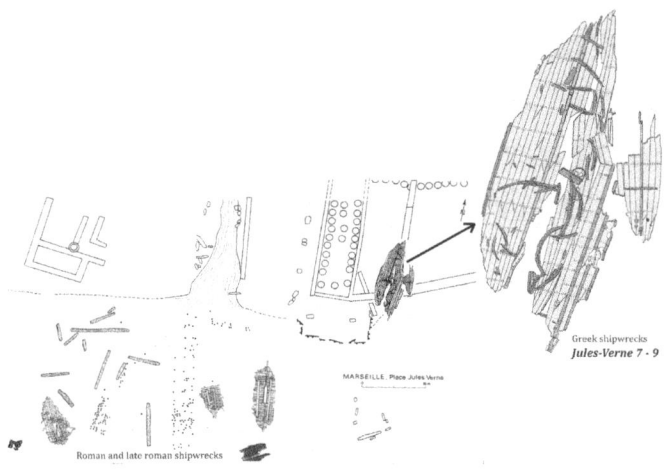

Figure 1. Localization map of the ancient shipwrecks of Place Jules-Verne in Marseille and plan of the Greek shipwrecks *Jules-Verne 7 et 9.* (Drawing M. Rival, Centre Camille Jullian, AMU-CNRS).

Figure 2. View of the Greek shipwrecks Jules-Verne 7 et *9* in course of excavation. In the foreground, at the centre, the *Jules-Verne 9* wreck. (Photo M. Derain, Centre Camille Jullian, AMU-CNRS).

The Jules-Verne 9 *Shipwreck: A Boat Assembled by Ligatures*

The shipwreck, kept over 5 m in length and 1.40 m in width, corresponds to a portion of the original watercraft and presents remains in a good state of preservation (Fig. 2). It is characterised by a rounded section at the main section, a keel without rabbet (height 7 cm; width 6.8 cm), a carvel planking and a shell reinforced by spaced frames. The strakes of the planking are carvel built and composed of planks (thickness 2.7 to 3 cm; width 15 to 20 cm) linked by diagonal scarf. A single floor timber (height 10 cm; width 8.5 cm) has been kept on site. It has at its ends the futtocks assemblies and in its centre the beginning of a small stanchion. According to the position of the other frames, known for their foot-print, the room reached 90 cm. Moreover, the frame was completed by top timbers taking place between the floor timbers in the upper part of the hull. The principle of construction is based on "shell" conception and the strakes were placed on the axial structure (keel, stem and stern posts) before the setting of the frames which essentially played a reinforcing role.

The most remarkable characteristic is the assembly system of the hull by means of ligatures, according to the archaic technique of "sewn boats", of which many links had been kept in place thanks to the sealing coat of the hull (Fig. 3). The strakes of the planking are placed first of all using pre-assembly dowels (diameter 1 cm; deviation 20.5 cm) pushed into the edge of the planks. Their purpose is to keep in position and in shape the planks and to prevent the play among the boards so as to avoid shear phenomena. Then they are fastened by a triple flax thread running through tetrahedral recesses (1.5 to 1.7 cm in size) spaced regularly (deviation 2.5 cm) along the edges of each plank and giving access to oblique channels (diameter 0.6 cm). These channels meet on the lower edge of the joint between the planks so that the links never protrude outwardly. They are thus protected against friction. Small tapered pegs, pushed into the oblique channels, then block the links and plug the passageways. Moreover, the water tightness of the assembly is ensured by flax fabric rolls placed on the joints and clamped by ligatures. Preliminary dry point marks indicated quite precisely the position of each assembly point. They provide for the regularity of the assembly with the tetrahedral. As for the running of the links, it goes back and forth and includes a double clamping turn, then goes obliquely to the following point, according to an IXIXIX-type scheme (Fig. 4).

Figure 3. Jules-Verne 9 wreck. Detail view of the remains of ligatures of the planking still in place. (Photo M. Derain, Centre Camille Jullian, AMU-CNRS).

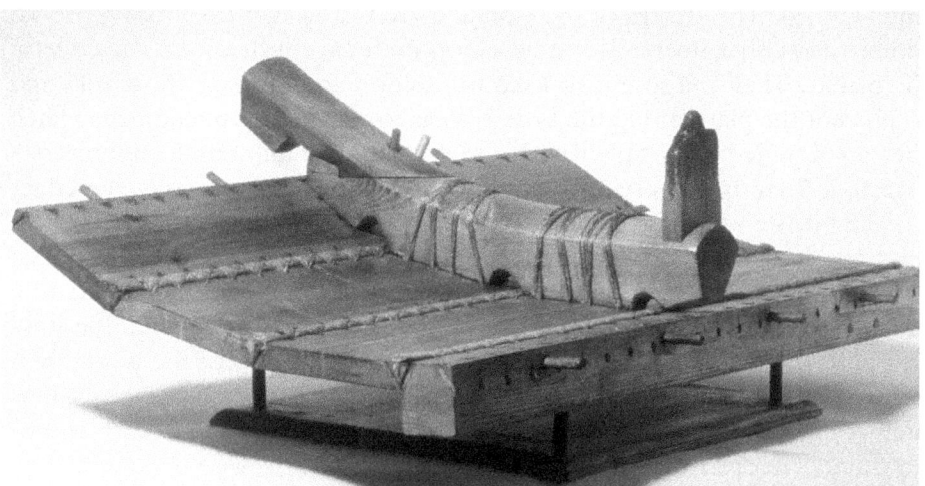

Figure 4. Jules-Verne 9 wreck. Study model (scale 1) of the assembly system by ligatures. (Model M. Rival, R. Roman, photo Ph. Foliot, Centre Camille Jullian, AMU-CNRS).

The frames are also lashed by links running through oblique channels cut into the planks then going on the back of the timber. Their morphology with a rounded back and a narrow foot (basis width 3 cm) obtains the most efficient clamping and their basis is cut regularly for letting through the ligatures of the planking (Fig. 4). Finally, a coat of beeswax and of conifer pitch covers the whole of the hull, inside and outside, to complete the tightness thereof.

Of local use, the watercraft was then built in the Massaliot shipyards with local essences resorting to oak for the keel, Aleppo pine tree for the planking and the frames, and olive tree for the dowels.

The Jules-Verne 7 *Shipwreck: A Mixed Construction Boat with Ligatures and Mortise-and-Tenon*

The shipwreck, over 14 m in length and close to 4 m in width seems, in spite of a few gaps, rather complete (Fig. 2). The keel is full and if the stem and the stern have disappeared, their profile is known nevertheless thanks to the strake heads. The transversal main section is rounded. The planking is carvel assembled and three wales are kept on the starboard side. The frame, although dispersed, is complete including in its upper portions.

The keel (length 10.70 m; height 11 cm; width 10 cm) is composed of two elements and exhibits rabbets at each end. The assemblies between the keel and the end parts, such as hook scarf with a vertical key, are similar to those of the *Jules-Verne 9* shipwreck. The planking is composed of strakes quite variable in length (14 to 28 cm) whose planks (thickness 2.5 to 3 cm) are linked by simple diagonal scarf in the bottoms and by three-planed scarf beyond. It entails three wales with a polygonal or semi-circular section (width 7 to 11 cm; thickness 8 to 12 cm). The frame is identical to that of *Jules-Verne 9* and is composed of floor timber (height 8 to 13 cm; width 7 to 11 cm) vastly spaced (0.90 m) and prolonged by futtocks assembled by a pegged hookscarf. They alternate in the upper portions of the hull with top timbers. The ends of the bottom frames bear the traces of lateral implantation of the transversal beams. Fastening elements of the mast step timber, the presence of a stanchion and of an element of a mast box enable us to reproduce the whole internal structure of the boat.

The structure and the morphology of the hull components are identical to those of the *Jules-Verne 9* shipwreck. Obviously, the boat belongs to the same architectural family and was built along the same "shell first" principle. But contrary to the previous shipwreck, several assembling techniques have been used. Thus, the planking is henceforth assembled by mortise-and-tenon joint. The tenons are long and narrow (14 x 3 cm), dowelled into widely spaced mortises (20 cm). The network of the assembly is rather loose, characteristic of the Archaic period, but not as dense as it was to become later (Fig. 5). Nevertheless, ligatures following a system identical to that of the *Jules-Verne 9* shipwreck, and are still used to assemble the planking in the rabbets of the ends of the keel, of the stempost and of the sternpost. Similarly, the numerous repairs of the hull always use ligatures. Moreover, the frames are henceforth nailed using iron nails with the tip clenched on the back of the timber whereas the top timbers are dowelled and their foot is ligatured. Nevertheless, the frames still keep their particular morphology with a narrow foot and a rounded back suited to ligature assembly. Everything suggests that the shipwreck points to a transition boat illustrating the evolution of shipbuilding techniques with the introduction of new assembly practices (mortise-and-tenon, iron nails) within the sewing tradition which still partially subsists.

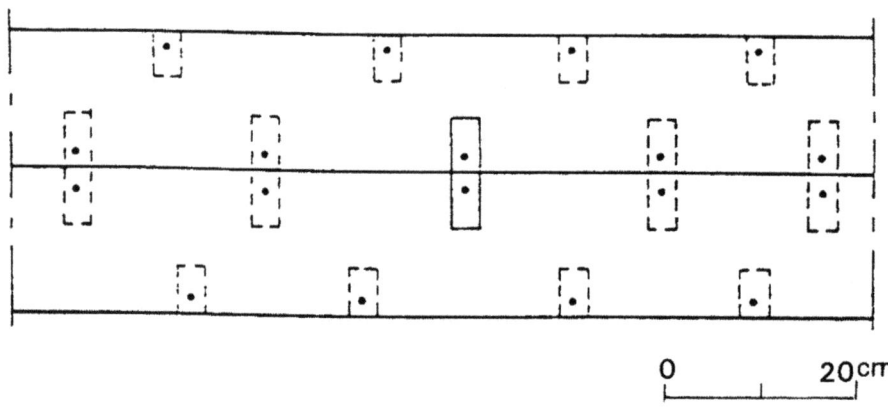

Figure 5. Jules-Verne 7 wreck. Schema of the mortise-and-tenon joint of the planking. (Drawing M. Rival, Centre Camille Jullian, AMU-CNRS).

The shipwreck exhibits numerous carpenter's marks which correspond to diverse construction phases. Thus, the first eight strakes were assembled before laying the floor timbers and the hull was checked for symmetry at the level of the eighth strake. Said strake, wider than the others and bearing special carpenter's marks, played the part of an adjusting strake. It will be noted that certain marks can be found identically on the *Jules-Verne 9* shipwreck, which means that the boat of the *Jules-Verne 7* shipwreck was also built in a Massaliot yard. The wooden planks supplied are also of local origin and include green oak for the keel, Aleppo pine for the planking, Aleppo pine, pinion pine and alder for the frames, and olive tree for the tenon and dowels.

A Coastal Craft and a Light Merchant Ship

Upon completion of the excavations, a long study was conducted with a view to restoring both original boats (Pomey 2003): restoration of the shape and structure plans, and reconstruction of the technical system with the propelling means and the steering apparatus. Beforehand, a first study model, partial but at full scale, was conducted so as to examine the assembly system by ligatures of the *Jules-Verne 9* shipwreck (Fig. 4). Then the original boats were sought to be reconstructed based on graphic reconstructions, which were controlled and validated at each step via 3D-models (⅒ or ⅕): mock-ups can be of different natures; model of the remains; models of the remains restored whereas parts were overhauled and connected back together; models restoring the overall shapes of the hull; final reconstruction model integrating the shapes of the hull, the general structure and the propelling (sails and oars) and steering systems. As for the *Jules-Verne 9* shipwreck, whereof one of the ends remains unknown, we had to examine the characteristics of other contemporary shipwrecks, of the same architectural family and of the same type (shipwrecks of *Villeneuve-Bargemon 1, Bon-Porté 1, Golo*). As for the final restoration with the rigging and the steering apparatus, contemporary iconographic data were used. Similarly, the restoration of the boat of the *Jules-Verne 7* shipwreck used shipwrecks of the same family and with similar characteristics (*Gela 1* shipwreck) as well as iconography.

Three levels of restoration can be obtained in total: the restorations deemed as certain, based directly on archaeological data; the restorations deemed as probable, based on elements of comparison from shipwrecks of similar types; the restorations deemed as possible, based on more general elements of comparison such as iconography. In all, in the case of the Marseille shipwrecks, where the certain and probable restorations are overwhelming, restorations can be considered as particularly reliable.

As for the *Jules-Verne 9* shipwreck, the study consisted of restoring a watercraft with symmetrical and streamlined shapes, 9.85 min length and 1.88 m in width. Light and fast, it was propelled by oars and sail (Fig. 6). Well suited to coastal navigation, the boat was used for nearby transport of light goods and for fishing, notably coral fishing, many fragments of which have been found on the wreck (Pomey 2000).

As for the *Jules-Verne 7* shipwreck, the restoration carried out corresponds to a small merchant ship with a rounded section hull, 15 m in length and 3.80 m in width (Fig. 7). Propelled by a square sail, it could transport a cargo of some fifteen tons and had sufficient nautical capacities for trans-Mediterranean navigations.

Figure 6. Final reconstruction model (¹⁄₁₀) of the boat of *Jules-Verne 9* wreck. (Photo Ph. Foliot, Centre Camille Jullian, AMU-CNRS).

Figure 7. Final reconstruction model (¹⁄₁₀) of the ship of *Jules-Verne 7* wreck. (Photo Ph. Foliot, Centre Camille Jullian, AMU-CNRS).

The *"Prôtis"* Experimental Archaeological Project and the Construction of the Gyptis, *a Sailing Replica of* Jules-Verne 9

To control the well-foundedness of the restorations, an experimental archae-ological programme has been implemented to validate and to better under-stand the construction methods, and to assess in real-scale the nautical quali-ties of the ships and their operating mode.

The opportunity provided by Marseille-Provence, the European capital of culture in 2013, has enabled us to put together the "Prôtis" project (the name of the legendary leader of the Phocaean settlers who founded Marseille) whose object was to build the sailing replica of the *Jules-Verne 9* shipwreck, denominated *Gyptis* (the name of the daughter of the local king who married Prôtis (Pomey 2014a, 2014b; Pomey & Poveda 2014).

The operation was conducted in the framework of a four-part conven-tion associating: Aix-Marseille University and the CNRS, as parent organ-isations and administrative supervisors of the Centre Camille Jullian, for the scientific part; and the Provence-Alpes-Côte d'Azur Region and the urban community of Marseille Provence Metropole for the financing side. The realisation was entrusted to the shipyard Borg of Marseille, specialised wooden traditional shipbuilding, and with the Arkaeos association, dedi-cated to the development and the dissemination of nautical archaeology, for an operations coordination mission. Finally, the Marseille-Provence 2013 organisation has taken on the preliminary tests and the first naviga-tions.

The work started at the beginning of 2013 and was subjected to prior experiments so as to get familiarised with the construction principles and methods of the time as well as the assembly technique which are completely forgotten. They should also enable us to specify the operating chain, to retrieve the gestures and the know-how and, finally to assess the working times of the various operations. These experiments have addressed in par-ticular: the "shell first" construction method, involving the assembly of the planking without frame elements nor mould elements; the selection of the best procedure and of the best suited tools for ligature-based assemblies; and the sealing coat of the hull based on beeswax and conifer pitch. In parallel, the boat was completely redrawn on 3D-software (Fig. 8) which moreover enabled us to outline and to complete the hydrostatic study of the watercraft and to model all the parts of the boat and its equipment.

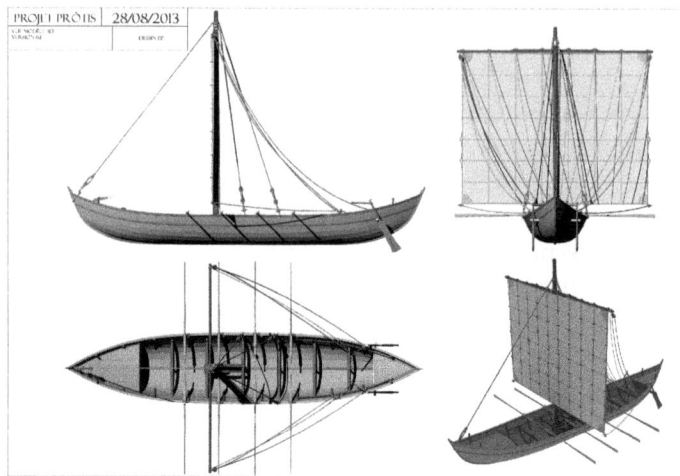

Figure 8. 3D computer views of the *Gyptis*, sailing replica of the boat of *Jules-Verne 9* wreck. (Views and plans P. Poveda, Centre Camille Jullian, AMU-CNRS).

Finally, the construction properly speaking started at the beginning of April 2013, for the ship, suitably rigged and seaworthy, to be put to water around mid-November after seven and a half months of intense work, which a team of some ten people permanently mobilised, among whom four were experienced shipwrights, with the assistance if needed of volunteers to carry out the 5 kilometres of ligatures necessary to the 10,000 assembly points (Fig. 9 and Fig. 10).

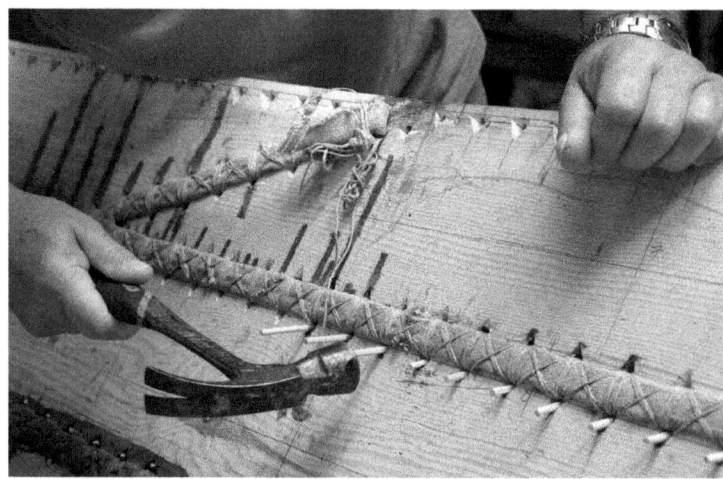

Figure 9. Gyptis. Detail view of the sewing system of the planking. (Photo C. Durand, Centre Camille Jullian, AMU-CNRS).

Figure 10. Interior view of *Gyptis* during finishing. Note the mast step timber and the mast box (foreground, at the centre); the framing system with floor timbers and top frames; the cross beams serving as bench for the rowers; the assemblages by ligatures; the sealing coat made of a mixture of beeswax and resin covering the bottom of the hull. (Picture L. Damelet, Centre Camille Jullian, AMU-CNRS).

The mixed propelled ship was fitted with four pairs of oars and an ancient rigging with a square sail (Fig. 11 and Fig. 12). The monoxylic mast (height 6.70 m), of fir tree, is maintained by a fore stay and two lateral shrouds on each side. It carries a yard hoisted by a double halyard. The 25 m², fitted with manoeuvring braces and sheets, is provided with brails for reducing or modifying its geometry to suit the needs. All the blocks and tackles for the rigging were carried out from elements found on ancient wrecks. The steering system consists of two lateral rudders arranged on both sides of the stern. Finally, for ballasting the watercraft, 720 kg pebbles from the Durance River, distributed in 20-kg bags were arranged on the bottom of the hull. Thus equipped, the *Gyptis* performed her first trials successfully in the bay of Marseille. The lateral rudders proved efficient, providing only the one situated leeward was used, and the square sail reached its maximum efficiency when downwind sailing, from wind astern to broad reach. Her capacities to sail upwind remain however limited, of the order of 75° to 70°, by reason of the nature of the sail and of the shape of the hull. However, they correspond to what can be expected from a square sail. The boat is light and fast, and can easily reach 3 knots by oars and 5–6 knots by sail, with an average breeze, with peak speeds above 7 knots. Although quite sensitive to the heeling force, the ship, once balanced, proves to be very stable. After these conclusive trials, *Gyptis* sailed along the coasts of Provence for a week, from Marseille to the Embiez and back to Marseille.

Figure 11. Gyptis under oars in the En Vau creek between Marseille and Cassis. (Photo L. Damelet, Centre Camille Jullian, AMU-CNRS).

Figure 12. Gyptis under sail in the bay of Marseille. Note the square sail and the lateral rudder. (Photo L. Damelet, Centre Camille Jullian, AMU-CNRS).

If the *Gyptis* has met with real popular success, the experiment has also been a success on the scientific plane. Her realisation has not only enabled us to test the justness of the ideas on ancient ship construction termed as "shell first" based, and the efficiency of the assemblies with ligatures, but also to raise and to answer many questions regarding the methods of construction used in Antiquity. Finally, the navigation enabled us to verify the life-sized nautical capacities of the ship and thus provided better understanding of her navigation space and her mode of use.

An Ancient Greek Tradition...

Beyond their patrimonial value, the Greco-Massaliot wrecks of the Place Jules-Verne interestingly offer, in the same historical context, two ships born in identical shipyards and belonging to the same architectural family, but exhibiting different assembly systems, which forebode the evolution thereof.

The *Jules-Verne 9* shipwreck testifies first of all to the pure ligature assembly techniques. The degree of sophistication observed shows that the technique reached its peak after a tradition whose longstanding character is attested by Homer (*Iliad*, II, 135; *Odyssey, V, 244–257*). According to the latter, the ships of the Achaean fleet of the Trojan War and Ulysses' boat "with many links" would be sewn boats assembled by ligature. As for the *Jules-Verne 7* shipwreck, it marks, within this tradition in the second half of the sixth century BC, the beginning of a significant evolution with the adoption of assembly techniques using mortise-and-tenon joints, which little by little replaced the ligature assemblies.

...and Its Long Evolution

Today, some ten other wrecks can be considered as part of this architectural family, clearly situated in a Greek context, and enable us to monitor its evolution over several centuries (Kahanov & Pomey 2004; Pomey 1997, 2010).

The ancient tradition illustrated by the *Jules-Verne 9* shipwreck include the Greco-Eastern wreck of Giglio (Tuscany, Italy), the Ionian wreck of Pabuç Burnu (Bodrum, Turkey) and the Massaliot wrecks of Cala Sant Vicenç (Majorca, Baleares) and of *Bon-Porté 1* (Saint-Tropez, France). All these wrecks can be dated to the sixth centry BC and have the same structural and morphological features as well as the same ligature technique assembly characterised by tetrahedral recesses giving birth to the passageways of ligatures. If most of them included cylindrical pre-assembly dowels, some like Pabuc Burnu and Cala Sant Vicenç have small tenons instead. Some authors preferred to consider it as the beginning of an internal evolution towards the adoption of the assembly by "mortise-and-tenon joint" (Polzer 2011). But the persisting usage of cylindrical pre-assembly dowels whereas the "mortise-and-tenon joint" assembly started to be widely adopted, tends to see them as different shipyard practices.

After the *Jules-Verne 7* shipwreck and the apparition of the "mortise-and-tenon joint" assembly system, we are dealing with a first so-called "transition" evolution phase. The latter also includes the Massaliot wreck of the Villeneuve-Bargemon square in Marseille (also called *César 1*), the Greek wreck of *Gela 1* (Sicily) and the wreck of the *Grand-Ribaud F* (Hyères—France). The latter, although transporting a cargo of Etruscan amphorae, nevertheless exhibits all the features of the *Jules-Verne 7* shipwreck and is demonstrably in line with this Greek tradition. This first transition phase can be dated back to the end of the sixth and the beginning of the fifth century BC. It is characterised by the adoption, within the previous tradition, of the mortise-and-tenon joint assembly for the planking, and of nails for the frames. It still keeps numerous characteristics referring to its filiation: same hull profile with rounded transversal section, same hull structure, and same frame morphology. Moreover, the same sewing system by ligature is still in use for the closing of the ends and repairs.

Since the middle of the fifth century BC, a second evolution phase represented by the Greek wreck *Gela 2* (middle of the fifth century, Sicily) and the wreck of Ma'agan Mikhaël (end of the fifth century, Israel), originated from the Ionian coast can be differentiated. On the technical plane, the evolution consecutive to the adoption of the mortise-and-tenon joint assembly continues. The ligatures are increasingly residual and limited to repairs (*Gela 2*) or to end knees (Ma'agan Mikhaël: Linder & Kahanov 2003) and the frames, henceforth nailed, tend towards a rectangular section, turning their back to their ancient morphology adapted to the ligatures. As for the hull shapes, this evolution translates in the apparition of a "wine-glass"-shaped transversal section, with sharp bottoms and a protuberant keel.

Finally, it can be considered that the Greek wreck of Kyrenia (end of the fourth century BC, Cyprus) marks the final stage of the evolution of this tradition and the starting point of what was to become the Greco-Roman tradition of the Hellenistic and Republican period. The mortise-and-tenon joint assemblies become systematic and the ligatures almost disappeared with the exception of rare reused elements. The "wine-glass"-shaped bottoms now associated with a rabbeted keel and the top timbers, prolonged into half-frames, form with the floor timbers an alternate tight-spaced frame. As for the mast step system, it remained unchanged in principle, since the *Bon-Porté 1* wreck, and is still embedded on the back of the floor timbers.

On the whole, it is the first time that we can characterise without error an architectural tradition through the same family of boats, relate that tradition to a specific context, in this instance a Greek and Ionian context, and monitor its evolution over three centuries, from the beginning of the sixth to the end of the fourth century BC.

The reasons of this evolution appear clear. The mortise-and-tenon joint assembly is more solid and longer-lasting than the ligature assembly. It enables building larger boats, with larger tonnage, and buildg new forms of more sophisticated and better performing hulls (Pomey 2011). This evolution will give birth to new types of ships, and this phenomenon is probably responsible for the development of the Greek trireme which appears in the combat fleets only at the end of the sixth century, precisely at the time when the Greeks adopted this assembly system using mortise-and-tenon joints. This evolution will also lead to the armament race and to the gigantic combat and commercial fleets of the Hellenistic period.

A Phoenician Influence

As for the origin of the assembly technique using mortise-and-tenon joint, it ought to be sought for around the coasts of the Levant (Wachsmann 1998; Polzer 2011) where it is attested for the first time the wrecks of the Bronze Age in the fourteenth and thirteenth centuries BC of Ulu Burun and Cape Gelidonya in Turkey (Pulak 2002). The technique would be inherited from the Cananeans and would have been developed by the Phoenicians and the Carthaginians, to the extent that Cato the Elder (*De agr.* XXI, 18, 9) designates this technique under the name of *coagmenta punicana,* that is, the "Punic assembly". Both wrecks of Mazzaron (Spain) testify in the second half of the seventh century of the usage of this technique in the midst of a Punic influence. It may be thought that further to contacts between the Greeks and the Punics during the conquest of the Western Mediterranean region during the sixth century BC the technological transfer took place, leading the Greeks to adopt the mortise-and-tenon joint assembly in lieu of their long-standing practice of ligature assembly. But, regardless of the circumstances of the adoption of this technique within the Greek tradition, no fewer than two centuries were necessary for the transition to be complete.

As we can see, the weight of tradition in shipbuilding has always been considerable, regardless of the epoch.

Bibliography

Bernard-Maugiron, H., 2007, Marseille, mille objets et trois épaves à conserver. In: H. Bernard-Maugiron, Ph. Cœuré, M. Clermont-Joly et al. (dir.), *Sauvé des eaux. Le patrimoine archéologique en bois, Histoires de fouilles et de restaurations*, Grenoble, Arc-Nucléart, 77–81.

Hesnard, A., 1994, Une nouvelle fouille du port de Marseille, place Jules-Verne. *CRAI*, janvier–mars, 195–217.

Kahanov, Y. & Pomey P., 2004, The Greek Sewn Shipbuilding Tradition and the *Ma'agan Mikhael* Ship: A Comparison with Mediterranean Parallels from the Sixth to the Fourth Centuries BC. *The Mariner's Mirror* 90, 1, 6–28.

Linder, E. & Kahanov, Y., 2003, *The Ma'agan Mikhael Ship. The Recovery of a 2400-Year-Old Merchantman*, Final report, vol. I., Haïfa.

Polzer, M., 2011, Early Shipbuilding in the Eastern Mediterranean. In: A. Catsambis, B. Ford, D. & L. Hamilton (eds.), *The Oxford Handbook of Maritime Archaeology*, Oxford Univ. Press, Oxford, 349–378.

Pomey, P., 1995, Les épaves grecques et romaines de la place Jules-Verne à Marseille. *CRAI*, avril–juin, 459–484.

Pomey, P., 1997, Un exemple d'évolution des techniques de construction navale antique: de l'assemblage par ligatures à l'assemblage par tenons et mortaises. In: D. Garcia & D. Meeks (éd.), *Techniques et économie antiques et médiévales, «Le temps de l'innovation», Colloque international Aix-en-Provence, mai 1996*, Errance, 195–203.

Pomey, P., 1998, Les épaves grecques du VIe siècle av. J.-C. de la place Jules-Verne à Marseille. In: P. Pomey & E. Rieth (dir.), *Construction navale maritime et fluviale. Approches archéologique, historique et ethnologique. 7th International Symposium on Boat and Ship Archaeology, île Tatihou, 1994* (Archaeonautica 14), 147–154.

Pomey, P., 2000, Un témoignage récent sur la pêche au corail à Marseille à l'époque archaïque. In: J.-P. Morel, C. Rondi-Costanzo & D. Ugolini (dir.), *"Corallo di ieri. Corallo di oggi", Atti del Convegno Ravello, 1996*, Bari, 37–39.

Pomey, P., 2001, Les épaves grecques archaïques du VIe s. av. J.-C. de Marseille: épaves Jules-Verne 7 et 9 et César 1. In: H. Tzalas (ed.), *Tropis VI, 6th International Symposium on Ship Construction in Antiquity, Lamia 1996 Proceedings*, Athènes, 425–437.

Pomey, P., 2003, Reconstruction of Marseilles 6th century BC Greek ships. In: C. Beltrame (ed.), *Boats, Ships and Shipyards. Proceedings of the IXth International Symposium on Boat and Ship Archaeology, Venice 2000*, Oxford, 57–65.

Pomey, P., 2010, De l'assemblage par ligatures à l'assemblage par tenons et mortaises. Introduction. In: P. Pomey (éd.), *Transferts technologiques en architecture navale méditerranéenne de l'Antiquité aux temps modernes: identité technique et identité culturelle, Actes de la Table Ronde Internationale d'Istanbul, mai 2007* (Varia Anatolica XX), 15–26.

Pomey, P., 2011, Les conséquences de l'évolution des techniques de construction navale sur l'économie maritime antique: quelques exemples. In: W.V. Harris & K. Iara (eds.), *Maritime Technology in the Ancient Economy* (Journal of Roman Archaeology, sup. 84), 39–55.

Pomey, P., 2014a, Le projet Prôtis. Reconstruire un bateau grec du VIᵉ siècle av. J.-C. *Archéologia*, 520, avril, 36–43.

Pomey, P., 2014b, Le projet «Prôtis» et le *Gyptis*: de l'épave à la réplique navigante d'un bateau grec du VIᵉ siècle av. J.-C. *Neptunia*, 275, septembre, 16–27.

Pomey, P. & Poveda, P., 2014, Le projet «Prôtis» et le *Gyptis*. Un programme d'archéologie expérimental. In: *Ports et navires dans l'Antiquité et à l'époque byzantine, Dossiers d'Archéologie*, 364, juillet–août, 42–47.

Pulak, C., 2002, The Ulu Burun hulls remains. In: H. Tzalas (ed.), *Tropis VII, 7ᵗʰ International Symposium on Ship Construction in Antiquity, Pylos 1999 Proceedings*, Athènes, 615–636.

Wachsmann, S., 1998, *Seagoing Ships and Seamanship in the Bronze Age Levant*. Texas A&M University Press, College Station.

15. Protohistoric Mediterranean Gaul as a Middle Ground

Michel Bats

For me, middle ground is not a performative concept, or a new example of contact. It is rather the label for a type of gathering still in progress at a given time, in a given context, a kind of "in between" (White 1991; Malkin 2011). I therefore consider this middle ground a virtual sphere that includes several actual and ever-evolving social spheres (economical, political, linguistic and cultural), and, that is, as such, never completed regarding the continuous construction of its constituents. These interconnected spheres, which correspond to the various social relationships, both between groups and with the outer world, compose "chains of society within which interact all social actors" (Amselle 1985).

Our goal is, therefore, to try and define how contacts were established through these fundamental spheres: with passing foreigners and with foreigners newly settled in specific areas—that is to say, firstly, the Phocaean Greeks. It is also to analyze the various areas of interactions, the manifestations of dynamics related to the environment and the outer world, as well as the inner changes likely to constitute starting points for the creation of social or ethnic groups. This is probably the best way to tackle the issue, based on the sole source of direct information that is available to us: archeology, a source that is silent unlike the oral traditions that feed all ethnological discussions. The best way to understand all the issues summarized in this chapter is definitely M. Dietler's book, *Archaeologies of Colonialism. Consumption, Entanglement and Violence in Ancient Mediterranean France* (2010).

In the course of the seventh century BC, various Greek items reached Mediterranean shores in Gaul, their itinerary remaining unknown. But the true contact among individuals on Gaul territory is the one resulting from the installation of Greeks from Phocaea, founders of Massalia around 600 BC.

Thus began five centuries of transactions before the Roman conquest and the creation of the Transalpine province (later known as *Gallia Narbonensis*), for a new middle ground which shaped new types of relationships.

The Greeks: Which Ones? Where?

The city of Massalia was established in a natural basin made up of a triangular depression, hilly rather than flat, about 18 km long north to south and 7 km west to east, cut across by a small river, the Huveaune, and surrounded by uplands some 500 to 600 m in height which, closer to the sea, take on the characteristics of massifs and form the city's natural geographical boundaries; including the lower slopes of these mountains, the total surface was close to 100 km².

Strabo (4. 1. 5) described the resources and constituent elements of the city's *chora*:

> [The Massaliots] possess a country which, although planted with olive-trees and vines, is, on account of its ruggedness, too poor for grain; so that, trusting the sea rather than the land, they preferred their natural fitness for a seafaring life. Later, however, their valour enabled them to take in some of the surrounding plains, thanks to the same military strength by which they founded their cities, I mean their stronghold-cities, namely, first, those which they founded in Iberia as stongholds against the Iberians...; secondly, Rhoë Agathe, as a stronghold against the barbarians who live round about the River Rhodanus; thirdly, Tauroentium, Olbia, Antipolis and Nicaea, against the tribe of the Sallyes and against those Ligures who live in the Alps.

Archeology has enabled us to reconstruct the stages of the evolution described by Strabo (Bats 2001):

> —The city, founded with the approval of the native people (hospitality granted by King Nannus and sealed with the marriage between Protis and Gyptis and the *locus condendae urbis* offering), was established on seemingly unoccupied land; the locals lived on higher sites, or even in caves, further inland, particularly on the north side of the 'chaîne de l'Étoile', on massifs dominating the upper Arc valley (necropolis with tumuli) and around the Étang de Berre. To the north, the limit of the *chora* may be indicated by the Maillans *oppidum* (Fig. 1, 40), to the east by that of the Baou de Saint-Marcel (Fig. 1, 27). As early as the last quarter of the sixth century, the Massaliots may have settled in Antibes (Antipolis), Arles (Theline) and Agde (Agathe).
> —From the fourth century, there was a reduction in the circle of *oppida* located on the higher ground surrounding the basin. The *chora*, linked directly to the city, experienced its maximum expansion towards the east (mid-Huveaune valley) and the north-west, where it reached the Rhône delta and where Strabo mentioned the presence of landmark towers, built to facilitate navigation on the

river, as well as a sanctuary to the Ephesian Artemis, which should probably be interpreted as a boundary sanctuary. On the coast, the *epiteichismata* of Olbia (around 325 BC), Tauroeis (early third century?) and Nikaia (second half of the third century?) were established.

At the time of the Roman conquest of the Transalpine province, the *chora* was fragmented, of varying depth, spreading along the coast of Gaul between Agde and Nice, with which a link was maintained by command of the sea. Massalia developed an *arche* with direct possessions (the Marseille basin, Rhône delta and the *epiteichismata*) and controlled areas (plains around the Étang de Berre). This limited territorial holding does not exactly represent a colonial conquest. There was, on the one hand, the immediate *chora*, devoted to specialised farming endowed with high trading value (vineyards and olive trees), and, on the other, coastal supporting sites meant to command maritime links, be they coastal or longer distance towards Spain and Italy (Bats 2008).

Means and Places of Contact

Literary and archaeological accounts invite us to consider several types of relationships between Greeks and natives.

Trade Relationships

Massalia's foundation (and possibly that of Mainake in the kingdom of Tartessos), closely followed by that of Emporion (Ampurias) in Iberia and of Alalia (Aleria) in Corsica, should be set in the context of the emporic trading developed by the Phocaeans in the western Mediterranean. During this initial phase, Gaul was not the sole objective of the Phocaeans, who were involved in the undoubtedly more lucrative markets of Etruria and Spain. They practised a type of commerce that, in terms of contacts with local populations, combined that of the aristocratic *prexis* with another form, new to the northwestern Mediterranean, in which professionals gradually supplanted these adventurers, based evidently on specific meeting places, *emporia*, opened at the initiative of local authorities (or with their agreement). In Gaul, the sites likely to have played this role are few: Tamaris and L'Arquet (Martigues, Bouches-du-Rhône: Fig. 1, 40, 44), Saint-Blaise (Saint-Mître-les-Remparts, Bouches-du-Rhône: Fig. 1, 62), settlements by the Étang de Mauguio (Lattes, Gard: Daveau & Py 2011; Py 2009), Agde (in contact with the settlement of the Hérault valley, Bessan and Pézenas) and Béziers (on the Orb), whence a few items reached the hinterland, essentially Etruscan amphorae and ceramics and East Greek and Massaliot pottery (Bats 1992; 1998; 2006).

From the last third of the sixth century BC, a multitude of new settlements started to appear in southern Gaul, mainly fortified, on high land or otherwise; to mention only those subject to excavations, from East to West: Le Montjean, Costebelle, Baudouvin, La Courtine d'Ollioule, Le Mont Garou at Sanary (Fig. 1, 64), Les Embiez, Le Baou-Roux at Bouc-Bel-Air, Auriol, Martigues (St-Pierre) (Fig. 1, 43), Carpentras (La Lègue), Cavaillon, Sorgues, Nimes, Villevieille, La Roche de Comps, Mauressip, Ambrussum, Le Marduel, Le Plan de la Tour, Florensac, Clermont l'Hérault and Montlaurès. Some others (Arles, Espeyran, Lattes, Bessan and Pech Maho), precisely on the location of the maritime interface, acted as gateway communities, centres for the distribution of Massaliot productions—wine amphorae, monochrome grey ware, light-coloured clay ware—as well as any other item, manufactured mainly in Greece, Magna Graecia, Etruria and the East (Bats 1992; 2015). These preferential relationships enabled the Greek city to achieve a monopoly as an entrepôt. What we witness here is the encounter of two distinctive economic and social systems: on the one hand, so-called primitive societies, with their complex network of kinship, production and power, where donations were the preeminent form of exchange and competition amongst individuals or groups; on the other hand, societies that were engaged in relationships between pre-capitalist, trade-based economies that were just as complex, where any item can be traded (Bats 2011b).

Let us recall Herodotus' comment on the direct participation of the locals in this trade (5. 9): "The Ligyes who dwell inland of Massalia use the word 'sigynnae' for hucksters"; and that by Polybius (3. 42): in 217, at the time when Hannibal was about to cross the Rhône, approximately four days' march from the sea for an army, that is somewhere north of Avignon, "he used all possible means to win over the riverside residents and bought all their boats, small and large, which were many as a large number of the Rhône residents use them to transport goods from the sea."

The Second Punic War and the conquest of Iberia by the Romans opened Gaul to Roman *negociatores*, their first intervention started from Spain moving towards the western Languedoc and the Aude-Garonne route (opening the Toulouse internal market). Greco-Italic amphorae reached coastal sites as early as the third century BC; they progressively took first place there, in spite of various levels of resistance from Massaliot supplies: strong in Arles, Espeyran, Mont Garou, and La Courtine, slight at Pech Maho and Lattes. The situation was similar farther inland: resistance was weaker in Provence than in the eastern Languedoc. In the second half of the second century, even before the Transalpine conquest, Italic productions had entirely replaced those from Massalia.

Hostilities

The myth of the foundation of Massalia suggests a pattern of contact between Greeks and locals based on a reciprocal understanding, symbolised by the mixed marriage between Protis, the Greek, and Gyptis, the Gaul, daughter of King Nannus. However, as early as the second generation, the Gauls started showing hostility, which would recur throughout the history, real or mythical, Massalia, going so far that it brought about Roman intervention in 125 BC on the side of the Massaliots. Unless we consider the presence of Elisyc mercenaries (that is from the Narbonne region) in the Punic army at the Battle of Himera as a sign of hostility towards the Greeks in general, and those of Massalia in particular, it was the close environment of the *chora* or of Massalian colonies (such as Antipolis and Nikaia in 154 BC) that brought about these hostilities. Obviously, the Massaliots and Gauls did not share the same conception of territory and borders. Once again, literature and archaeology complement one another to produce a picture of these hostile relationships. According to Trogus Pompeius, after Comanus, son of Nannus, had tried to take the city, Massalia drove back a joint attack from the surrounding populations, led by king Catumandos. The Baou de Saint-Marcel *oppidum* was abandoned. A Massaliot police operation reached the site of the Île in Martigues (Fig. 1, 41), which was completely destroyed. Of developments at the end of the third century (permanent abandonment of the Notre-Dame-de-Pitié fortified *oppidum*, temporary desertion of the second settlement in Martigues) and the beginning of the second century (destruction by fire and abandonment of the fortified *oppidum* of the Teste-Nègre at Pennes-Mirabeau, violent destruction by balista-balls and fire at the site of Roquepertuse in Velaux (Fig. 1, 74), and of the *oppidum* of Baou-Roux at Bouc-Bel-Air), archaeology does not tell us if they reflect Massaliot expansion or a reaction to Gallic advance. After an alert in 154 BC, when, according to Polybius (34. 8), the Massaliots were held up while Antipolis and Nikaia were besieged, incursions from the Salyens (Livy *Per.* 60: "Fines Massiliensium populabantur") forced the Massaliots to call on Rome (the campaigns of 125–123 BC and the creation of the Transalpine province), and a series of settlements (St-Pierre-les-Martigues and the Île in Martigues, St-Blaise, the Baou de St-Marcel, the Baou-Roux at Bouc-Bel-Air, the Baou-Rouge at Auriol, the Tête-de-l'Ost at Mimet), though not at the Cloche in Pennes Mirabeau or at Entremont in Aix-en-Provence, were destroyed and abandoned in the last quarter of the second century BC.

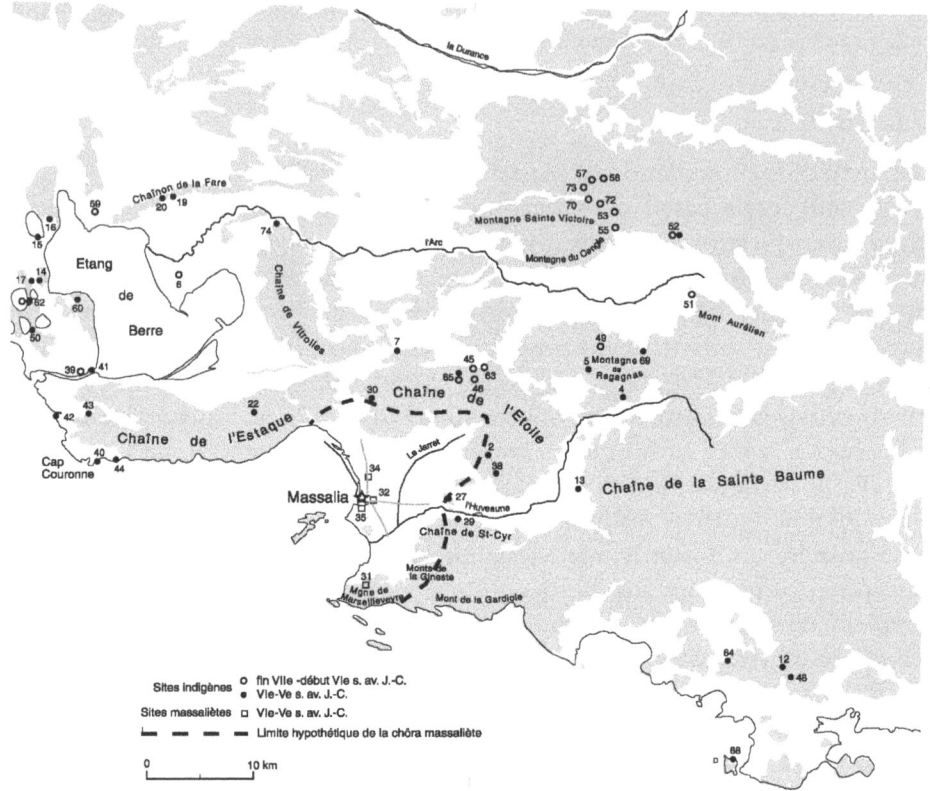

Figure 1. Massalia's territory and native sites in the sixth–fifth century BC (DAO M. Bats).

Partnership and Pacific Coexistence

We have seen that the Phocaeans' initial objective was the creation of commercial meeting places rather than territorial conquest. Clearly, trading relationships held a better chance of prospering against a pacific background than one of permanent hostilities. The development of a true monopoly over Mediterranean trade by the Massaliots (through the successive elimination of Etruscan and Punic intermediaries) led to control of the mechanism of exchange, with an alternation between partnership and submission depending on the balance of power.

Thus, from the fourth century, we observe a dual phenomenon in southern Gaul:

—abandonment or retreat from settlements in certain sectors, particularly in Provence, in parallel with the emergence or reinforcement of large structured settlements;

—reduction in imports of Massaliot amphorae by the interior, whilst their diffusion on the coast held up and did not waver until the end of the third century BC.

These two events may well be an illustration of the reinforcement of the role of coastal stations as both gateway communities and places of consumption, and the organisation of redistribution in an increasingly linear hierarchical pattern. This would seem to correspond, in social terms, to a reinforcement of the communities' autonomy and the implementation of a more hierarchical internal structure. Regarding the eastern Languedoc (but the explanation can also be applied to other regions of Provence), M. Py (1990) also considers the possibility that the Massaliots established dependent relationships that I would prefer to translate in terms of *philia* or *xenia*. We have the proof of the existence of these thanks to the literature from the end of the third century: At the occasion of Hasdrubal's passage, Livy (27. 36) hints at the existence of hospitality relationships between *principes gallorum* and *duces massiliensium*, while at the time of the siege of Massalia by Caesar's troops, he speaks of the Albic people "qui in [Massiliensium] fide antiquitus erant" (*BC* 1. 34). Still at the time of Hannibal, Polybius (3. 41) alludes to Celtic mercenaries in the pay of the Massaliots, who appointed the former as guides for Scipio's army. Finally, we should mention a bronze hand, "sign of reconnaissance by Ouelaunoi" if the Greek inscription it carries (*SUMBOLON PROS OUELAU-NIOUS*) is to be believed, and which may be the property of a Massaliot on an assignment with the Ouelaunoi people in eastern Provence.

Mixed Settlements?

It remains difficult to define the criteria that would allow us to confirm the existence of such settlements beyond doubt. We still know very little about Massalia's architecture and urbanism; moreover, no native site echoes them in any way. Only one area of the town of Arles, dated to the beginning of the fifth century BC, presents an orthogonal plan unknown anywhere else (Arcelin 1995); however, this is probably the Massaliot colony referred to as Theline by Avienus. It was demonstrated long ago (Tréziny 1986) that, despite appearances, the Saint-Blaise and Glanum fortifications, which can be dated to the second century, were different in terms of both their technique and function from the contemporary walls of Massalia with which they had been compared.

Although the study of the characteristics and pattern of consumption of ceramics, which I have previously investigated (Bats 1988a), enables a Greek settlement to be differentiated from a native one, it is not sufficiently accurate to identify a mixed settlement. The convergence of several criteria is necessary. It should also be made clear that a mixed settlement may simply include a few foreign families among a native population. Here are some avenues for further exploration.

After analysis of individual names written in the Iberic alphabet in Ensérune between the fourth and first centuries BC, Jürgen Untermann (1969) found almost half of them were Iberic names, the rest being divided between Gaul and "Ligurian" names (that is, neither Gaul nor Iberic). The pattern of ceramics from the settlement and the necropolis is similar to that of regional native sites. Within the Celtic regional background, Iberic appears as a vehicular rather than as a vernacular language and the transcribed names are representative of economic (tradesmen) and social (upper classes) contexts rather than of the demographic background. It is, however, clear that Iberics lived in Ensérune on a permanent basis.

In Lattes, in an area close to the harbour, excavation uncovered several rooms built at the end of the sixth/beginning of the fifth century BC, whose organisation, implementation, building techniques and ceramic items seem to differ from the rest of the settlement: The walls were made from rammed earth upon a stone socle, covered with coloured clay coatings; one partition is in adobe, doorsteps are made of wood. Almost all pottery items are of Etruscan origin—whole amphorae but also common ceramics, sometimes bearing graffiti in Etruscan characters. All these elements evoke the existence of an Etruscan warehouse, already considered by previous finds of Etruscan graffiti and by a high percentage of Etruscan amphorae (Py 1995; Lebeaupin 2014). However, two mid-fifth-century lead tablets were found in that same area, inscribed in Greek alphabet and Ionian language, giving information about trade deals of oil and garos, carried out by Greeks, Kleanax and Kleosthenes (Bats 2010). Another short later lead tablet inscribed in Greek was found at the Ruscino site. These items complement the lead tablet from Pech Mao (Lejeune et al. 1988) where a Greek individual named Heronoios may have resided, in connection with Emporion harbour (Ampurias).

In Lattes again, but in the third–second centuries BC, some elements suggest the presence of Greek families in the settlement: houses with several rooms organised around a courtyard, concrete with broken brick floors, sometimes decorated, Greek-type cooking ceramics (*lopades* and *caccabai*) and, unique in southern Gaul, two Greek *abecedaria*, proof that the Greek language was being learnt (Fig. 2) (Bats 1988b; 2004).

Figure 2. Greeks *abecedaria* of Lattes on campanian A ceramic (early second century BC).

Acculturation Fields

We have seen that outside the area situated between the city of Massalia and the Rhône delta, under their direct control, the Greeks did not extend their "colonial" activity and, therefore, did not find themselves in a directly dominant position towards native populations. Free acculturation relationships were established instead.

Conservatism and Resistance

Modelled Urn. The modelled urn remained the fundamental form of cooking ware on all native sites in southern Gaul. It probably expresses, through its lasting resistance to innovation, one of the clearest cultural signs of the assertion of identity against the "other" Greek user of chytrai, caccabai and lopades. It is even possible to use this type of cooking pot to distinguish cultural areas, based upon home production or a poorly distributed local craft industry:

1. Eastern Provence from Italy to Marseille—S-profile urn without shoulder, only suggested by a printed or incised decoration, and flaring rim: *DICOCER* CNT-PRO U6;
2. Western Provence between the Rhône and Durance—urn with lightly marked shoulder, underlined by a decoration, and a high rectilinear neck finished by a flaring rim: *DICOCER* CNT-PRO U4;
3. Eastern Languedoc—urn with more or less pronounced shoulder, underlined by an incised or printed decoration, with a low, rectilinear neck: *DICOCER* CNT-LOR U2b/U3a;
4. Western Languedoc and Roussillon—urn without shoulder, often suggested by a corrugated fillet, with a sub-rectilinear neck and straight rim: *DICOCER* CNT-LOC U3a-U4a3.

One workshop is an exception to this rule, producing so-called Rhodanian urns, with an inward neck, small flaring rim, comb-decorated wall with oval-prints decorations at the neck-body junction, distributed on either side of the Lower Rhône from the second quarter of the fifth century.

Sculpture. Sculpture, often considered representative of the Hellenistic influence on a primitive, local substratum, has in recent years undergone a typo-chronological revision to place it in a Celtic context. A recent study by P. Arcelin and A. Rapin (2003) suggests a four-phase evolution from the figured stelai of the Late Bronze Age and the appearance of the statuary in the round, possibly from as early as the seventh century BC. The authors consider that the first Greek influences may have appeared in the "realistic modelling and stone work" of works of the "Western Provence school" towards the end of the sixth century (Glanum, Roquepertuse) in the representation of a seated figure that will remain, until the end of the second century, the emblematic illustration of the Celtic ideology, praising war and heroic values (Fig. 3).

Figure 3. Seated warrior of Glanum (late sixth century BC).

Decapitation by Celts. The practice of chopping-off and exposing the heads of defeated enemies is widely attested in literature (Diodorus of Sicily 5. 29 and Strabo 4. 4. 5, after Poseidonius' account) and archaeology (statuary groups, reliefs, cavities for the fitting of heads and nailed skull remains) at several sites in Provence and the Languedoc. According to Strabo (4. 4. 5), "the Romans put an end to these customs", clearly condemned by the Greeks (Hermary 2003).

Hybridity

This process appears clearly through several pottery products.

Grey monochrome pottery. Grey monochrome pottery produced in the sixth and fifth centuries BC in a series of workshops scattered from the Var to the Roussillon (but with a significant gap in the eastern Languedoc), including, and more particularly, outside Greek establishments. The technical borrowing of turning and of reduced-firing is present everywhere, along with the creation of a mixed repertoire, which differs between the Languedoc and Provence. There are several production groups in the Languedoc: in the lower valleys of the Hérault (Agde area), Orb (Béziers) and Aude. Besides forms of Greek origin such as the marl bowl, the most frequent, or the trefoiled-neck oinochoe, vases carry on native tradition forms (goblets, urns and bowls). In Provence, Charline Arcelin-Pradelle (Arcelin-Pradelle 1984) isolated seven production groups that may correspond to different workshops located in Massalia as well as around the Étang de Berre or the hinterland (Vaucluse, Var). This repertoire is also mixed: both Greek (bowls, cups with handles, oinochoe and olpe) and native forms (streamlined bowl, most frequent form of all, and urns and basins) experience differentiated distribution depending on geography and the identity of consumers.

Subgeometric pottery. Light-coloured clay painted pottery (so-called Subgeometric), produced throughout the fifth century BC in the Lower Rhône (Goury 1995) and, in the fourth century, in the Hérault valley (Garcia 1993). One detects the existence of several workshops, none of which has yet been located. This production, although it covers all the functions of table- and household ware, still remains, like the Iberic-Languedocian light-co-loured clay painted pottery in the western Languedoc, in a minority com-pared with handmade traditional ware. The forms represented are borrowed from both the Greek (jugs, column-krater, stamnos, lip cups near of B2 cups) and "traditional" repertoires (urns, shallow bowls, one-handle cups). The brown-red decoration seems inspired by the stripe-decoration present on Massaliot light-coloured clay ware and Ionian pottery, but also includes abundant, highly personalised patterns (herringbones, checks, semicircles, figurative designs such as birds or riders) that only partly re-use those already adopted for incising or printing on handmade pottery (Fig. 4). Diffusion of this ceramic is confined to native sites of production area (Bats 2007).

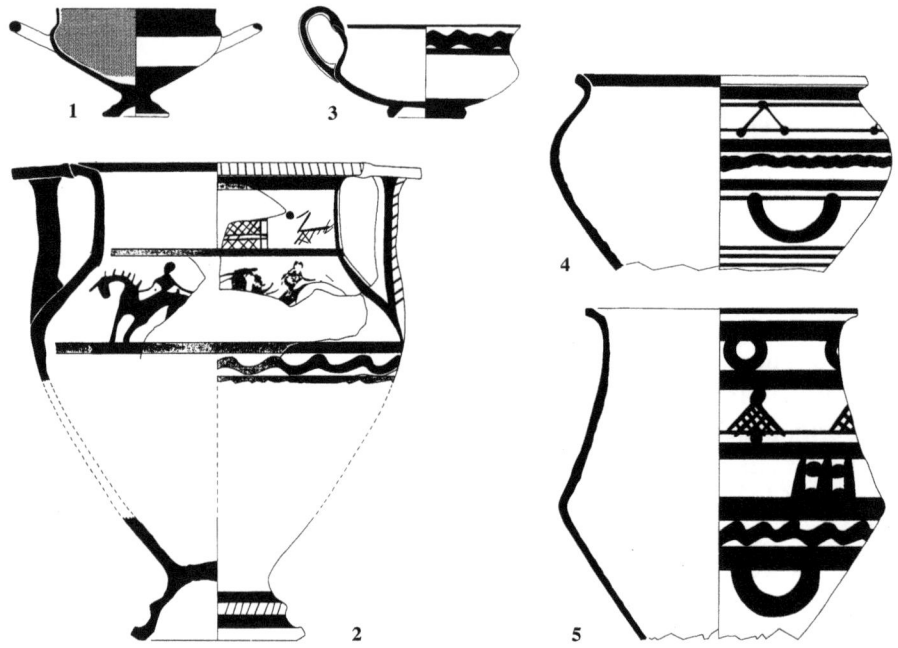

Figure 4. Light-colored clay painted pottery of the lower Rhône area (fifth century BC).

Cooking Pottery from the Étoile Range (Arcelin 1985). In the second–first centuries BC, a workshop near Massalia produced the majority of the handmade lopades and caccabai used in Massalia and its colonies in Olbia and Antibes, as well as most of the urns used on the native sites of western Provence (Fig. 5).

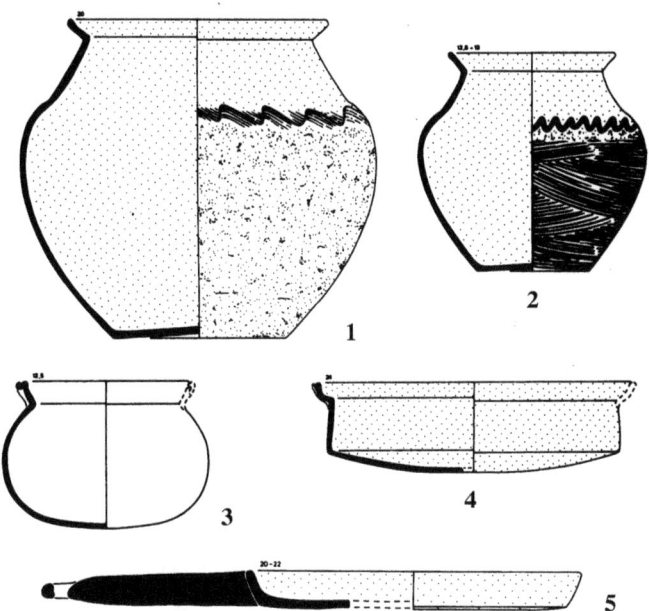

Figure 5. Non-turned cooking pottery from the Etoile range (second–first century BC).

Reinterpretation and Syncretism

Contacts with the Greeks were at the origin of wine consumption: for the Gauls, Hellenism was synonymous with the civilisation of wine consumption. The analysis of tombs in the Ensérune necropolis may provide an expression of a syncretism in funeral practices through a change from local wine consumption to its inclusion within a new ideology of death (Bats 2002). The contents of these tombs reflect the complex encounters between items originating from different cultures: Celtic weapons and fibulae, clearly imported, and Greek-origin vases, also imported, in association to local products. In the first phase tombs (425–375 BC), drinking vessels (Attic cups and skyphoi) were considered to be the deceased's personal objects and as such were burnt with him on the pyre. The first change occurs in the next phase (375–325 BC): while drinking vessels disappear, the bones of the deceased are placed inside a vessel, usually a light-coloured clay container of Iberic-Languedocian type, but sometimes a krater, possibly associated with weapons or jewellery (depending on the sex)—all personal items recovered from the pyre. The third phase confirms the use of the krater as the main cinerary vessel; the additional containers are not specifically drinking vessels, but rather multi-purpose, and come with handmade pots, often containing animal remains (eggs, shells, the bones and skeletons of poultry, rabbits, cattle and sheep, more rarely fish). Indeed, the allusion to wine consumption seems to take on a different meaning between the first phase (drinking vessels only) and the second and third (use of kraters as cinerary containers) with the addition of a "reference to symposion culture, the collective and social consumption of wine", and a funerary function for the krater. However, a new dimension to the allusions to libations and sacrifices is added during the third phase: beside the personal social status of the dead—still present—an ideology of death is put forward, which is concerned with the salvation of the soul and indicates group participation.

Borrowing and Building Identity: Gallo-Greek Literacy

The use of writing has not been attested in south Gaul before the foundation of Masalia in ca. 600 BC. Based on our current knowledge, the Gauls started to write their own language only four centuries later. We know that Celtic society belonged to a type that put the accent on the oral transmission of culture. Beside druids, masters of a sacred education which was, according to Caesar, marked by a religious prohibition against the use of writing, an important place was held by bards, other masters of the oral communication. Diodorus of Sicily and Strabo, according to Poseidonius, Ammianus Marcellinus, according to Timagenes (himself dependent on Poseidonius), describe them as poets, composers and singers who, accompanying themselves on the lyre, told heroic and satirical pieces: for instance, the bard from the Bituit tribe, evoked by Appian (4. 12), improvised before Roman representatives a hymn recounting the achievements of the Allobroges and their king. This preference for oral story-telling would continue until the time of pagan Ireland, in which neither the druids nor the poets entrusted their knowledge to the Ogamic alphabet; only at the time of conversion to Christianity would monks start to transcribe this epic and literary legacy into Latin. Although the 'literary' field escaped preservation through writing, Strabo and Caesar report the use in the first century BC of writing in the secular field, especially in the private and political areas.

In any case, starting from the early second century, some sites in southern Gaul (Teste Nègre at the Pennes-Mirabeau, Martigues, Lattes, Saint-Blaise), finds from which testify to their close contact with Massalia, suddenly provide such written testimonies as proper nouns in the Greek alphabet on pottery items (Fig. 6 & 7). Why then? The reason should probably be sought in the implementation of a new type of relationship between Greeks and locals on some sites, of which this written outburst would be a sign. Let us say that, from a cultural point of view, they attest to an assertion of identity, an awareness of one's existence against the 'others' that did not previously exist in this area. However, this process seems to have unfolded in two separate stages. I would be tempted to suggest that at first the situation involved individual contacts in which exchanges (or geographical proximity), possibly associated with the permanent presence of Greek families on the native sites where these contacts occurred, encouraged the development of bilingualism, and Greek was primarily the written vehicular language. In this context of technical borrowing, Gallo-Greek writing was created, whose main remains, and more particularly lapidary inscriptions, date essentially from the end of the second century and even more prominently from the first century BC (Fig. 8). Yet this is also the time of a sudden change in the socio-political environment: with the Roman conquest, encounters gave way to domination. Aside from the Greek language, which continued to be used until the middle of the first century BC, Gallo-Greek developed and reached its peak in the context of the Transalpine province. For the Gauls, it then represented more than just a means to communicate, and possibly to count and record; it had also become a way to assert themselves and their identity, personally, socially and politically. This last aspect is obviously favoured by the archaeological remains, such as stone or coin inscriptions. Beside Latin, the written and spoken language of the conqueror and his administration, the development of Gallo-Greek would appear to have been linked to a will to identify as Gauls facing the Romans (Bats 2004; 2011a).

Figure 6. Martigues (Saint-Pierre) (B.-du-Rh.). Two vases with owner's name, *Ritumos* (Cl. J. Chausserie-Laprée).

Figure 7. Les Pennes-Mirabeau (B.-du-Rh.). La Cloche. Vase with owner's name, *Attilos* (Cl. Chr. Durand, CCJ, Aix-en-Provence).

Figure 8. Velleron (Vaucluse). Gravestone of Caios Indoutilos Samolatis and his wife Anektia (Cl. M. Bats).

Bibliography

Amselle, J.-L., 1985, Ethnies et espaces: pour une anthropologie topologique. In: J.-L. Amselle & E. M'Bokolo (eds.), *Au cœur de l'ethnie. Ethnies, tribalisme et état en Afrique.* Paris, 1985 (2nd ed. 1999), 11–48.

Arcelin, P., 1985, Ateliers de céramique non tournée en Provence occidentale à la fin de l'Age du fer. In: *Histoire des techniques et sources documentaires* (Aix-en-Provence), 115–28.

Arcelin, P., 1995, Arles protohistorique, centre d'échanges économiques et culturels. In: *Sur les pas des Grecs en Occident. Hommages à A. Nickels,* Paris-Lattes (*EtMass* 4), 325–28.

Arcelin, P. & Rapin, A., 2003, Considérations nouvelles sur l'iconographie anthropomorphe de l'âge du Fer en Gaule méditerranéenne. In: O. Buchsenschutz et al. (eds.), *Décors, images et signes de l'âge du Fer européen.* Actes du XXVIᵉ colloque de l'Association Française pour l'Étude de l'Age du Fer, Paris et Saint-Denis, 9–12 mai 2002 (Tours), 183–219.

Arcelin-Pradelle, C., 1984, *La céramique grise monochrome en Provence* (Paris), *RAN* Sup. 10.

Bats, M., 1988a, *Vaisselle et alimentation à Olbia de Provence (v. 350–v. 50 av. J.-C.). Modèles culturels et catégories céramiques* (Paris), *RAN* Sup. 18.

Bats, M., 1988b, La logique de l'écriture d'une société à l'autre en Gaule méridionale protohistorique. *RAN* 21, 121–48.

Bats, M., 1992, Marseille, ses colonies et les relais indigènes du commerce massaliète en Gaule méridionale. In: M. Bats et al. (dir.), *Marseille grecque et la Gaule.* Actes des colloques de Marseille (1990). Lattes-Aix-en-Provence (*EtMass* 3), 263–78.

Bats, M., 1998, Marseille archaïque: Étrusques et Phocéens en Méditerranée nord-occidentale. *MEFRA* 110, 609–33.

Bats, M., 1999, Identités ethno-culturelles et espaces en Gaule méditerranéenne (principalement aux VIᵉ-Vᵉ s. av. J.-C.). In: *Confini e frontiera nella Grecità d'Occidente.* Atti XXXVII Convegno intern. di studi sulla Magna Grecia (Taranto, 1997) (Napoli), 381–418.

Bats, M., 2001, La chôra de Massalia. In: *Problemi della chora coloniale dall'Occidente al Mar Nero.* Atti XL Convegno intern. di studi sulla Magna Grecia (Taranto, 2000) (Napoli), 491–512.

Bats, M., 2002, Du cratère sympotique au stamnos funéraire: tombes aristocratiques du Midi de la Gaule (IVᵉ–Iᵉʳ s. av. J.-C.). In C. Müller & F. Prost (eds.), *Identités et cultures dans le monde méditerranéen antique. Hommage à F. Croissant* (Paris), 277–302.

Bats, M., 2003, Les Gaulois et l'écriture aux IIᵉ–Iᵉʳ s. av. J.-C. In: *Articulations entre culture matérielle et sources antiques dans la recherche sur l'Age du fer européen* (Actes du XXIIIᵉ colloque de l'Association Française pour l'Étude de l'Age du Fer, Nantes, 1999) (Rennes), 369–80.

Bats, M., 2004, Grec et gallo-grec: les graffites sur céramique aux sources de l'écriture en Gaule méridionale (IIᵉ-Iᵉʳ s. av. J.-C.). *Gallia* 61, 7–20.

Bats, M., 2006, Systèmes chronologiques et mobiliers étrusques du Midi de la Gaule au premier Age du fer (v. 600–v. 480 av. J.-C.): les rythmes de l'archéologie et de l'histoire. In: *Gli Etruschi da Genova ad Ampurias* (Atti del XXIV convegno di studi etruschi ed italici, Marseille-Lattes, 26 septembre–1er octobre 2002) (Pisa/Rome), 81–92.

Bats, M., 2007, Entre Grecs et Celtes en Gaule méridionale: de la culture matérielle à l'identité ethnique. In: *Identités ethniques dans le monde grec antique* (Actes du Colloque international de Toulouse, 2006) (=Pallas 73), 191–98.

Bats, M., 2008, Le colonie massaliote (VI–II s. a.C.). In *Colonie di colonie: le fondazioni sub-coloniali greche tra colonizzazione e colonialismo* (Atti del convegno internazionale di studi, Lecce, 22–24 giugno 2006) (Lecce), 203–208.

Bats, M., 2010, Une lettre sur plomb à Lattes (Hérault). In: Th. Janin (dir.), *Premières données sur le Ve s. av. n.è. dans la ville de Lattara*. T. 2. Lattes, 749–756 (Lattara, 21).

Bats, M., 2011a, Emmêlements de langues et de systèmes graphiques en Gaule méridionale (VIᵉ–Iᵉʳ s. av. J.-C.). In: C. Ruiz Darasse & E. R. Lujan (éd.), *Contacts linguistiques dans l'Occident méditerranéen antique* (Actas del Coloquio internacional, Madrid, 23–24 avril 2009) (Madrid), 197–226 (Coll. CVZ 126).

Bats, M., 2011b, Métal, objets précieux et monnaie dans les échanges en Gaule méridionale protohistorique (VIᵉ–IIᵉ s. av. J.-C.). In: *Barter, money and coinage in the Ancient Mediterranean (10th–1st Centuries BC)* (Actas del IV Encuentro peninsular de numismatica antigua, 2010) (Madrid), 97–109.

Bats, M., 2015, Parcours commerciaux et culturels de la céramique grecque en Gaule méridionale du VIIᵉ au Vᵉ s. av. J.-C. In: M. Guggisberg & S. Bonomi (dir.), *Griechische Keramik nördlich von Etrurien: mediterrane Importe im archäologischen Kontext.* Internationale Tagung Basel (14.–15. Oktober 2011) (Wiesbaden), 69–77.

Daveau, I. & Py, M., 2015, Grecs et Etrusques à Lattes: nouvelles données à partir des fouilles de La Cougourlude. In: *Contacts et acculturations en Méditerranée occidentale, Hommages à Michel Bats* (Actes du colloque de Hyères, 2011) (Aix-en-Provence), 31–42 (BiAMA 15).

De Hoz, J., 1999, Los negocios del señor Heronoiyos. Un documento mercantil, jonio clásico temprano, del sur de Francia. In: J. A. López Férez (ed.), *Desde los poemas homéricos hasta la prosa griega del siglo IV d.C* (Madrid), 61–90.

Dietler, M., 2010, *Archaeologies of Colonialism. Consumption, Entanglement and Violence in Ancient Mediterranean France* (Berkeley & Los Angeles).

Garcia, D., 1993, *Entre Ibères et Ligures. Lodévois et moyenne vallée de l'Hérault protohistoriques* (Paris).

Goury, D., 1995, Les vases pseudo-ioniens des vallées de la Cèze et de la Tave (Gard). In: *Sur les pas des Grecs en Occident... Hommages à A. Nickels* (Lattes-Aix-en-Provence), 309–24 (*EtMass* 4).

Hermary, A., 2003, Grecs et barbares cloueurs de têtes: compléments au témoignage de Poseidonios. In: M. Bats, B. Dedet, P. Garmy, T. Janin, C. Raynaud & M. Schwaller (eds.), *Peuples et territoires en Gaule méditerranéenne. Hommage à Guy Barruol* (Montpellier), 525–530 (*RAN* Sup 35).

Lebeaupin, D. (dir.), 2014, *Les origines de Lattara et la présence étrusque. Les données de la zone 27* (Lattes) (Lattara 22).

Lejeune, M., Pouilloux J., & Solier Y., 1988, Étrusque et ionien archaïques sur un plomb de Pech Maho (Aude), *RAN*, 22, 1988, 19–59.

Malkin, I., 2011, *A Small Greek World, Networks in the Ancient Mediterranean* (Oxford).

Py, M., 1990, *Culture, économie et société protohistoriques dans la région nimoise* (Rome) (Coll. EFR 131).

Py, M., 1995, Les Etrusques, les Grecs et la fondation de Lattes. In: *Sur les pas des Grecs en Occident. Hommages à A. Nickels,* Paris-Lattes (*EtMass* 4), 261–76.

Py, M, 2009, Lattara : Lattes, Hérault comptoir gaulois méditerranéen entre Etrusques, Grecs et Romains, Errance, Paris, 343p.

Tréziny, H., 1986, Remarques sur la fonction du rempart hellénistique de Saint-Blaise. In: *Le territoire de Marseille* (Actes de la table ronde d'Aix-en-Provence, 1985) (Aix-en-Provence), 145–51 (*EtMass* 1).

Untermann, J., 1969, Lengua gala y lengua ibérica en la *Gallia Narbonensis. Archivo de Prehistoria Levantina* 12, 99–161.

White, R., 1991, The Middle Ground: Indians, empires and republics in the Great Lakes Region (1650–1815), Cambridge/New York/Melbourne, Cambridge Univ. Press, 544p.

Contributors

Michel Bats
ASM, Archéologie des sociétés méditerranéennes, UMR 5140, Université Paul-Valéry Montpellier 3, CNRS, MCC, Montpellier, France
batcha@club-internet.fr

Loup Bernard
Université de Strasbourg, UMR7044, MISHA,
loup.bernard@unistra.fr

Philippe Boissinot
Ecole Pratique des Hautes Etudes, TRACES/CRPPM Toulouse
Philippe.boissinot@free.fr

Sophie Bouffier
Aix Marseille Univ, CNRS, MinistCulture & Com, CCJ, Aix-en-Provence, France
sophie.bouffier@univ-amu.fr.

Marc Bouiron
CEPAM (UMR 7264)
mbouiron@hotmail.com

Emmanuèle Caire,
Aix Marseille Univ, CNRS, TDMAM, Aix-en-Provence, France
emmanuele.caire@univ-amu.fr

Marie-Brigitte Carre
Aix Marseille Univ, CNRS, MinistCulture & Com, CCJ, Aix-en-Provence,
France
carre@mmsh.univ-aix.fr

Bernard Dedet
ASM, Archéologie des sociétés méditerranéennes, UMR 5140, Université
Paul-Valéry Montpellier 3, CNRS, MCC, Montpellier, France
bernard.dedet@cnrs.fr

Rachel Feig Vishnia†
Department of History, Tel Aviv University

Dominique Garcia
Aix Marseille Univ, CNRS, MinistCulture & Com, CCJ, Aix-en-Provence,
France
Dominique.garcia@inrap.fr

Delphine Isoardi
Aix Marseille Univ, CNRS, MinistCulture & Com, CCJ, Aix-en-Provence,
France
isoardi@mmsh.univ-aix.fr

Antoine Hermary
Aix Marseille Univ, CNRS, MinistCulture & Com, CCJ, Aix-en-Provence,
France
Ahermary@mmsh.univ-aix.fr

Philippe Leveau,
Aix Marseille Univ, CNRS, MinistCulture & Com, CCJ, Aix-en-Provence,
France
leveau.phil@wanadoo.fr

Patrice Pomey
Aix Marseille Univ, CNRS, MinistCulture & Com, CCJ, Aix-en-Provence,
France
pomey@mmsh.univ-aix.fr

Jean-Christophe Sourisseau
Aix Marseille Univ, CNRS, MinistCulture & Com, CCJ, Aix-en-Provence, France
sourisseau@mmsh.univ-aix.fr

Henri Tréziny
Aix Marseille Univ, CNRS, MinistCulture & Com, CCJ, Aix-en-Provence, France
Treziny@mmsh.univ-aix.fr; henri.treziny@orange.fr

LANG
Classical
Studies

This monograph series concentrates on the history and literature of the Greek and Roman world, embracing all subjects relevant to Classical Humanities: ancient religion and anthropology, cultural and intellectual history, comparative literature, historiography and political theory, and literary genres. Rather than specific technical studies, this series promotes scholarship that in one way or another addresses the larger concerns of modern Classical scholarship.

For additional information about this series or for the submission of manuscripts, please contact the series editor:

Daniel H. Garrison
Northwestern University
Department of Classics
Kresge 18
Evanston, Illinois 60208-2200

To order other books in this series, please contact our Customer Service Department:

(800) 770-LANG (within the U.S.)
(212) 647-7706 (outside the U.S.)
(212) 647-7707 FAX

Or browse online by series:

www.peterlang.com